ASSESSING FOR LEARNING

ASSESSING FOR LEARNING

Building a Sustainable Commitment
Across the Institution

SECOND EDITION

PEGGY L. MAKI

Stylus

STERLING, VIRGINIA

To my husband for his enduring patience and support

Published by Stylus Publishing, LLC
22883 Quicksilver Drive
Sterling, Virginia 20166-2102

Library of Congress Cataloging-in-Publication Data

Maki, Peggy.
   Assessing for learning : building a sustainable commitment across the institution / Peggy L. Maki.—2nd ed.
      p.   cm.
   Includes bibliographical references and index.
   ISBN 978-1-57922-440-0 (cloth : alk. paper)—ISBN 978-1-57922-441-7 (pbk. : alk. paper)
   1. Universities and colleges—United States—Examinations.   2. Education, Higher—United States—Evaluation.   I. Title.

LB2366.2.M35   2010
378.1'671—dc22   2010017526

13-digit ISBN: 978-1-57922-440-0 (cloth)
13-digit ISBN: 978-1-57922-441-7 (paper)

Printed in the United States of America

All first editions printed on acid free paper that meets the American National Standards Institute Z39-48 Standard.

Bulk Purchases
Quantity discounts are available for use in workshops and for staff development.
Call 1-800-232-0223

First Edition, 2010

10 9 8 7 6 5 4 3 2 1

CONTENTS

5   IDENTIFYING OR DESIGNING TASKS TO ASSESS THE DIMENSIONS OF LEARNING   155

7   DESIGNING A CYCLE OF INQUIRY   255

8 BUILDING A CORE INSTITUTIONAL PROCESS OF INQUIRY OVER TIME 283

ACKNOWLEDGMENTS

Breathing life into this book are examples of assessment practices from institutions across the United States and developments in national organizations. Not only do I acknowledge the individuals who contributed those examples, but I hereby also celebrate their work and their institutions' or organizations' work in advancing educational assessment as a core institutional process. Thank you to the following institutions and individuals, including two graduating seniors, for committing to this important process in higher education and for allowing me to make public your practices throughout the book:

Alverno College: Kathy Lake, Georgine Loacker, and Glen Rogers for describing some methods of assessment and the process of validating assessment methods

Association of American Colleges & Universities for contributing four of its VALUE rubrics

Association for Authentic, Experiential and Evidence-Based Learning: Trent Batson for sharing his thoughts about the future of e-portfolios

Azusa Pacific University: Connie Austin, Vicky Bowden, Julie Jantzi, and Shila Wiebe for Nursing Program learning outcome statements

Bowling Green State University: Milton Hakel for the University's Learning Outcomes

California State University, Monterey Bay: Amy Driscoll for the University's General Education Learning Outcomes

Clarke College: Kate Hendel, Lynn Lester, Kate Zanger, and the Chemistry Department for describing and illustrating leadership commitment and assessment processes at the College

Community College of Rhode Island: Daniel Donovan for describing the Paralegal Studies assessment portfolio and the integrative capstone course for Law Enforcement majors

Eastern Connecticut State University: Salvatrice Keating and Marsha Davis for describing the use of *Maple T.A.* in the Department of Mathematics and Computer Science

Eastern Kentucky University: Rose Perrine for an example of a syllabus footer to identify general education outcomes addressed in department-level courses

George Washington University: Randy Bass for contributing the opening quotation in chapter 4

Goddard College: Shelley Vermilya and Sarah L. Van Hoy for contributing documents that describe the College's learning portfolio and progress review

Hamline University: graduating senior Natalie Self for the diversity learning outcomes and methods of assessment proposed in her social justice capstone project

Hampden-Sydney College: Robert Herdegen III for contributing a scoring rubric for a psychology thesis

Indiana University-Purdue University in Indianapolis: Trudy W. Banta for describing and representing the University's assessment process; Michele J. Hansen, Scott E. Evenbeck, and Cathy A. Buyarski for describing methods to assess the advising process

Keystone College: Judith Keats, David Porter, and William Tersteeg for describing assessment methods used in the Fine Arts Department

Marion College: Carleen VandeZande for describing the culminating project in the educational leadership program

Mesa Community College: Andrea Greene, Elizabeth Hunt Larson, and Gail Mee for describing the College's assessment practices and processes

Miami Dade College: President Padrón for contributing the College's 2007 Learning Outcomes Covenant

New Jersey City University: William Craven, John Egan, Marilyn Ettinger, Richard Fabris,

Shimshon Kinory, Patricia McGuire, Robert Matthews, Leonard Nass, Barbara O'Neal, Jeanette Ramos-Alexander, Afaf Shalaby, Joseph Stern, Susan Williams, and Rosalyn Young for the business administration curriculum map

North Carolina State University: Sarah Ash and Patti Clayton for describing a method to assess service learning; and Jo Allen, James Anderson, and Marilee Bresciani for the University's principles-of-commitment statement

The Ohio State University: Katherine Kelley for the Pharmacy Program's curriculum map

Portland State University: Terrel Rhodes and Devorah Lieberman for describing the University's assessment practices

Ramapo College of New Jersey: Emma Rainforth for her poster on redesigning a general education science course

Rochester Community and Technical College: Anne High and Tammy Lee for the College's principles of commitment statement

Rose-Hulman Institute of Technology: Gloria Rogers for a curriculum map and description of the role of institutional research in the assessment process

Rutgers University: Calvin Y. Yu for results of his study on student behaviors in note-taking and studying

St. Olaf College: Jo Beld for the College's principles of commitment statement

Simmons College: Peter Hernon and Candy Schwartz for a description of ongoing assessment in a doctoral program; Peter Hernon, Robert E. Dugan, and Mildred F. Schwarz for contributing an exercise.

South Florida Community College: Erik Christensen for the physics curriculum map that incorporates general education outcomes

United States Naval Academy: Peter Gray for the description and graphic representation of the assessment process

University of Colorado: Wendy Adams and Karl Wieman for descriptions and graphic representations of the assessment process in physics

University of Florida: graduating music major Sandee Katz for the table of contents in her e-portfolio

University of Maryland: Student Affairs Outcome Group, Andrea Goodwin, and Rhondie Vorhees for documents about their assessment plans and processes, sample scoring rubrics, and interpretations of findings

University of Michigan: Matt Mayhew (currently at New York University) for describing methods to assess students' spirituality

University of Nebraska-Lincoln: Jessica Jonson and Jeremy Penn for a description and graphic representations of the University's assessment management system

University of Portland: Mark Eifler, Terrence Favero, Becky Houck, Ken Kleszynski, Marlene Moore, Elayne Shapiro for the University's principles of commitment statement

University of Rhode Island: Student Affairs Assessment Committee for the scoring rubric to assess student affairs employees

University of South Florida: Teresa Flateby for describing a process to assess writing

University of Washington: Richard Roth and members of the Geography Department faculty for describing their learning outcomes project

University of West Florida: Jane Halonen for describing promotion and tenure criteria related to assessment; Edward Ranelli and faculty in the Master of Accountancy for representative curriculum maps

University of Wisconsin-River Falls: Michael Middleton, Faculty Assessment Committee, for describing the institution's assessment fair

Valencia Community College: Karen Borglum and faculty for describing the online course outline builder worksheet

Washington State University: Diane Kelley-Riley for contributing a student consent form from the Critical Thinking Project

This book draws its inspiration from research on learning presented through the work of the National Research Council and other researchers cited throughout the chapters. Their work challenges educators to draw upon research on learning to inform the design of educational practices, as well as the design of assessment methods. I thank those researchers for laying important groundwork for this book.

I also thank the 12 assessment management system developers for preparing brief descriptions of their online assessment systems (chapter 8, Appendix 8.2) so that readers new to these technological options develop an overview of how these systems may advance their institutions' assessment efforts.

Finally, I wish to express an author's gratitude to John Von Knorring, President and Publisher, Stylus Publishing, LLC, whose early commitment to this book sustained both the first and second editions.

Thanks to the following individuals and publishers for allowing me to include copyrighted material:

The Australian Council for Educational Research for the introductory quotation in chapter 3 from "Towards a Theory of Quality in Higher Education" by Ference Marton, p. 84, from *Teaching and Learning in Higher Education*, edited by Dart and Boulton-Lewis, 1998.

Elsevier Publishing for Figures 1.1, 1.2, and 1.3 in chapter 1, originally published in the *Journal of Academic Librarianship*, *28*, 2002, pp. 8–13, from the article by Peggy Maki titled "Developing an Assessment Plan to Learn About Student Learning."

HarperCollins Publishers for the quotation that opens chapter 7 from Jim Collins. *From Good to Great: Why Some Companies Make the Leap and Others Don't*. Copyright © 2001 by Jim Collins.

Jossey-Bass for the quotation that opens chapter 6 from Paul Dressel (1976). *Handbook of Academic Evaluation*. San Francisco, CA: Jossey Bass.

Kogan Page for the quotation that opens chapter 1 from Derek Rowntree. (1987). *Assessing Students: How Shall We Know Them?* (2nd Ed.). London: Kogan Page.

Mentkowski & Associates, 2000, for material contributed for Box 5.7 in chapter 5 by Glen Rogers, Senior Research Associate, Educational Research and Evaluation, and Kathy Lake, Professor of Education, Alverno College, with citations from: Alverno College Faculty. (1979/1994).

Student Assessment-as-Learning at Alverno College. Milwaukee, WI: Alverno College Institute. Original work published 1979, revised 1985 and 1994; and Mentkowski, M., & Associates. (2000). *Learning That Lasts: Integrating Learning, Development, and Performance in College and Beyond*. San Francisco: Jossey-Bass.

The Modern Languages Association for the quotation in chapter 5 from E. White et al., *Assessment of Writing: Politics, Politics, Practices*, New York: MLA, 1996.

National Research Council for permission to reproduce the quotation that opens chapter 5 from *Knowing What Students Know: The Science and Design of Educational Assessment*, 2001. Washington, D.C.: National Academy Press

The Perseus Books Group for permission to reproduce the opening quotation of chapter 7 from John Gardner, *The Unschooled Mind: How Children Think and How Schools Should Teach*, 1991, New York: Basic Books.

Stylus Publishing for permission to reproduce a quotation in chapter 1, page 11 from Paul Gaston, *The Bologna Process: What United States Higher Education Has to Learn From Europe, and Why It Matters That We Learn It* by Paul Gaston, 2010 and a quotation in chapter 1, page 24 from Jean Mach in *Coming to Terms With Assessment: Faculty and Administrators' Journeys to Integrating Assessment in Their Work and Institutional Culture*, edited by Peggy Maki, 2010. Sterling, VA: Stylus Publishing.

Taylor & Francis Books for permission to reproduce a quotation in chapter 4 from Diane Laurillard, *Rethinking University Teaching: A Framework for the Effective Use of Educational Technology*, 1993, London: Routledge.

Bill Tucker for permission to reproduce a quotation in Chapter 5 from "Beyond the Bubble: Technology and the Future of Assessment," *Education Sector Report*, 2009, Washington: D.C: Education Sector.

PREFACE TO THE SECOND EDITION

The second edition of *Assessing for Learning: Building a Sustainable Commitment Across the Institution* springs less from an author's chronologically persistent need to revise—often an immediate urge that arises the moment an author hands off her work to her publisher—and more from the need to take stock of and reflect on the state of assessment 6 years later. Much has happened or developed over those 6 years that warranted taking a fresh look at the earlier edition, resulting in expanding, building upon, illustrating, updating, and developing new content to contribute to advancing our assessment practices. An overview of those 6 years is in order.

Over those years, accreditors; national, professional and disciplinary organizations; and foundations have continued to contribute to the assessment movement as a core institutional practice. These entities have chronologically produced resources and offered workshops, institutes, symposia, and conferences on assessment, disseminating knowledge about assessment practices in undergraduate and graduate education at the institution, program, and department levels. Foundations such as the Lumina Foundation and the Teagle Foundation have generously supported small- and large-scale projects focused on using results to improve student learning. Accreditors have coupled their expanding resources with an increased focus on institutions' abilities to use assessment results to improve learning. Almost annually, a professional or disciplinary organization that may not heretofore have taken a step toward assessment comes forward to address the topic or announce a publication on it. Also, contributing to the elevation of assessment's national profile has been the proliferation of publications such as journal articles and books, including books about assessment in particular majors and about assessment at our highest levels of education—the master's and doctoral level. Both the *Chronicle of Higher Education* and *Inside Higher Education* routinely cover developments in assessment and accountability. In fact, *Inside Higher Education* has dedicated a section of its publication to assessment and accountability.

We have also seen the emergence of two new national organizations specifically focused on assessment: (1) the National Institute for Learning Outcomes Assessment (NILOA), a research organization that promotes better use of assessment tools and communicates about the actual assessment practices at our institutions, and (2) The New Leadership Alliance for Student Learning and Accountability, which will become a "public voice" for assessment and accountability.

Assessment of student learning has increasingly become a visible rhythm across our colleges and universities. Indeed, most of the chief academic officers or their designated representatives (78%) who responded to a 2009 Association of American Colleges & Universities' online survey of its 906 member institutions, representing public and private institutions and 2- and 4-year institutions, stated that they have a common set of intended learning outcomes for all undergraduate students. Ninety-eight percent stated that their institutions had developed learning outcome statements in at least "some" of their departments. Finally, one need only look at the numerous annual updates to the current Internet database on assessment, Internet Resources for Higher Outcomes Education Assessment, to document the national focus that has taken hold (www2.acs.ncsu.edu/UPA/assmt/resource.htm).

Over these 6 years, as well, institutions' demonstration of accountability for their students' learning also became a national focus. "Charting the Future of U.S. Higher Education, A Report of the Commission," appointed by secretary of education Margaret Spellings and published in 2006 (www.ed.gov/about/bdscomm/list/hiedfuture/reports/final-report.pdf), included among its findings documentation of the declining literacy among college graduates and the absence of accountability mechanisms that systematically report student achievement levels. Fueled in part by this document, heated debates ensued through the late summer of 2008 among Spellings's commission members, accreditors, employers, and college and university representatives about how institutions should publicly represent their students' learning in efficient ways, such as through national tests of general education outcomes.

Although higher education escaped a mandated federal threat of across-the-board use of standardized tests, focus on how institutions will represent their educational effectiveness through documentation of student learning continues to loom over our colleges and universities as a national issue. Moreover, a divide exists between those who support national tests and want to use results to compare institutions' educational effectiveness and those who believe that valid assessment of student achievement is based on assessing the work that students produce along and at the end of their educational journeys. Two national responses illustrate that divide: (1) the Association of Public and Land-grant Universities request that its member institutions post results of student performance on one of three general education standardized tests on its Voluntary System of Accountability site and (2) the Association of American Colleges & Universities' development of 15 national scoring rubrics that institutions can now apply to student work to assess students' achievement of the range of general education outcomes our institutions expect students to demonstrate—an integrated and authentic approach to providing evidence of student learning that this book espouses given the demographic spread of our students and the ways in which students demonstrate integration of those outcomes.

The need to humanize assessment, as opposed to standardizing it, and the need to democratize results are in order given the demographics of our institutions—students do not all start at the same place in their learning. These needs are also relevant given the Obama administration's 2009 call to higher education to provide increased educational opportunities to Americans to reach the "the highest proportion of college graduates in the world" by 2020 (www.whitehouse.gov/the_press_office/remarks-of-president-barack-obama-address-to-joint-session-of-congress/). In particular, the current secretary of education, Arne Duncan, has focused on the importance of increasing access for underrepresented and economically disadvantaged students. This educational priority calls for institutions to assess the progress of those new to or unfamiliar with higher education to learn about the efficacy of our educational practices for these new learners. It also requires that colleges and universities learn how to nimbly institutionalize recommended changes in educational practices based on analysis and discussion of assessment results. That is, they will need to learn how to scale up, so to speak, those new practices through the necessary structures,

processes, curricula, faculty development, and support services. Concurrent with this need for expanded access, President Obama fueled online education as the means to accommodate our new populations. Specifically, the President has committed annual financial support to community colleges to develop online or open classes, a concept popularized in 2001 at the Massachusetts Institute of Technology with its development of 1,900 online courses and further expanded by Carnegie Mellon University's offerings at its Open Learning Initiative. These newly proposed open courses would "reach students through multiple devices, such as computers, handheld devices, and e-book readers like Kindles. They would be modular, and therefore easily updated. Both nonprofit and for-profit entities could compete for the money to build them" (http://chronicle.com/article/Obamas-Great-Course-Giveaway/47530). Planning for competitive grants for the community college sector, focused on leveraging best practices and innovations in teaching and learning, is underway.

Two large-scale surveys over the last few years provide national perspectives on our actual assessment practices, confirming that assessment has taken hold but also pointing out some concerns. The 2009 AAC&U survey cited previously reported on its membership commitment to assessment and to various methods of assessment but also found a "lack of understanding of these goals [learning outcomes] among many students" (www.aacu.org/membership/documents/2009MemberSurvey_Part1.pdf). That is, we need to identify and implement ways to educate students about the assessment process as well as engage them in the process. In a second survey of assessment practices summarized in October 2009 in "More Than You Think, Less Than We Need," NILOA's principal investigators, George Kuh and Stan Ikenberry, reported that most institutions use assessment results primarily to respond to an external driver—accreditation. Not surprisingly, the first recommendation at the end of the 2009 survey focuses on institutions' need to demonstrate their ability to effectively use assessment results to improve student learning—a pattern that has not yet taken hold as national practice: "Integrating assessment into faculty practice and using assessment findings to guide pedagogical change and improved learning outcomes are as yet unrealized goals on many campuses" (http://www.learningoutcomeassessment.org/documents/full reportrevised-L.pdf). Within the aforementioned context, then, the second edition of this book was developed. It addresses new developments in assessment practices over the last 6 years. It identifies new methods and practices to respond to areas that we can improve, such as more fully including students in our work and positioning ourselves to ask open-ended research or study questions to guide inquiry into our students' products and thinking-learning processes so that we can use answers to our questions to inform our educational practices. Given the growth of online learning and blended courses and the Obama administration's focus on opening up access via technology, this revision also expands the pool of direct and indirect assessment options to include representative options in technology-enabled assessment, including the current and emerging sources of evidence of learning emerging from Web 2.0 applications in electronic portfolios. In the midst of the demands for evidence of our students' learning, it views standardized methods as an option among many others that now enable us to humanize the assessment process.

We cannot sign off on standardized test results as representative of our diverse learners' achievements or our institutions' educational effectiveness. We can, however, be conscientious about identifying who our students are, what we know about their strengths and weaknesses when they enter our institutions, what we learn about patterns of weakness in their learning, how we respond to improving those patterns through developments in educational practices, and what kinds of progress they make. That is, we need to humanize assessment as part of the teaching-learning process and democratize the results we report based on our diverse learners. Finally, it describes and illustrates systematic ways that institutions are documenting, storing, and drawing on their findings through either homegrown or commercially designed assessment management systems that serve as an institution's central assessment repository and framework to support human judgment about student work and interpretation of assessment results.

To sustain, refine, or mature institutional practices, the second edition includes the following kinds of updates, developments, improvements, models, institutional practices, and new content:

- Strategies to connect students to an institution's or a program's assessment commitment
- Integration of student voices, experiences, and self-reflections as part of the assessment process in direct and indirect methods

- Description of the components of a comprehensive institutional commitment that engages the institution, educators, and students—all as learners
- Expanded identification, description, and inventory of direct and indirect assessment methods, including technology-enabled methods that prompt students to represent their learning products and their thinking-learning processes—heretofore untapped invisible processes that provide us with new evidence about our learners that contributes to improving educational practices
- Case studies illustrating successful use of assessment results to improve teaching and educational practices and, thus, student learning
- An expanded range of campus examples from undergraduate to graduate education and across academic and support services
- A new chapter that describes a backward-designed problem-based assessment process to chronologically pursue answers to open-ended research or study questions about students' products and thinking-learning processes that lead to results that, in turn, inform discussions about how to improve student learning.
- Integration of developments across professional, scholarly, and accrediting bodies, across national and disciplinary organizations, and across foundations that support assessment as a means of improving student learning
- Descriptions and illustrations of homegrown or commercially designed assessment management systems that provide a central repository for supporting the assessment process and helping educators to chronologically analyze and interpret assessment results
- Additional examples, worksheets, guides, and exercises that align with new content

PROGRESSION OF THE BOOK

Assessing for learning is a systematic and systemic process of inquiry into what and how well students learn over the progression of their studies and is driven by intellectual curiosity about the efficacy of collective educational practices. That professional context anchors assessment as a core institutional process guided by questions about how well students learn what we expect them to learn—based on pedagogy; the design of curricula and co-curricula, instruction, and new web-based or technology-based learning environments; and other educational opportunities. Through examining students' products and thinking-learning processes we gain knowledge about the efficacy of our work. This book is designed to help colleges and universities build a sustainable commitment to assessing student learning at both the institution and program levels. This collective inquiry among faculty, staff, administrators, and students seeks evidence of students' abilities to integrate, apply, and transfer learning, as well as to construct their own meaning. Thus, this book focuses on the "bigger picture" of student learning—the kind of learning that students will draw and build on as they move into the workplace, graduate school, their local communities, and an increasingly global community. To that end, assessment is a process of ascertaining how well students achieve higher education's complex expectations through the multiple experiences and avenues inside and outside the classroom as well as online. This process that is embedded in our professional commitment to develop undergraduate and graduate students' knowledge, understanding, abilities, habits of mind, and ways of thinking, knowing, and behaving, then, becomes the collective responsibility of all educators in our higher education institutions. It brings constituencies together from across a campus and across a program, as well as external constituencies who contribute to our students' education through team research projects, internships, practica, and community-based projects.

The chapters focus on program- and institution-level assessment within the context of collective inquiry about student learning. Moving often in fits and starts, assessment is not initially a linear startup process or even necessarily sequential. Institutions develop their own processes. For that reason this book does not take a prescriptive or formulaic approach to building this commitment. What it does present is a framework, processes, strategies, and structures that help faculty, staff, administrators, and campus leaders develop a sustainable and shared core institutional process. This process enables institutions and programs to determine the fit between agreed-upon expectations for learning and students' representation or demonstration of that learning at points along their educational careers. Each chapter explores nested sets of decisions, tasks, and interdependent kinds of dis-

course that characterize collective inquiry. Institutional examples punctuate the text to illustrate how colleges and universities develop practices that embed assessment into institutional life. The "Additional Resources" listed at the end of each chapter, including metasites to larger sets of resources, enable you to pursue particular foci to deepen your institution's or your program's efforts. In addition, each chapter ends with worksheets, guides, and exercises designed to build collaborative ownership of assessment. These chapters progress as follows:

Chapter 1, "Developing a Collective Institutional Commitment," provides an overview of institution- and program-level assessment as a process of intellectual inquiry anchored in institutional and professional values and collective principles of commitment. This chapter also introduces a framework for planning assessment backward to deepen inquiry into student learning, including integrating students' own responses to or reflections on their learning experiences as a means of more deeply exploring patterns of strength and weakness in student work. It takes time out to describe who our students are, asking us to then determine what and when we want to learn about their progress to provide a more realistic accounting of their journeys, in contrast to allowing standardized tests to tell our stories, often based on a small sample of our student body. Presenting assessment as a process built on inclusiveness, this chapter also describes how to position educators, students, and the institution itself to engage in inquiry about learning. Updated worksheets, guides, and exercises at the end of this chapter contribute to strengthening a collective commitment to assessing for learning that is anchored in the following:

1. Intellectual curiosity about student learning
2. The demographic spread of students at each of our institutions that leads to chronological reporting of results against that spread to humanize and democratize the assessment process, not standardize it
3. Positions of inquiry that enable educators, students, and the institution itself to view and self-reflect on learning
4. Scholarly inquiry into assessment of student learning to deepen the usefulness of assessment results
5. Roles and responsibilities across an institution to sustain an institutional commitment to the assessment process

Chapter 2, "Beginning With Dialogue About Teaching and Learning," focuses on the coordinating role of institution- and program-level assessment committees that initiate, orchestrate, and sustain cycles of inquiry into student learning. To root assessment practices into teaching and learning, these committees initiate rounds of dialogue that lead to consensus about shared expectations for student learning, followed by collaborative strategies that explore the curricular and co-curricular coherence that contributes to these expectations. Institution- and program-level visual representations of the landscape of students' learning opportunities, maps and inventories of educational practice, become the bedrock on which educators develop institution-, program-, and department-level claims about student learning in learning outcome statements. The worksheets, guides, and exercises at the end of this chapter are designed (1) to establish collaboration as a principle that underlies the work of assessment committees and their relationship with members of the academic community, (2) to promote institution- and program-level dialogue about teaching and learning as the context for embedding assessment, and (3) to guide the development of curricular and co-curricular maps and inventories of practice that document where and how students learn what an educational community values.

Chapter 3, "Making Claims About Student Learning Within Contexts for Learning," takes the work of the previous chapter to a greater level of specificity, helping educators to articulate sentences that describe what they expect students to demonstrate, represent, or produce as a result of what and how they have learned at the institution and its programs. This chapter describes strategies for translating and achieving agreement on collective institution-, program-, and department-level expectations for student learning, represented in maps and inventories of educational practice, and turning them into learning outcome statements—sentences that describe what students should be able to demonstrate. The worksheets, guides, and exercises at the end of this chapter (1) foster collaborative authorship of learning outcome statements, (2) foster collective review and approval of these statements, and (3) orient students to institution- and program-level learning outcomes.

Chapter 4, a new chapter, "Raising and Pursuing Open-Ended Research or Study Questions to Deepen Inquiry Into and Improve Student Learning," positions faculty and other educators to take a problem-based scholarly approach to the remaining assessment decisions and tasks detailed in succeeding chapters. Specifically, it assists faculty and other educators to collaboratively identify and pursue student-focused learning problems or pedagogically focused issues translated into open-ended research or study questions that educators care about—often prompted by developing a Taxonomy of Student Weaknesses, Errors, or Fuzzy Thinking in student work. It assists educators to identify the kinds of evidence or data that will contribute to answering those questions, including learning about how students learn and make meaning. And it assists educators to focus on how students do or do not develop sustained or enduring learning—learning for the long haul as opposed to learning solely for the end of a course or a single educational experience. Case studies incorporated into this chapter demonstrate how deepening inquiry into patterns of student performance promotes collaborative discussions, reflection, and actions to improve or maximize student learning. The worksheets, guides, and exercises at the end of the chapter position inquiry groups or communities of practice to engage in scholarly assessment as either a formal or an informal process that can lead to two by-products: (1) actions to improve or maximize student learning and inquiry-based findings and (2) interpretations that contribute to or build on knowledge and practices in the teaching profession.

Chapter 5, "Identifying or Designing Tasks to Assess the Dimensions of Learning," identifies the considerations that surround the choices we make among methods to assess our students' learning. Specifically, it focuses on engaging core working groups in identifying the considerations that surround the methods of assessment they choose, including how well a method aligns with what and how students learn and receive feedback of that learning and how well a method "fits" its purpose. It also expands the pool of direct and indirect assessment methods to include those now possible through technology and discusses the current and emerging assessment possibilities available through Web 2.0 tools now integrated into electronic portfolios and students' personal learning environments. The worksheets, guides, and exercises at the end of this chapter, together with the Inventory of Traditional and Technology-Enabled Direct and Indirect Assessment Methods, are designed to deepen discussions leading to decisions about assessment methods by focusing on (1) the parameters of decision making that lead to choices, (2) the properties of methods that make them fit for use, and

(3) the range of traditional and technology-based direct and indirect methods that capture the dimensions of learning.

Chapter 6, "Reaching Consensus About Criteria and Standards of Judgment," describes how observers or raters interpret student work, projects, or assignments in response to methods of assessment. Developing criteria and quality standards of judgment—such as scoring rubrics—provides a means to document and interpret patterns of student achievement. Demonstrating how scoring rubrics have become mainstreamed into assessment practice in higher education, this chapter includes four scoring rubrics from the Association of American Colleges & Universities' national VALUE Project (Valid Assessment of Learning in Undergraduate Education) and several examples of scoring rubrics used in the co-curriculum. The worksheets, guides, and exercises at the end of this chapter are designed to assist core working groups as they (1) develop scoring rubrics, (2) pilot-test scoring rubrics, and (3) develop interrater reliability among scorers as they prepare to apply scoring rubrics to student work.

Chapter 7, "Designing a Cycle of Inquiry," helps institution and program-level assessment committees or working groups orchestrate and then move through one cycle of assessment. Specifically, this chapter describes strategies for collecting evidence of student learning; scoring student responses; analyzing, representing, and interpreting results to make decisions about ways to improve educational practices; and then reentering the assessment cycle. Progressing through one cycle of inquiry helps an institution and its programs and services determine how to position assessment as a core institutional process—how to adapt existing processes, structures, and channels of communication or how to create new ones. The worksheets at the end of this chapter are designed to guide two processes: (1) an institution- or program-level cycle of inquiry and (2) the development of periodic reports that chronicle the assessment process, results, and next steps for each cycle of inquiry. These reports build institution- and program-level knowledge about student learning. They also become a way for colleges and universities to document their achievements, as well as their continual learning.

Chapter 8, "Building a Core Institutional Process of Inquiry Over Time," focuses on the characteristics of a maturing commitment to assessment as it becomes embedded into institutional life as a core process. The maturational process occurs by establishing intentional links or connections with other campus structures, processes, decisions, and channels of communication, often resulting in complementary or new relationships or new institutional behaviors. Further, it advances through a commitment of human, financial, educational, and technological support. In addition, it manifests itself through new campus practices that publicly and intentionally recognize the enduring value of this work in advancing both institutional and student learning. Representative campuses included in this chapter illustrate some of the ways that institutions are strengthening their commitment, including developing or purchasing an assessment management system to provide a means to centralize and record assessment work leading to human judgment about student work and assessment results. The worksheet, guides, and exercises at the end of this chapter are designed (1) to promote institutional self-reflection about a campus's current commitment to assessing for learning and (2) to stimulate collective discussion about ways in which that current commitment might deepen or expand into a core institutional process focused on advancing institutional and student learning.

As with the first edition, institutions in the early stages of launching assessment may wish to follow the processes, strategies, and developments in each successive chapter. Institutions that have developed more mature practices may benefit from delving into specific chapters or sections of chapters that deepen or refine their current practices.

Educators are by nature curious: they observe and analyze from multiple perspectives. Learning more about how well students translate our intentions into their own work extends that curiosity into the profession of teaching. What we learn promotes programmatic and institutional self-reflection about our practices. This self-reflection, in turn, stimulates innovations, reform, modification, revisions, or rethinking of educational practices to improve or strengthen student learning.

As institutions develop systemic and systematic core processes of inquiry, they will also increasingly be able to represent their students' achievement to external audiences in ways that reflect educational practices, institutional values, and the diverse ways in which students represent and demonstrate their learning. The significant learning outcomes of our colleges and universities are not discrete abilities; they are complex. Moreover, they are understood through multiple methods of assessment that capture integrated learning.

Chapter 1

DEVELOPING A COLLECTIVE INSTITUTIONAL COMMITMENT

If we wish to discover the truth about an educational system, we must look into its assessment procedures. What student qualities and achievements are actively valued and rewarded by the system? How are its purposes and intentions realized? To what extent are the hopes and ideals, aims and objectives professed by the system ever truly perceived, valued, and striven for by those who make their way within it? The answers to such questions are to be found in what the system requires students to do in order to survive and prosper. The spirit and style of student assessment defines the de facto curriculum.

—Derek Rowntree, 1987

OVERVIEW: Driven by intellectual curiosity about the efficacy of collective educational practices, assessment of student learning pursues questions about teaching and learning. This chapter provides an overview of institution- and program-level assessment as a systemic and systematic process of inquiry along the continuum of students' learning to determine over time who learns what, when, where, why, how, and how well. In addition, it presents an anatomy of the process that unfolds more specifically through succeeding chapters and argues for planning the assessment process backward to answer research or study questions about students' abilities to develop sustained learning. Joined to one or more outcomes, these collaboratively agreed-upon questions guide and channel deeper inquiry into the efficacy of pedagogy and other educational practices that students demonstrate in their work, as well as in their own analyses or descriptions of what and how they learn. This first chapter also engages educators in dialogue about an institution's collective commitment to assessing for learning that is anchored in (1) intellectual curiosity about learning and learners; (2) shared institutional principles of commitment; (3) interrelated positions of inquiry in a learning organization among the institution, its students, and its educators; and (4) roles and responsibilities across the institution. Additional Worksheets, Guides, and Exercises at the end of this chapter are designed to deepen educators' commitment to prioritizing assessment as a professional commitment that engages an institution into inquiry into and improvement of the teaching-learning process.

A CULTURE OF INQUIRY

How humans learn is complex. Ask a group of people to identify strategies, contexts, and conditions for how they learn. That list will probably include some of the following responses: repetition; practice in multiple contexts and over multiple times; feedback from peers, colleagues, or trusted others; self-reflection; motivation; risk taking; modeling behavior against that of another; observation; preference for learning in a certain way to ground new learning, such as the need to visualize; and even the instructiveness of failure. More than a process of ingesting information, learning is a multidimensional process of making meaning. This process differs from human being to human being and may even vary within each of our own selves depending on the nature of the task we face. What is easy for one person to learn may be difficult for another.

Insert the complexity of learning into the complexity of what we expect our students to achieve while studying at our colleges and universities. At the undergraduate level we aim to develop complex, higher-order thinking abilities that, in turn, inform or shape behaviors, values, attitudes, and dispositions. We educate individuals to respond to muddy problems within environmental, political, social, technological, scientific, and international contexts or developments. We develop students' communication skills so that they are versatile in their ability to represent their thoughts in written, oral, and visual forms for different audiences and purposes and through different kinds of media. We prepare students to develop lifelong learning habits of mind and ways of knowing that contribute to their personal and professional development. In addition, we educate our students to become morally and socially responsible citizens who contribute to their local and even global communities, cognizant of the ethical dimensions of their work, decisions, and actions. We also expect students to understand and practice the conventions, behaviors, disciplinary logic, and problem-solving strategies of their major field of study, as they become our future biologists, chemists, accountants, artists, journalists, physicians, researchers, and public figures. Increasingly, we also expect them to be able to apply various disciplinary modes of inquiry or perspectives. For example, arguing that a "sick patient does not represent a biochemistry problem, an anatomy problem, a genetics problem, or an immunology problem," a Harvard medical dean proposed in 2008 that undergraduates preparing to apply to medical schools should take sequences of interdisciplinary courses that span areas of biology, chemistry, and physics most "germane to advanced medical studies," as opposed to discrete scientific disciplines," and "take biologically-relevant quantitative skills and the basic statistics needed to understand scientific literature" ("Harvard Medical Dean," 2008).

Higher education is also cognizant of projected workforce and societal needs for the 21st century. Specifically, in 2007, the New Commission on the Skills of the American Workforce projected the need for "a very high level of preparation in reading, writing, speaking, mathematics, science, literature, history and the arts" as an "indispensable foundation for everything that comes after for most members of the workforce" (New Commission, 2007, pp. 6–7). "Developing students' abilities to think creatively, work creatively, and implement solutions should be central educational priorities as well" (Partnership for 21st Century Skills, 2004). Identifying the more advanced skills required of today's college students, workers, and citizens (which also require new ways of assessing), Elena Silva, senior policy analyst at Educator Sector, identifies "solving multifaceted problems by thinking creatively and generating original ideas from multiple sources of information" as pervasive intellectual demands of the 21st century (Silva, 2008, p. 1).

At the graduate level we educate people to become experts who explore new territories in their fields or professions and question findings, challenge claims, or rethink tradition-bound perspectives on or approaches to issues that lead to new directions in research and lines of inquiry. We educate them to work effectively in teams, to cross or connect disciplinary boundaries, to become "scholar-citizens who connect their work to the needs of society" and understand "ethical conduct as researchers, teachers, and professionals, including issues of intellectual property" (Nyquist, 2002, p. 19). Increasingly, graduate programs, as well, prepare students to think and behave in crossdisciplinary, multidisciplinary, or transdisciplinary ways to bring new knowledge and perspectives to bear on their professional work. For example, Charles Redman, inaugural director of the Schools of Sustainability at Arizona State University, views work in sustainability as "collaborative, transdisciplinary and problem-oriented to address the enmeshed environmental, economic, and social challenges of the 21st century." He believes that the problems of the world are to be solved and addressed by people who can make connections and understand cascading implications and do all these things in a rigorous way so they can really make statements and make connections for the future. Otherwise, we're just trying to add the parts together and we've proven that doesn't work. (Schools of Sustainability, 2009)

How well do we achieve our educational intentions at both the undergraduate and graduate levels of learning? How well do we position our students to integrate, apply, reapply, and deepen their knowledge, understanding, and ways of knowing and behaving, including repositioning or challenging long-held theories or beliefs or attitudes about a subject? How do undergraduate and graduate students construct meaning along the continuum of their learning journey? Even more fascinating are the questions we should now be raising about how our undergraduate and graduate students learn in what Yancey, Cambridge, and Cambridge (2009) describe as "this new world of distributed learning sites . . . that mandates investigation into how learning occurs in these new environments."

Therein lies the wellspring of an institutional commitment to assessment—intellectual curiosity about what and how well our students learn at both the undergraduate and graduate levels and across professional programs. Assessment is the means of answering those questions of curiosity about our work as educators. This systemic and systematic process of examining student work against our standards of judgment enables us to determine the fit between what we expect our students to be able to demonstrate or represent and what they actually do demonstrate or represent at points along their educational careers. Beyond its role of ascertaining what students learn in individual courses, assessment, as a collective program or institutional process of inquiry, examines students' learning over time. It explores multiple sources of evidence that enable us to draw inferences about how students make meaning based on our collective educational practices and the classroom, experiential, and web-based or virtual contexts or environments in which they learn.

This book presents a framework, processes, strategies, illustrative campus practices, key resources, guides, worksheets, and exercises that assist institutions offering undergraduate, graduate, and professional programs in developing a sustainable culture of inquiry about students' learning. This inquiry builds on the successful practices of classroom-based assessment to explore students' cumulative learning at various points in their educational careers represented in their "texts," that is, their behaviors, interactions, reactions, reflections, and visual and verbal products or performances that include paper and paperless modes of representation, including those possible now through media technologies. Specifically, this book focuses on assessing how well students achieve at two levels:

1. The program level (department, division, school, or service within an institution)
2. The institution level, based on a college's or university's mission statement, educational philosophy, or educational objectives

At these two levels of assessment, collective questions such as the following initiate inquiry into student learning:

- How well do undergraduate and graduate students transfer and apply concepts, principles, processes, ways of knowing, and problem solving across their major program of study?
- How well do undergraduate students integrate their core curriculum, general studies, or liberal studies into their major program or field of study?
- How well do undergraduate and graduate students develop understanding, behaviors, attitudes, values, and dispositions that a program asserts it develops?
- How do open resources, digitized collections, virtual learning environments, social networks, and collaborative online research deepen learning, foster research skills, and shape the ways in which undergraduate and graduate students construct meaning and present their work?
- How do graduate students organize and produce knowledge amid emerging technologies and digital environments that are rapidly developing open-access collections (often making more widely available heretofore limited-access documents or even unpublished materials), such as the Open Humanities Press, which has created five new open-access monograph series focused on critical and cultural theory that invite readers to "annotate, tag, edit, add to, remix, reformat, reversion,

reinvent, and reuse" the material? (Howard, 2009)

- In graduate education, what pedagogies and uses of emerging technologies in disciplines and across disciplines contribute to developing "experts" in a field of study?
- How do we educate our graduate students to take risks, develop creative solutions or approaches to problems or issues, and challenge existing paradigms?

This book also presents inquiry into student learning as a systemic and systematic core process of institutional learning—a way of knowing about our work—to improve educational practices and, thus, student learning. Becoming learning organizations themselves, higher education institutions deepen understanding of their educational effectiveness by examining processes and products: (1) the various learning processes or pathways students follow or pursue, and (2) the various ways in which students make their learning visible. Each chapter explores ways to position intellectual inquiry into program- and institution-level processes, decisions, structures, practices, forms of dialogue, and channels of communication. Some campuses have embedded or woven this institutional commitment into existing institutional structures and practices. Others have developed new ways of behaving that accommodate the depth and breadth of this commitment.

DIALOGUE ABOUT TEACHING AND LEARNING ACROSS THE INSTITUTION

Driven by compelling questions about how students translate what they have learned into their own set of practices, assessment promotes sustained institutional dialogue about teaching and learning. A complex process, learning occurs over time inside and outside the classroom, including in virtual spaces and places, but not at the same time for all learners or under the same set of educational practices or experiences. Compatible with the intellectual curiosity that characterizes educators—a desire to explore and question issues from multiple perspectives—assessment channels intellectual curiosity into investigating students' learning (Maki, 2002c). This investigation occurs through the multiple lenses of individuals who contribute to students' learning: faculty, staff, administrators, graduate and undergraduate students, teaching or grad-

uate assistants, local community leaders, internship or field advisers, alumni, counselors, coaches, mentors, and peers.

Building a collective commitment to assessing student learning also involves establishing new or different kinds of relationships and opportunities for dialogue. Some of these relationships involve deepening or transforming working relationships that already exist, such as among faculty in a department, program, or division, or among professional staff in a service. Other relationships involve crossing boundaries to create lasting new partnerships, such as among academic affairs, student affairs, student support services, and those in library and information resources. Still other relationships require breaking new ground to build an organic and systematic focus on learning and improving learning. Establishing learning circles or inquiry groups that track student learning over time to understand how students construct meaning along different dimensions of their educational experiences is one kind of groundbreaking relationship. Developing communication structures and processes that channel assessment results into program- and institution-level planning, budgeting, and decision making is yet another kind of new relationship. These kinds of relationships characterize a culture of inquiry that relies on evidence of student learning to inform institutional actions, decisions, and long- and short-term planning focused on improving student achievement.

Learning as defined in this book encompasses not only knowledge leading to understanding, but also abilities, habits of mind, ways of knowing and problem solving, attitudes, values, and other dispositions that an institution and its programs and services claim to develop. Identifying patterns of student performance represented in various kinds of student "texts"—written, visual, oral, and interactive, including embedding image and audio in online sites—provides robust evidence of how well undergraduate and graduate students progress toward and achieve our expectations for their learning. Exploring reasons why students are not achieving our expectations or why educational practices are not maximizing students' learning stimulates specific discussion about ways to improve the following:

- Pedagogy
- Instructional design for face-to-face, hybrid, and online learning environments
- Curricular and co-curricular design

- Institutional programs and services that support, complement, and advance student learning
- Educational resources and tools that offer alternative ways for students to learn
- Educational opportunities, such as research, internships, or study abroad
- Educational practices such as writing across the curriculum or learning communities
- Advising and mentoring

Situated within our sets of educational practices, assessment becomes integral to teaching and learning. Within this context we become more aware of how well we translate our intentions into multiple, varied, and frequent opportunities for students to learn. What an institution and its programs and services learn through students' work promotes programmatic and institutional dialogue and self-reflection about the processes of teaching and learning and their relationship to levels of student achievement. Dialogue and self-reflection, in turn, stimulate innovation, reform, modification, change, and revision or rethinking of educational practices and pedagogy to improve or strengthen student achievement.

ANATOMY OF THE COLLABORATIVE ASSESSMENT PROCESS

Providing a global view of assessment at this point in the book illustrates the dimensions of this internally driven commitment. As you read the following chapters, you will be able to flesh out the process for your institution and its programs and services. If you already have a process in place, the remaining chapters may help refine or deepen it.

Viewing the Process at Work

The collaborative process has no universal model that fits all institutions. Rather, individual institutions embed or evolve practices that enable them to sustain a culture of inquiry. (Internet resources for assessment glossaries and online institutional handbooks, listed under "Additional Resources" at the end of this chapter, illustrate the range of campus approaches.) Further, assessment is an iterative process—moving forward often depends on exploring or unearthing information that shapes a decision or on establishing new procedures or lines of communication that ad-

vance the process (Maki, 2002a). Assessment is also a process of nested discussions, decisions, and actions. Two examples illustrate this point:

- Developing institution- or program-level *outcome statements,* sentences that describe what students should be able to demonstrate during or at the end of their undergraduate or graduate careers, is not simply a matter of word craft. Educators must agree on how, when, and where they address these outcomes. Clear outcome statements emerge from this kind of collaborative work.
- Determining a schedule to assess students' cognitive development in a discipline or graduate students' development of increasingly more complex conceptual understanding rests on discussions among faculty and others who contribute to students' learning about how they design their courses, the curriculum, and educational experiences to advance undergraduate or graduate students' cognitive or conceptual abilities. Agreement about collective intent, then, becomes the backbone of a schedule to assess student learning.

Figures 1.1, 1.2, and 1.3 provide an anatomy of the collaborative assessment process. These figures are not designed to prescribe a lockstep institution- or program-level strategy. Rather, they identify major tasks that occur in a sustainable inquiry process. Chapters 2 through 8 elaborate on these major tasks, describe various strategies for carrying them out, and incorporate institutional examples that illustrate representative campus practices. Figure 1.1 focuses on the collective tasks and decisions involved in describing major program- and institution-level outcomes, on developing methods to assess those outcomes, and on developing criteria and standards of judgment to assess student work. Figure 1.2 focuses on collective tasks and decisions related to identifying when to assess students' work to ascertain how well they are achieving or have achieved program- or institution-level outcomes. Figure 1.3 focuses on collective tasks and decisions related to interpreting the results of assessment methods and using them to verify students' achievement or to identify patterns of weakness. It also focuses on the importance of implementing changes to improve learning, an action that stimulates anew the inquiry process.

A. State Expected Outcomes at the Appropriate Level	B. Identify Where Expected Outcomes Are Addressed	C. Determine Methods and Criteria to Assess Outcomes	D. State Institution's or Program's Level of Expected Performance	E. Identify and Collect Baseline Information
Examples: • Derive supportable inferences from statistical and graphical data • Analyze a social problem from interdisciplinary perspectives • Evaluate proposed solutions to a community issue	*Examples:* • Courses • Programs • Services • Internships • Community service projects • Work experiences • Independent study	*Examples:* • Test • In-class writing sample • In-class analysis of a problem • In-class collaborative problem solving project • Portfolio • Performance • Simulation • Focus group	*Examples:* • Numerical score on a national examination • Numerical score on a licensure examination • Holistic score on ability to solve a mathematical problem • Mastery-level score on a culminating project • Mastery-level score on writing samples	*By means of:* • Standardized tests • Locally designed tests or other instruments • In-class writing exercise • In-class case study • Portfolio • Performance

FIGURE 1.1 Assessment Guide: Determining Your Expectations at the Institution and Program Levels

A. Determine Whom You Will Assess	B. Establish a Schedule for Assessment	C. Determine Who Will Interpret Results

For example:
 • All students
 • Student cohorts, such as
   • At-risk students
   • Historically underrepresented students
   • Students with SATs over 1200
   • Traditional-aged students
   • Certificate-seeking students
   • International students
   • First-generation students
	For example:
	 • Upon matriculation
	 • At the end of a specific semester
	 • At the completion of a required set of courses
	 • Upon completion of a certain number of credits
	 • Upon program completion
	 • Upon graduation
	 • Upon employment
	 • A number of years after graduation
		For example:
		 • Outside evaluators:
		   • Representatives from agencies
		   • Faculty at neighboring institutions
		   • Employers
		   • Alumni
		 • Inside evaluators:
		   • Librarian on team for natural science majors
		   • Student affairs representative on team to assess general education portfolio
		   • Interdisciplinary team
		   • Assessment committee
		   • Writing center
		   • Academic support center
		   • Student affairs office

FIGURE 1.2 Determining Timing, Identifying Cohort(s), and Assigning Reponsibility

A. Interpret How Results Will Inform Teaching/Learning and Decision Making	B. Determine How and With Whom You Will Share Interpretations	C. Decide How Your Institution Will Follow Up on Implemented Changes
For example: • Revise pedagogy, curricula, sequence of courses • Ensure collective reinforcement of knowledge, abilities, habits of mind by establishing, for example, quantitative reasoning across the curriculum • Design more effective student orientation • Describe expected outcomes more effectively • Increase connections between in-class and out-of-class learning • Shape institutional decision making, planning, and allocation of resources	*For example:* • General Education Sub-committee of the Curriculum Committee, through an annual report • Departments, through a periodic report • Students, through portfolio review day • College planning/budgeting groups, through periodic reports • Board of trustees, through periodic reports • Accreditors, through self-studies	• Repeat the assessment cycle after you have implemented changes or innovations: **Assessment Cycle** 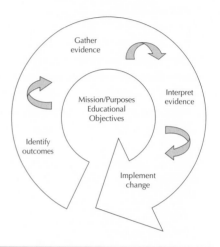

FIGURE 1.3   Interpreting and Sharing Results to Enhance Institutional Effectiveness

Planning the Assessment Process Backward

Figures 1.1, 1.2, and 1.3 represent the subtasks that are involved in the assessment process once it is initiated; however, collaboratively planning assessment backward before initiating the process—thinking through what you want to discover about student learning and what sources of evidence you will draw on along the students' learning continuum—leads eventually to useful and robust results that inform dialogue about patterns of student performance. Assessment becomes an opportunity to explore the efficacy of pedagogy, instructional design, use of current and emerging technologies (such as virtual learning environments), and other educational experiences or contexts for learning that we draw on to position students to learn. Exploring how students learn, how different contexts promote sustained learning—that is, how students transfer and apply their learning beyond a course—should be the driving forces behind the assessment process.

Planning the assessment process backward before initiating it slows us down to think about not only what we want to assess, but also whom we want to assess,

how we want to assess, and when we want to derive evidence of students' enduring learning along their educational journey. Without raising and answering questions about our students and what and when we want to learn about their achievements—before launching into the assessment process—our results may not be all that useful or may lend themselves to limited generalizations, such as "students do not show development of their analytical abilities by the end of four years." All students? Some students? Which students? Failure to identify whom you will assess may well lead to questions about the usefulness of results except to make overarching generalizations about "students." Answering the following two sets of questions early on in the backward planning process will shape who, what, when, where, why, and how you sample and collect evidence of student learning that leads to highly useful results.

1. Who Are Your Students?

From multitasking millennial students who were born into the digital age to nontraditional students who did not grow up in a technologically driven world, our student bodies increasingly reflect the demographics of our country and the world. A partial list of student descriptors may look like the following, including any combination of descriptors such as *part-time, nonresidential non-native speakers* or *full-time, residential millennial students:*

- Part-time
- Full-time
- Residential
- Nonresidential
- Distance or online
- Certificate-seeking
- One-course-seeking
- Traditional-aged, millennial, Generation X, 21st-century who may already have developed their own personal online learning environment (Barrett & Garrett, 2009)
- Non-traditional-aged
- First-generation
- Non-native-speaking
- Honors
- Advanced-placement
- Prior-learning
- Learning-disabled
- Physically disabled
- GED
- Historically underrepresented
- Degree-seeking
- Non-degree-seeking
- Developmental or underprepared
- Transfer
- International
- Degree returnees seeking a new profession or training for a changing economy and workforce
- Working

Initially, documenting what your students already know or can do, establishing a baseline for your diverse student population, provides you with a way to track your students' achievement levels within the context of your educational practices. The National Governors Association's Center for Best Practices, in particular, has recently called for establishing benchmarks for underachieving students in developmental and core courses (National Governors Association, 2009). Given the diversity of learners at our institutions, as well as students' varying abilities, motivation, and readiness to learn, it is useful to know about their levels of achievement as they enter a college or university or declare their major program of study. Otherwise,

you may end up with generalizations about your students that may not be true of all of your student cohorts. (A list of major readings on characteristics of different student populations appears in the "Additional Resources" at the end of this chapter). The demographics of our colleges and universities have changed dramatically: there are diverse learners at our institutions, not one-of-a-kind learners. Indeed, three of President Obama's educational challenges—(1) the challenge to Americans to attend at least one year of college, (2) the challenge to colleges and universities to graduate more students ("Obama's Bold Goals," 2009; "Obama to Propose Graduation Goal," 2009), and (3) the challenge to improve remedial education with particular focus on and support for community colleges (Killough, 2009)—press institutions to identify their student populations as well as expand the repertoire of teaching-learning strategies to prepare increased numbers of historically and economically underrepresented students.

Identifying who our students are and what we know about their entry-level abilities is an important way to anchor a chronological commitment to assessing student progress. The more you know about your student populations' performance, the better able you will be to make changes in pedagogy or educational practices for groups that do not perform at the expected level. Thus you can engage in focused dialogue about changes you may want to make for certain populations, such as underprepared students or non-native speakers.

2. *What Do You Want to Learn About Your Students' Learning and When Do You Want to Learn?*

Also, given the diversity of our student bodies, it is important to plan your assessment process by agreeing on what you want to learn about cohorts in your demographic spread and when you want to learn about their progress. Collecting evidence of student learning at the end of a program in students' undergraduate or graduate studies is too late to identify patterns of weakness across cohorts of students. Identifying patterns of weakness early on in students' coursework leads to early intervention to address the reasons for those weaknesses. A useful way to think about course-based assessment is in relation to program- and institution-level expectations: specifically, when and where will students be asked to apply or use what they have learned in a course in the progression of their program of study? For example, some learners in a basic statistics course will need to apply basic statistical knowledge and procedures in upper-level courses; thus, determining how well students apply what they learned in the basic course to their upper-level coursework in their major program of study would be a valuable question to answer through assessment. Do these students do well in recall and recognition of statistical terms but have a weak ability to apply the correct statistical processes to solve a specific kind of problem? Identifying students' future use or application of learning shapes who and when and how students will be assessed.

There also needs to be more than one opportunity to assess student achievement of an expected learning outcome: identifying two assessment times, at least, is important in your overall program- or institution-level assessment process after you have established baseline data about your student populations:

1. *Formative* assessment captures students' progress toward institution- or program-level outcomes based on applying agreed-upon criteria and standards of judgment to student work at chronological times or milestones in their learning journey, such as the end of the second year, after a certain number of credits, before acceptance into a program of study, after a gateway course, or at a significant transition point in a program of study
2. *Summative* assessment captures students' achievement at the end of their program of study in their undergraduate or graduate education based on applying agreed-upon criteria and standards of judgment.

Coupling your learning-outcome statements with a research or study question—a question of curiosity about what, how, how well, when, where, or why students learn or have difficulty learning—also shapes the design of your assessment process, leading to robust evidence. (Chapter 4 focuses on the importance of coupling research or study questions with learning outcomes as a way to ground the assessment process to identify, track, and address barriers to student learning.) Research or study questions articulate collaboratively agreed-upon issues about learning, such as the following: What kinds of cognitive or conceptual impediments do specific cohorts of students experience as they shift from thinking arithmetically to thinking algebraically? Raising such questions contributes to identifying both the kinds of evidence you

will assess and when you will seek that evidence along the continuum of students' coursework.

Consisting of more than isolated cells of activity, assessment becomes an institutional way of behaving, an institutional rhythm involving educators within and outside the institution in examining evidence of student learning at significant points in students' undergraduate and graduate programs. For example, results of asking undergraduates in a major to solve a case study at the end of their second year may reveal that some students cannot apply necessary analytical reasoning that upper-level courses are designed to build on. A milestone examination that captures how well master's or doctoral students apply disciplinary or cross-disciplinary knowledge, processes, methods of inquiry, and perspectives at a significant transition point in their programs' curricula could identify not only students' accumulated strengths but also existing patterns of weakness that, left unaddressed, remain as obstacles to developing expertise.

PRINCIPLES OF AN INCLUSIVE COMMITMENT

An inclusive commitment to assessment of student learning is established when it is (1) meaningfully anchored in the educational values of an institution—articulated in a principles-of-commitment statement; (2) intentionally designed to foster interrelated positions of inquiry about the efficacy of educational practices among educators, students, and the institution itself as a learning organization; and (3) woven into roles and responsibilities across an institution from the chief executive officer through senior administrators, faculty leaders, faculty, staff, and students. Without meaningful institutional anchors, the commitment to assessment may become periodic, transitory, or marginalized—an action that has to be performed but not necessarily for any meaningful purpose. The following anchors represent possible ways institutions can ground a sustainable inclusive commitment across the institution.

Accountability

Overall, institutions have responded to assessment of student learning because it is an essential commitment that accreditors review as an indication of institutional effectiveness.

Regional and National Accreditation
National focus on institutions' demonstration of their students' learning continues to be a major focus of

regional and national accreditors, who have increasingly raised the bar for institutions over the last several years. Creating additional resources, workshops, institutes, and guidelines, accreditors are pressing institutions to prioritize as well as mature the assessment process so that it leads to changes in pedagogy, curricular and instructional design, and educational practices. Among the kinds of developments across regional accreditors are the following:

- Annual series of workshops or conferences that focus on assessment, such as those offered by the Accrediting Commission for Senior Colleges and Universities of the Western Association of Schools and Colleges (www.wascsenior.org); the Middle States Commission on Higher Education (www.msche.org); the Higher Learning Commission's Academy for Assessment of Student Learning, designed to offer its member institutions "a four-year sequence of events and interactions that are focused on student learning, targeted at accelerating and advancing efforts to assess and improve student learning, and designed to build institution-wide commitment to assessment of student learning" (www.ncahlc.org); and the New England Educational Assessment Network (NEEAN), a collaboration between the Commission on Institutions of Higher Education of the New England Association of Schools and Colleges (http://neean.southernct.edu)
- New accreditation pathways, under some regional accreditation agencies, that offer institutions the option of focusing on institutional improvement, including student learning, such as the Quality Enhancement Plan (QEP) of the Commission on Colleges of the Southern Association of Colleges and Schools, a component of accreditation that describes a "carefully designed course of action that addresses a well defined or focused topic or issue related to enhancing student learning" (www.sacscoc.org), or the Higher Learning Commission's proposed Pathways Construction Project, designed to separate the continued accreditation process into the Assurance Process and the Improvement Process (www.ncahlc.org)

Though legislators, policy makers, and accreditors become external drivers of an institutional commitment to assessment, it is important to shift from an externally driven process to an internally driven one. It is vital to position assessment as integral to our professional work and to a commitment to teaching and learning that is responsive to our students' needs. Developing a sustainable, internally driven core process of inquiry to improve student learning, as opposed to an externally driven periodic activity, is what accreditors aim to promote in higher education. Regional accreditors seek evidence of an institution's ability to build a systemic process from the inside out. National and specialized accreditors seek the same process with a focus at the level of a program or service. An institution's ability to demonstrate its commitment to student learning involves, as the following standards from some of the regional accreditors illustrate, a holistic approach to student learning that focuses not only on the curricular but also co-curricular intentions in educating students and the efficacy of the practices that carry out those intentions.

- Standard II of the standards of the Accrediting Commission for Community and Junior Colleges of the Western Association of Schools and Colleges (2002), "Student Learning Programs and Services," requires that an institution demonstrate how instructional programs, as well as student support services, and library and learning support services, facilitate the achievement of an institution's stated student learning outcomes. Results need to become a part of an "institution wide dialogue" (p. 1) focused on how well a campus achieves its mission and purposes.
- Standard 2 of the standards of the Accrediting Commission for Senior Colleges and Universities of the Western Association of Schools and Colleges (2008), "Achieving Educational Objectives Through Core Functions," requires that student learning outcomes and expectations be "reflected in academic programs and policies, curriculum, advisement, library and information resources, and the wider learning environment" (p. 15).
- Standard 14 of the standards of the Middle States Commission on Higher Education (2009) requires that institutions develop clearly articulated written statements, "expressed in observable terms, of the knowledge, skills, and competencies that students are expected to exhibit upon successful com-

pletion of a course, academic program, co-curricular program, general education requirement, or other specific set of experiences" (p. 41).

- Criterion Three, "Student Learning and Effective Teaching," under the accreditation standards of the Higher Learning Commission of the North Central Association of Schools and Colleges (2003), calls for patterns of evidence documenting that "Faculty and administrators routinely review the effectiveness and uses of the organization's program to assess student learning" (p. 3.1–4).

Specialized Accreditation

Specialized accrediting bodies, as well, seek evidence of a sustained commitment to assessment at the department, program, or school level—an indicator of quality and a commitment to improving student learning. The Association to Advance Collegiate Schools of Business (AACSB; www.aacsb.edu); the two leading education program accreditors, the Teacher Education Accreditation Council (TEAC; www.teac.org) and the National Council for Accreditation of Teacher Education (NCATE; www.ncate.org); nursing accreditors such as the Commission on Collegiate Nursing Education (CCNE; www.aacn.nche.edu) and the National League for Nursing Accrediting Commission (NLNAC; www.nlnac.org); and other healthcare accrediting bodies such as those for kinesiology and pharmacy focus on assessment of student learning (often based on explicit competencies) as part of their standards and criteria for evaluating programs. Some accrediting associations, such as the Accreditation Board for Engineering and Technology (ABET), hold programs responsible for assessing learning outcomes that the institution values as well (see Criterion 5 in the 2009–2010 accrediting standards of ABET (2008, p. 2). A list of specialized and regional accrediting agencies can be found at the Council for Higher Education Accreditation (CHEA) website (www.chea.org).

The International Context: The Bologna Process

A larger international context, established through the Bologna Process begun in 1999, may provide American colleges and universities with yet another context to deepen their commitment to assessment of student learning. As described on the project's website (www.ond.vlaanderen.be/hogeronderwijs/bologna/), the Bologna Process has been a multiyear European commitment across higher education that has established how degrees are defined, how disciplines are structured, how higher degrees build on students' previous degrees, how student learning is documented in a degree, and how documented student achievement facilitates students' transfer to other European institutions. This process has also migrated to Latin America, North Africa, and Australia. Adelman (2009) argues that "the core features of the Bologna Process have sufficient momentum to become the dominant global higher education model" (p. viii). In a recent publication on the Bologna Process that explores both the positive developments in this commitment as well as its remaining challenges, Gaston (2010) urges American colleges and universities to pay attention to the Bologna Process as it has addressed current American higher education foci and concerns:

. . . higher educators in the United States should regard as significant the challenges [the Bologna Process] poses and collaborate on a judicious and constructive response. The primary issue is not that Europe has created an agenda for reform that the U.S. must emulate in order to remain competitive—though that is a consideration. Rather, the aspirations that inform Bologna are for the most part ones we share and at least to some extent are pursuing already. With the exception of Bologna's stated determination to assert a new European ascendancy, the action lines of the Process reflect issues that have been of concern in the U.S. for many years: consistency (how degrees are defined, how disciplines are structured), continuity (how one degree level should encourage students to attempt the next), quality assurance ("accountability ideas"), and mobility (issues of transferability and transcript transparency). But if the European priorities are familiar, they should also be compelling because Europe has embarked on a course of reform far better coordinated and comprehensive than any the U.S. can offer—and has done so with a far greater sense of urgency" (p. 9).

Migration of Bologna-like work has now made its way to the United States through support from the Lumina Foundation. Specifically, in its Tuning USA project (*tuning* refers to a faculty-led approach that involves seeking input from students, recent graduates, and employers to establish criterion-referenced learning outcomes and competencies—an approach that has been used in the Bologna Process), Lumina has launched a pilot project involving higher education institutions in the states of Indiana, Minnesota, and Utah. Each state will draft learning outcomes and map the relations between these outcomes and graduates' employment options for at least two of the following disciplines: biology, chemistry, education, history, physics, and graphic design. According to the foundation, the aim of this project is to "create a shared understanding among higher education's stakeholders of the subject-specific knowledge and transferable skills" that students in these six fields must demonstrate upon completion of a degree program ("Tuning USA," 2009).

The Science of Learning

More compelling reasons exist for integrating assessment into institutional life than responding solely to external drivers. For one, research on the complexity of learning is increasingly challenging educators to examine the assumptions underlying teaching and learning in face-to-face and online learning environments, as well as those underlying methods of assessment. Halpern and Hakel (2002) make the compelling case that the business of educators is indeed to engage in research on teaching to promote students' long-term retention and recall or, at least, to draw on existing research to inform educational practices. They explore the effects of various pedagogies on long-term retention. Integral to this arena of work is assessment, a means to ascertain the effectiveness of different kinds of pedagogy and instructional tools, including technology tools, in fostering desired learning. Since the early 21st century, the National Research Council's publications on research on learning have stimulated deeper thinking about how we design for learning. Publications that demonstrate how the science of learning shapes pedagogy, such as Reif (2008), should become required reading for faculty as they design their courses and programs and develop aligned assessment methods.

In addition, there is an ever-expanding body of research on the effects of educational technology on learners; examples include what and how well students transfer and apply learning in virtual environments such as Second Life (SL) and how well they represent their learning in wikis, podcasts, and blogs (see, for example, Educause [2010]). The ever-growing number of blended courses and programs (ones that combine online and face-to-face learning) in higher education received a boost from recent research reported by the Department of Education—a meta-analysis of 1,000 empirical studies from 1996–2008 focusing on student achievement of outcomes in online versus face-to-face learning environments particularly for undergraduate and graduate students (U.S. Department of Education, 2009). Results of this meta-analysis reveal that, on average, students who took all or part of their courses online performed better than those who learned the same outcomes in face-to-face instruction. Although this report does not state that online learning is superior to face-to-face instruction, it does give an edge to certain online elements that promote learning, such as the expansion of learning time. Continuing to draw on research on how people learn and research on the efficacy of online, face-to-face, and blended learning environments should directly shape the design of pedagogy, curricula, and learning environments. If we simply layer assessment methods onto students' work as afterthoughts, as opposed to designing them based on (1) dialogue about our educational philosophies, practices, and intentions; (2) knowledge about how students learn through different modes of delivery, such as through tutorials or self-paced online programs; and (3) acceptance of the fact that students learn differently, then we cannot learn about the efficacy of our designs or determine how to improve them. It is reasonable, then, that the National Research Council called for "a richer and more coherent set of assessment practices that align with what and how students learn" (2001, p. 3). Engaging in research on learning or drawing on research on learning in the design of pedagogy, curricula, educational experiences, educational technology, and the use of technology to assess our students serves as a professional underpinning for an institutional commitment to assessment.

The Scholarship of Teaching and Learning

Since Ernest Boyer's (1990) landmark reconsideration of scholarship as four interrelated priorities for the professoriate—discovery, integration, application, and teaching—inquiry into teaching and learning has become an avenue for scholarship. In that inquiry, assessment, a means of providing evidence about the effectiveness of teaching practices, has received scholarly status as well. Shulman (1998) contributes to this status by describing the scholarship of teaching as entailing a public account of some or all of the full act of teaching—vision, design, enactment, outcomes, and analysis—in a manner susceptible to critical review by the teacher's professional peers and amenable to productive employment in future work by members of that same community (p. 6). A year later, Hutchings and Shulman (1999) described the stance that characterizes the Carnegie Academy for the Scholarship of Teaching and Learning (CASTL) approach to teaching: It requires a kind of "going meta," in which faculty frame and systematically investigate questions related to student learning—the conditions under which it occurs, what it looks like, how to deepen it, and so forth—and to do so with an eye not only to improving their own classroom but to advancing practice beyond it (p. 13). A 2002 collection of CASTL scholars' essays notably advanced dialogue about and inquiry into the scholarship of teaching and learning through 10 disciplinary perspectives. Discussions of disciplinary styles of teaching necessarily raise questions about the relationship between methods of teaching and methods of assessing disciplinary learning. For example, some of the pedagogical disciplinary questions Calder, Cutler, and Kelly raise in "Historians and the Scholarship of Teaching and Learning" focus on identifying the "best ways to help students develop historical knowledge" and on identifying the kinds of assessment that "count as evidence for the understanding" they hope to build (Huber & Morreale, 2002, pp. 59–60).

Litterst and Tompkins (2001) and Banta and Associates (2002) have made a compelling case for viewing assessment as scholarship. For Litterst and Tompkins, assessment "belongs to the scholarship of teaching" because it is a systematic study of "situated teaching practices . . . using particular forms of research and knowledge" (2001, p. 10). Banta and Associates' book, the most exhaustive collection of writings to date dedicated to exploring assessment as scholarship, draws together the writings of scholars, researchers, and practitioners that provide different disciplinary rationales for and perspectives on this approach to assessment, including the scholarly assessment of student development. For institutions that value or intend to value a commitment to assessment as a form of scholarship, Banta and Associates' book provides a rich resource on procedures and methods that define the scholarly parameters of this work.

The STEM disciplines (science, technology, engineering, and mathematics) have built an impressive history of focusing on the "scholarship of instruction"

through assessment. For example, a report by the Center for Education of the National Academy of Engineering (2003), based on a workshop organized by the National Research Council's Committee on Undergraduate Science Education, assesses the efficacy of pedagogy beginning with the first course that students take in STEM fields. Among the reported findings is that lectures and recipe-based laboratory sections alone are not sufficient preparation for students to "foster inquisitiveness, cognitive skills of evidence-based reasoning, and an understanding and appreciation of the processes of scientific investigation" (p. 25).

Continuing to leverage a focus on scholarly teaching, a publication of the National Academy of Engineering seeks to change how institutions recognize and reward the importance of "instructional scholarship" as central to the profession of teaching, noting that historically promotion and tenure decisions reward research as the most important measure of faculty performance, but value teaching effectiveness less regardless of the stated weighting of research, teaching, and service (King, Ambrose, Arreola, & Watson, 2009). Aimed at shifting this imbalance, the report proposes metrics for evaluating faculty instruction to meet institution- and program-level expectations for student learning. Drawing from Arreola, Theall, and Aleamoni (2003), King and colleagues identify five skills that faculty should demonstrate as key to ensuring student learning: content expertise, instructional design skills, instructional delivery skills, instructional assessment skills, and course management skills (p. 23).

Reporting and discussing assessment results becomes not only an institutional responsibility but also a larger academic community responsibility so that educators build knowledge about the efficacy of teaching-learning practices and disseminate that knowledge for others to adapt, refine, or use directly. Thus, publishing; presenting at regional, professional, or national conferences; and sharing results of inquiry into our students' learning through the current technologies represent a wider scholarly context for our assessment work, as proposed by Iiyoshi and Kumar (2008). An online locus for the scholarship of teaching, learning, and assessment is the Academic Commons, sponsored by the Center of Inquiry in the Liberal Arts at Wabash College (www.academiccommons.org). This website brings together faculty, academic technologists, librarians, administrators, and other academic professionals focused on liberal arts education. It aims to "share knowledge, develop collaborations, and evaluate and disseminate digital tools and innovative practices for teaching and learning with technology." Among the site's resources are scholarly contributions on the educational uses of the new technologies and the ways in which they are making visible what and how students are learning or representing their learning—ways that were not previously visible to us.

Disciplinary and Professional Organizations' Focus on Student Learning

Disciplinary and professional organizations continue to advance assessment as a means of upholding educational quality as well as improving teaching and learning. In 2006 the National Council of Teachers of English (NCTE), through its Conference on College Composition and Communication (CCCC), updated its position statement on assessment of writing, "Writing Assessment: A Position Statement." This statement articulates principles of effective assessment design in relation to the pedagogy of teaching writing, including using multiple samples of student work in the assessment process (NCTE, 2006). Thus, this public position on assessment practices is congruent with current pedagogy. In its position statement on "Teaching, Learning and Assessing Writing" prepared two years earlier (NCTE, 2004), CCCC recognized the importance of developing students' "literacy of the screen," but opposed the use of machine scoring in the assessment of writing. For first-year writing programs, the Council of Writing Program Administrators (WPA) describes the "common knowledge, skills, and attitudes sought by first-year composition programs in American postsecondary education" (Council of Writing Program Administrators, 2008). This statement also reflects research on how students learn to write, as well as current practices in the teaching of writing. NCTE and WPA have collaboratively written a white paper on assessment of writing that "helps teachers, administrators, and other stakeholders articulate the general positions, values, and assumptions on writing assessment that both these national organizations jointly endorse" (http://wpacouncil.org/whitepaper, n.d.).

The sciences and mathematics continue to demonstrate an impressive staying power in their commitment to advancing assessment as integral to teaching and learning (see also page 34 in this chapter). Project Kaleidoscope, an informal national alliance working to build learning environments for undergraduate students in mathematics, engineering, and various fields of science, focuses on assessing learning through its workshops, seminars, and publications (www.pkal .org). Since the late 1980s, the Mathematical Association of America (MAA) has focused on assessing undergraduates' quantitative reasoning, best represented in *Quantitative Reasoning for College Graduates: A Complement to the Standards* (Sons, 1996), which established quantitative literacy requirements for recipients of undergraduate degrees and called for institutions to take responsibility for assessing students' achievement of those requirements. A year earlier, the American Mathematical Association of Two-Year Colleges (AMATYC) had established requirements for its undergraduates (AMATYC, 1995). In 1999 the MAA published *Assessment Practices in Undergraduate Mathematics,* later expanded as *Supporting Assessment in Undergraduate Mathematics* (Steen, 2005), containing 26 case studies resulting from a four-year National Science Foundation–supported MAA project. The MAA's Committee on Assessment continues to work on its National Science Foundation and MAA-sponsored project to help departments of mathematical sciences develop effective assessment plans (www.maa.org/saum/).

The National Academies have maintained a consistently high profile in the advancement of teaching, learning, and assessment in the sciences, engineering, and medicine. Their publications represent a commitment to improving education for future scientists and to promoting assessment as integral to teaching and learning (National Research Council, 2002a, 2002b, 2003). Sustained focus on assessment is also evident in funding opportunities supported by the National Science Foundation. Among its categories of funding is Instructional Materials Development, which supports creating methods to assess student learning that are linked to nationally developed standards and to current thinking about how students learn math and science (www.nsf.gov-Funding/).

Other disciplines have developed guidelines, competencies, and resources that have contributed to a body of assessment practices that assist their members. The American Library Association (ALA) is a well-known pioneer in establishing standards to assess students' information literacy learning outcomes (www.ala.org/ala/mgrps/divs/acrl/issues/infolit/standards/standardstoolkit.cfm). Additionally, in 2008 the ALA developed information literacy competencies for political science research (www.ala.org/ala/mgrps/divs/acrl/standards/PoliSciGuide.pdf). The National

Communication Association (NCA) has developed a rich resource site (www.natcom.org) that presents a conceptual framework for assessment; identifies competencies in speaking and listening and assessment techniques and methods to assess those competencies; and provides guidelines for developing department assessment plans. The American Psychological Association (APA) has taken a leadership role in assessment demonstrated through the creation of its Assessment Cyberguide (www.apa.org/ed/guide_outline.html). This guide articulates undergraduate psychology learning goals and outcomes and lists resources on assessment in the field. And the American Historical Association recently published *Assessment in History: A Guide to Best Practices* (2008).

National organizations have also advanced their focus on assessment though the institutes, conferences, and resources they annually offer. Taking a lead in the focus on assessment of general education outcomes is the Association of American Colleges & Universities (AAC&U) through its VALUE Project, Valid Assessment of Learning in Undergraduate Education (AAC&U, 2009; see also www.aacu.org/value). This project has developed 15 national scoring rubrics (see chapter 6) that educators can use to assess student work in their general education (GE) program as well as in the work students produce in their major programs of study as they continue to build on these GE outcomes. A response to greater calls for accountability in higher education, these rubrics represent an alternative to standardized instruments that are unable to capture all of the desired GE outcomes, including students' abilities to integrate their learning over time. In addition, these rubrics provide a means for institutions to chronologically assess student learning over time, as opposed to standardized tests' snapshot in time, providing evidence of patterns of strength and weakness in students' work. AAC&U provides a wealth of resources, guides, and examples of assessment methods on its assessment website (www.aacu.org/resources/assessment). The Association of General and Liberal Education Studies has also expanded its reach to include attention to assessment of general education, leading to creation of an electronic mailing list and a guide for assessment and program review (www.bsu.edu/web/agls/).

Under its Global Learning for All project, the American Council on Education embarked on a project with eight institutions of varying sizes to develop international learning outcomes and models to assess these outcomes (www.acenet.edu/). Results

of this project, translated into campus practices and models, are published in Olson, Green, and Hill (2006).

The following national organizations have woven assessment into the work of student affairs professionals and student support programs:

- The American College Personnel Association (ACPA), along with its focus on assessment in its conferences and institutes, has published a guide for assessing student learning, the *ASK Standards* (Henning, 2008). This publication describes both the tasks that underlie assessment and the kinds of assessment methods that student affairs professionals may use or adapt to assess student learning. ACPA also offers assessment resources at www.myacpa.org/pub/pub_books_assessment.cfm.
- NASPA—Student Affairs Administrators in Higher Education—has also woven assessment into its conferences. NASPA has developed an Assessment Framework to guide integration of assessment into the organization's conferences and to help professionals charged with assessment to identify appropriate staff training (February, 2009). NASPA has also created a link to student affairs assessment websites (www.naspa.org/kc/saaer/websites.cfm) and recently published a book focused on assessment as collaborative work among faculty, student affairs, administrators, and students (Keeling, Wall, Underhile, & Dungy, 2008).
- The National Academic Advising Association (NACADA) has woven assessment into advising through its institutes, a CD (*Guide to Assessment of Academic Advising*), and a website that provides space for professionals to share and update assessment methods (www.nacada.ksu.edu/Commissions/C32/C32-AdvisingAssessmentTools.htm).
- The Council for the Advancement of Standards (CAS), a consortium of more than 35 professional organizations focused on student support services and programs for undergraduate and graduate students, frequently updates a set of publications focused on standards for and methods of assessment. Chief among its publications is *The CAS Professional Standards for Higher Education* (www.cas.edu/catalog/index.cfm).

Focus on assessment of graduate student learning has also received national attention in professional organizations and through publications. From 2000 to 2006, the Woodrow Wilson National Fellowship Foundation, under its Responsive Ph.D. Program, developed a Ph.D. Professional Development Assessment Project that attended to "program assessment at the graduate level," among other foci (www.woodrow .org/policy/responsivephd). The Carnegie Initiative on the Doctorate (CID; www. carnegiefoundation.org/ CID/partners_allies.htm) was a five-year action and research project that worked with doctoral-granting departments committed to restructuring their programs to better prepare graduates in six disciplines: chemistry, education, English, history, mathematics, and neuroscience. Some participating doctoral programs identified assessment of their graduate students' learning as a component of their plans to restructure, documented in Maki and Borkowski (2007). The Council for Graduate Studies (CGS) published a policy statement that includes guidelines for integrating assessment of student learning into program review (CGS, 2005).

Barbara Lovitts's publications also have contributed to integrating assessment into doctoral programs. *Making the Implicit Explicit: Creating Performance Expectations for the Dissertation* (Lovitts, 2007d) makes the case, based on her multiyear research project with Ph.D. programs, that doctoral programs should develop scoring rubrics to help graduate students understand what is required of them in writing a strong dissertation. That is, students should be introduced to these criteria early in their studies so that they develop the abilities necessary to write successful dissertations. Accompanying this work are three guides for graduate students that contain criteria for writing successful dissertations in the sciences, humanities, and social sciences (Lovitts & Wert, 2007a, 2007b, 2007c).

Finally, major funding organizations have been awarding grants to individual institutions or consortia to improve learning through assessment. Among those funding large-scale assessment-focused projects are the following:

1. The Fund for the Improvement of Post-Secondary Education, along with State Farm Companies Foundation, has supported AAC&U's VALUE Project (www.aacu.org/ value/) and the Association of Public and Land-grant Universities' (APLU) current study of the degree of comparability among

the three standardized tests APLU offers institutions to measure their students' achievement of general education outcomes under its Voluntary System of Accountability (VSA): Measure of Academic Proficiency and Progress (MAPP), Collegiate Learning Assessment (CLA), and Collegiate Assessment of Academic Proficiency (CAAP) (www.aplu.org/).

2. Lilly Endowment Inc. (www.lillyendowment .org/) has partially funded the Wabash National Study of Liberal Arts Education, a longitudinal study of 49 liberal arts-focused institutions with a wide range of selectivity that is focused on (1) identifying the teaching practices, programs, and institutional structures that support liberal arts education and (2) developing methods to assess liberal arts education (www.liberalarts.wabash.edu/ study-overview/). This project is also supported by the Teagle Foundation. (See also page 37 in this chapter.)

3. The Lumina Foundation (www.lumina foundation.org) among other higher education initiatives, supports Achieving the Dream: Community Colleges Count, a national multi-year project begun in 2004 to help more community colleges succeed in educating students (www.achievingthedream.org/). This initiative involves a partnership of 20 organizations and 83 community colleges in 15 states that focuses on institutions' use of data to "drive change," including the goal of increasing what we in higher education know about the efficacy of teaching strategies that increase student learning, thus, student success. (Examples from this grant appear on page 23). In addition, the Lumina Foundation supports the Tuning USA project described on pages 11–12.

4. The National Science Foundation supports all fields of the fundamental sciences and engineering, including research and developments in education across those disciplines and fields of study (www.nsf.gov/funding/ pgm_summ.jsp?pims_id=5468).

5. The Teagle Foundation identifies higher education's focus on assessing student learning as one of its funding priorities. Its website lists consortial projects it has funded or is funding in assessment and provides a robust

assessment resource site that also includes reports from institutions about their assessment results and white papers on assessment (www.teagle.org/about/ar08/resources/grants.aspx).

Institutional Focus on Learning-Centeredness

Yet another anchor for assessment is institutions' declaration of their focus on learning-centeredness. Increasingly, institutions across the country are characterizing themselves as learning-centered or student-centered, a term that appears in many college and university mission and purpose statements. Learning-centered institutions view students as active learners, creators of or contributors to knowledge and understanding, while at the same time reflecting on how well they are learning. Students are shaped by the contexts of their learning inside and outside the classroom, just as they shape their own learning. Learning-centered institutions shift away from being what Barr and Tagg (1995) describe as providers of instruction to being providers of learning. Faculty become designers of learning environments and tasks that foster student engagement, leading to students' own discovery and construction of meaning rather than predominantly being the transmitters of knowledge. Under this paradigm, the learning environment expands beyond the classroom to include, for example, face-to-face and online learning, interactive distance education, virtual studio classrooms, virtual simulations and engagement in environments such as Second Life, interaction in electronic media environments, online social networks, knowledge-building sites such as wikis, web-based instruction, self-paced learning, peer-to-peer learning, cooperative learning, and service learning.

Learning-centered institutions also focus on how programs and services outside the formal curriculum contribute to, support, and complement the curriculum, thereby contributing to students' achievement of an institution's mission and purposes. How do the programs and services of librarians and information resource staff, student affairs staff, learning support staff, and other professional staff or administrators contribute to student achievement? An institution that develops ethical decision making or civic responsibility would wish to explore not only how these dispositions develop in the classroom, but also how they develop or manifest themselves in residence life, athletics, governance, stu-

dents' interactions online, and student work on and off campus. Students' participation in multiple social contexts or in communities within and outside the academy offers opportunities for them to learn and reflect on their learning and offers educators opportunities to learn about the efficacy of our teaching or educational practices and experiences. Within an ever-expanding learning environment propelled through developments in technology, faculty, staff, administrators, students, teaching assistants, graduate assistants, alumni, community members, community leaders, and employers contribute to student learning.

Exploring how different complementary relationships contribute to learning, as illustrated in Figure 1.4, enables an institution to understand the efficacy of these relationships in contributing to its students' education (Maki, 2002b). In this figure, the learner transfers, deepens, or affirms learning in social contexts with people in various roles and responsibilities. Relationships with one or more individuals contribute to students' learning in the following ways:

- Advancing, challenging, and building on new or previous learning
- Providing feedback that corrects misunderstandings or affirms understanding
- Extending contexts for learning that illustrate the relevance or usefulness of new or previous learning
- Providing models of a particular behavior or ability

Faculty, staff, peers, mentors, advisers, administrators, internship supervisors, community leaders, and students, for example, assume teaching roles, offering diverse opportunities for students to apply or transfer knowledge, understanding, ways of knowing, and behaving. Consider the power of the following contexts in enabling students to deepen understanding:

- Observing how another peer or teaching assistant solves a chemistry problem
- Applying business principles to a student-run organization
- Applying principles of effective writing in preparing a proposal to undertake an independent study
- Serving as a resident assistant in a dormitory or a member of a judiciary board and wrestling with the ethical dimensions of a student's behavior

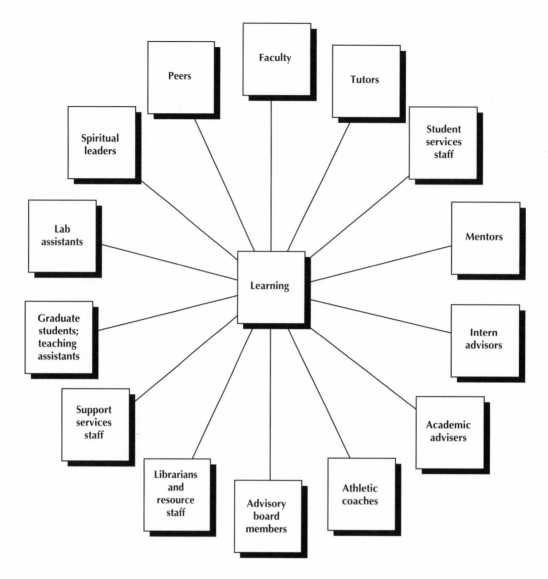

FIGURE 1.4 Some Contributors to Student Learning
Source: Adapted from Maki, P. (2002, October). Learning contexts inside and outside of the academy. *AAHE Special Report.* www.aahe.org/specialreports/part2.htm

- Challenging a decision made in a committee or group meeting that demonstrates a bias or violates agreed-upon working principles
- Applying principles of design to a community-based public art project
- Creating a wiki or podcast with fellow classmates focused on addressing a problem through interdisciplinary approaches.

Directing professional energy and curiosity into what and how students learn, then, is an essential process in a learning-centered institution. Questioning how students develop understanding, professional,

or disciplinary habits of mind; how they recall and use what they have learned and transfer it into new contexts; and how they move beyond long-held misconceptions to develop new understanding represents a challenging avenue of exploration in learning-centered institutions. What specific intellectual capacities or ways of understanding, for example, do problem-based collaborative projects, learning communities, and service-learning experiences promote that other educational experiences may not? How different pedagogies or learning experiences contribute to students' behaviors or values represents still another line of inquiry.

Institutional Focus on Becoming a Learning Organization

Evolving an institution into a learning organization—one that engages in ongoing inquiry into teaching and learning and is responsive to research findings about student learning and about the science of learning—may also anchor an institution's commitment to assessment. This commitment is reflected in the kinds of institutional structures, processes, and practices that evolve to answer and reflect on such questions about student learning as the following:

- How do institutions systematically learn about research on the science of learning or other faculties' teaching-based research?
- How does an institution use emerging open knowledge and open resources about teaching, learning, and assessment, as proposed by Iiyoshi and Kumar (2008), to inform or develop new educational practices?
- What support exists to enable educators to apply new knowledge or assessment findings or translate them into large-scale educational practices?
- How does an institution gather, store, and provide easy access to information about student learning that contributes to greater understanding about the efficacy of educational practices and experiences for cohorts of students (see descriptions of assessment management systems in chapter 8)?
- How do students, alumni, faculty, other campus professionals, and members of the surrounding community contribute to institutional discourse on teaching and learning?

Individuals and groups working across traditional boundaries to focus on student learning from multiple perspectives are indicative of a behavior that defines an institution's commitment to learn about its work. In their learner-centered paradigm, Barr and Tagg (1995) envision the "institution itself as a learner—over time, it continuously learns how to produce more learning with each graduating class, each entering student" (p. 14). An institution may ground its principles of commitment within the context of becoming a learning organization dedicated to continuously exploring its educational effectiveness. Institutions may in this way decide to view themselves as learners, shaped by what they learn from and about their students.

Indeed, two of the central outcomes of the Achieving the Dream: Community Colleges Count national initiative, supported by the Lumina Foundation (see also pages 23 and 35), illustrate the importance of institutions becoming learning organizations. Specifically, this project asserts that participating institutions will become "'learning organizations' and will use data to identify problems, set goals, establish institutional priorities, allocate resources and measure progress," as well as use the results of their inquiry to "make lasting changes in policies, structures, programs and services to improve student outcomes" (www.achieving thedream.org/aboutatd/expectedoutcomes.tp). Laurillard (2008) makes a case for the importance of institutions acting "like a learning system—one that makes knowledge of what it takes to learn explicit, adapts it, tests it, refines practice, reflects, rearticulates, and shares that new knowledge" (p. 328).

ESTABLISHING INTERRELATED POSITIONS OF INQUIRY IN A LEARNING ORGANIZATION

Three interrelated positions of inquiry characterize a college or university that is a learning organization—one fully committed to inquiry into student learning and use of its inquiry to effect change: (1) the institution's positions of inquiry, (2) students' positions of inquiry, and (3) educators' positions of inquiry, represented in Figure 1.5.

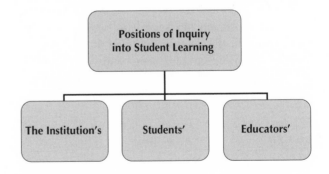

FIGURE 1.5 Positions of Inquiry

The Institution's Positions of Inquiry

More than an environment in which assessment takes place, a college or university needs to organize itself to raise and answer questions about how well students learn across their life of learning. That is, the institution becomes a collector of evidence to build knowledge about the efficacy of educational practices that may well lead to institution- or program-level changes to address patterns of student weakness. This kind of commitment involves creating campus-wide *soft times* (informal but regularly scheduled discussion times) and *neutral zones* (times and places that do not threaten honest dialogue) to engage members of the community in discussion about and reflection on evidence of student learning. These contexts promote the likelihood that large-scale structural or curricular or pedagogical changes based on inquiry into students' learning are widely and deeply addressed.

The institution itself needs to position itself to become reflective about what it learns from the assessment process, ensure broad campus discussion that includes major constituencies about findings that build collective knowledge, and develop the structures and processes that implement agreed-upon changes, as illustrated in chapter 8. Without establishing these goals and annually identifying the times and places to draw together the community, assessment remains a mechanical process of reporting, not a process of inquiry leading to dialogue about agreed-upon actions. Annual or semiannual formal and informal times to (1) share institution- and program-level results, both good news and not-so-good news; (2) collectively reflect on results; and (3) discuss and then propose innovations in educational practices, such as pedagogy or closer alignment of the curriculum with the co-curriculum, characterize the kinds of activity that occur in soft times and neutral zones. Engaging in collective discussion about research on effective online or face-to-face pedagogies to address a well-documented pattern of weakness in student achievement represents one way in which an institution could position itself as a learning organization.

Students' Positions of Inquiry

Students' positions of inquiry focus on what and how they learn and build on their learning so that they become responsible for their learning; that is, they own it as an ongoing process. Keeping stock of what they have mastered through their work such as in electronic portfolios; what they are able to transfer, apply, or build on in new contexts; and what they struggle to master or have yet to learn become the foci of their inquiry. Engaging students in reflection on their work as they hand it in, as they receive comments from faculty and peers or mentors, and as they chronologically

progress through their studies are ways to deepen students' understanding about what they do and do not know. Simultaneously, these kinds of engagement foster students' understanding of learning as a continual process, a patterning for lifelong learning. Involving students in discussions about their work, about how they learn, or about why they are unable to learn through in-class or online social spaces empowers them as learners and provides educators with other sources of evidence about the efficacy of educational practices besides the work students produce. (Chapter 5, pages 115–117 and page 159, lists some of the methods through which we can learn about students' learning experiences and processes as part of the assessment process.)

Acculturating students to take chronological responsibility for their learning initially requires faculty and staff to publicly orient students to undergraduate and graduate learning outcomes at both the institution and program or department levels, officially launching them into their educational journey. This acculturation process should position students to view learning as an ongoing, connected process as opposed to the accretion of discrete courses or units of learning that traditionally have, in students' view, no long-term relevance or usefulness. Across a coherently designed curriculum and co-curriculum, students continue to learn more about and demonstrate these outcomes in numerous contexts and experience, as well as identify how these outcomes are translated into disciplinary or interdisciplinary contexts (see also pages 97–98 and 115–117 in chapter 3). Additionally, students require faculty and staff guidance to learn how to become self-reflective learners, periodically pausing to analyze how well they are learning or building on learning outcomes across their educational journey, or how well they are applying previous learning, such as disciplinary concepts, into new contexts or situations.

A unique means of introducing students to an institution's general education learning outcomes is the Learning Outcomes Covenant, developed in 2007 by the leadership of Miami Dade College. This covenant was publicly and officially signed by campus and community leaders—the president, the provost for academic and student affairs, the chair of the board of trustees, the chair of the chamber of commerce (on behalf of employers and businesses in Miami), and student representatives from each campus in the college system. As Box 1.1 illustrates, this signed

---

BOX 1.1   INSTITUTIONAL EXAMPLE: *Miami Dade College's Learning Outcomes Covenant*

Learning Outcomes Covenant
October 19, 2007

We, the students and faculty of Miami Dade College, establish a covenant this day, **October 19, 2007,** to work together to achieve the Miami Dade College Learning Outcomes, and to build a foundation for the success of future students.

We acknowledge that liberal learning is essential to a free society and that the Miami Dade College Learning Outcomes hold the promise of guiding principles and practices that lead to empowered, informed and responsible citizens.

We, the students, accept our responsibility to become intentional learners and promise to engage actively and continually in preparation and study, and to articulate these learning outcomes in our lives and work.

We, the faculty, accept our obligations as teachers and mentors to design engaging coursework, programs and activities that intentionally address the learning outcomes and actively engage students.

Collectively, we—Miami Dade College students and faculty— pledge ourselves to the development of knowledge, skills, and attitudes that foster effective citizenship and lifelong learning.

Toward that end, we accept our shared responsibility to accomplish learning that will enable Miami Dade College graduates to:

- Use quantitative analytical skills to evaluate and process numerical data.
- Solve problems using critical and creative thinking and scientific reasoning.
- Formulate strategies to locate, evaluate, and apply information.
- Demonstrate knowledge of diverse cultures, including global and historical perspectives.
- Create strategies that can be used to fulfill personal, civic, and social responsibilities.
- Demonstrate knowledge of ethical thinking and its application to issues in society.
- Communicate effectively using listening, speaking, reading, and writing skills.
- Use computer and emerging technologies effectively.

Source: Used with permission from President Padrón, Miami Dade College.

document holds faculty, administrators, and students accountable for achieving the college's institutional learning outcomes.

Graduate students, as well, deserve to know upon matriculation what a program expects them to demonstrate along the trajectory of their doctoral or master's degree work and how this learning is specifically fostered throughout the courses and experiences that together form their program of study. Chapter 3, pages 118–119, provides some examples of graduate-

level learning outcome statements in a master's degree program.

Educators' Positions of Inquiry

Those who teach and those who provide programs and services for students such as those in student affairs or student support should be intellectually curious about the efficacy of their practices in fostering, promoting, and maximizing student learning. This curiosity should stretch beyond determining what students have or have not learned at the end of a course or service or educational opportunity to inquiry into students' longer-term abilities to draw and build on, apply, practice, and integrate learning over time. Additionally, educators should be responsive to the need to diversify pedagogy, instruction, and educational practices in light of the following variables: shifting or changing demographics at an institution; diverse learners' needs, such as those of first-generation students; and current and emerging technologies that offer alternative ways of teaching and learning. Those who teach, then, are positioned to design as well as develop sustained focus on and inquiry into the following:

- Learning about research and emerging practices in teaching and learning through various modes of delivery
- Examining and adjusting or revising the curriculum and co-curriculum to ensure coherence among the parts of students' experiences
- Aligning course and service outcomes with program-level, department-level, and institution-level learning to foster students' learning as well as provide students with a road map of their journey
- Constructing syllabi that identify learning outcome statements to help students understand what they are responsible for demonstrating, the pedagogy that promotes those outcomes, and the methods that will capture students' learning of those outcomes (syllabi will be addressed in more detail in chapter 3)
- Identifying research or study questions about student learning to be answered at the end of a cycle of inquiry (chapter 4 focuses on developing these kinds of questions in a problem-based assessment process)
- Identifying and chronologically using assessment methods that capture students' learning in the work students produce, as well as capture what students say about how they learn and transfer learning (learn more about this student focus in chapter 5, pages 162 and 177–178).
- Developing collaboratively agreed-upon criteria and standards of judgment by which to assess student work chronologically to ascertain how well students are making progress and eventually achieve expected levels of institution-level and program-level learning

- Analyzing and interpreting students' results within the context of educational practices that educators believe promote desired learning
- Collaboratively reflecting on and discussing interpretations of assessment results that lead to agreed-upon changes in educational practices based on patterns of weakness in student work
- Identifying a time to implement proposed agreed-upon changes as well as a time to reassess student work within the context of these changes to ascertain the efficacy of those changes

ROLES AND RESPONSIBILITIES ACROSS THE INSTITUTION

A shared commitment to assessing our students' learning involves initial and sustained interdependence among levels of constituencies across an institution. These constituencies are discussed in the following sections.

Presidents, Chancellors, System Heads, and Senior-Level Administrators

Communicating the value of assessing student learning within an institution—learning about the efficacy of our work through our students' work, for example—is a primary responsibility of presidents, chancellors, and system heads. Situating assessment within an institution or system as a core inquiry process is also primarily an executive leader's responsibility (as demonstrated in Box 1.1). A campus executive is also responsible for making sure that his or her senior administrators or policy makers are empowered to carry through program- and institution-level assessment recommendations—particularly those that focus on changing practices for cohorts of students, such as, for example, underprepared, historically underrepresented students or non-traditional-aged students. That is, senior-level administrators need to put into large-scale practice faculty and staff recommendations to improve student learning that have emerged from the assessment process—including structuring or restructuring the curriculum, aligning the curriculum with other resources or services that complement learning inside the classroom or online, and implementing new policies or practices that emerge as necessary ones at the end of the assessment process. Empowering senior-level administrators ensures that proposed recommended educational changes lead to systemic change.

Additionally, senior-level administrators need to channel assessment findings and recommendations into scheduled times for institutional self-reflection, decision making, budgeting, strategic long- and short-range planning, and allocation or reallocation of resources. The institutional example in Box 1.2 illustrates how the president at Clarke College has integrated or developed many leadership practices across her institution to maintain institutional focus on assessing student learning. These practices include positioning assessment in strategic planning as well as program review and integrating assessment's prominence in the annual State of the College Address with celebrating faculty and staff commitment.

Incorporating assessment results into institutional decisions and actions demonstrates a collective commitment to improving programs and services to advance student learning. Without these kinds of forward movement, assessment results gather dust on the shelf and lead to faculty and staff inertia. Forward movement that uses assessment data to improve student learning, and thus student success, is illustrated in the multiyear national project begun in 2004 and supported by the Lumina Foundation, Achieving the Dream: Community Colleges Count. In "Courageous Conversations" (2009), several community colleges reported on their organizational ability to use assessment results to institutionally scale up educational practices that were formerly restricted to a limited number of developmental courses. Institutionalizing efficacious practices across all developmental courses has led to improved student learning in those courses as well as in successive courses, such as in mathematics sequences. Based on results of faculty-led assessment projects that explored student achievement in courses that used pedagogies or modes of instruction that had not been mainstreamed into curricula for all developmental students, such as learning communities and cooperative learning, community colleges such as Valencia Community College, Cuyahoga Community College, and New Brunswick Community College have enabled broad changes in developmental students' curricula. Scaling up has meant that these institutions committed to identifying financial and human resources, supporting faculty development to integrate practices into the curricula, redesigning gateway courses, and developing student success courses and forms of intervention.

BOX 1.2   INSTITUTIONAL EXAMPLE: *Clarke College*

Based on the following kinds of annual events, follow-up activities, support, and forms of engagement, members of the Clarke College Community know that assessment is an institutional priority.

- At the annual opening workshop, the president gives the "State of the College" address to faculty and staff detailing the specific initiatives and objectives that she and the cabinet have highlighted to focus the year's efforts. Academic and student life program reviews are consistently included among these objectives.
- After each meeting of the board of trustees, an open "Townhall" is held in which the president provides a progress report detailing how the objectives are being met.
- The president is an active member of the Strategic Planning Committee and consequently engages in all conversations regarding program review.
- The president shares executive summaries of the program reviews with the board of trustees.
- When specific follow-up is required for a particular program review, the provost keeps the president apprised of the progress.
- Institutional support is reflected in the provision of Assessment Day—one day each semester devoted to study, discussion, and practice of assessment at the institutional and departmental levels. Departments and individuals who are recognized for best-practice models are invited as presenters in group and break-out sessions.
- Faculty may apply for summer development grants to work on assessment (or other development) projects.

Source: Kate Hendel, vice president of academic affairs, Clarke College, personal communication, March 12, 2009.

Channeling assessment results and decisions into institutional planning still remains a challenge to most colleges and universities for several major reasons: (1) Institutional decision making and planning calendars do not match those of assessment reporting cycles; (2) other institutional priorities, often involving budgeting, take precedence over implementing assessment recommendations; and (3) effecting changes based on assessment results requires that institutions position themselves to address meaningful questions about student learning and then implement desired large-scale changes in educational practices. As Mach (2010) points out:

> An educational environment must be willing to confront real questions that it really does want answered, and students must be involved in the whole process. If finding answers requires changes that extend beyond a single course, institutions must be willing and able to support both the collection of data and college-wide discussions of all relevant educational structures, despite the traditional territorial boundaries that make such discussions difficult. (pp. 72–73)

In addition, (4) institutions have not yet been willing to reward or recognize this work as a contribution to the scholarship of teaching and learning, often treating it as "extra" work that educators must endure. There are some institutional exceptions, however: the University of West Florida recognizes that faculty commitment to assessment of student learning in each of their courses is essential in ensuring that students achieve collaboratively agreed-upon departmental learning outcomes. Newly established promotion and tenure criteria now include evaluation of a faculty member's effectiveness in assessing student learning, as demonstrated in Box 1.3.

Boards of Trustees

Learning about student achievement is a responsibility of boards of trustees. Beyond being fiscally responsible, board members are also champions of our colleges and universities, their educational quality, and students' achievement. Establishing structures and channels to learn about assessment results and recommendations, in collaboration with the chief executive officer, faculty, staff, administrators, and student representatives, ensures that board members remain informed about students' achievement. Nowadays it is common practice for provosts or vice presidents or faculty or student affairs committees to periodically report assessment results and plans for improving patterns of weakness at meetings of the board of trustees or other annual or semiannual retreats. Through these convenings, assessment results can inform and shape board deliberations and decisions about institutional priorities, commitment of resources, allocation or reallocation of resources, fundraising priorities, and strategic planning. Student learning becomes, then, a focus at the level of institutional decision making and planning, a focus that marks a serious commitment to improving programs and the quality of education.

BOX 1.3   INSTITUTIONAL EXAMPLE: *University of West Florida*

The provost and president of faculty senate jointly appointed a committee that included one administrator, a senator, a union person, three administrators from each of the university's colleges, and three faculty from the faculty councils of each college—a balance that turned out to be critical for the progress/success of the group. The first year the committee studied what other regional institutions had been doing to identify criteria for promotion and tenure. Ultimately the committee decided to develop overarching principles that include behavioral criteria in relation to poor, fair, good, excellent, and distinguished performance. One of the dimensions that cuts across teaching is "effectiveness of assessment practices" along with "quality of syllabi and course goals." Specifically, the criterion for assessment states that a faculty member must demonstrate that his or her assessment practices enhance student learning and contribute to department needs. Formally, assessment is now built in as an expectation for how one achieves the highest ratings.

Source: Jane Halonen, dean of arts and sciences, University of West Florida, personal communication, March 9, 2009.

Campus Leaders

Establishing structures, processes, and channels of communication at the institution and program levels is the responsibility of campus leaders—provosts, vice presidents, deans, chairs, and department heads. Provosts and vice presidents facilitate the establishment of an institution-level process and a central committee, such as an institution-wide assessment committee, that consists of faculty, staff, administrators, and undergraduate and graduate student representatives. This committee sets a timetable for receiving institution-level and program-level reports that present findings and interpretations based on cycles of assessing student learning. Results of these reports shape a chief academic officer's budgets and academic plans to improve student learning. Similarly, provosts, deans, chairs, and department heads ensure that each of their undergraduate or graduate schools, divisions, departments, programs, and services establishes an assessment process and cycles of inquiry. Results and interpretations of program-level assessment shape annual budgets, priorities, and plans to improve student learning. Two other major responsibilities fall within the role of campus leaders in collaboration with faculty and staff:

1. Determining how an institution will value a commitment to assessing student learning as a core institutional learning and improvement process:
   - How will an institution recognize and reward this professional work?
   - Will such work be valued in promotion, tenure, and renewal processes as a form of scholarship as opposed to a form of service? If so, under what criteria?
   - Will this work also be valued in periodic reviews of staff?
   - How does this commitment translate into the ways in which people spend their professional time?
2. Ensuring that there are forms of support and resources to initiate, build, and sustain this commitment as a core institutional process:
   - What kinds of human, financial, technological, and educational resources are necessary to build and sustain program- and institution-level capacity? (See also chapter 8.)

Responses to these questions vary from institution to institution. The framework presented in this book, including the institutional examples, offers campus leaders a range of approaches to determine how they will develop, design, support, and sustain assessment as a core institutional process of inquiry leading to improvement.

Faculty, Administrators, Staff, Students, and Other Contributors to Student Learning

Those who teach and those who learn form the fabric of the actual process of assessment. Thus, a collective institutional commitment to assessing student learning engages all who contribute to the educational process, including students themselves. Faculty, administrators, and staff design the curriculum, co-curriculum, sets of educational experiences and opportunities, and support services to provide multiple ways of learning. Individuals in local communities educate students as they participate in internships, service-learning programs, and other experiential opportunities, thus extending learning opportunities beyond a campus environment. Graduate teaching assistants and undergraduate tutors bring fresh perspectives to the assessment process as both teachers and observers of student learning. Expanding the range of contributors brings different lenses to assessing student learning that broaden interpretations of students' experiences and achievement. And engaging students in the design of the assessment process invests them in their learning as well, such as seeking their contributions to identifying or designing relevant assessment methods or developing criteria and standards to assess student work. A case in point is illustrated in Box 1.4. A graduating senior in the social justice major at Hamline University undertook a capstone project researching what students should specifically learn under Hamline University's commitment to educating students for a diverse world. She identified for the university three categories of outcomes—multicultural knowledge, skills, and awareness—and ways in which students could provide evidence of those outcomes throughout their undergraduate education. Involving students' voices and experiences in institution- and program-level assessment brings learners' perspectives into this collective effort and encourages students to take responsibility for their learning.

BOX 1.4   A Senior Student's Proposed Learning Outcomes and Assessment Methods for Hamline University's Institution-Wide Focus on Diversity

Learning Outcomes	Assessment Method
Articulate problems in their disciplines from multiple points of view using multiple theories of oppression and power	After identifying a theory a student is most comfortable with, that student could serve on a panel with other students, using the preferred theory of a different student on the panel to make meaning.
Create sustainable and inclusive additions to scholarship and practices of their discipline	Students create lesson plans that contribute to the scholarship of their discipline. This would allow future students the opportunity to see what their peers have done and give an individual's research multiple uses.
	Students create lesson plans to teach their contributions to scholarship of their discipline, then implement them in the same way they would a class presentation.
Trace and determine the impact of their scholarship locally, nationally and internationally	Students create wikis to show relationships among multiple different ideas through the strategic organization of text and image. These wikis could also be used in future instruction or built on in later courses.
Demonstrate active listening skills that lead to effective understanding of other class participants	Small-group discussions assessed by both faculty and fellow students give students a platform to demonstrate their listening skills and other students the opportunity to learn through observation.
Successfully complete group assignments and describe their group's developmental process	Beyond completing the assigned project, students could design and present group development activities aimed at teaching the skills each group developed over the course of the group project.
Outline the development of personal attitudes toward groups different than their own, including influences on those attitudes and possible effects of those attitudes on other constituencies	Through text and images, students may create maps, timelines, or concept webs that articulate and represent their personal development and effect on others.
Develop culturally appropriate responses in large- and small-group discussion that reflect students' comfort with the ambiguity and complexity of cultural issues	Students find or create an original case study relevant to the course topic and develop appropriate answers to it. They then switch their case study with their peers and develop responses to that one as well.

Source: Natalie Self, social justice major senior project, "Another Vision of Cultural Breadth: A Proposal for Radical, but Possible Curriculum and Pedagogical Changes," Hamline University, May 2009.

AN INSTITUTION'S PRINCIPLES-OF-COMMITMENT STATEMENT

Establishing public and shared principles of a collective commitment to assessment is a necessary foundation in signaling the institutional value of this work within the context of a college or university. Drawing members of an educational community together to develop a principles-of-commitment statement symbolically represents the collaborative nature of assessment. Through collaborative authorship, a college's or university's principles-of-commitment statement anchors assessment within the mission, purposes, and values of an institution, thereby providing an institutionally meaningful context for this work. Eventually, the language of an institution's vision and mission statements may also incorporate one or more of the anchors described in the preceding pages, indicating campus ownership of assessment as a way of knowing, learning, and evolving.

Identifying the purposefulness of this commitment also engages individuals across an institution because they see the place of this work within their profession. Involving representatives from across an institution or system—as well as representatives from external stakeholders such as community leaders, legislators, or policy makers—demonstrates the collaborative nature of this work at the outset. The following list identifies those who may work together to draft and circulate principles of commitment that provide an institutional context for this work:

- President, chancellor, or system head
- Board of trustees' representative
- Faculty, including those involved in governance
- Academic and administrative leaders
- Staff from student affairs, support services, and library and information resources
- Undergraduate and graduate students
- Alumni
- Employers
- Local community leaders
- Parents
- Other interested parties

A principles-of-commitment statement from St. Olaf College reflects how that institution has positioned assessment as inquiry into teaching and learning—a professional commitment. An excerpt from the St. Olaf website appears in Box 1.5. A statement from the University of Portland in Box 1.6 illustrates how that institution has woven assessment into the scholarship of teaching and learning.

CONTEXTS TO GROUND THE COMMITMENT

Where and how an institution and its programs and services position an institutional commitment to assessing for learning is dependent on their current contexts. There are no absolute places to start, but there are contexts, issues, or institutional developments that become opportunities to initiate or ground the effort. The following occasions may initiate your institution's commitment:

- Developing a new mission statement or educational philosophy for the institution or an

---

BOX 1.5   INSTITUTIONAL EXAMPLE: *St. Olaf College*

A conceptualization of assessment as a form of inquiry in support of student learning can affect what we assess, how we assess, and why we assess. Inquiry in support of student learning, like other kinds of inquiry, springs from questions or puzzles originating in the lived professional experiences and disciplined reflections of committed teacher-scholars. Moreover, it can draw on a wide array of methodological tools originating in those same experiences and reflections. Assessment need not be restricted to quantitative research conducted within the positivist social science tradition. It can draw on multiple methodologies (feminist, postpositivist, historical, etc.) and multiple kinds of evidence (narratives, portfolios, interviews, content analysis, etc.), to provide richer and more persuasive evidence of the process and outcomes of student learning. But equally important, it will facilitate the effort to make the *process* of conducting inquiry inherently educational. If such inquiry is to be embedded in our academic programs, the methods of inquiry need to be grounded in the disciplines characterizing these programs. We need to inquire into our teaching in ways that fit what and how we teach; we need to inquire into student learning in ways that fit what and how students learn. This effort supports faculty learning as well as student learning. The better the fit between inquiry in support of student learning and the roles, responsibilities, and rewards of faculty and staff, the more likely it is that such inquiry will be undertaken and used for improvement.

Source: Jo Beld, director of evaluation and assessment and professor of political science, St. Olaf College, www.stolaf.edu/offices/ir-e/assessment/principles/inquiry.htm

BOX 1.6   INSTITUTIONAL EXAMPLE: *University of Portland*

The University of Portland has anchored its institutional commitment in its definition of scholarly teaching. The following statement and descriptors provide the context within which assessment takes place. Significant are the ways in which the descriptors embed assessment within the broader scope of teaching and improving student learning:

Scholarly teaching is an intellectual activity designed to bring about documented improvements in student learning. Scholarly teaching reflects a thoughtful engagement and integration of ideas, examples, and resources, coupled with pedagogically informed strategies of course design and implementation to bring about more effective teaching and learning. Scholarly teaching documents the effectiveness of student learning in a manner that models or reflects disciplinary methods and values.

THE SCHOLARLY TEACHER
- exhibits curiosity about his/her students, student learning, and students' learning environments;
- identifies issues/questions (problems) related to some aspect of student learning;
- develops, plans, and implements strategies designed to address/enhance student learning;
- documents the outcomes of his/her strategies using methodology common to the discipline;
- reflects upon and shares with others his/her ideas, designs and strategies, and outcomes of his/her work;
- consistently and continually builds upon his/her work and that of others (i.e., process is iterative).

The desire to create a new core curriculum at the University of Portland became the opportunity to initiate an institutional commitment to assessing student learning. As faculty, staff, administrators, and students created the new core and articulated learning outcomes, they also simultaneously designed an assessment program. A governing body oversees the implementation of the core, as well as the assessment program that cuts across disciplines, to ascertain how well students are able to address seven questions common to this curriculum.

Source: Statement developed by the University of Portland 2002 AAHE Summer Academy Team and contributed by Marlene Moore, Dean, College of Arts and Sciences. Reproduced with permission.

academic department, school, program, or service
- Responding to national developments in professional educational organizations such as AAC&U's work on articulating learning outcomes for General Education in its LEAP Project (Liberal Education and America's Promise: www.aacu.org/LEAP/index.cfm) and developing national scoring rubrics to assess those outcomes in its VALUE Project.
- Embarking on institutional strategic planning
- Reconceptualizing or revising faculty and staff roles and rewards
- Designing a new core curriculum or revising a core curriculum at the undergraduate or graduate level
- Developing new programs or services

- Selecting a new institutional leader
- Responding to voiced or documented dissatisfaction about student learning, such as perceived weaknesses in quantitative reasoning or critical thinking or students' inability to transfer lower-level course knowledge and abilities into upper-level coursework
- Recognizing achievements in classroom-based assessment as a foundation for institution- and program-level assessment
- Recognizing that changing demographics at our institutions requires a chronological look at how these populations are performing
- Accepting that learning occurs through different media that requires developing knowledge about how students effectively learn through those media

- Preparing documentation to respond to legislators, accreditors, policy makers, or other public audiences

HIGHER EDUCATION'S OWNERSHIP

How we situate assessment as a process of collective inquiry matters. Driven solely by external forces, such as legislators or accreditors, assessment probably resides on the margins of our institutions, eliciting periodic attention. This peripheral location divorces us from our institutional missions and values and the educational practices that translate our intentions into multiple contexts for learning. Driven by internal curiosity about the nature of our work, assessment becomes a core institutional process, embedded into definable processes, decisions, structures, practices, forms of dialogue, channels of communication, and rewards. By taking ownership of assessment and developing an internally driven core process, colleges and universities can profile their students' learning within institutional educational practices and intentions. Moreover, within this context, assessment becomes an institution's means to examine its educational intentions on its own terms within the complex ways that humans learn and within the populations an institution serves. Undertaken systematically, assessment can provide longitudinal documentation or profiles of student learning for external bodies, such as accreditors or legislators, demonstrating patterns of students' performance over time, as opposed to one point in time. In the midst of many sectors' proposed use of standardized tests to represent our students' learning and even to compare institution's educational effectiveness, Driscoll and Wood's (2007) cautionary words to faculty continue to ring true: "The seriousness of this situation makes it compelling for you, as a faculty member, in collaboration with administrators, students, community, and accrediting agencies, to take and maintain stewardship of the process of determining learning outcomes and assessing their achievement" (p. 17).

Dialogue that focuses on teaching and learning is the necessary professional context within which the assessment process develops and matures. As discussed in the following chapters, this context is essential to establish and sustain a collective commitment to inquiry into teaching and learning. Without this context, assessment runs the risk of remaining or becoming marginalized. Worse yet, it remains an empty and intellectually unfulfilling activity.

WORKS CITED

Accreditation Board for Engineering and Technology. (2008). *Criteria for accrediting engineering programs.* *www.abet.org/Linked%20Documents-UPDATE/ Criteria%20and%20PP/E001%2009-10%20EAC% 20Criteria%2012-01-08.pdf*

Accrediting Commission for Community and Junior Colleges of the Western Association of Schools and Colleges. (2002). *Accreditation standards.* *www.accjc.org/pdf/ACCJC_WASC_Accreditation_ Standards.pdf*

Accrediting Commission for Senior Colleges and Universities of the Western Association of Schools and Colleges. (2008). *Handbook of accreditation.* *www.wascsenior.org/findit/files/forms/Handbook_of_ Accreditation_2008_with_hyperlinks.pdf*

Adelman, C. (2009, April). *The Bologna Process for U.S. eyes: Relearning higher education in the age of convergence.* *www.ihep.org/assets/files/EYESFINAL.pdf*

American Council on Education: Global learning for all project. www.acenet.edu.

American Historical Association, Teaching Division. (2008). *Assessment in history: A guide to best practices.* Washington, DC: American Historical Association.

American Mathematical Association of Two-Year Colleges. (1995). *Crossroads in mathematics: Standards for introductory mathematics before calculus.* *www .amatyc.org/Crossroads/CROSSROADS/V1/index.htm*

Arreola, R. A., Theall, M., & Aleamoni, L. M. (2003). *Beyond scholarship: Recognizing the multiple roles of the professoriate.* Paper presented at the 2003 American Educational Research Association Convention, Chicago, IL. *www.cedanet.com/meta/Beyond%20 Scholarship.pdf*

Association of American Colleges & Universities. (2009, Winter). *The VALUE Project overview.* *www.aacu.org/peerreview/pr-wi09/pr-wi09_overview.cfm*

Association of Public Land-grant Universities. *www.aplu.org.*

Banta, T. W., & Associates. (2002). *Building a scholarship of assessment.* San Francisco: Jossey-Bass.

Barr, R. B., & Tagg, J. (1995, November–December). *From teaching to learning: A new paradigm for undergraduate education. Change, 27,* 13–25.

Bernard, B. L. (Ed.). (1999). *Assessment of student learning in college mathematics: Towards improved programs and courses.* Tallahasse, Florida Association for Institutional Research.

Boyer, E. L. (1990). *Scholarship reconsidered: Priorities of the professoriate*. Princeton, NJ: Carnegie Foundation for the Advancement of Teaching.

Calder, L., Cutler, W. W., & Kelly, T. M. (2002). Historians and the scholarship of teaching and learning. in Huber, M. T., & Morreale, S. P. (Eds.). (2002). *Disciplinary styles in the scholarship of teaching and learning: Exploring common ground*. Washington, DC: American Association for Higher Education

Center for Education of the National Academy of Engineering. (2003). *Improving undergraduate instruction in science, technology, engineering, and mathematics: A report of a workshop. http://books.nap.edu/openbook .php?reodrd_id=10711&page=25*

Council for Graduate Studies. (2005). *Assessment and review of graduate programs*: A policy statement. Washington, DC: Author.

Council of Writing Program Administrators. (2008). WPA *outcomes statement for first-year composition. http://wpacouncil.org/positions/outcomes/html*
———. (n.d.). "*Writing Assessment in Colleges and Universities.*" *http://wpacouncil.org/whitepaper.*

Courageous conversations: Achieving the dream and the importance of student success. (2009, January–February). *Change. www.changemag.org/ Archives/Back%20Issues/January-February%202009/ full-achieving-dream.html*

Driscoll, A., & Wood, S. (2007). *Developing outcomes-based assessment for learner-centered education: A faculty introduction*. Sterling, VA: Stylus.

Educause. (2010). *Resources. www.educause.edu/resources.*

Gaston, P. (2010). *The Bologna Process: What United States higher education has to learn from Europe, and why it matters that we learn it*. Sterling, VA: Stylus.

Halpern, D., & Hakel, M. (2002, Spring). *Applying the science of learning to university teaching and beyond. New directions for teaching and learning*, 89. San Francisco: Jossey-Bass.

Harvard medical dean urges a rethinking of the pre-med curriculum. (2008, July 16). *Chronicle of Higher Education. http://chronicle.com/article/Harvard-Medical-Dean-Urges-a/41314/*

Henning, G. W. (2008). ASK *standards*. Washington, DC: ACPA.

Higher Learning Commission of the North Central Association of Schools and Colleges. (2003). *Handbook of Accreditation* (3rd ed.). *www.ncahlc.org/ download/Handbook03.pdf*

Howard, J. (2009, August 12). New open-access monograph series is announced. *Chronicle of Higher Education. http://chronicle.com/blogPost/*

New-Open-Access-Monograph/7613/?sid=pm&utm_ source=pm&utm_medium=en

Hutchings, P., & Shulman, L. S. (1999). The scholarship of teaching: New elaborations, new developments. *Change*, 31, 11–15.

Iiyoshi, T., & Kumar, M. S. V. (Eds.). (2008). *Opening up education: The collective advancement of education through open technology, open content, and open knowledge*. Cambridge, MA: MIT Press.

Keeling, R. P., Wall, A. F., Underhile, R., & Dungy, G. J. (2008). *Assessment reconsidered: Institutional effectiveness for student success*. Washington, DC: NASPA.

Killough, A. C. (2009, June 15). Obama administration joins efforts to fix remedial education. *Chronicle of Higher Education. http://chronicle.com/ article/Obama-Administration-Joins-/44478/*

King, J. C., Ambrose, S. A., Arreola, R. A., & Watson, K. (Eds.). (2009). *Developing metrics for assessing engineering instruction: What gets measured is what gets improved. A report from the Steering Committee for Evaluating Instructional Scholarship in Engineering*. Washington, DC: National Academies Press. *http:// books.nap.edu/openbook.php?record_id=12636& page=R1*

Laurillard, D. (2008). Open teaching: The key to sustainable and effective education. In T. Iiyoshi & M. S. V. Kumar (Eds.), *Opening up education: The collective advancement of education through open technology, open content, and open knowledge* (pp. 319–336). Cambridge, MA: MIT Press.

Lilly Endowment Inc. *www.lillyendowment.org.*

Litterst, J. K., & Tompkins, P. (2001, January). Assessment as a scholarship of teaching. *Journal of the Association for Communication Administration*, 1–12.

Lovitts, B. (2007). *Making the implicit explicit: Creating performance expectations for the dissertation*. Sterling, VA: Stylus.

Lovitts, B., & Wert, E. (2007a). *Developing quality dissertations in the humanities: A graduate student's guide*. Sterling, VA: Stylus.

Lovitts, B., & Wert, E. (2007b). *Developing quality dissertations in the sciences: A graduate student's guide*. Sterling, VA: Stylus.

Lovitts, B., & Wert, E. (2007c). *Developing quality dissertations in the social sciences*. Sterling, VA: Stylus.

Mach, J. (2010). Wanted: Nutrient-rich environments for genuine assessment. In Maki, P. (Ed.), *Coming to terms with assessment: Faculty and administrators' journeys to integrating assessment in their work and institutional culture* (pp. 59–76). Sterling, VA: Stylus.

Maki, P. (2002a, January/February). Developing an assessment plan to learn about student learning. *Journal of Academic Librarianship*, 28, 8–13.

Maki, P. (2002b, October). Learning contexts inside and outside of the academy. AAHE *Special Report* *www.aahe.org/specialreports/part2htm*

Maki, P. (2002c, May). Moving from paperwork to pedagogy: channeling intellectual curiosity into a commitment to assessment. AAHE *Bulletin*. *www.aacsb.edu/resource_centers/assessment/Maki-Reprint.asp*

Maki, P. L., & Borkowski, N. A. (Eds.). (2007). *The assessment of doctoral education: Emerging criteria and new methods for improving outcomes*. Sterling, VA: Stylus.

Middle States Commission on Higher Education. (2009). *Characteristics of excellence in higher education: Requirements of affiliation and standards for accreditation*. *www.msche.org/publications/CHX06_Aug08 REVMarch09.pdf*

NASPA. (2009, February). *Assessment Framework*. *www.uncc.edu/stuaffairs/FrameworkBrochure-Feb09.pdf*

National Council of Teachers of English. (2004). *Teaching, learning and assessing writing*. *www.ncte.irg/cccc/resources/positions/digitalenvironments*

National Council of Teachers of English. (2006). *Writing assessment: A position statement*. *www.ncte.org/cccc/resources/positions/writingassessment107610.htm*

National Governors Association. (2009, November 9). *Measuring student achievement at postsecondary institutions*. *www.nga.org/Files/pdf/0911measuring achievement.pdf*

National Research Council. (2001). *Knowing what students know: The science and design of educational assessment*. Washington, DC: National Academies Press.

National Research Council. (2002a). *BIO2010: Transforming undergraduate education for future research biologists*. Washington, DC: National Academies Press.

National Research Council. (2002b). *BIO2010: Undergraduate education to prepare biomedical research scientists*. Washington, DC: National Academies Press.

National Research Council. (2003). *Evaluating and improving undergraduate teaching in science, technology, engineering, and mathematics*. Washington, DC: National Academies Press.

National Science Foundation. (n.d.). *Instructional Materials Development*. *www.nsf.gov./funding/pgm_sumjsp?pims_id=5468*.

New Commission on the Skills of the American Workforce. (2007). *Tough choices or tough times*. *www.skillscommission.org/pdf/exec_sum/ToughChoices_EXECSUM.pdf*

Nyquist, J. D. (2002, November/December). The Ph.D.: A tapestry of change for the 21st century. *Change*, 34, 13–20.

Obama's bold goals for higher education. (2009, February 25). *Chronicle of Higher Education*. *http://chronicle.com/blogPost/Obamas-Bold-Goals-for-High/6684/*

Obama to propose graduation goal and $12-billion in programs for 2-year colleges. (2009, July 14). *Chronicle of Higher Education*. *http://chronicle.com/article/Obama-to-Propose-Graduation/47375/*

Olson, C., Green, M., & Hill, B. (2006). *A handbook for advancing comprehensive internationalization: What institutions can do and what students should learn*. Washington, DC: American Council on Education.

Partnership for 21st Century Skills. (2004). *Framework for 21st century learning*. *www.21stcenturyskills.org/index.php?option=com_content&task=view&id=262& Itemid=120*

Reif, F. (2008). *Applying cognitive science to education: Thinking and learning in scientific and other complex domains*. Cambridge, MA: MIT Press.

Rowntree, D. (1987). *Assessing students: How shall we know them?* (2nd ed.). London: Kogan Page.

Schools of Sustainability, Colleges of the Environment. (2009, July 23). *Inside higher education*. *www.insidehighered.com/news/2009/07/23/sustainability*.

Shulman, L. S. (1998). *The course portfolio*. Washington, DC: American Association for Higher Education.

Silva, E. (2008). *Measuring skills for the 21st century*. Washington, DC: Education Sector.

Sons, L. A. (Ed.). (1996). *Quantitative reasoning for college graduates: A complement to the standards*. Washington, DC: Mathematical Association of America.

Steen, L. A. (Ed.). (2005). *Supporting assessment in undergraduate mathematics*. Washington, DC: Mathematical Association of America.

Tuning USA. (2009). The Lumina Foundation: *www.luminafoundation.org/newsroom/news_releases/2009-04-08.html*

U.S. Department of Education, Office of Planning, Evaluation, and Policy Development. (2009). *Evaluation of evidence-based practices in online learning: A meta-analysis and review of online learning studies*. *www.ed.gov/about/offices/list/opepd/ppss/reports.html*

Wabash National Study of Liberal Arts Education. *www.liberalarts.wabash.edu/study-overview/*.

Yancey, K., Cambridge, B., & Cambridge, D. (2009, January 7). *Making common cause: Electronic portfolios, learning, and the power of community.* www.academic commons.org/commons/essay/making-common-cause-electronic-portfolios

ADDITIONAL RESOURCES

Metasite for Assessment Categories and Institutional Assessment Sites
Internet Resources for Higher Education Assessment: *www2.acs.ncsu.edu/UPA/assmt/resource.htm*

Metasite for Online Assessment Handbooks:
Internet Resources for Higher Education Assessment: *www2.acs.ncsu.edu/UPA/assmt/resource.htm #hbooks*

Attributes of Learning-Centered Institutions
Doherty, A., Riordan, T., & Roth, J. (Eds.). (2002). *Student learning: A central focus for institutions of higher education: A report and collection of institutional practices of the student learning initiative.* Milwaukee, WI: Alverno College Institute.

Huba, M. E., & Freed, J. E. (2000). *Learner-centered assessment on college campuses: Shifting the focus from teaching to learning.* Needham Heights, MA: Allyn & Bacon.

Koester, J., Hellenbrand, H., & Piper, T. D. (2005, September–October, 2005). Exploring the actions behind the words "learning-centered" institution. *About Campus, 10*(4), 10–16.

McClenney, K. M. (2003, Spring). The learning centered institution: Key characteristics. *Inquiry & Action, 1,* 2–6.

O'Banion, T. (1997). *A learning college for the 21st century.* Washington, DC: Oryx Press.

O'Banion, T. (1997). *Creating more learning-centered community colleges.* Mission Viejo, CA: League for Innovation.

Tagg, J. (2003). *The learning paradigm college.* Boston: Anker Press.

Characteristics of Diverse Learners in Higher Education
Adams, J. M., & Carfagna, A. (2006). *Coming of age in a globalized world: The next generation.* Bloomfield, CT: Kumarian Press.

Allen, J. K., Bracken, S. J., & Dean, D. R. (2007). *Most college students are women: Implications for teaching, learning, and policy.* Sterling, VA: Stylus.

Anderson, J. A. (2008). *Driving change through diversity and globalization: Transformative leadership in the academy.* Sterling, VA: Stylus.

Bash, L. (2003). *Adult learners in the academy.* Boston: Anker Press.

Bowl, M. (2003). *Non-traditional entrants to higher education: They talk about people like me.* Sterling, VA: Stylus.

Branche, J., Mullennix, J., & Cohn, E. R. (Eds.). (2007). *Diversity across the curriculum: A guide for faculty in higher education.* Boston: Anker Press.

Burke, P. J. (2002). *Accessing education: Effectively widening participation.* Sterling, VA: Stylus.

Carroll, D. D. (2005). *First generation college students: Identifying the precollegiate characteristics of first generation students who persist into their second fall semester.* Columbia: University of Missouri.

Duderstadt, J. J., Atkins, D. E., & van Houweling, D. (2002). *Higher education in the digital age: Technology issues and strategies for American colleges and universities.* American Council on Education/Praeger Series on Higher Education. Westport, CT: Praeger.

Economist Intelligence Unit. (2008). *The future of higher education: How technology will shape learning.* *http://eric.ed.gov/ERICDocs/data/ericdocs2sql/content_ storage_01/0000019b/80/44/0e/20.pdf*

Field, J. (2006). *Lifelong learning and the new educational order* (2nd ed.). Sterling, VA: Stylus.

Flowers, L. A., & Pascarella, E. T. (in press). *The impact of institutional racial composition on student development and educational outcomes.* Sterling, VA: Stylus.

Gibson, C. C. (Ed.). (1998). *Distance learners in higher education: Institutional responses for quality outcomes.* Madison, WI: Atwood.

Gurung, R. A. R., & Prieto, L. R. (2009). *Getting culture: Incorporating diversity across the curriculum.* Sterling, VA: Stylus.

Hayes, E., & Flannery, D. D. (2000). *Women as learners: The significance of gender in adult learners.* San Francisco: Jossey-Bass.

Heller, D. E., & D'ambrosio, M. B. (2008). *Generational shockwaves and the implications for higher education.* Northampton, MA: Elgar.

Howard-Hamilton, M. F., Morelon-Quainoo, S. D., Johnson, S. D., Winkle-Wagner, R., & Santiague, L. (Eds.). (2008). *Standing on the outside looking in: Underrepresented students' experiences in advanced degree programs.* Sterling, VA: Stylus.

Inoue, Y. (Ed.). (2007). *Technology and diversity in higher education: New challenges.* Hershey, PA: Information Science.

Landsman, J., & Lewis, C. W. (2006). *White teachers/ diverse classrooms: A guide to building inclusive schools, promoting high expectations, and eliminating racism.* Sterling, VA: Stylus.

Magolda, M. B. (1992). *Knowing and reasoning in college: Gender-related patterns in students' intellectual development.* San Francisco: Jossey-Bass.

Magolda, M. B., & Terenzini, P. T. (n.d.). Learning and teaching in the 21st century: Trends and implications for practice. In C. S. Johnson & H. E. Cheatham (Eds.), *Higher education trends for the next century: A research agenda for student success.* *www.eric.ed.gov/PDFS/ED430446.Pdf*

Moore, A. H., Fowler, S. B., Jesiek, B. L., Moore, J. F., & Watson, C. E. (2008, April 1). Learners 2.0? IT and 21st century learners in higher education. *Educause Center for Applied Research: Research Bulletin.* *www.educause.edu/ECAR/Learner20ITand 21stCentury Lear/162820 S*

Oblinger, D. C., & Oblinger, J. L. (Eds.). (n.d.). *Educating the net generation.* *www.educause.edu/educating thenetgen*

Ortiz, A. M., & Santos, S. J. (2009). *Ethnicity in college: Advancing theory and improving diversity practices on campus.* Sterling, VA: Stylus.

Palfrey, J., & Gasser, U. (2008). *Born digital: Understanding the first generation of digital natives.* New York: Basic Books.

Perez, W. (2009). *We are Americans: Undocumented students pursuing the American dream.* Sterling, VA: Stylus.

Pollack, D. (2006). *Learning life histories of students identified as dyslexic.* Sterling, VA: Stylus.

Reay, D., & David, M. E. (Eds.). (2005). *Degrees of choice: Social class, race and gender in higher education.* Sterling, VA: Stylus.

Reiss, M. J. (Ed.). (2007). *Marginality and difference in education and beyond.* Sterling: VA: Stylus.

Riddell, S., Tinklin, T., & Wilson, A. (2005). *Disabled students in higher education: Perspectives on widening access and changing policy.* New York: Routledge.

Scott, D. (2009). *Growing up digital: How the next generation is changing your world.* New York: McGraw-Hill.

Smith, W., & Bender, T. (Eds.). (2008). *American higher education transformed, 1940–2005: Documenting the national discourse.* Baltimore: Johns Hopkins University Press.

Thomas, L., Cooper, M., & Quinn, J. (2003). *Improving completion rates among disadvantaged students.* Sterling, VA: Stylus.

Tippiconic, M. J., Lowe, S. C., & McClellan, G. S. (Eds.). (2005, April). *Serving Native American students. New directions for student services,* 109. San Francisco: Jossey-Bass.

Wan, G. (Ed.). (2008). *The education of diverse student populations: A global perspective. Explorations of educational purpose* (Vol. 2). New York: Springer.

Watson, L., Terrell, M. C., Wright, D. J., Bonner, F., Cuyjet, M., Gold, J., et al. (2002). *How minority students experience college: Implications for planning and policy.* Sterling, VA: Stylus.

Zamel, V., & Spack, R. (Eds.). (2004). *Crossing the curriculum: Multilingual learners in college classrooms.* Mahwah, NJ: Erlbaum.

Learning Organizations

Angelo, T. A. (1997). The campus as learning community: Seven promising shifts and seven powerful levers. AAHE *Bulletin,* 49, 3–6.

Boggs, G. R. (1999, January). What the learning paradigm means for faculty. AAHE *Bulletin,* 51, 3–5.

Ewell, P. T. (1997). Organizing for learning: A new imperative. AAHE *Bulletin,* 50, 10–12.

Freed, J. E. (2001, January–February). Why become a learning organization? *About Campus,* 5(6), 16–21.

Fuchs, M. (2006). Higher education—Is the learning organization refusing to learn? In E. Pearson & P. Bohman (Eds.), *Proceedings of world conference on educational multimedia, hypermedia and telecommunications.* (pp. 1373–1376). Chesapeake, VA: AACE.

Jeffery, J. (2008). *Institutions of higher learning and learning organizations: An annotated bibliography.* *www.teagle foundation.org/learning/report/LearningAB.aspx*

Kezar, A. J. (Ed.). (2005). *Organizational learning in higher education. New directions for higher education,* 131. San Francisco: Jossey-Bass.

Law, N., Yuen, A., & Fox, R. (Eds.). (2010). *Educational innovations beyond technology: Nurturing leadership and establishing learning organizations.* New York: Springer.

McMillin, L., & Berberet, J. (Eds.). (2002). *A new academic compact: Revisioning the relationship between faculty and their institutions.* Boston: Anker Press.

Senge, P. M. (1990). *The fifth discipline: The art and practice of the learning organization.* New York: Doubleday.

Tinto, V. (1997). Universities as learning organizations. *About Campus,* 1, 2–4.

National, Regional, and Specialized Accreditors

To locate regional, national, and specialized accreditors' standards and criteria for assessing student learning, search through the Council of Higher Education Association's (CHEA) directories at *www.chea.org/Directories/index.cfm.*

Representative Professional and Disciplinary Organizations Focusing on Assessment

American Council on Education (ACE) Global Learning for All Project: *www.acenet.edu*

American Educational Research Association (AERA): *www.aera.net*

American Psychological Association (APA): *www.apa.org*

Association of American Colleges & Universities (AAC&U): *www.aacu.org*

Association of College and Research Libraries (ACRL): *www.ala.org/acrl/ilcomstan.html*

Association for Institutional Research (AIR): *www.airweb.org*

Association for the Study of Higher Education (ASHE): *www.ashe.ws*

Higher Education Research Institute (HERI): *www.gseis.ucla.edu/heri/heri.html*

LibQUAL+: *www.libqual.org*

The National Academies lists current research projects focused on the science of learning and assessment of learning. To view a list of projects, see *www.nationalacademies.org/cp/keywordsearch.aspx*

National Association of Student Personnel Administrators (NASPA): *www.naspa.org*

National Council of Teachers of English (NCTE): *www.ncte.org*

National Learning Infrastructure Initiative (NLII) of Educause: *www.educause.edu/eli*

National Science Foundation (NSF): *www.nsf.gov*

Project Kaleidoscope (PKAL): *www.pkal.org*

Scholarship of Teaching and Learning

Angelo, T. A. (Ed.). (1998). *Classroom assessment and research: An update on uses, approaches, and research findings.* San Francisco: Jossey-Bass.

Angelo, T. A., & Cross, K. P. (1993). *Classroom assessment techniques: A handbook for college teachers* (2nd ed.). San Francisco: Jossey-Bass.

Becker, W. E., & Andrews, M. L. (Eds.). (2004). *The scholarship of teaching and learning: Contributions of research universities.* Bloomington: Indiana University Press.

Biggs, J. (1999). *Teaching for quality learning at university.* Birmingham, UK: Society for Research into Higher Education and Open University Press.

Cross, K. P., & Steadman, M. H. (1996). *Classroom research: Implementing the scholarship of teaching.* San Francisco: Jossey-Bass.

Glassick, C. E., Huber, M. T., & Maeroff, G. I. (1997). *Scholarship assessed: Evaluation of the professoriate.* San Francisco: Jossey-Bass.

McKeachie, W. J. (1994). *Teaching tips: Strategies, research, and theory for college and university teachers* (11th ed.). Boston: Houghton Mifflin.

McKinney, K., & Cross, K. P. (2007). *Enhancing learning through the scholarship of teaching and learning: The challenges and joys of juggling.* San Francisco: Jossey-Bass.

Menges, R. J. (1996). *Teaching on solid ground: Using scholarship to improve practice.* San Francisco: Jossey-Bass.

Rice, E. (1991). The new American scholar: Scholarship and the purposes of the university. *Metropolitan Universities, 4,* 7–18.

Shulman, L. S. (1999). Taking learning seriously. *Change, 31,* 10–17.

Weimer, M. (2006). *Enhancing scholarly work on teaching and learning: Professional literature that makes a difference.* San Francisco: Jossey-Bass.

Metasites on the Scholarship of Teaching and Learning

The Carnegie Foundation for the Advancement of Teaching offers a rich collection of print and online publications focused on the scholarship of teaching and learning and assessment:

1. Its e-library contains downloadable and printable articles that may well jump-start dialogue about the philosophies, assumptions, theories, research, or practices that underlie teaching in a discipline or that underlie how curricula are structured for learning (*www.carnegiefoundation.org/general/sub.asp?key=21&subkey=72&topkey=21*).

2. An updated version (2002) of *The Scholarship of Teaching and Learning in Higher Education: An Annotated Bibliography* (Pat Hutchings, Senior Scholar; Marcia Babb, Program Associate; and Chris Bjork, Research Assistant) is available at *www.carnegiefoundation.org/sites/default/files/CASTL_bibliography.pdf*

3. Carnegie position papers and perspectives on assessment are available at *http://bondessays.carnegiefoundation.org.*

McKinney, K. (2009, Summer). *The scholarship of teaching and learning: Selected bibliography. www.sotl.ilstu.edu/resLinks/selBibl.shtml*

Science of Learning as It Relates to Teaching and Learning

Bereiter, C., & Scardamalia, M. (1989). Intentional learning as a goal of instruction. In L. Resnick (Ed.), *Knowing, learning, and instruction: Essays in honor of Robert Glaser* (pp. 361–392). Hillsdale, NJ: Erlbaum.

de Jong, T., van Gog, T., Jenks, K., Manlove, S., van Hell, J., Jolles, J., et al. (2008). *Explorations in learning and the brain on the potential of cognitive neuroscience for educational science.* New York: Springer.

Leamnson, R. (1999). *Thinking about teaching and learning: Developing habits of learning with first year college and university students.* Sterling, VA: Stylus.

Leamnson, R. (2000, November–December). Learning as biological brain change. *Change, 32,* 34–40.

Mentkowski, M., & Associates. (2000). *Learning that lasts: Integrating learning, development, and performance in college and beyond.* San Francisco: Jossey-Bass.

Merrill, M. D., Zhongmin, L., & Jones, M. K. (1990, December). ID2 and constructivist theory. *Educational Technology, 52–55.*

National Research Council. (1999). *How people learn: Bridging research and practice.* Washington, DC: National Academies Press.

National Research Council. (2000). *How people learn: Brain, mind, experience, and school* (expanded ed.). Washington, DC: National Academies Press.

Oxford Centre for Staff Development. (1992). *Improving student learning.* Oxford, UK: Oxford Brookes University.

Svinicki, M. D. (Ed.). (1999, November). *Teaching and learning on the edge of the millennium: Building on what we have learned. New directions for teaching and learning, 80.* San Francisco: Jossey-Bass.

Wiske, M. S. (Ed.) (1998). *Teaching for understanding: Linking research with practice.* San Francisco: Jossey-Bass.

Zull, J. E. (2002). *The art of changing the brain: Enriching teaching by exploring the biology of learning.* Sterling, VA: Stylus.

Some Metasites on the Science of Learning
Halpern, D.

Halpern's site (*http://berger.research.claremontmckenna.edu/asl/tp.asp*) is dedicated to sharing research, publications, and other resources on developments in the science of learning and research on learning through assessment. Her current project, along with Milton Hakel and others, is focused on making public what the science of learning is revealing and identifying and assessing innovations in teaching that advance the profession of teaching.

Huitt, B.

Huitt's site (*http://chiron.valdosta.edu/whuitt/interact.html*) provides a wealth of readings, Internet resources, articles, and books focused on teaching and learning, problem solving and decision making, systems theory applied to human behavior, and theories of learning.

Some Major National Projects Focused on Assessing Student Learning
Achieving the Dream: Community Colleges Count

Supported by the Lumina Foundation, this multiyear national project initiated in 2004 (*www.achievingthedream.org/default.tp*) aims to help more community colleges succeed in educating students. This initiative involves a partnership of 20 organizations and 83 community colleges in 15 states that focuses on institutions' use of data to "drive change," including the goal of increasing what we in higher education know about the efficacy of teaching strategies that increase student learning, thus, student success.

Association of American Colleges & Universities' Projects

1. The Association of American Colleges & Universities' Collaborative Project with the Carnegie Foundation for the Advancement of Teaching, Integrative Learning: Opportunities to Connect

This project was designed to engage campuses in developing comprehensive approaches aimed at providing students with "purposeful, progressively more challenging, integrated educational experiences." For information about this project and institutions' efforts to assess integrative learning, read "Integrative Learning: Mapping the Terrain," the background paper for this project (www.carnegiefoundation.org/dynamic/publications/elibrary_pdf_636.pdf), which focuses on deliberate promotion of integrative learning in students' undergraduate studies.

2. The Association's Project on Accreditation and Assessment, a component of the Association's national initiative, Greater Expectations: The Commitment to Quality as a Nation Goes to College

This major national project (www.aacu-edu.org/paa/index.cfm) has focused on identifying and assessing the outcomes of liberal education. Specifically, this project developed a "shared understanding of the desired outcomes of a liberal education"; identified "the curricular design principles that help students reach these outcomes"; and identified the "criteria for 'good practice' in assessing liberal education as collaborative and integrative." Having identified the Essential Learning Outcomes for General Education in its LEAP Project (Liberal Education and America's Promise), under its VALUE Project (Valid Assessment of Learning in Undergraduate Education), the association developed 15 national scoring rubrics—released in September 2009—that institutions can apply to their students' work to assess students' progress toward and eventual achievement of the relevant general education outcomes at an institution. Rubrics have been developed for the following LEAP outcomes:

Intellectual and Practical Skills

- Inquiry and analysis
- Critical thinking
- Creative thinking
- Written communication
- Oral communication
- Reading
- Quantitative literacy
- Information literacy
- Teamwork
- Problem solving

Personal and Social Responsibility

- Civic knowledge and engagement—local and global
- Intercultural knowledge and competence
- Ethical reasoning
- Foundations and skills for lifelong learning

Integrative Learning

- Integrative learning

These rubrics are an alternative to standardized tests to document and represent students' GE learning that students also build on in their major programs of study. For a summary of this project, see www.aacu.org/value/.

Indiana University Center for Postsecondary Research and Planning and Indiana University Center for Survey Research

The National Survey of Student Engagement (NSSE) and the Community College Survey of Student Engagement (CCSSE) ask students to respond to their college and university experiences under benchmarks of effective educational practices that foster student learning such as level of academic challenge, active and collaborative learning, student-faculty interaction, enriching educational experiences, and supportive campus environment (www.iub.edu). The importance of relating these results to other sources of student performance is discussed in Kuh, G. W. (2003, March-April), "What We're Learning About Student Engagement From NSSE: Benchmarks for Effective Educational Practices," *Change*, 24–32. See, especially, p. 31.

Illustrating how institutions are now using their survey results to improve student learning is a recent publication: *Using NSSE to Assess and Improve Undergraduate Education: Lessons From the Field* 2009 (www.nsse.iub.edu/links/lessons).

John N. Gardner Institute on Excellence in Undergraduate Education

The Gardner Institute focused on "developing assessment-based action plans with measurable outcomes" for undergraduate education with a particular emphasis on improving students' first year of study. Publications relevant to assessing educational practices and student learning are listed at www.jngi.org/research_and_publications.

Mathematical Association of America

Supporting Assessment in Undergraduate Mathematics (SAUM) is an association project supported by a grant from the National Science Foundation. This project is designed to help departments effectively assess one or more goals common to undergraduate mathematics departments in the major, in preparing future teachers, in college placement programs, in mathematics-intensive programs, and in general education courses (www.maa.org/saum/).

Tuning USA

Modeled after the European Bologna Process (see pages 11–12), the Tuning USA pilot project, supported by the Lumina Foundation, involves higher education institutions in Indiana, Minnesota, and

Utah (www.luminafoundation.org/newsroom/news_releases/2009-04-08.html) and is aimed at developing a "shared understanding among higher education's stakeholders of the subject-specific knowledge and transferable skills" that undergraduate students in the following six fields must demonstrate at the end of their program of study: biology, chemistry, education, history, physics, and graphic design. Each state will draft learning outcomes and map the relations between these outcomes and graduates' employment options for, at least, two of these disciplines.

The Wabash National Study of Liberal Arts Education

Currently, The Wabash National Study of Liberal Arts Education is a longitudinal investigation of students at 49 institutions that has as its goal identifying and augmenting undergraduate experiences that promote student success in a range of cognitive and affective outcomes. The Wabash National Study uses a longitudinal approach, assessing first-year students shortly after they arrive on campus and then following them for at least four years. To gauge how much students change during their time at college, institutional and student data are collected at multiple points during the study, supplementing quantitative data from surveys and assessments with interviews at a subset of institutions. The Wabash National Study staff collaborate with institutions to ensure that they can use study data to address their unique concerns and improve student learning. Specifically, this study relies on results from the following methods to help institutions track student learning:

1. CAAP (critical-thinking test)
2. Need for Cognition Scale (provides indicators for how inclined students are to engage in effortful cognitive activities
3. In-depth interviews of student learning to discern integration of learning
4. Miville-Guzman Universality-Diversity Scale–Short Form (multiple-choice form about attitudes, cognitions, and behaviors about diversity)
5. Socially Responsible Leadership Scale
6. Defining Issues Test (DIT) (see www.liberalarts .wabash.edu/nationalstudy)
7. Ryff Scales of Psychological Well-Being (measure six dimensions of psychological well-being: self-acceptance, environmental mastery, positive re-lations with others, personal growth, purpose in life, and autonomy)

A Representative List of Research Projects That Integrate Assessment

Research on teaching and learning contributes to our understanding of the effectiveness of pedagogies, educational tools, and practices in developing disciplinary habits of mind and problem-solving abilities. Some representative projects that incorporate assessment are the following.

Center for Innovative Learning Technologies

Founded in 1997 with a grant from the National Science Foundation, the Center for Innovative Learning Technologies (CILT) focuses its work on developing and studying technology-enabled solutions to teaching science, mathematics, engineering, and technology in K–14. In its commitment to assessing for learning, CILT develops methods of assessment that enable educators to "see qualities of student achievement that are invisible on traditional, standardized tests" (www.cilt.org/themes/assessments .html). Current work focuses on developing scoring rubrics that capture how students make meaning during the processes of instruction (www.cilt.org/ themes/assessments.html/Shell/Open/Command).

Massachusetts Institute of Technology (MIT)

A part of the Office of the Dean for Undergraduate Education, MIT's Teaching and Learning Laboratory (TLL) increases campus understanding about the process of learning in science and engineering. It achieves this goal by conducting research that can be applied to the classroom and by developing innovative educational curricula, pedagogy, technologies, and methods of assessment. Allied with several programs and centers across the institution, the laboratory disseminates its work on campus as well as nationally and internationally. For published work that focuses on teaching, learning and assessment, see http://web.mit.edu/tll/research/articles-working-papers/articles-working-papers.html.

Vanderbilt University, Northwestern University, the University of Texas at Austin, and the Health Sciences and Technology Program of Harvard and MIT

Bioengineering and learning sciences faculties from these institutions, with support from the National

Science Foundation, have established a center to conduct research on bioengineering educational technologies within the various domains of this science. In conjunction with developing new learning materials that relate to the structure of knowledge in bioengineering domains, the center is developing assessment methods to determine the effectiveness of these new materials and methods of instruction (www.vanth.org).

Visible Knowledge Project

The five-year Visible Knowledge Project was aimed at "improving the quality of college and university teaching through a focus on both student learning and faculty development in technology-enhanced environments." The project involved more than 70 faculty from 21 campuses nationwide. Assessment of student learning in technology-enhanced environments is built into many of these projects (www.crossroads.georgetown.edu/vkp).

Recently, the Teagle Foundation extended this work to focus on electronic portfolios.

Some Journals That Publish Research on Teaching, Learning, and Assessment, Including New Technologies

Active Learning in Higher Education
American Educational Research Journal
Assessment and Evaluation in Higher Education
Cognition and Instruction
Educational Researcher
Educational Technology Research and Cognition
English Journal
Innovative Higher Education
International Journal of Computing for Mathematical Learning
International Journal of Science Education
Journal of Applied Research at Community Colleges
Journal of Assessment and Institutional Effectiveness
Journal of Computer Assisted Learning
Journal of Computing in Higher Education
Journal of Curriculum Studies
Journal of Deaf Studies and Deaf Education
Journal of Education for Business
Journal of Educational Multimedia and Hypermedia
Journal of Educational Psychology
Journal of Technology, Learning, and Assessment
Language Learning
Learning and Instruction
On the Horizon
Research in Science Education
Review of Higher Education
Teaching English in the Two-Year College

WORKSHEETS, GUIDES, AND EXERCISES

The following worksheets, guides, and exercises are designed to anchor assessing for learning as a core institutional process.

1. *Principles of Commitment:* Developing a principles-of-commitment statement positions assessment within an institution or system and establishes a context for collective engagement. As an institutional or system leader, draw from the following list of possible individuals who might work together to draft that document within the context of your institution's or system's mission, purposes, and values:

   ❏ Administrators
   ❏ Alumni
   ❏ Faculty—full- and part-time
   ❏ Librarians and information resource staff
   ❏ Local community members, including advisory committee members
   ❏ Members of the board of trustees
   ❏ Other staff
   ❏ Parents
   ❏ Representative employers
   ❏ Representatives from professions or professional organizations
   ❏ Student affairs and support staff
   ❏ Students
   ❏ Other stakeholders inside or outside the institution

2. *Principles of Commitment:* As an institutional or system leader, once you have identified a cross-representation of individuals to draft a principles-of-commitment document, you may want to ask the authoring group to read one or more of the following documents before members of the group collaboratively draft a statement and then send it out for wider institutional review. Focused on principles of learning and assessment, these documents may inform your institution's or system's discussion and resulting statement:

   (a) Chickering, A. W., & Gamson, Z. F. (1987). Seven principles of good practice in undergraduate education. *AAHE Bulletin, 39,* 7. Summaries of these principles that appear on numerous institutional websites, such as www.rochester.edu/ITS/edtech/documentation/Pedagogy/7principles.pdf.

   (b) The American Association for Higher Education's "Nine Principles of Good Practice for Assessing Student Learning," which follows:

American Association for Higher Education

Nine Principles of Good Practice for Assessing Student Learning

1. **The assessment of student learning begins with educational values.** Assessment is not an end in itself but a vehicle for educational improvement. Its effective practice, then, begins with and enacts a vision of the kinds of learning we most value for students and strive to help them achieve. Educational values should drive not only *what* we choose to assess but also *how* we do so. Where questions about educational mission and values are skipped over, assessment threatens to be an exercise in measuring what's easy, rather than a process of improving what we really care about.

2. **Assessment is most effective when it reflects an understanding of learning as multidimensional, integrated, and revealed in performance over time.** Learning is a complex process. It entails not only what students know but what they can do with what they know; it involves not only knowledge and abilities but values, attitudes, and habits of mind that affect both academic success and performance beyond the classroom. Assessment should reflect these understandings by employing a diverse array of methods, including those that call for actual performance, using them over time so as to reveal change, growth, and increasing degrees of integration. Such an approach aims for a more complete and accurate picture of learning, and therefore firmer bases for improving our students' educational experience.

3. **Assessment works best when the programs it seeks to improve have clear, explicitly stated purposes.** Assessment is a goal-oriented process. It entails comparing educational performance with educational purposes and expectations—those derived from the institution's mission, from faculty intentions in program and course design, and from knowledge of students' own goals. Where program purposes lack specificity or agreement, assessment as a process pushes a campus toward clarity about where to aim and what standards to apply; assessment also prompts attention to where and how program goals will be taught and learned. Clear, shared, implementable goals are the cornerstone for assessment that is focused and useful.

4. **Assessment requires attention to outcomes but also and equally to the experiences that lead to those outcomes.** Information about outcomes is of high importance; where students "end up" matters greatly. But to improve outcomes, we need to know about student experience along the way—about the curricula, teaching, and kind of student effort that lead to particular outcomes. Assessment can help us understand which students learn best under what conditions; with such knowledge comes the capacity to improve the whole of their learning.

5. **Assessment works best when it is ongoing, not episodic.** Assessment is a process whose power is cumulative. Though isolated, "one-shot" assessment can be better than none, improvement is best fostered when assessment entails a linked series of activities undertaken over time. This may mean tracking the process of individual students, or of cohorts of students; it may mean collecting

the same examples of student performance or using the same instrument semester after semester. The point is to monitor progress toward intended goals in a spirit of continuous improvement. Along the way, the assessment process itself should be evaluated and refined in light of emerging insights.

6. **Assessment fosters wider improvement when representatives from across the educational community are involved.** Student learning is a campus-wide responsibility, and assessment is a way of enacting that responsibility. Thus, while assessment efforts may start small, the aim over time is to involve people from across the educational community. Faculty play an especially important role, but assessment's questions can't be fully addressed without participation by student-affairs educators, librarians, administrators, and students. Assessment may also involve individuals from beyond the campus (alumni, trustees, employers) whose experience can enrich the sense of appropriate aims and standards for learning. Thus understood, assessment is not a task for small groups of experts but a collaborative activity; its aim is wider, better-informed attention to student learning by all parties with a stake in its improvement.

7. **Assessment makes a difference when it begins with issues of use and illuminates questions that people really care about.** Assessment recognizes the value of information in the process of improvement. But to be useful, information must be connected to issues or questions that people really care about. This implies assessment approaches that produce evidence that relevant parties will find credible, suggestive, and applicable to decisions that need to be made. It means thinking in advance about how the information will be used, and by whom. The point of assessment is not to gather data and return "results"; it is a process that starts with the questions of decision-makers, that involves them in the gathering and interpreting of data, and that informs and helps guide continuous improvement.

8. **Assessment is most likely to lead to improvement when it is part of a larger set of conditions that promote change.** Assessment alone changes little. Its greatest contribution comes on campuses where the quality of teaching and learning is visibly valued and worked at. On such campuses, the push to improve educational performance is a visible and primary goal of leadership; improving the quality of undergraduate education is central to the institution's planning, budgeting, and personnel decisions. On such campuses, information about learning outcomes is seen as an integral part of decision making, and avidly sought.

9. **Through assessment, educators meet responsibilities to students and to the public.** There is a compelling public stake in education. As educators, we have a responsibility to the publics that support or depend on us to provide information about the ways in which our students meet goals and expectations. But that responsibility goes beyond the reporting of such information; our deeper obligation—to ourselves, our students, and society—is to improve. Those to whom educators are accountable have a corresponding obligation to support such attempts at improvement.

Authors: Alexander W. Astin; Trudy W. Banta; K. Patricia Cross; Elaine El-Khawas; Peter T. Ewell; Pat Hutchings; Theodore J. Marchese; Kay M. McClenney; Marcia Mentkowski; Margaret A. Miller; E. Thomas Moran; Barbara D. Wright. 1992.

This document was developed under the auspices of the AAHE Assessment Forum with support from the Fund for the Improvement of Postsecondary Education with additional support for publication and dissemination from the Exxon Education Foundation. Copies may be made without restriction.

(c) The collaborative document, "Powerful Partnerships: A Shared Responsibility for Learning," written by a joint task force consisting of representatives from the American Association for Higher Education, the American College Personnel Association, and the National Association of Student Personnel Administrators, June 1998 (www.aahe.org/teaching/tsk_frce.htm). This document presents 10 principles for learning drawn from research and practice. Three other American College Personnel Association publications also focus on principles and practices to promote discussion about ways to intentionally enhance student learning, including collaborating with others across a campus:

"The Student Learning Imperative: Implications for Student Affairs" (www.acpa.nche.edu/sli/sli.htm)
"Principles of Good Practice for Student Affairs" (www.acpa.nche.edu/pgp/principle.htm)
Learning Reconsidered 2: Implementing a Campus-Wide Focus on the Student Experience.
    Washington, DC

(d) Angelo, T. (1999, May). Doing assessment as if learning matters most. *AAHE Bulletin.* www.aahebulletin.com/public/archive/angelomay99.asp

(e) Maki, P. (2002, May). Moving from paperwork to pedagogy: Channeling intellectual curiosity into a commitment to assessment. *AAHE Bulletin.* www.aacsb.edu/resource_centers/ assessment/Maki-Reprint.asp

3. *Principles of Commitment:* Another way to draft a principles-of-commitment statement is to ask representatives from across your institution to identify institutional anchors that link assessment to mission, values, and vision. North Carolina State University anchored its commitment to assessment within four contexts. Read the following summary of the university's approach and then, using the chart following the summary, ask individuals to identify institutional anchors as a way to draft a collaborative statement for wider review.

INSTITUTIONAL EXAMPLE: *North Carolina State University*

North Carolina State University, a premier research-extensive institution, has anchored its commitment to assessment in four ways: (1) responsiveness to professional and public accountability, including its primary constituents, students; (2) clarity about its institutional descriptors—"high-quality programming," "institutional excellence," and "effectiveness"—and its status as a premier research-extensive institution focused on learner-centeredness; (3) desire to provide evidence of student learning to better inform decision makers and planners as they direct and allocate resources that support the institution's work; and (4) desire to promote dialogue across the institution about student learning. The meaningful beginning point for the university has been its decision to focus annually on student outcomes within programs across the institution and to integrate this work as part of program review. Thus assessment at the program level is a continuous process of raising and answering a significant question or questions about student learning that each program chooses to assess each year. Program review, then, characterizes the university's meaningful beginning.

Source: Jo Allen, James A. Anderson, and Marilee J. Bresciani, North Carolina State University.

To address institution- or program-level readiness for a collective commitment to assessing student learning, ask individuals to explain how one or more of the following principles might anchor your institution's shared commitment to assessing student learning. Ask individuals to fill out the following chart as a way to stimulate discussion leading to a draft:

Possible Anchors for an Institutional Commitment

Research on learning or the integration of research on learning into educational practices	
Scholarship of teaching and learning	
Responsiveness to developments in disciplinary and professional organizations' work focused on assessment	
Focus on learning-centeredness	
Focus on organizational learning	
Responsiveness to accountability	
Other	

4. *Meaningful Beginnings:* Having authored a draft principles-of-commitment statement, ask individuals of that authoring group to list meaningful ways in which the institution (or a program) can launch a shared commitment to assessing student learning. Use the following scenario from Rochester Community and Technical College as a way to think about how your institution will initiate a meaningful and shared commitment:

INSTITUTIONAL EXAMPLE: *Rochester Community and Technical College*

Rochester Community and Technical College (RCTC), the oldest community college in Minnesota, established in 1915, began its institutional commitment to assessing student learning by linking institution-wide planning, a commitment to ensuring quality throughout the institution, and accreditation. It has realigned its mission and vision for the 21st century, has identified design criteria and academic performance indicators to determine points of reference for assessing quality performance, and has begun to implement comprehensive assessment of student learning. The college's focus on performance indicators at all levels of its work has provided an institutional context within which the community now works. RCTC established a college-wide assessment committee consisting of representatives from across the institution that has established broad commitment. The college launched its initial commitment to assessment through pilot projects in general education and in certain programs, including connecting its work to a larger statewide system office project that is piloting a data software program designed to track student learning results. Key to the institution's sustained commitment was the president's recognition that a budget line needed to be established in the institutional budget, a clear recognition that this work is recognized and valued. An institutional website (www.acd.roch.edu/asl) describes assessment work in departments and programs, highlights work that the faculty are undertaking, provides resources on assessment, and provides committee meeting minutes.

Source: Anne M. High, R.D.H., M.S., director of dental hygiene, co-coordinator of assessment, and Tammy J. Lee, M.B.A., Ed.D., business instructor, co-coordinator of assessment, Rochester Community and Technical College.

5. *Meaningful Beginnings:* Another way to develop a meaningful beginning is to reach consensus with representatives across the campus about ways to initiate institution- and program-level assessment. Ask members of this group to discuss the possibilities listed in the following chart or to generate other approaches that may be more appropriate for your institutional context.

Meaningful Beginnings

Development of a new mission statement or educational philosophy for the institution or an academic department, school, program, or service	
Initiation of strategic planning	
Reconceptualization or revision of faculty and staff roles and rewards	
Design or revision of a core curriculum	
Development of a new program or service	
Selection of a new institutional leader	
Response to voiced dissatisfaction about student learning	
Recognition of classroom-based assessment as a foundation for institution- and program-level assessment focus	
Preparation of documentation to respond to legislators, accreditors, policy makers, or other public audiences	
National developments on teaching, learning and assessment, such as AAC&U's LEAP and VALUE Projects, the Wabash National Study, and the Lumina Tuning USA Project	

6. *Relationships to Explore Compelling Questions:* As institution- and program-level groups begin to identify collective questions that initiate inquiry, such as those listed on pages 3–4, identify constituencies within and outside your institution who contribute to students' learning. Determine how representatives from some of these constituencies might become involved in assessing institution- or program- level compelling questions. For example, if your institution or program wants to inquire into how well students integrate interdisciplinary perspectives into problem solving, which of those constituencies might become involved in exploring how and how well students develop these perspectives over the continuum of their studies? What new kinds of working relationships might you develop to assess the development of this kind of perspective-taking?

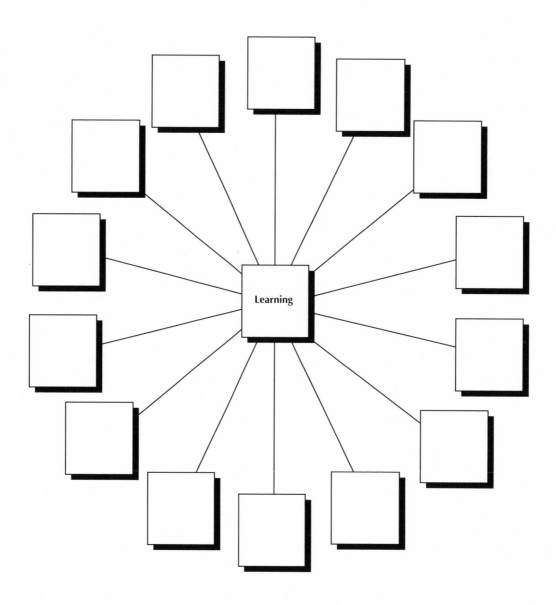

7. Focusing separately on the level of commitment of the institution, students, and educators, use the following templates to identify (a) the existence of a particular assessment commitment (yes or no); (b) the evidence that demonstrates a particular commitment; and (c) the level at which each commitment is rooted or established (1 = no commitment; 2 = some commitment; 3 = routinized or well-established commitment) as indicators of the depth and breadth of your institution's commitment to assessing student learning. Based on your results, discuss with appropriate faculty and staff and senior-level administrators how you might broaden, strengthen, or deepen your institution's commitment to assessment:

(a) Institution-level evidence: processes, practices, norms, structures, forms, and channels of communication and decision making

Specific Kinds of Commitment (Y/N)	Evidence of This Commitment	Level of Commitment (1–3)
Collaboratively developed principles-of-commitment statement		
Established soft times and neutral zones to discuss teaching, learning, and assessment		
Established soft times and neutral zones to discuss, reflect, and act on assessment results		
Recognition of the professional significance of a commitment to assessment		
Institution-level structures into which assessment is rooted, such as curriculum committee; assessment committee; center for teaching, learning, and assessment; and decision-making and planning bodies		
Institutional processes into which assessment is rooted, such as orientation of new students and new and adjunct faculty and staff; tenure and promotion; annual evaluations or review; and program review		
Forms of communication that inform both students and other stakeholders about student learning outcomes (SLOs) and students' accomplishment of those SLOs		
Forms of communication that annually channel assessment results and proposed actions to improve patterns of student weakness to department- and institution-level decision-making and planning bodies		
Evidence that decision-making and planning bodies use or act on communicated assessment results and recommended actions to improve student learning		
Financial, human, technological, and educational resources to support and sustain an institutional commitment to assessment		

(b) Student-level evidence: engagement

Specific Kinds of Commitment (Y/N)	Evidence of This Commitment	Level of Commitment (1–3)
Chronological documentation of achievement of SLOs at the institution and department levels through work assessed against publicly shared criteria and standards of performance		
Chronological evaluation of courses and programs based on students' own perceptions of their learning and their demonstrated achievement of SLOs		
Involvement in assessment-related bodies or activities, such as an institution-wide assessment committee or annual or semiannual assessment days		
Provider of chronological feedback to peers on their achievements against publicly shared criteria and standards of performance		
Recipient of chronological feedback from peers, faculty, and other educators and professionals based on publicly shared criteria and standards of performance		
Ability to articulate strengths, weaknesses, and accomplishments along their educational journey		

(c) Educators' evidence at course, department, service, or program levels

Specific Kinds of Commitment (Y/N)	Evidence of This Commitment	Level of Commitment (1–3)
Engagement in ongoing faculty and staff development on the interrelationship among teaching, learning, and assessment		
Orientation of new or part-time faculty and staff to SLOs and the assessment process		
Incorporation of a commitment to assessment into annual or periodic review of faculty and staff		
Integration of the assessment process into the teaching and learning process (for more detail, see #8)		
Regularly scheduled soft times and neutral zones to discuss teaching, learning, and results of assessment		
Establishment of soft times and neutral zones to discuss, reflect and act on assessment results		
Development of channels of communication to report assessment results and actions to improve student learning for department- or program-level decision making, planning, and budgeting as well as institution-level decision making and planning		
Recognition of assessment as a professional commitment to teaching and learning		
Public recognition of individuals and groups for their achievements in assessment of student learning		
Integration of assessment into program review		

8. Use the following template to take a closer look at how well your department or program has woven the assessment process into educational practices:

Department- or Program-Level Template for Assessing Students' Learning

Has your department or program collaboratively:

❏ Articulated and made public department- or program-level learning outcome statements?

❏ Mapped where and how students progressively learn these outcomes and identified points along the curriculum, as well as at the culmination of the program of study, when students demonstrate these collaboratively agreed-upon outcomes?

❏ Discussed the design of the curriculum as reflected in a department- or program-level curricular map, focusing on (1) pedagogies or educational practices that chronologically foster desired learning outcomes and (2) ways faculty intentionally build on each others' courses and educational experiences to continue to foster students' learning?

❏ Oriented and chronologically acculturated students to these outcomes?

❏ Oriented new and adjunct faculty or staff to these outcomes?

❏ Integrated these outcomes into syllabi so that students continue to deepen and build on their learning in multiple contexts?

❏ Identified times along students' program of study to position them to assess their learning gains across their program of study, such as in focus groups or at the end of courses, and used these results for departmental discussions?

❏ Identified or designed methods to assess students' progress toward and achievement of your SLOs?

❏ Identified appropriate times along students' program of study to assess their progress toward and achievement of your SLOs?

❏ Developed and distributed criteria and standards of judgment, scoring rubrics, to assess students' progress toward and achievement of your department- or program-level outcomes and to position students to self- or peer-assess?

❏ Identified times to convene department members to analyze, interpret, and use results of assessment to identify patterns of weakness in student work that lead to discussion about and identification of ways to improve student achievement through changes in pedagogy, curricular and instructional design, or other educational practices?

❏ Identified times to implement and assess collaboratively agreed-upon changes to ascertain how well these changes improve student learning?

Chapter 2

BEGINNING WITH DIALOGUE ABOUT TEACHING AND LEARNING

It is essential for any organization, academic or not, to assess the extent to which individual work contributes to collective needs and priorities. No organization can function effectively as a collection of autonomous individuals in which everyone pursues personal priorities and the overall achievements consist, in essence, of a casual, nonoptimal aggregate of activities. If universities are to have the resilience and adaptability they will need in the decades to come, they must find better ways to make individual faculty members' work contribute to common organizational needs, priorities, and goals.

—Ernest Lynton, 1998

OVERVIEW: This chapter focuses on the coordinating role of institution- and program-level assessment committees that initiate, orchestrate, and sustain cycles of inquiry into student learning. To root assessment practices into teaching and learning, these committees initiate rounds of dialogue that lead to consensus about shared expectations for student learning, followed by collaborative strategies that explore the curricular and co-curricular coherence that contributes to these expectations. Institution- and program-level representations of the landscape of students' learning opportunities become the bedrock on which assessment methods and practices are shaped. The Worksheets, Guides, and Exercises at the end of this chapter are designed to (1) establish collaboration as a principle that underlies the work of assessment committees and their relationship with members of the academic community; (2) promote institution- and program-level dialogue about teaching and learning as the context for embedding assessment; and (3) guide the development of curricular and co-curricular maps and inventories of practice that document where and how students learn what an educational community values.

THE CONTINUUM OF LEARNING: BEYOND AN AGGREGATION OF COURSES, CREDITS, AND SEAT TIME

With the exception of a small percentage of institutions in the United States that provide narrative tran-scripts of students' achievement, providing contexts for students' learning, typically colleges and universities record student achievement through a system of numbers and grades. Number of courses, number of credit hours, and grades document student learning. For example, somewhere in the range of 120 to 135 credits equal an undergraduate degree that is, in turn, divided into credits and courses delineating majors, minors, concentrations, electives, and general education. At both the graduate and the undergraduate levels, a certain number of courses or credits certifies a focus of learning—an area of specialization in graduate school, for example, or a minor in undergraduate school. This number-grade system is based on the assumption that students progressively transfer and build on previous learning as they advance through courses.

More than an aggregation of courses and credits, learning is a process of constructing meaning, framing issues, drawing on strategies and abilities honed over time, reconceptualizing understanding, repositioning oneself in relation to a problem or issue, and connecting thinking and knowing to action. Institution- and program-level assessment extends inquiry about student learning beyond students' achievement in individual courses to their achievement over time. This chapter describes structures and strategies for institution- and program-level tasks focused on (1) identifying collective expectations for student learning and (2) verifying how well pedagogy and the design of curriculum, co-curriculum, instruction, and other educational experiences or practices intentionally contribute to students' achievement of these expectations. The tasks described in this chapter are essential for embedding assessment into the processes of teaching and learning. Further, the initial ways in which members of an academic community work together to identify shared expectations for student learning pave the way for the collective dialogue, tasks, and decisions that characterize assessment as a core institutional process.

A FOCUS ON INTEGRATION

A focus on institution- and program-level learning moves beyond students' achievement in single courses to their achievement over time, in different contexts, through different kinds of educational experiences and modes of learning, and ways of representing learning. This focus, then, examines the integration, rather than the separation, of the domains of learning identified by Bloom and collaborators (1956); later extended by Krathwohl, Bloom, and Masia (1964); and more recently revised by Anderson and Krathwohl (2001). Within a context students demonstrate their learning through one of the three following domains:

1. The *cognitive domain*, which includes the development of the following intellectual abili-

ties listed in ascending order, although that order does not exclude simultaneous development of multiple abilities—remembering, understanding, applying, analyzing, evaluating, and creating (now at the top of the revised Bloom's Taxonomy)—such as a medical student's knowledge of anatomy, a graduate linguistic student's abilities to select and apply a method of discourse analysis to a text, an undergraduate business student's evaluation of multiple solutions to a problem in a case study, or a graduate or an undergraduate's new solution to or way of approaching a problem or issue.

2. The *psychomotor domain*, which includes the development of physical movement, coordination, and sets of physical skills, such as the intricately timed movements of a dancer, the precision of a neurosurgeon, or the task-centered procedures involved in human-computer interactions.

3. The *affective domain*, which includes the development of values, attitudes, commitments, and ways of responding, such as valuing others' perspectives, identifying situations that disadvantage a group of people, exercising tenacity in practicing an ability to improve it over time, or demonstrating a passion for learning.

A fourth domain that I believe actualizes these three domains is the *expressive domain*—a domain that integrates, represents, and at times even humanizes the other three domains or combinations of them within a specific context, such as in a performance, in a situation, or through a medium such as a podcast, an interactive website, or a video.[1] This domain includes humans' ways of representing or conveying ideas, knowledge, understanding, and even feelings,

---

1. The development of this fourth domain came about years ago as I worked with several visual and performing arts faculty, leading me to think more deeply about how individuals draw on the other three domains to represent or express their learning, beliefs, or ideas and themselves to others and for others. I am especially indebted to Professors Ronald Warners, honors program director, and Peter Hainer, professor of anthropology, Curry College, for validating my description of this domain and acknowledging its relevance to the relationship among teaching, learning, and assessment.

through body movement, facial expressions representing emotional responses, creative work in the visual and performing arts, short stories, novels, poems, narratives, visual and auditory media presentations, or nonverbal and nonlinear modes of representation. The expressive domain, then, actualizes what we know or understand, how we interpret, how we demonstrate understanding, or how we make meaning based on what we have learned. It also connects us as humans—even across language differences—shaping or deepening perspectives or positions on issues or problems, including enabling humans to discover new meaning. This fourth domain, then, includes the range of ways in which humans represent or demonstrate their knowledge, understanding, abilities, values, and attitudes within contexts or environments and through modes of communication. A nurse's or aide's empathetic facial expression may, for example, immediately place a worried patient at ease; similarly, a painting, a concerto, a dance, or a short story may deepen our sense of some aspect of the human condition; that is, it may connect us through time and space. Although some may argue that this fourth dimension is a form of one of the other three domains, I argue that this domain humanizes the cognitive, psychomotor, and affective domains. How students behave in a situation or what they produce expresses or represents what

they know, what they are actually able to do, and what they value. The integration of these four domains in a particular context, environment, or situation, represented in Figure 2.1, illustrates the focus of institution- and program-level assessment: students' construction of meaning represented or demonstrated through their interactions, responses, commitments, creations, projects, research, interpretations, chronological self-reflections, and multimedia expressions of ideas, now occurring in new online places and spaces. An architectural student needs to demonstrate more than the ability to draw; the ability to draw does not by itself define an architect. Knowledge and understanding of the properties of building materials, environmental and climatic conditions, and building codes, for example, as well as a predisposition to research limitations of a particular building site, as well as an ability to express a sense of place through building design and structure, work together to produce an architect's final design for a particular context—a building site. Faculty who teach drawing courses assess architectural students' ability to design a structure to represent or express or evoke a sense of place; faculty who teach environmental courses assess architectural students' knowledge about how environments limit designs. Program-level assessment focuses on how students integrate their learning across these and

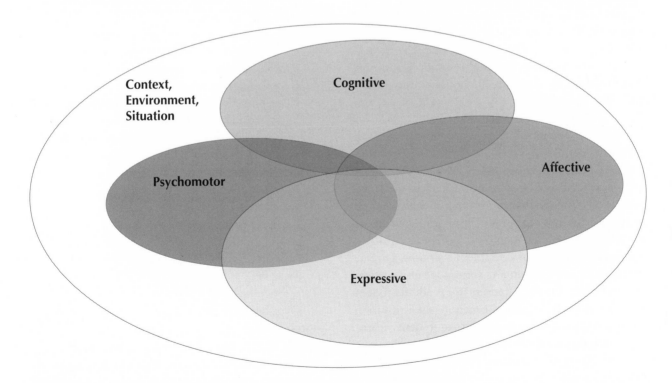

FIGURE 2.1 Integration of Domains in a Context, Environment, or Situation

other courses to actualize their learning as architects. Identifying appropriate times to assess for integrated learning, then, defines the role of institution- and program-level assessment.

COORDINATING COMMITTEES

Reaching consensus about collective expectations for student learning at both the institution and program levels marks the first stage of the assessment process. Initiating this first stage is typically the role of a coordinating body—an assessment committee—that seeks community consensus about expectations for student learning based on an institution's or a program's mission, purpose, and values. Generally, there are two levels of assessment committees within a college or university: (1) a campus-wide committee and (2) a program- or department-level committee (also established in schools, divisions, departments, or services).

A Campus-Wide Assessment Committee

A campus-wide assessment committee develops an institutional student learning assessment plan (see pages 139–140 and 146–151 in chapter 4). This plan, often developed in concert with other constituencies of an institution and in collaboration with a college or university institutional research and planning office, develops a timetable that triggers annual cycles of inquiry into student learning at both the institution and program levels. A campus-wide committee becomes both the structure that initiates and the engine that drives sustainable assessment of student learning across an institution.

Generally, members on this committee serve term appointments, 2 to 3 years, after which a new representative from each constituency joins the committee for a term period. There may be permanent members such as a representative from institutional research or the institution's vice president of academic affairs or provost. Rotational membership broadens institutional understanding of assessment over time. Diverse membership on this standing committee also ensures that there are sustained conversations about student learning and achievement throughout the institution and among the various contributors to students' learning. The following list includes those who might serve on a campus-wide assessment committee or in an advisory capacity:

- Institution's chief academic leader
- Institution's assessment director or coordinator, often someone who works separately on academic and co-curricular assessment but also in conjunction with a director of institutional research
- Representative from the institution's faculty and staff governance
- Representative from each academic program, department, division, or school within an institution
- Representative from the institution's center for teaching and learning or from a faculty development center
- Representative from academic support services such as services for students with learning differences
- Representative from student support services
- Representative from student affairs
- Representative from library and information resources
- Full- and part-time graduate and undergraduate student representative
- Teaching assistant representative
- Representative from instructional design or instructional technology
- Student tutor representative who experiences firsthand the levels of difficulties students confront in learning
- Representative from the local community who educates students in internships, cooperative education programs, or community service
- Representative from alumni
- Representative employer who contributes knowledge about what students bring to their employment and identifies new abilities students will need to bring into the workplace or into civic life
- Member of an institution's business or advisory board
- Representative from institutional research and planning who provides guidance and support along the life of the assessment process

Over time, campus-wide assessment committees morph from an initially appointed small task force to a larger permanent committee, representing the enduring commitment of assessment on a campus. As assessment committees mature, they form or appoint core working groups, task forces, or cluster groups, consisting of faculty, staff, administrators, students, and others who contribute to students' education to carry out specific assessment tasks, as represented in Figure 2.2. An assessment committee and its working groups sustain an institutional commitment to assessment by taking responsibility for overseeing the following institution-level tasks:

- Articulating institution-level (such as general education) student learning outcome statements and ensuring wide dissemination of these to students and other stakeholders on the institution's website and through other forms of communication

- Overseeing the design or selection of methods to assess students' institution-level outcomes represented in students' work and in their perceptions of their learning
- Developing a cycle of inquiry—a timetable— to assess one or more agreed-upon institution-level learning outcome statements each year that includes identifying the following:

  When and how student work will be collected, scored, and analyzed

  When analysis of scoring results will be presented for community interpretation, discussion, reflection, and action, such as revisions, changes, or innovations in educational practices

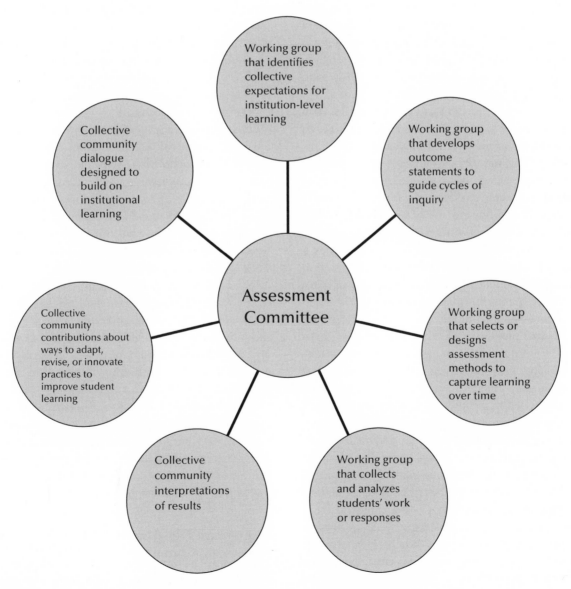

FIGURE 2.2 Assessment Committee Core Working Groups and Tasks

When proposed changes will be implemented
When assessment results and proposed
changes will be annually channeled to
institution-wide decision-making, planning, and budgeting bodies to inform
those bodies' actions
When student work will be reassessed after
implementation of changes to ascertain
the efficacy of those changes

At many institutions, a campus-wide assessment committee also serves as a body that peer-reviews department- and program-level multiyear assessment plans to ensure that these plans include the major assessment tasks, use multiple sources of student evidence of learning, and chronologically cycle through its outcomes. Figure 2.3 represents part of a student affairs plan that illustrates how the student life division at Clarke College annually cycles through institution-level outcomes that are incorporated into its range of programs and services. To ensure that each program or department's plan is carried out, even after a plan is peer-approved, the campus-wide committee also sets up a reporting schedule to learn about how each program or department's findings, analyses, and interpretations of student performance led to collaborative decision making about ways to improve areas of lower-than-expected student performance. (Appendix 7.1 also represents one example of a reporting template that programs or departments may use to represent results and actions after assessing a set of outcomes; a variation on that template could also be used to submit an initial assessment plan that would indicate dates for carrying out each task in the template.)

An assessment committee shapes or informs the work of other campus entities such as centers for teaching and learning, now often named centers for teaching, learning, and assessment, or centers for faculty development to ensure that there are sustained educational opportunities for current, new, full-time, and part-time faculty and staff to learn about developments in assessment in online, blended, and face-to-face learning environments. Contemporary developments include designing or identifying methods to assess online learning, using assessment methods built into learning management systems, working with instructional designers and educational technology experts to design methods to assess students in alternative modes of instruction. An institution's curriculum committee also adapts to the work of a campus-wide assessment committee through developing policies and guidelines for syllabi, course, and program approval, such as a syllabi policy that requires all courses to state intended learning outcomes in relation to overarching program or department-level outcomes or a policy that requires a program demonstrate how its outcomes will be addressed in the courses and experiences that altogether contribute to that program. (Key components of outcome-based syllabi are identified in chapter 3, pages 99–102.)

Often in conjunction with the institution's director of assessment or in conjunction with the director of institutional research, the institutional assessment committee oversees developing and updating a campus assessment website that houses all relevant assessment documents, decisions, reports, actions, resources, and institution- or department-level outcomes—such as minutes of meetings, annual department reports and actions to improve student learning, and lists of on-campus resources (such as workshops and publications) and off-campus resources (such as state, regional, national, or international assessment conferences). Some institutions have even developed short "how to" videos for their websites that focus on individual assessment tasks, such as writing learning outcome statements. Department or program assessment reports, including periodic program reviews that now address assessment of student learning as a central component of the review (this development is discussed in chapter 8 and illustrated on pages 304–314) are often included on institutional assessment websites, containing the results of assessment of student work and the actions departments have taken or will take to improve identified areas of weak performance. A fine example of an institutional assessment site is the Student Achievement and Assessment Committee site at Bowling Green State University (www.bgsu.edu/offices/assessment/index.html)—a comprehensive website that, along with other information, lists the university- and department-level learning outcomes, scoring rubrics used to assess the university's learning outcomes, annual department and program assessment reports, resources, and departments and programs that have been recognized for excellence in this commitment—a testament of how well assessment is woven into the institution's culture.

Program- or Department-Level Assessment Committees

Overall, in small or large departments or programs there is at least an appointed liaison who ensures that

The Student Life area at Clarke College includes the following offices: Athletics, Student Activities, Multicultural Student Services, Campus Ministry, Counseling Center, Career Services, Residence Life, and Health Services. These offices are scheduled to evaluate student learning, according to the seven Student Life outcomes, on a 3-year cycle.

Semester	Department Outcomes	Offices/Programs	
Year 1			
Fall 06	**Outcome 2.** Develop self-confidence. *[Aligns with Institutional Outcomes 5 and 9]*	Athletics Student Activities Multicultural Student Services Campus Ministry	Counseling Center Career Services Health Services Residence Life
Spring 07	**Outcome 3.** Develop leadership skills. *[Aligns with Institutional Outcomes 2, 6, 7, and 9]*	Athletics Student Activities Multicultural Student Services Campus Ministry	Counseling Center Career Services Health Services Residence Life
Year 2			
Fall 07	**Outcome 4.** Develop a personal code of values and ethics. *[Aligns with Institutional Outcome 3]*	Athletics Student Activities Multicultural Student Services Campus Ministry	Counseling Center Career Services Health Services Residence Life
Spring 08	**Outcome 5.** Deepen spiritual values. *[Aligns with Institutional Outcome 3]* **Outcome 6.** Develop respect for people of different ethnic and cultural backgrounds. *[Aligns with Institutional Outcomes 2 and 8]*	Athletics Student Activities Multicultural Student Services Campus Ministry	Counseling Center Career Services Health Services Residence Life
Year 3			
Fall 08	**Outcome 7.** Demonstrate skills and behaviors to achieve personal and professional goals. *[Aligns with Institutional Outcomes 3, 6, and 7]*	Athletics Student Activities Multicultural Student Services Campus Ministry	Counseling Center Career Services Health Services Residence Life
Spring 09	**Outcome 1.** Develop self-understanding. *[Aligns with Institutional Outcomes 3, 7, and 9]*	Athletics/Team and individual statistics and year-ending evaluations Student Activities/CSA, Class, Club, and Organization Officers Multicultural Student Services/Kwanzaa Celebration Campus Ministry/New Orleans Service Trip Career Services/Internship-for-Credit program Health Services/Student Health Visits and Health Screenings (NASD, NDSD, NESD)	

FIGURE 2.3   3-Year Student Life Timeline to Assess Institution-Level Outcomes
Source: Kate Zanger, vice president for student life, Clarke College.

assessment of student learning is integrated into the routine life of a department or program. In large programs or departments there may well be a small group that takes on this responsibility: members of that group may serve for several years, after which a new group takes over. Either a liaison or a group initiates and drives the assessment process through all of its tasks—such as developing consensus about learning outcomes, agreeing on actions to improve or innovate educational practices based on students' performance, and ensuring that recommendations move through established channels within the department or pro-

gram for decision making, planning, budgeting, and allocation or reallocation of resources as well as through institution-level decision-making, planning, and budgeting channels that make campus-wide decisions and recommendations. Not a onetime or sometime commitment, assessment becomes an annual way of behaving; typically, departments and programs assess one to two outcomes a year (often looking at more than one outcome in students' work, such as a student's writing and critical thinking in a sophomore-level paper) until they have cycled through the agreed-upon set of department or program outcomes.

Then they begin anew to assess chronologically that same set of outcomes, taking time to update outcomes or include new ones based on developments in a discipline or field.

Working in much the same way as the campus-wide assessment committee, program-level assessment committees may act as a committee of the whole program or distribute tasks through core working groups. In large programs, schools, or divisions, a central committee that focuses on core learning for students studying in that school may establish satellite committees that focus more specifically on assessing learning in areas of specialization, such as in a school of natural sciences. Program-level committees also consist of broad representation from their educational constituencies and contributors, including students and representatives from advisory boards, professions, or organizations in the local community. In addition to considering representation from the pool of constituencies listed on page 54, program-level committees may draw membership from the following groups:

- Administrative heads of individual departments in a program, school, or division
- Full- and part-time faculty who teach in programs
- Faculty from graduate schools who bring perspectives on accepted students
- Laboratory assistants
- Graduate assistants
- Graduates from the program
- Employers who directly hire graduates of a program

Program-level assessment committees mirror the responsibilities and inquiry process described for institution-level assessment committees, described on pages 56–57. In both campus-wide and program-level committees, dialogue about teaching and learning and students' achievement based on those processes ensures that assessment reflects educators' values.

DIALOGUE FOCUSED ON EXPECTATIONS FOR STUDENT LEARNING

Marking the first phase of a campus-wide or program-level assessment plan is dialogue focused on identifying shared expectations for student learning:

- What do members of a college or university and members of specific programs expect

their students to be able to demonstrate or represent based on pedagogy; the design of the curriculum, co-curriculum, and instruction; other educational opportunities and practices; and the use of educational tools?
- What should students be able to demonstrate or represent at points along their studies based on these educational practices?
- What do the curricula and other educational experiences "add up to"?

These kinds of questions initiate institution- and program-level dialogue that eventually leads to consensus about what members of an academic community wish to explore along students' chronology of learning, such as their ability to perform the following tasks:

- Reason quantitatively in different kinds of contexts outside quantitatively based courses
- Solve complex global problems through interdisciplinary perspectives
- Integrate general education learning into their major fields of study
- Apply disciplinary habits of mind and ways of behaving to solve a range of representative problems

A core working group within an institution- or program-level assessment committee may be appointed to respond to or gather responses to these kinds of questions. This core working group may progress through this consensus-building phase in several ways, such as the following:

1. Draft responses to questions about what students should be able to demonstrate at the end of their undergraduate or graduate studies. To focus on institution- or program-level core curricula, a committee may appoint, select, or elect a more specialized group consisting of individuals who specifically teach courses in an institution's or program's core curriculum or who contribute to it through programs and services, such as representatives from academic support services.
2. Schedule several occasions for community dialogue to address questions about what students should be able to demonstrate at the end of their undergraduate or graduate studies, developing cross-disciplinary and cross-

functional groups (such as academic affairs and student affairs groups).

3. Conduct a syllabi audit to derive a list of recurring foci that courses attend to as well as a list of foci that are less frequently addressed but may deserve full discussion across the department or program. The results of this audit would serve as an underpinning for discussing and eventually agreeing on shared expectations for students among faculty. The results may also identify expectations that should be more widely agreed upon but momentarily are not.

4. Schedule one or more occasions for upper-level undergraduate and graduate students to come together to identify what they believe they have learned in their program of study and where and how they learned what they identify.

These occasions for dialogue also contribute to and foster collaboration, a key ingredient in an institutional commitment to assessing for learning that values collective and diverse contributions to student learning as students construct meaning over time.

Positioning assessment as a collaborative process begins in this initial phase of information gathering. The following strategies also engage the wider community:

1. Posting results of core working groups' responses or the results of community dialogue on a campus website

2. Inviting larger response—even from other constituencies outside a campus or program who contribute to students' learning or have a vested interest in their learning, such as members from the local businesses that hire students

3. Redrafting and posting a final list of expectations for student learning on a campus website with a deadline for recommended additions or proposed changes to the draft.

Building institutional knowledge across the assessment process promotes dialogue about teaching and learning and the practices that contribute to students' learning. Program-level assessment committees also contribute to institution-wide dialogue about shared expectations for student learning. For example, a university composed of schools or divisions may structure occasions for interrelated dialogue about how schools or divisions and the separate programs or departments within them contribute to university-wide expectations for student learning, such as those for general education. Specifically, if a university asserts that its graduates develop the ability to explore the ethical dimensions of their decisions, then verifying that schools, divisions, and their programs contribute to the development of this attribute—beyond a required course—becomes a focus of dialogue. On the other hand, an institution's focus on developing leadership abilities and qualities may, in turn, contribute to a program's focus on that quality as well. Program-level dialogue also focuses on identifying disciplinary, cross-disciplinary, or professional expectations for fields of study. For example, members of a biology department, together with students, members of an advisory board, and local biologists, may agree that they expect students to communicate disciplinary principles and concepts to different audience levels—from expert to lay audiences. They may also agree that as part of solving representative biology problems, students should be able to demonstrate that they follow disciplinary procedures and draw upon ways of knowing and behaving that characterize the work of biologists.

DIALOGUE FOCUSED ON THE DESIGN OF THE CURRICULUM AND CO-CURRICULUM

Bringing to the surface and agreeing on shared expectations for student learning at both the institution and program levels pave the way for a second level of community dialogue. This level focuses on exploring where, when, and even how the design of curriculum, co-curriculum, instruction, pedagogy, and educational opportunities intentionally promotes these shared expectations. Specifically, it examines coherence—how well collective expectations translate into intentional educational practices, providing multiple and varied opportunities for students to learn. These kinds of conversations extend across academic programs and services, across the co-curriculum, and even into the surrounding local community that educates our students in internships, residencies, cooperative learning experiences, field experiences, community service, and work-study opportunities.

This kind of dialogue also may reveal gaps in students' opportunities to learn. For example, within a department or program, colleagues may believe they have adequately sequenced courses in a major program of study based on a developmental model of how students learn. However, a collective look at course content, curricular design, and pedagogy and other educational practices may reveal insufficient opportunities for students to build on or use previous learning. Courses may exist as separate entities, disconnected from students' previous learning. Students may be responsible for memorizing formulas, principles, or concepts in one course in a major program of study with little opportunity to practice, apply, and extend this learning until later in their studies.

Therefore, members of a department or program or members who contribute to an institution's general education or core curriculum, including representatives from other programs and services that contribute to students' learning, must engage in collaborative discussion about the educational philosophy, set of assumptions, and research on learning or effective educational practices (such as the "high impact" practices documented by Kuh [2008]) that underlie the design of the curriculum and sequencing of or choices of courses and educational experiences. An example of how one institution has redesigned its general education courses in light of knowledge about student-centered course design, high-impact educational practices, and a desire for students to develop longer-term retention of geology than students who had enrolled in a more traditional lecture and lab model course is represented in the poster presentation in Appendix 2.1. Using learning circles, faculty at Ramapo College have collaboratively redesigned general education courses, drawing on current student-centered course design principles and anchoring the design in a "dream statement—what faculty want their students to retain long after a course is over—and learning outcomes that drive course redesign."

The following list represents the kinds of questions that may be generated from planned occasions to collaboratively explore and identify the curricular/co-curricular terrain that contributes to students' learning:

- How intentionally do members of an academic community provide curricular and co-curricular opportunities for students to learn what an institution and its programs assert that they teach or inculcate?
- How do faculty, staff, and other contributors to student learning build on each other's work?
- Do students have multiple and diverse opportunities to build on previous learning, receive feedback, and reflect on their progress toward achieving what an institution and its programs expect?
- How do academic programs, services, and educational opportunities promote institution- and program-level understanding, abilities, habits of mind, ways of thinking, and behaving?
- What educational processes and experiences contribute to and reinforce collective educational expectations?
- What forms of online or face-to-face pedagogy (or combinations of modes of delivery), instruction, and use of educational experiences such as online labs, case studies, or data mining in virtual sites foster agreed-upon expectations for student learning?

The Works Cited and Additional Resources at the end of this chapter provide a range of possible texts that can prompt collaborative discussion about the design of courses and the design of a program or department's curriculum and related co-curriculum, including Rose (2009), calling on those who teach developmental courses to rethink the assumptions and practices that underlie traditional approaches to educating underprepared students, based on a possible new approach he and others have designed; Richlin (2006); Gurung, Chick, and Haynie (2008); Fink (2003); and Gabriel (2008). Other texts discuss curricular design for online or blended learning, such as Garrison and Vaughan (2008). Principles and practices of a universally designed curriculum (Universal Design for Learning [UDL]), focused on developing multiple means of representation, expression, and engagement to address all learners, are described by the Center for Applied Special Technology (2008) and applied to teaching in higher education by Burgstahler and Cory (2008). These representative texts can generate important exchanges among colleagues focused not only on how individuals independently teach or position students to learn, but also on how colleagues can build on or continue to contribute to each other's courses to move students to achieve enduring and more complex levels of learning. These texts may also generate research or study questions, such as the ones addressed in chapter 4, that colleagues wish to pursue through the assessment process in order to deepen their own understanding about who, why, how, or how well students develop enduring, transferable learning—a repertoire from which they can draw by the time they complete their program of study. Without threaded opportunities in the curriculum or related educational experiences to apply early learning such as memorized facts, processes, procedures, or concepts, students will probably be unable to recall, much less apply, what they once learned or memorized. As a result, learning for students remains course-bound because opportunities to use and build on initial learning simply do not exist between an early course and later courses that aim to build on students' previous learning.

CURRICULAR AND CO-CURRICULAR MAPS AND INVENTORIES OF EDUCATIONAL PRACTICES

A way to visualize the range of interdependent relationships that foster student learning through multiple learning opportunities is to develop curricular and co-curricular maps and inventories of educational practices. These representations may be used to verify collective expectations across actual educational practices; that is, they reveal the distribution of opportunities to learn across an institution and its programs and services. More important, these representations provide a rich context for writing learning outcome statements, sentences that describe what students should be able to demonstrate, represent, or produce based on how and what they have learned, the subject of chapter 3. Dialogue and work focused on what students' learning continuum looks like lead to collectively agreed-upon and clear outcome statements. Without this preparatory work leading to the development of outcome statements, disjunctures may exist between shared expectations for student learning and actual opportunities for students to achieve these expectations along their chronologies of learning. Developing a broad view of students' progression enables us to see how frequently students have or have had opportunities to hone a particular ability, for example, or to build a repertoire of strategies to solve discipline-specific problems.

Maps

Maps provide information about what students learn over time; they profile intentionality over the continuum of students' learning. Representing the underlying logic of curricular and co-curricular design, they provide a shared context for authoring outcome statements, methods to assess outcome statements, and

criteria and standards by which to judge student work, topics addressed in chapters 3 through 6.

A curricular map or a co-curricular map, one that identifies learning outcomes addressed in life outside the classroom, charts where faculty and others who contribute to student learning integrate educational opportunities that address institution- and program-level expectations for student learning. These maps also identify gaps in student learning opportunities or identify concentrations of learning experiences without further opportunity for students to transfer, build on, or apply learning. Most important, in the early dialogue that grounds assessment, maps help us see whether the learning priorities we collectively articulate translate into underlying coherence among our efforts. If not, during these early discussions we can reprioritize learning outcomes, identify other outcomes that have taken precedence because of societal or workplace changes, or reassert their significance as core outcomes by discussing ways to deepen and broaden attention to them in the curriculum and co-curriculum. Maps of the curriculum and co-curriculum serve four main purposes in building a collective institutional commitment to assessment:

1. They stimulate discussion about and critical reflection on collective learning priorities.
2. They illustrate how well collective expectations align with educational practices that foster those priorities.
3. They provide a visual representation of students' contexts for learning that may assist faculty and staff later on when they interpret assessment results.
4. If made available to students, they focus them on program-, department-, and institution-level expectations for learning, holding them accountable for their learning and encouraging them to develop their own learning map as they progress through their undergraduate or graduate studies. Sharing and discussing a curricular and a co-curricular map with students upon matriculation is also a way to acculturate them to learning as a building process, not a credit-counting exercise.

Because students learn in different ways, under different pedagogies and educational practices, holding a couple of courses solely responsible for developing students' ability to write, for example, assumes that students continue to retain from year to year what they learned in those courses (see the resources for teaching different learners, including online learning environments, under "Additional Resources" at the end of this chapter). In fact, students need to continue to apply and build on that learning over the remainder of their undergraduate and graduate studies, including learning about and using disciplinary conventions, formats, rhetorical styles, and ways of presenting information or evidence to solve problems for different audiences and purposes. Valuing multiple educational opportunities that contribute to students' writing abilities broadens institutional responsibility and students' opportunities to learn. For example, besides responding to assignments in their coursework, students have multiple opportunities to extend their writing abilities outside the classroom through the following:

- Contributions to a college's or university's newspaper or other publications
- Proposals for independent study
- Proposals for honors projects
- Documentation of meeting discussions and results
- Summaries and analyses of campus surveys
- Wikis, blogs, podcasts, online discussion boards, and chat rooms

The institutional value placed on writing translates into the life of the institution in multiple learning contexts or opportunities and thereby expands and deepens students' learning about the various forms, strategies, and conventions of writing. Maps of the curriculum and co-curriculum, then, chart not only courses that initially focus on or integrate writing,

but also complementary learning experiences that expand students' opportunities to write (see Box 2.1 and Box 2.2). Appendix 2.2 at the end of this chapter illustrates the curricular map described in Box 2.1.

Inventories of Educational Practices

Maps provide an overview of students' learning journey—a place to locate where educational opportunities are specifically designed to address institution- and program-level expectations. Inventories drill down into actual educational practices to develop shared understanding of and discussion about how students learn over time and how educators value that learning through assessment methods. These kinds of inventories build institution- and program-level knowledge and provide the foundation on which to design and develop the "bigger picture" assessment methods described in chapter 5. Agreeing on shared expectations initiates the process of assessment. Exploring questions about the efficacy and relevance of collective educational practices, however, sustains collective curiosity. The following set of questions is useful at either the institution or program level to initiate dialogue about how students actually learn what an institution and its programs expect them to learn:

- What educational philosophy, principles, theories, models of teaching, research on learning, or shared assumptions underlie curricular or co-curricular design, instructional design, pedagogy, or use of educational tools?
- What pedagogies or educational experiences develop the knowledge, understanding,

---

BOX 2.1 INSTITUTIONAL EXAMPLE: *New Jersey City University*

At New Jersey City University, the business administration program's curriculum map locates where both program- and institution-level learning outcomes are addressed and distributed across the program (see Appendix 2.2 at the end of this chapter). Using a labeling system of *I* (introduce), *R* (reinforce), and *E* (emphasize), members of the program indicate how courses build on desired learning over time, providing a sense of relationships among and between courses and a chronology of how students learn. Listed in the left-hand column are both institution- and program-level learning outcomes. The map and the labeling system provide a visual representation of students' curricular progression as it relates to shared expectations among faculty in the business administration program and as it relates to institution-level expectations. An important collaborative strategy, mapping provides a picture of the whole that may prompt further dialogue about ways to distribute or redistribute learning opportunities.

BOX 2.2 INSTITUTIONAL EXAMPLE: *Rose-Hulman Institute of Technology Curricular Map*

At Rose-Hulman Institute of Technology, faculty map where and how they address institution-level learning outcomes, referred to as learning objectives, such as students' awareness of the ethical dimensions of engineering problems for engineers. Faculty receive an electronic form that lists institutional learning objectives, along with criteria that further identify those objectives. This form asks faculty to respond to four questions about how intentionally they address these objectives in their courses, including whether students are asked to demonstrate objectives and whether faculty provide feedback to students on these objectives, an indicator of intentionality. A composite curriculum map of these practices provides evidence about program- and institution-level intentionality. This evidence may demonstrate sustained attention over programs and across the institution, or it may demonstrate declining or sporadic attention. Declining or sporadic attention raises the following questions for faculty and staff to answer:

- Is this outcome still one of our priorities?
- If so, how do we redirect attention to it?
- If not, why do we state that it is a priority?

Objective Explicit. This objective is explicitly stated as being a learning objective for this course.
Demonstrate Competence. Students are asked to demonstrate their competence on this objective through homework, projects, tests, etc.
Formal Feedback. Students are given formal feedback on their performance on this objective.

Not covered. This objective is not addressed in these ways in this course.

Note: Clicking on the link "view criteria" will bring up the list of criteria for that particular institutional objective in a floating window.

Objective	Objective Explicit	Demonstrate Competence	Formal Feedback		Not Covered
1. Recognition of ethical and professional responsibilities. view criteria or make a comment (optional)	☐ Yes	☐ Yes	☐ Yes		☐
2. An understanding of how contemporary issues shape and are shaped by mathematics, science, and engineering. view criteria or make a comment (optional)	☐ Yes	☐ Yes	☐ Yes		☐
3. An ability to recognize the role of professionals view criteria or make a comment (optional)		Yes	☐ Yes		☐
4. An ability to understand diverse cultural and the view criteria or make a comment (optional)		Yes	☐ Yes		☐
5. An ability to work effectively in teams. view criteria or make a comment (optional)		Yes	☐ Yes		☐
6. An ability to communicate effectively in oral, wi forms. view criteria or make a comment (optional)	☐ Yes	Yes	☐ Yes		☐
7. An ability to apply the skills and knowledge necessary for mathematical, scientific, and engineering practices. view criteria or make a comment (optional)	☐ Yes	☐ Yes	☐ Yes		☐
8. An ability to interpret graphical, numerical, and textual data. view criteria or make a comment (optional)	☐ Yes	☐ Yes	☐ Yes		☐
9. An ability to design and conduct experiments. view criteria or make a comment (optional)	☐ Yes	☐ Yes	☐ Yes		☐
10. An ability to design a product or process to satisfy a client's needs subject to constraints. view criteria or make a comment (optional)	☐ Yes	☐ Yes	☐ Yes		☐

When given the opportunity, students will;
1. **Demonstrate knowledge of professional codes of ethics.**
2. **Evaluate the ethical dimensions of a problem in their discipline.**

Submit/Reconfirm

Rose-Hulman Institute of Technology
2002–2003 Curriculum Map
www.rose-hulman.edu

habits of mind, ways of knowing, and problem solving that the institution or its programs value?

- How do students become acculturated to the ways of thinking, knowing, and problem solving in their field of study?
- How do faculty and staff intentionally build on each other's courses and educational experiences to achieve programmatic as well as institutional learning priorities?
- Which students benefit from various teaching strategies, educational processes, or educational experiences in face-to-face and online learning environments?

Identifying course-based or module-based teaching methods, course-based assessment methods, or methods to assess students as they complete educational opportunities or experiences, such as community service projects, is a second type of inventory. This inventory provides longitudinal documentation of the range and frequency of educational practices and assessment methods that students experience during their education. An agreed-upon coding system identifies how students learn in a module or course (such as through online laboratories or simulations or webcasts) and how they are assessed for desired learning, such as through a final project or presentation. Identifying patterns of course-based assessment methods over a program of study shapes and informs program- and institution-level assessment methods that build on students' previous assessment experiences, the subject of chapter 5. Asking students to make inferences based on multiple sources of data is one way to determine their critical-thinking abilities. If, however, an inventory of course-based assessment practices reveals that students have had limited experience making inferences and, instead, have been asked primarily to recall or recognize information, then a program-level inference-drawing assessment method would not fairly and appropriately match students' learning history. Knowing when to assess chemistry students' ability to formulate a hypothesis or when to assess computer science students' ability to apply rules of formal logic rests on collective understanding of the chronological educational practices that have fostered these abilities as well as the chronological value faculty have placed on these abilities in their assessment methods. The following prompts invite conversation about how individuals design assessment tasks in response to institution- and program-level expectations:

- Describe how you design a course or experience to contribute to students' demonstration or representation of an institution- or program-level expectation.
- Identify ways in which students learn what you intend—for example, in collaboratively based projects, through virtual simulations, through memorization, through the use of equipment, or through self-reflection in response to a task.
- Describe your assessment method and the context within which students respond to it—for example, at the end of an internship, in a multiple-choice test, or as part of an online laboratory module quiz.
- Describe the content, abilities, habits of mind, and so on that you expect students to demonstrate when they respond to your assessment method—for example, conceptual or procedural knowledge or analytical or interpretive abilities.

The accumulated results of individual inventories profile the frequency, diversity, and modes of delivery of educational practices and the frequency, diversity, modes, and methods of assessment that occur along students' studies. Represented together in a map, individual efforts illustrate how intentionally institution- or program-level learning priorities are distributed, addressed, and valued across students' studies. Without mapping where and how our expectations for student learning are addressed, we can only hope that students learn what we intend them to learn. Through maps and inventories of practice we can see and talk about our students' learning experiences—how they have opportunities to learn what we expect them to learn.

Appendix 2.3 at the end of this chapter is part of a map from a physics department, representing how a community college's general education outcomes are woven across and reinforced within the context of the physics curriculum. Codes used in this map document where and how students continue to learn general education outcomes in a disciplinary context and how they are assessed for that learning along the chronology of their learning. Appendix 2.4 at the end of this chapter is a coding system for a professional program, pharmacy, that chronologically identifies how both the level and type of pedagogy promotes students' abilities to build on and advance their professional learning. Other coding systems can be developed for curricular or co-curricular maps, such as systems that reflect a developmental design of the curriculum or systems that reflect a chronological level of expected achievement, performance, application, or mastery. (See also Appendix 3.3 in Chapter 3.)

Curricular mapping that also documents educational practices and methods of assessment has now become a common component of web-based assessment management systems, many of which are described in chapter 8. It is becoming common practice across colleges and universities that educators document where they address institution- and program-level outcomes in an online curricular map that can be annually or periodically updated with ease. In addition, other software developers have designed online curricular maps such as CurrMITT, the Curriculum Management & Information Tool, which is used in medical programs (www.aamc.org/meded/curric/start.htm).

THE DESIGN OF OUR WORK

Given that learning is a complex process, that students learn as a result of different pedagogies, and that they face different obstacles based on misunderstanding or long-held beliefs, exploring the design of our collective work enables us to identify underlying connections and avenues for learning. Additionally, exploring the design of our collective work positions us to identify how we may strengthen connections or build additional avenues for learning. Routine discussions about teaching and learning with representatives from across a campus or from across a program, department, school, or division provide an essential platform for verifying the coherence that underlies collective intentions for student learning. Department or program chairs and directors of services and programs can integrate these discussions within the fabric of their units' work—a rhythm of professional life. In a collective commitment to assessment, our complex intentions for students, such as their ability to solve disciplinary problems or their ability to evaluate and choose among compelling and competing solutions to a problem, are achieved across our programs and services. Focus is not on what "I" do; focus is on what "we" do. Ownership of teaching stretches across courses, services, and educational practices. It holds us collectively responsible for contributing to learning over students' studies, providing multiple and varied opportunities for them to learn and practice what we value. Conversations about how we translate our teaching philosophies, sets of assumptions about learning, or theories of learning into pedagogy and curricular and co-curricular design establish a common ground for how we choose to assess our students based on their learning chronologies. Representation of multiple voices in assessment dialogue contributes to achieving consensus about what an institution values and how those values are integrated into institutional culture. This representation also begins to establish institutional channels of communication among all who educate to enhance understanding of the myriad ways in which students learn within and outside a college or university. Without this context, assessment becomes divorced from our professional work.

WORKS CITED

Anderson, L. W., & Krathwohl, D. R. (Eds.). (2001). *A taxonomy for learning, teaching, and assessment: A revision of Bloom's taxonomy of educational objectives.* New York: Longman.

Bloom, B. S., & Collaborators. (1956). *The taxonomy of educational objectives: Cognitive domain.* New York: McKay.

Burgstahler, S. E., & Cory, R. C. (Eds.). (2008). *Universal design in higher education: From principles to practice.* Cambridge, MA: Harvard Education Press.

Center for Applied Special Technology. (2008). *Universal design for learning guidelines.* Version 1.0. Wakefield, MA: Author. *www.udlcenter.org/aboutud/udguidelines*

Fink, D. (2003). *Creating significant learning experiences: An integrated approach to designing college courses.* San Francisco: Jossey-Bass.

Gabriel, K. F. (2008). *Teaching unprepared students: Strategies for promoting success and retention in higher education.* Sterling, VA: Stylus.

Garrison, R. D., & Vaughan, N. D. (2007). *Blended learning in higher education: Framework, principles, and guidelines.* San Francisco: Jossey Bass.

Kuh, G.D. (2008). *High impact educational practices: What they are, who has access to them, and why they matter.* Washington, D.C.: AAC&U.

Lynton, E. A. (1998, March). Reversing the telescope: Fitting individual tasks to common organizational ends. AAHE *Bulletin, 50,* 8–10.

Richlin, L. (2006). *Constructing college courses to facilitate, assess, and document learning.* Sterling, VA: Stylus.

Rose, M. (2009, August 3). *Colleges need to remediate re-mediation. http://chronicle.com/article/Colleges-Need-to-Re-Mediate/47527/*

ADDITIONAL RESOURCES

Teaching Practices, Theories, and Research on Learning That Guide Dialogue About Curricular and Co-Curricular Coherence

Anderson, J. A., Reder, L. M., & Simon, H. A. (1996). Situated learning and education. *Educational Researcher, 25*(4), 5–11.

Angelo, T. A. (1993, April). A teacher's dozen: Fourteen research-based principles for improving higher learning in our classrooms. AAHE *Bulletin, 13,* 3–7.

Association of American Colleges & Universities. (1991). *The challenge of connecting learning.* Washington, DC: Author.

Association of American Colleges & Universities. (1998). *Statement on liberal learning.*

Balsom, P. D., & Tomie, A. (Eds.). (1985). *Context and learning.* Hillsdale, NJ: Erlbaum.

Bean, J. C. (1996). *Engaging ideas: The professor's guide to integrating writing, critical thinking, and active learning in the classroom.* San Francisco: Jossey-Bass.

Biggs, J. (1999). *Teaching for quality learning at university: What the student does.* Birmingham, UK: Society for Research Into Higher Education and Open University Press.

Brookfield, S. D. (1987). *Developing critical thinkers.* San Francisco: Jossey-Bass.

Brown, J. S., Collins, A., & Duguid, P. (1989). Situated cognition and the culture of learning. *Educational Researcher, 18,* 32–42.

Clement, J. J. (2008). *Creative model construction in scientists and students: The role of imagery, analogy, and mental simulation.* New York: Springer.

Colby, A., Ehrlich, T., Beaumont, E., & Stephens, J. (2003). *Educating citizens: Preparing America's undergraduates for lives of moral and civic responsibility.* San Francisco: Jossey-Bass.

Diamond, R. M. (1997). *Designing and assessing courses and curricula: A practical guide.* San Francisco: Jossey-Bass.

Donald, J. D. (2002). *Learning to think: Disciplinary perspectives.* San Francisco: Jossey-Bass.

Edgerton, R., Hutchings, P., & Quinlan, K. (1995). *The teaching portfolio: Capturing the scholarship of teaching* (3rd reprinting). A publication of the AAHE Teaching Initiative. Washington, DC: AAHE.

Entwhistle, N. (1983). *Understanding student learning.* New York: Nichols.

Fink, D. L. (2003). *Creating significant learning experiences: An integrated approach to designing college courses.* San Francisco: Jossey-Bass.

Gabelnick, F., MacGregor, J., Matthews, R. S., & Smith, B. L. (1990). *Learning communities: Creating connections among students, faculty, and disciplines. New directions for teaching and learning,* 41. San Francisco: Jossey-Bass.

Gardner, H. (1993). *Multiple intelligences: The theory into practice.* New York: Basic Books.

Hutchings, P. (Ed.). (1998). *The course portfolio: How faculty can examine their teaching to advance practice and improve student learning.* A publication of the AAHE Teaching Initiative. Washington, DC: AAHE.

Kuh, G. D. (2001). Assessing what really matters to student learning: Inside the national survey of student engagement. *Change, 33*(3), 10–17, 66.

Lehrer, J. (2008). *How we decide.* New York: Houghton Mifflin.

Light, R. J. (2001). *Making the most of college: Students speak their minds.* Cambridge, MA: Harvard University Press.

Light, R. J., Singer, J. D., & Willett, J. B. (1990). *By design: Planning research on higher education.* Cambridge, MA: Harvard University Press.

McLaughlin, T., & MacGregor, J. (1996). *Curricular learning communities directory.* Olympia, WA: Washington Center for Improving the Quality of Undergraduate Education.

Mentkowski, M., & Associates. (2000). *Learning that lasts: Integrating learning, development and performance in college and beyond.* San Francisco: Jossey-Bass.

Mezirow, J., & Associates. (2000). *Learning as transformation: Critical perspectives on theory in progress.* San Francisco: Jossey-Bass.

Michaelsen, L. K., Knight, A. B., & Fink, L. D. (2004). *A transformative use of small groups in college teaching.* Sterling, VA: Stylus.

Miller, J. E., Groccia, J., & Miller, M. (Eds.). (2001). *Student-assisted teaching: A guide to faculty-student teamwork.* Boston: Anker Press.

Palmer, P. J. (2000). *The courage to teach: Exploring the inner landscape of a teacher's life.* San Francisco: Jossey-Bass.

Pascarella, E. T., & Terenzini, P. T. (1991). *How college affects students: Findings and insights from twenty years of research.* San Francisco: Jossey-Bass.

Perry, W. G. (1999). *Forms of intellectual and ethical development in the college years: A scheme.* San Francisco: Jossey-Bass. (Originally published in 1970)

Poindexter, S. (2003, January/February). Holistic learning. *Change, 35*(1), 25–30.

Prosser, M., & Trigwell, K. (1999). *Understanding learning and teaching: The experience in higher education.* Buckingham, UK: Open University Press.

Schon, D. A. (1990). *Educating the reflective practitioner.* San Francisco: Jossey-Bass.

Seldin, P., & Associates. (2000). *Improving college teaching.* Boston: Anker Press.

Sheckley, B. G., & Keeton, M. T. (1997). *A review of the research on learning: Implications for the instruction of adult learners.* College Park: Institute for Research on Adults in Higher Education, University of Maryland.

Shulman, L. S. (1999, July/August). Taking learning seriously. *Change, 31*(4), 10–17.

Shulman, L. S. (2002, November/December). Making differences: A table of learning. *Change, 34*(6), 36–44.

Smith, B. L., & McCann, J. (2001). *Reinventing ourselves: Interdisciplinary education, collaborative learning, and experimentation in higher education.* Boston: Anker Press.

Stark, J. S., Shaw, K. M., & Lowther, M. A. (1989). *Student goals for college and courses.* Report No. 6. Washington, DC: School of Education and Human Development, The George Washington University.

Stirnberg, R. J. (1997, March). What does it mean to be smarter? *Educational Leadership,* 20–24.

Strassburger, J. (1995). Embracing undergraduate research. *AAHE Bulletin, 47*(9), 3–5.

Tinto, V., et al. (1997). *Building learning communities for new college students: A summary of findings from the collaborative learning project.* Syracuse, NY: National Center on Postsecondary Teaching, Learning, and Assessment, Syracuse University.

21st Century Learning Initiative. *www.21learn.org*

Wehlburg, C. M., & Chadwick-Blossey, S. (Eds.). (2003). *To improve the academy: Resources for faculty, instructional, and organizational development.* Boston: Anker Press.

Weimer, M. (2002). *Learner-centered teaching: Five key changes to practice.* San Francisco: Jossey-Bass.

Wiggins, G., & McTighe, J. (1998). *Understanding by design.* Alexandria, VA: Association for Supervision and Curriculum Development.

Wiske, M. S. (Ed.). (1998). *Teaching for understanding: Linking research with practice.* San Francisco: Jossey-Bass.

Zahornik, J. A. (1997, March). Encouraging—and challenging—students' understandings. *Educational Leadership,* 30–33.

Resources That Focus on Teaching Diverse Learners and on Diverse Learning Styles

Anderson, J. (2001). Developing a learning/teaching style assessment model for diverse populations. In L. Suskie (Ed.), *Assessment to promote deep learning* (pp. 21–30). Washington, DC: AAHE.

Barkley, E. (2009). *Student engagement techniques: A handbook for college faculty.* San Francisco: Jossey-Bass.

Bash, L. (2003). *Adult learners in the academy.* Boston: Anker Press.

Brookfield, S. D. (1987). *Developing critical thinkers: Challenging adults to explore alternative ways of thinking and acting.* San Francisco: Jossey-Bass.

Brookfield, S. D. (1991). *Understanding and facilitating adult learning.* San Francisco: Jossey-Bass.

Caffarella, R. S. (2002). *Planning programs for adult learners: A practical guide for educators, trainers, and staff developers.* San Francisco: Jossey-Bass.

Cranton, P. (2003). *Finding our way: A guide for adult educators.* San Francisco: Jossey-Bass.

Farmer, J. A., Jr., Buckmaster, A., & LeGrand, B. (1992, Fall). Cognitive apprenticeship: Implications for continuing professional education. In V. J. Marsick & H. K. Baskett (Eds.), *Professionals' ways of knowing: New findings on how to improve professional education. New directions for adult and continuing education, 55* (pp. 41–49).

Merriam, S. (2008). *The third update on adult learning theory.* San Francisco: Jossey-Bass.

Nilson, L. B. (2003). *Teaching at its best: A research-based resource for college instructors* (2nd ed.). Boston: Anker Press. See, especially, the chapter on teaching to different learning styles.

Rendon, L. I. (2008). *Sentipensante (sensing/thinking) pedagogy: Educating for wholeness, social justice and liberation.* Sterling, VA: Stylus.

Ross-Gordon, J. M. (Ed.). (2002). *Contemporary viewpoints on teaching adults effectively.* San Francisco: Jossey-Bass.

Stein, D. S., & Imel, S. (Eds.). (2002). *Adult learning in community. New directions for adult and continuing education.* San Francisco: Jossey Bass.

Taylor, K., Marienau, C., & Fiddler, M. (2000). *Developing adult learners.* San Francisco: Jossey-Bass.

Tennant, M., & Pogson, P. (2002). *Learning and change in the adult years: A developmental perspective.* San Francisco: Jossey-Bass.

Three Paths to Better Teaching. (2009). *http://chronicle .com/article/3-Paths-to-Better-Teaching/47950/*

Wilson, A. L., & Hayes, E. R. (2000). *Handbook of adult and continuing education*. San Francisco: Jossey-Bass.

Wlodkowski, R. J., & Ginsberg, M. B. (2003). *Diversity and motivation: Culturally responsive teaching*. San Francisco: Jossey-Bass.

Zohar, A., & Dori, Y. J. (Eds.). (2010). *Metacognition in science education: Trends in current research*. New York: Springer.

Zubrowski, B. (2009). *Exploration and meaning making in the learning of science: Vol. 18*. New York: Springer.

Resources for Collaboration Between Academic Affairs and Student Affairs

About Campus. A bimonthly journal sponsored by the American College Personnel Association, *About Campus* is dedicated to the idea that student learning is the responsibility of all educators on campus. It is, therefore, designed to foster work between student affairs and academic affairs. *About Campus* is abstracted/indexed in *Current Index to Journals in Education* (ERIC) and Higher Education Abstracts (www.interscience.wiley.com).

R. P. Keeling, *Learning Reconsidered: A Campus-Wide Focus on the Student Experience* (2004; www.myacpa.org/ pub/documents/LearningReconsidered.pdf) and *Learning Reconsidered 2: Implementing a Campus-Wide Focus on the Student Experience* (2006) focus on the integrated use of all of higher education's resources and educators to educate the whole student.

Some Resources on Online Teaching and Learning

Aldrich, C. (2004). *Simulations and the future of learning*. San Francisco, CA: Wiley.

Aldrich, C. (2005). *Learning by doing:A comprehensive guide to simulations, computer games, and pedagogy in e-learning and other educational experiences*. San Francisco, CA: Wiley.

Aldrich, C. (2009). *The complete guide to simulations and serious games: How the most valuable content will be created in the age beyond Gutenberg to Google*. San Francisco, CA: Wiley.

Aldrich, C. (2009). *Learning online with games, simulations, and virtual worlds: Strategies for online instruction*. San Francisco, CA: Wiley.

Bender, T. (2003). *Discussion-based online teaching to enhance student learning: Theory, practice and assessment*. Sterling, VA: Stylus.

Brown, D. G. (Ed.). (2000). *Teaching with technology*. Boston: Anker Press.

Brown, J. S. (2000). Growing up digital: How the web changes work, education, and ways people learn. *Change, 32*(2), 11–20.

Clark, R. C., & Mayer, R. E. (2002). *E-learning and the science of instruction*. San Francisco: Jossey-Bass.

Comeaux, P. (2002). *Communication and collaboration in the online classroom: Examples and applications*. Boston: Anker Press.

Conrad, R., & Donaldson, J. A. (2004). *Engaging the online learner: Activities and resources for creative instruction*. San Francisco: Jossey-Bass.

Finkelstein, J. (2006). *Learning in real time: Synchronous teaching and learning*. Online Teaching and Learning Series. San Francisco: Jossey-Bass.

French, D., Hale, C., Johnson, C., & Farr, G. (1998). *Internet-based learning: A framework for higher education and business*. San Francisco: Jossey-Bass.

Garrison, R. (2003). *E-learning in the 21st century*. San Francisco: Jossey-Bass.

Garrison, R., & Vaughan, N. (2008). *Blended learning in higher education*. San Francisco: Jossey-Bass.

Hoefling, T. (2003). *Managing people for successful virtual teams and organizations*. San Francisco: Jossey-Bass.

Johnson, K., & Magusin, E. (2005). *Exploring the digital library: A guide for online teaching and learning*. San Francisco: Jossey-Bass.

Jolliffe, A., Ritter, J., & Stevens, D. (2001). *The online learning handbook: Developing and using web-based learning*. The Times Higher Education Supplement. London: Routledge.

Oblinger, D. G., & Rush, S. C. (1997). *The learning revolution: The challenge of information technology in the academy*. Boston: Anker Press.

Oblinger, D. G., & Rush, S. C. (Eds.). (1998). *The future compatible campus: Planning, designing, and implementing information technology in the academy*. Boston: Anker Press.

Palloff, R. M., & Pratt, K. (2001). *Lessons from the cyberspace classroom*. San Francisco: Jossey-Bass.

Palloff, R. M., & Pratt, K. (2003). *The virtual student: A profile and guide to working with online students*. San Francisco: Jossey-Bass.

Palloff, R. M., & Pratt, K. (2005). *Collaborating online: Learning together in community*. San Francisco: Jossey-Bass.

Palloff, R. M., & Pratt, K. (2007). *Building online learning communities: Effective strategies for the virtual classroom* (2nd ed.). San Francisco: Jossey-Bass.

Pitler, H., Hubbell, E. R., Kuhn, M., & Malenoski, K. (2007). *Using technology with classroom instruction that works: Effective strategies for the virtual classroom*. Alexandria, VA: ASCD

Richardson, W. (2009). *Blogs, wikis, podcasts, and other powerful web tools for classrooms* (2nd ed.). Thousand Oaks, CA: Sage.

Smith, R. (2008). *Conquering the content: A step-by-step guide to web-based course development*. San Francisco: Jossey-Bass.

Solomon, G., & Schrum, L. (2007). *Web 2.0: New tools, new schools*. Washington, DC: International Society for Technology in Education.

Warlick, D. F. (2007). *Classroom blogging: A teacher's guide to blogs, wikis, and other tools that are shaping a new information landscape* (2nd ed.). Raleigh, NC: The Landmark Project.

West, J. A., & West, M. L. (2009). *Using wikis for online collaboration: The power of the read-write web*. San Francisco: Jossey-Bass.

Metasites on Active Learning and Teaching and Learning Inventories

The Texas Collaborative for Teaching Excellence (www.texas collaborative.org/activelearning.htm) provides links to research on active learning. roadblocks to active student participation, and use of active learning strategies, including those in assorted disciplines..

Effective Teaching Practices Bibliography and Electronic Resources. Selectively lists articles and chapters on effective teaching practices as well as teaching and learning centers in higher education that demonstrate effective teaching strategies online. http://units.sla .org/division/dbio/publications/resources/teaching %20bib%209-08.pdf

The Learning Styles Resource Center. Sponsored by the University of Maryland University College and Towson University, the Learning Styles Resource Center (http://polaris.umuc.edu/~rouellet/learning/about .htm) provides teaching and learning inventories that may contribute to dialogue about the ways in which students learn and the ways in which faculty teach (site requires a user login). Learning inventories help educators understand how students perceive, organize, and process information. Teaching inventories stimulate and promote discussion about the range or lack of range of ways in which educators teach, thus occasioning dialogue about the multiple, varied, and ample opportunities students experience to learn and develop over time.

Learning Styles Resources at Questia. For more information about publications and research on learning styles, go to Learning Styles Resources at Questia,

an online library of books, journals, magazines, and newspapers (www.questia.com).

The Kolb Learning Styles Inventory. Among the most well-recognized learning inventory is the Kolb Learning Styles Inventory, designed to identify students' preferences in learning and the ways in which they process ideas and experiences. For information about this inventory, go to www.infed.org/biblio/b_explm.htm

Solomon and Felder. Solomon and Felder have integrated several learning inventories, including perceptual ways of learning, into one inventory. To learn more about their inventory and its relationship to teaching strategies, go to www.4ncsu.edu/ unity/lockers/users/f/felder/public/ILSdi

Metasite on Educational Technology Journals

www.educational-software-directory.net/publications/ journals

Metasite on Educational Technology Organizations

www.educational-software-directory.net/organizations

Metasite on Open Courseware and Open Educational Resources Available in Higher Education

http://iberry.com/cms/OCW.htm

Metasite on Library Instruction for Diverse Populations

www.ala.org/ala/mgrps/divs/acrl/about/sections/is/ projpubs/fullbib.pdf

After a section of "General Resources" on teaching diverse populations within academic libraries, the bibliography addresses the following groups in alphabetical order:

- African American students
- Asian American students
- First-generation college students
- Gay, lesbian, bisexual, and transgender students
- Hispanic and Latino/a students
- International students
- Native American students
- Nontraditional students
- Students with disabilities
- Transfer students

WORKSHEETS, GUIDES, AND EXERCISES

1. *A Coordinating Body.* Campus leaders oversee the formation of a campus assessment committee to initiate, coordinate, and orchestrate cycles of inquiry into student learning. Provosts, vice presidents, faculty, staff, and students work together to design a campus assessment committee purposefully composed of representatives from across an institution who bring different sets of lenses to explore student learning. As a campus leader, in conjunction with key members of your college or university, identify the range of members who will serve on or contribute to a campus committee. If you already have a committee, discuss how you might expand its membership or its relationship to other members of the campus. Membership in either case may include those in the local business community, advisory board members, parents, and representatives of the wider public, for example. Division heads or department chairs may follow a similar process to design a program-level committee that invites representation from other internal or external constituencies. Use the following list to help identify these constituencies as representatives on your committee or as ad hoc members:

❏ Institution's chief academic leader
❏ Institution's assessment director or coordinator, often someone who works separately on academic and co-curricular assessment but also in conjunction with a director of institutional research
❏ Representative from the institution's faculty and staff governance
❏ Representative from each academic program, department, division, or school within an institution
❏ Representative from the institution's center for teaching and learning or from a faculty development center
❏ Representative from academic support services such as services for students with learning differences
❏ Representative from student support services
❏ Representative from student affairs
❏ Representative from library and information resources
❏ Full- and part-time graduate and undergraduate student representative
❏ Teaching assistant representative
❏ Representative from instructional design or instructional technology
❏ Student tutor representative who experiences firsthand the levels of difficulties students confront in learning
❏ Representative from the local community who educates students in internships, cooperative education programs, or community service
❏ Representative from alumni
❏ Representative employer who contributes knowledge about what students bring to their employment and identifies new abilities that students will need to bring into the workplace or into civic life
❏ Member of an institution's business or advisory board
❏ Representative from institutional research and planning who provides guidance and support along the life of the assessment process.

2. *Expectations for Student Learning.* Use Figure 2.1 in this chapter as a way to generate discussion and consensus about institution- and program-level expectations for student learning. Initially, discussion may begin by identifying discrete abilities, such as critical thinking. However, because program- and institution-level assessment focuses on how students integrate over time, work toward articulating what you expect them to be able to accomplish at the middle and end of their studies, such as evaluating alternative solutions to disciplinary problems, identifying behavioral patterns that lead to a specific diagnosis, or integrating disciplinary or interdisciplinary perspectives into solutions to problems. An institution-, or program- or department-wide committee may use this figure as a way to focus on articulating what it believes all students who graduate from an institution should be able to demonstrate, represent, or produce. A program-level committee may use this figure to promote dialogue about what it believes all students who graduate from that program should be able to demonstrate, represent, or produce. Programs and services that contribute to and support student learning, such as in the areas of library and information resources or student affairs and support services, may use this figure to promote similar discussions. Representatives from these areas should also participate in academic institution- and program-level discussions to ensure coherence in curricular and co-curricular intentions.

Additionally, use this figure to promote discussion about the various existing ways students enact their learning in online and face-to-face environments so that you begin to develop an inventory of current assessment practices that capture the multiple ways students demonstrate their learning, including integrating learning outcomes over time.

3. *Integration.* You may wish to select one or more of the readings listed under "Additional Resources" in this chapter as a way to deepen dialogue about how students learn over time in a department, school, program, or service at the institution.

For example, your department may read Donald's book, *Learning to Think: Disciplinary Perspectives,* to stimulate discussion about how learning develops in a discipline over time. Perry's book, *Forms of Intellectual and Ethical Development in the College Years: A Scheme,* may guide institution-level dialogue about how a theory of development translates itself into the design of the curriculum and co-curriculum to develop students' attitudes and dispositions. Brown's article, "Growing Up Digital: How the Web Changes Work, Education, and Ways People Learn," may focus dialogue on the design of delivery systems as they contribute to program- and institution-level learning outcomes. Huber and Hutchings' 2005 work on integrative learning, *Integrative Learning: Mapping the Terrain,* could generate discussion about the learning relationships between students' majors and their liberal education. Mentkowski & Associates' seven principles of learning, in *Learning That Lasts: Integrating Learning, Development and Performance in College and Beyond* (pp. 227–246), may focus dialogue on ways to deepen student learning at the program and institution levels.

4. *Coherence.* Once your institution- or program-level committee has agreed on expectations for student learning, discuss the range of ways in which people teach or create learning environments that contribute to students' learning. Dialogue may involve discussing philosophies of teaching, principles of or assumptions about teaching and learning, theories of learning, research on learning and development, or research on learning in a discipline, topics that lead to collective understanding of the ways in which students learn over time. Use the following set of questions to guide institution-level discussions focused on how students learn what an institution and its programs and services value:

- What educational philosophy, principles, theories, models of teaching, research on learning, or shared assumptions underlie curricular or co-curricular design, instructional design, pedagogy, or use of educational tools to promote institution- or program-level expectations for student learning?
- What pedagogies or educational experiences develop the knowledge, understanding, habits of mind, ways of knowing, and problem solving that the institution or its programs value?
- How do students become acculturated to the ways of thinking, knowing, and problem solving that the institution or its programs value?
- How do faculty and staff intentionally build on each other's courses and educational experiences to achieve institution- and program-level learning priorities?
- Which students benefit from specific teaching strategies, educational processes, or educational experiences?

5. *Mapping.* Appendixes 2.2 through 2.4 are useful after working groups have achieved consensus about shared expectations for student learning. At the institution, department, or program level, these maps document the distribution of learning opportunities that contribute to shared expectations for student learning—learning outcome statements. Representatives from institutional constituencies and even constituencies that contribute to student learning outside the institution fill out these maps as a way to verify curricular and co-curricular coherence using coding systems such as those represented in Appendixes 2.2 through 2.4. Using a coding system, individuals indicate the level of students' learning in the courses they teach and the educational experiences or opportunities they provide. Focusing on where students continue to learn and practice core curricular outcomes in their major programs of study should also be chronologically coded, as illustrated in Appendixes 2.2 and 2.3.

If graduate programs also expect students to demonstrate core outcomes that exist for all graduate programs at an institution, then program-level graduate curricular maps should also document where these core outcomes are chronologically addressed, as illustrated in the master's-level curricular map in Appendix 3.3.

Referring to Appendixes 2.2 through 2.4, use the blank format that follows to determine how you will code the level of students' learning in the courses, modules, or educational experiences that contribute to institution, department, or program outcomes.

Blank Format for a Program-, Department-, or Institution-level Map

Coding System:	Course, Module, or Educational Experience	Course, Module, or Educational Experience	Course, Module, or Educational Experience	Course, Module, or Educational Experience	Course, Module, or Educational Experience	Course, Module, or Educational Experience	Course, Module, or Educational Experience	Course, Module, or Educational Experience
Learning Outcomes:								
1.								
2.								
3.								
4.								
5.								
6.								
7.								

6. *Inventories.* After you have mapped collaboratively agreed-upon outcomes, discuss and then develop a way to code (a) how students learn these outcomes and (b) how they are chronologically assessed as illustrated in Appendixes 2.3 and 2.4. This collaborative work often jettisons questions about the assumptions or philosophy of teaching and learning that underlie the design of a program. If, for example, a program is developmentally designed, does the actual coding of learning and assessment methods reveal that approach? If colleagues believe that a problem-based approach underlies the design of the curriculum or programs in the co-curriculum, what degrees of complexity are intentionally developed over time?

7. *Inventories.* The following two inventories (a and b) can be used at a program, department, or institution level to develop a rich understanding of how educational practices promote shared learning outcomes. They are particularly useful after groups have developed a map. That is, they provide a deeper look at educational practices and individual assessment methods that promote expected learning. Collective discussion of these worksheets identifies gaps in the continuum of students' learning, focusing on how educators can integrate or redistribute opportunities for students to build on and demonstrate their learning over time.

Inventory a: Analysis of Assessment Method Used in a Course, Module, or Educational Experience to Assess Students' Achievement of or Progress Toward Institution- or Program-Level Outcomes

Design	Pedagogy and Use of Educational Tools	Assessment Method: Context	Assessment Method: Content, Abilities, Habits of Mind, etc.
Describe how you design a course, module, or educational experience to contribute to students' demonstration or representation of an institution- or program-level outcome(s)	Identify ways in which students actually learn what you intend, for example, through online simulations or data mining, memorization, the use of equipment, or the use of self-reflection in response to a task	Describe your assessment method and the context within which students respond to it, for example, at the end of an internship, in a multiple choice test, or in a laboratory report	Describe the content, abilities, habits of mind, etc., that you expect students to demonstrate when they respond to your assessment method, for example, conceptual or procedural knowledge or analytical abilities

Inventory b: Documentation of Focus on and Assessment of Institution-, Program-, or Department-Level Learning Outcomes

Program-, Department-, or Institution-Level Learning Outcome	Course, Module, or Education Experience Explicitly States This Outcome in Its Description	Students Demonstrate or Represent Their Learning of This Outcome	Students Receive Formal Feedback About Their Demonstration or Representation of This Outcome	This Outcome Is Not Addressed in This Course, Module, or Educational Experience
	Yes/No If yes, document where	Yes/No If yes, describe how	Yes/No If yes, describe how	Addressed Not addressed
1.				
2.				
3.				
4.				
5.				
6.				
7.				

RAMAPO COLLEGE OF NEW JERSEY

Student Engagement in a General Education Science Course

Dr. Emma C. Rainforth

Environmental Science Convening Group, Ramapo College, Mahwah, NJ 07430; erainfor@ramapo.edu

I. Abstract

This poster describes how a non-laboratory science course, 'Introduction to Geology' (aka 'rocks for jocks'), was redesigned with the goal of improving student engagement and learning at a time when the college's general education science curriculum has been reduced. Although it previously included lab and field exercises, the course has been redesigned to focus on giving students the skills to think critically about science issues long after they have taken this course; the experiential component has been greatly augmented, with greater emphasis on interpreting data.

II. Why Redesign the Course?

Pre-redesign:

- Content-driven general education science course
- Lecture-based - no formal lab time, although it had ~12 hours/semester of in-class hands-on exercises and capstone field trip
- Students don't want to have to take general education science courses – so need to engage them better in order to enhance learning
- Results of cumulative final exam indicate students are neither *retaining* content information nor able to *apply* information in critical thinking exercises

Goal of Redesign

- *To produce more significant student learning*
- Are non-lecture components designed with *all* course goals in mind (rather than simply addressing content goals)?
- Are all topics appropriate for this audience?
- Enable connections to be made between geology and life outside the classroom

Context: College-wide Curricular Revision

Fall 2006: implementation of *Curriculum Enhancement Program*.

- Course remains 4 credits, in-class time *reduced* to 3 hours/week, 5 hours out-of-class-time component.
- Field trip moved to the out-of-class time, freeing up 3 hours of in-class time
- Expanded in-class experiential components
- Reduced lecture time: lectures revised, additional topic added.

III. The Redesign Process

A. Develop 'Dream Statement'

'Three years after the course ends, I want my students to be able to know: what science 'is' and how it differs from other endeavors; the basic earth processes and principles; why it is important to know about geology; and be able to apply this scientific and geologic background in order to think critically about any scientific issue (e.g. as portrayed in the media).'

B. Refine Course Goals

Simplify existing language (italics) and add one goal (bold)

1. Understand the Scientific Method.
2. Identify & understand the processes of formation of the major *geologic materials (rocks/minerals, resources)*.
3. Appreciate the Earth's *interior and surface processes*.
4. Gain an overview of the physical and biological history of the Earth, including its formation.
5. *Identify the ways in which geology affects your life.*
6. **Discover interactions between geology and other realms of knowledge*.**

*previously mentioned in passing, but not a major goal

C. Modify Existing Course Structure

Goals

1) To increase student engagement
2) To increase development of critical thinking skills
3) To increase integration between in-class lab exercises, field trip, and lectures
4) To increase student awareness of the relevance of geology to everyday life
5) To increase student awareness of their own learning

Methods

- Increase collaborative learning opportunities
- Increase in-class experiential component, decrease lecturing on a topic (which requires a greater student commitment to reading the text)
- Redesign activities (*see next column*)

Examples of New and Redesigned Activities

Module Tests (new)

Class is organized into 3 modules. The first 2 have tests. Students take the test individually & then, for 25% of the grade, take the test in small groups, using scratch-off test sheet.

Advantages: immediate feedback; group learning.

Lab exercises

Rock/mineral labs:
Before: ID & interpret how the materials formed. *After:* students also have to construct a dichotomous key so that they can re-identify specimens at a later date (e.g., on the field trip, in the final exam).

Geologic time:
Before: determine geologic history from an outcrop. *After:* also determine outcrop configuration from written description

Advantages: develop critical analysis skills; apply prior knowledge (integration)

Field Trip

Before: observe outcrop. ID rocks, interpret their formation, determine geologic history. *After:* also - file to a new 'lab exercise' on NJ geology, stress application of scientific method throughout field trip

Advantages: develop critical analysis skills; application of prior knowledge

Other course modifications include:

- Geologic journals: weekly entries on geologic news, reflection at end of semester
- Add content topic on geologic resources (fossil fuels, minerals, water)
- Use of 'clickers' in classroom
- 'Think-pair-share'
- Rubrics provided for all written assignments

IV. Results

Course Assessment and Observations

- Increased active participation in class
- Geological journals highly effective for student engagement and 'relevance of geology'
- Results of cumulative final exam in Fall 2006 improved over previous semesters.

Goals Survey

- Goals Survey designed and administered to both sections of GEOL 101 in Fall 2006.
- Survey has 3 sections: course content goals, RCNJ general education goals, and significant learning goals (Fink). Note: not all goals were specifically treated in this course, but were included in the survey for completeness.
- Results (below) are generally favorable:
  - *Course content goals:* 73-92% responded 'SA' or 'A'
  - *Gen. Ed. goals:* 50-85% responded 'SA' or 'A' (except the writing question (38%)]
  - *Significant learning goals:* 77-96% responded 'SA' or 'A' for those goals specifically targeted in the course.

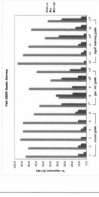

Combined results for both sections. *Course goals:* see left. (*Gen. ed. goals:* critical reading, writing, analytic skills, academic skills, information literacy. *Significant learning goals:* foundational knowledge, application of knowledge/skills, integration, learning how to learn, caring, human dimension [Fink, see fig. on overview poster]. *NOTE: asterisked goals were not targeted in course, but included on survey for completeness.*

V. References and Acknowledgements

- Fink, L.D., 2003, *Creating Significant Learning Experiences*. Jossey-Bass, San Francisco, 295 pp.
- For discussion on course redesign: RCNJ Faculty Resource Center Teaching Circles on course redesign, Fall 2005 - Fall 2006.
- For discussion and comments on this poster: Fall 2006 Teaching Circle participants (Phil McLewin, Kay Fowler, Lysandra Perez-Strumolo).
- Course site: phobos.ramapo.edu/~erainfor/Courses/GEOL101.html

APPENDIX 2.2 Sample Pages from Business Administration Map

BUSINESS ADMINISTRATON
COMPETENCIES/EXPECTED OUTCOMES
FOR THE COMMON PROFESSIONAL COMPONENT

I=Introduce; R=Reinforce; E=Emphasize

Competency	Econ 207 Macro-Economics	Econ 208 Micro-Economics	CS 214 Microcomp App for Bus	Eng 200 Writing for Bus	Math 1165 Pre-Calc (Bus)	Busi 201 Intro to Bus	Busi 203 Bus Statistics	Busi 211 Prin Mgmt	Busi 231 Prin Mktg	Busi 241 International Bus	Busi 251 Prin Acctg I	Busi 252 Prin Acctg II	Busi 281 Bus Law I	Busi 371 Mgtl Finance	Busi 411 Bus Policy
Writing Competencies															
Identify a subject and formulate a thesis statement				I											E
Organize ideas to support a position				I				R	R						E
Write in a unified and coherent manner appropriate to the subject matter				I					R						E
Use appropriate sentence structure and vocabulary				I									R		E
Document references and citations according to an accepted style manual				I									R		E
Critical Thinking Competencies															
Identify business problems and apply creative solutions								R	R	R	R	R	R		E
Translate concepts into current business environments							I	R	R	R	R	R	R		E
Analyze complex problems by identifying and evaluating the components of the problem							I								E
Quantitative Reasoning Competencies															
Apply quantitative methods to solving real-world problems							R				R	R	R		E
Perform necessary arithmetic computations to solve quantitative problems					I						R	R	R		
Evaluate information presented in tabular, numerical, and graphical form					I		R	R		R	R	R	R		E
Recognize the reasonableness of numeric answers					I		R	R			R	R	R		E
Oral Communications Competencies															
Organize an oral argument in logical sequence that will be understood by the audience						I		R	R					E	E
Use visual aids effectively to support an oral presentation						I		R	R						E
Demonstrate professional demeanor, speak clearly in well-modulated tone, and engage the audience						I		R	R						E
Exhibit good listening skills when others are speaking						I		R	R						E

81

BUSINESS ADMINISTRATON
COMPETENCIES/EXPECTED OUTCOMES
FOR THE COMMON PROFESSIONAL COMPONENT

I=Introduce; R=Reinforce; E=Emphasize	Econ 207 Macro-Economics	Econ 208 Micro-Economics	CS 214 Microcomp App for Bus	Eng 200 Writing for Bus	Math 1165 Pre-Calc (Bus)	Busi 201 Intro to Bus	Busi 203 Bus Statistics	Busi 211 Prin Mgmt	Busi 231 Prin Mktg	Busi 241 International Bus	Busi 251 Prin Acctg I	Busi 252 Prin Acctg II	Busi 281 Bus Law I	Busi 371 Mgrl Finance	Busi 411 Bus Policy
Technology and Information Literacy															
Identify problem/topic								R						R	
Demonstrate familiarity with information resources and technologies								R						R	
Conduct search query								R						R	
Evaluate sources of information								R						R	
Computer Literacy															
Demonstrate computer literacy in preparation of reports and presentations			I					R						E	E
Demonstrate ability to use software application to solve business problems														E	E
Conduct search queries through the use of the Internet						I								E	
Values Awareness															
Recognize ethical issues						I	R	R	R				E	E	
Identify ethical issues						I	R	R	R				E	E	
Identify theoretical frameworks that apply to corporate social responsibility							R	R	R	R				E	
Translate ethical concepts into responsible behavior in a business environment						I	R	R	R					E	
Develop values awareness						I	R	R	R					E	
CONTENT-SPECIFIC COMPETENCIES															
Global Business Competencies															
Demonstrate knowledge of contemporary social, economic, and political forces; their interrelationship; and their impact on the global business environment	I							R	R					R	
Identify the integration of global markets from both financial and product/service perspectives.										I				R	
Incorporate diverse cultural perspectives into business decisions						I				I				R	
Accounting Competencies															
Understand the role of the accounting information system within an organization's overall information system											R				
Demonstrate knowledge of the accounting cycle and the ability to perform necessary procedures at each step of the cycle for both corporate and non-corporate entities											R				

BUSINESS ADMINISTRATON
COMPETENCIES/EXPECTED OUTCOMES
FOR THE COMMON PROFESSIONAL COMPONENT

I=Introduce; R=Reinforce; E=Emphasize	Macro-Economics Econ 207	Micro-Economics Econ 208	Microcomp App for Bus CS 214	Writing for Bus Eng 200	Pre-Calc (Bus) Math 1165	Intro to Bus Busi 201	Bus Statistics Busi 203	Prin Mgmt Busi 211	Prin Mktg Busi 231	International Bus Busi 241	Prin Actg I Busi 251	Prin Actg II Busi 252	Bus Law I Busi 281	Mgl Finance Busi 371	Bus Policy Busi 411
Describe, prepare, and interpret comparative financial statements using analytical techniques such as ratios and common-size statements												R		E	
Understand the differences between financial and managerial accounting											I				
Understand the role of managerial accounting analysis, control, and planning of costs within the corporation										I		R			
Finance Competencies															
Integrate knowledge of economics, accounting, and quantitative analysis in the process of making financial decisions	I	I												IRE	
Access and interpret financial market data using both Internet and print sources								R	R					RE	
Apply basic computational techniques and/or spreadsheet software to solve financial problems						I									
Compute return and risk measures for basic financial assets (stocks and bonds)							I							E	
Analyze corporate financial statements to pinpoint strengths and weaknesses										R			I	E	
Identify the impact of investment, financing, and dividend policy decisions on the value of an enterprise										I				E	R
Use financial tools for life decisions about items such as housing, credit, retirements, and investments													I	R	

Source: William Craven, John Egan, Marilyn Ettinger, Richard Fabris, Shimshon Kinory, Patricia McGuire, Robert Matthews, Leonard Nass, Barbara O'Neal, Jeanette Ramos-Alexander, Afaf Shalaby, Joseph Stern, Susan Williams, and Rosalyn Young.

APPENDIX 2.3   Partial Department Curriculum Map Identifying Where and at
                What Level General Education Outcomes Are Addressed in the
                Physics Curriculum, How Students Learn Those Outcomes, and
                How They Are Assessed for Their Learning

GENERAL EDUCATION OUTCOMES
Natural Science Department

PHYSICS ASSESSMENT MAP

GEN ED SLO	Performance Measures	PHY 1000	PHY 2053	PHY 2054	PHY 2048	PHY 2049	PSC 1121	AST 1002
1. Be able to think critically	a. Identify the validity of collected data.		I L,T	E L	I L	E L		
	b. Use graphical and numerical methods to organize, analyze, and interpret natural phenomena from collected data.		I L	E L	I L	E L		
	c. Use graphs, tables, and charts to summarize, analyze, and interpret information to solve problems.		I W	E T	I W	E T		I T
2. Demonstrate facility in written and oral communications	a. Speak clearly, project voice sufficiently, and use appropriate vocabulary.	E P	E C	M C	E C	M C	I C	
	b. Write effective lab reports and project reports.	I P	E LR		E LR			I P
	c. Present information clearly in tables, charts, and graphs.	I P	E LR		E LR			

Method of Learning	Method of Assessment
L = Laboratory Experiment	Written document using a scoring rubric
C = Class Discussion	Portfolio entry scored with scoring rubric
LR = Lab Report	Exam or quiz scored against benchmark
P = Project	Oral presentation using a scoring rubric
T = Quiz or Test	Rising Junior Milestone Exam using rubric and benchmark score
W = Homework	Other

Source: Erik Christensen, South Florida Community College.

APPENDIX 2.4   Coding for Curricular Mapping (Ohio State University: Pharmacy)

CONNECTION CODES—DEGREE OR LEVEL OF CONNECTION BETWEEN COURSE AND OUTCOME

Not Applicable or Level 0

There is no relationship between the course and the outcome.

I—Introductory/Background or Level 1

There is an **indirect relationship** between the course and the outcome. The outcome itself is not the focus of the course, but at least one element of the course serves as a building block to the achievement of the final outcome. For example, course elements may provide either the knowledge, skills, or attitudes necessary for the ultimate achievement of the outcome.

M—Intermediate/Transitional or Level 2

There is **more of a direct relationship** between the course and the outcome than at Level 1. A mixture of course elements supports the final achievement of the outcome, but the final integration of the knowledge, skills, and attitudes necessary for its achievement is not accomplished in this course. For example, knowledge, skills, and/or attitudes (at least two of the three) required for the achievement of the outcome may be the focus of the course or course element, but the integration of all three is not.

E—Emphasized or Level 3

There is a **direct relationship** between the course and the outcome. At least one element of the course focuses specifically on the complex integration of knowledge skills and attitudes necessary to perform the outcome.

PEDAGOGY CODES—HOW OUTCOME IS TAUGHT

- **L** = Lecture
- **LD** = Lecture/discussion
- **C** = Cases—any type of problem-based learning, learning applied to realistic scenarios
- **E** = Experiential—actual practice of the outcome in a real or simulated environment; may include the use of live "subjects" (patients, patient actors, health care practitioner, etc.)
- **I** = Independent study

ASSESSMENT CODES—HOW THE OUTCOME IS EVALUATED

- **B** = Building blocks—students are assessed primarily on their grasp of basics (i.e., recall of information) rather than their ability to apply and or synthesize knowledge, skills, and/or attitudes.
- **A** = Application/synthesis—students are assessed on their ability to apply and synthesize knowledge, attitudes, and/or skills. This includes simulated experiences.
- **D** = Demonstration—students demonstrate their abilities; they are assessed based on their ability to show mastery of the elements of the outcome. The "demonstration" may occur in either a simulated environment (e.g., OSCE or professional practice laboratory) or a realistic setting (e.g., patient care setting).

Source: Katherine A. Kelley, assistant dean for assessment, The Ohio State University, College of Pharmacy.

Chapter 3

MAKING CLAIMS ABOUT STUDENT LEARNING WITHIN CONTEXTS FOR LEARNING

If the students are dealing with a narrow range of problems in their studies, the likelihood of their being able to deal with other kinds of problems in relation to which their studies are potentially relevant would be much less than if they had encountered more variation. In order to be able to make use of what one has learned in a course of studies, a new situation has to be seen by the individual in such a way that certain knowledge and certain skills appear relevant, and what we can make use of and apply depends on how we see, interpret, and define the situation. This also makes the most fundamental form of learning into learning to see, learning to experience, and learning to understand certain things in certain ways, as for instance when a scientist develops a scientific way of seeing scientific phenomena, a lawyer develops a juridical way of seeing legal problems, or a physician develops a medical way of listening to heartbeats, seeing x-ray pictures, and so on.

—Ference Marton, 1998

OVERVIEW: The dialogue and tasks described in chapter 2 provide the foundation for making claims about student learning, the focus of chapter 3. These claims reflect the kinds of learning that the institution and its programs value and that emerge more specifically from the dialogue, maps, and inventories described in the previous chapter. This chapter takes the work of the previous chapter to a greater level of specificity to develop learning outcome statements that describe what students should be able to represent, demonstrate, or produce based on how and what they have learned. Building on the verification strategies described in the previous chapter, it presents strategies for developing and reviewing learning outcome statements to ascertain how well they align with institution- and program-level expectations and practices. The Worksheets, Guides, and Exercises at the end of this chapter are designed to (1) foster collective authorship of and agreement on learning outcome statements; (2) foster collective review and approval of these statements; and (3) orient students to institution- and program-level learning outcome statements. This chapter positions educators to couple learning outcome statements with collectively agreed-upon research or study questions, the focus of chapter 4. Agreement about research or study questions that drive the assessment process, in turn, contributes to identifying or designing chronologically developed assessment methods, the focus of chapter 5. These methods provide ongoing evidence of what students are or are not able to do, represent, or demonstrate, such as inability to transfer or apply previous learning into new contexts or inability to analyze complex disciplinary problems.

OUTCOME STATEMENTS

The dialogue, mapping, and inventorying in chapter 2 establish generally agreed-upon outcomes. This chapter aims to achieve consensus about the public claims institutions make about student learning and learning outcome statements. These statements build on the consensus achieved in chapter 2 but are more specific based on further dialogue about the design of curriculum, co-curriculum, instruction, educational experiences and opportunities, and students' learning histories that were the ending focus of the previous chapter. They describe what students should demonstrate, represent, or produce in relation to how and what students have learned.

Characteristics of Institution- and Program-Level Learning Outcome Statements

Collectively developed across an institution or a program, a learning outcome statement is a sentence that meets the following criteria:

- Describes what students should be able to demonstrate, represent, or produce based on their learning histories

- Relies on active verbs that identify what students should be able to demonstrate, represent, or produce over time—verbs such as *create, apply, construct, translate, identify, formulate,* and *hypothesize*
- Aligns with collective program- and institution-level educational intentions for student learning translated into the curriculum and co-curriculum
- Maps to the curriculum, co-curriculum, and educational practices that offer multiple and varied opportunities for students to learn
- Is collaboratively authored and collectively accepted
- Incorporates or adapts professional organizations' outcome statements when they exist
- Can be quantitatively and/or qualitatively assessed during students' undergraduate or graduate studies

The institutional example in Box 3.1 illustrates the specificity of learning outcome statements developed at California State University—Monterey Bay.

BOX 3.1   INSTITUTIONAL EXAMPLE: *California State University—Monterey Bay*

Ethics, one of the foci in California State University—Monterey Bay's general education curriculum, seeks to develop students who "recognize the complexity and importance of choices available to humans in their personal, professional and social lives"; are aware of deeply held beliefs about how humans relate to each other in specific contexts; are able to recognize and understand others' approaches to ethical decision making; and are able to "participate meaningfully and successfully in dialogue across these differences" (www.csumb.edu/academic/ulr/index.html). What capacities identify students' achievement of this requirement? That is the focus of a learning outcome statement. The following five learning outcome statements identify those capacities in graduates of the university:

Outcome 1: Graduates are able to identify and analyze real-world ethical problems or dilemmas, and identify those affected by the dilemma.

Outcome 2: Graduates are able to describe and analyze the complexity and importance of choices that are available to the decision makers concerned with this dilemma.

Outcome 3: Graduates are able to articulate and acknowledge their own deeply held beliefs and assumptions as part of a conscious value system.

Outcome 4: Graduates are able to describe and analyze their own and others' perceptions and ethical frameworks for decision making.

Outcome 5: Graduates are able to consider and use multiple choices, beliefs, and diverse ethical frameworks when making decisions to respond to ethical dilemmas or problems.

Drawn from multiple and varied opportunities to learn at the university, these outcomes identify the ways of thinking and knowing that students should demonstrate within societal and personal frameworks. In addition, these outcomes reflect the university's focus on developing learners who are predisposed to self-reflection about their own value system and ethical decision-making process.

Source: California State University Monterey Bay: University Learning Requirements, 2002. Reproduced with permission.

Difference Between Program or Institutional Objectives and Learning Outcomes or Learning Objectives

As the example in Box 3.1 illustrates, learning outcome statements are anchored in verbs that identify the actions, behaviors, dispositions, and ways of thinking or knowing that students should be able to demonstrate. Confusion sometimes exists between the terms *program* or *institutional objectives* and *learning outcome statements*, sometimes also referred to as *learning objectives* or *educational objectives*. Program or institutional objectives identify content or learning parameters—what students should learn, understand, or appreciate because of their studies. Mission statements often contain the language of program or institutional objectives, providing an overall description of what an institution and its programs intend students to learn. Learning outcome statements, learning objectives, or educational objectives identify what students should be able to demonstrate, represent, or produce because of what and how they have learned at the institution or in a program. That is, they translate learning into actions, behaviors, and other texts from which observers can draw inferences about the depth and breadth of student learning. Box 3.2 illustrates how the faculty in the geography department at the University of Washington moved from learning objectives to more specific learning outcome statements that articulate what students are expected to demonstrate as a result of curricular design.

BOX 3.2   INSTITUTIONAL EXAMPLE: *University of Washington*

The following figure illustrates how faculty in the Development and Regional Studies Concentration at the University of Washington have translated two of their program objectives into outcome statements. These outcome statements describe what students should be able to do based on the concentration's content and curricular sequence, students' learning experiences, and the ways in which they learn in that program. Notice how the descriptors of what students should understand in the two program objective statements translate into a complex intellectual process: analysis. As the figure also illustrates, program-level outcome statements are more specific statements than institution-level statements. That is, these statements reflect the purposes and intentions of a specific field or focus of study or work.

Program Objective:	Understand the processes of urbanization and modernization in the developing world.
⇩	
Student Learning Outcome:	Analyze cities as products of modernization, as expressions of various processes, such as investment and employment.
Program Objective:	Understand ways political and economic relationships are shaped by history and geography.
⇩	
Student Learning Outcome:	Differentially analyze colonialism according to geographical and scalar variation: how different colonial regimes and technologies have affected development in different places—how structural tools look and are used differently in various places.

Development and Regional Studies Concentration in Geography at the University of Washington: Sample Program Objectives Translated into Student Learning Outcome Statements

Source: Richard Roth and members of the Geography Department, University of Washington. Reproduced with permission.

LEVELS OF LEARNING OUTCOME STATEMENTS

Across an institution exist levels of outcome statements. At an institutional level, outcome statements are more general statements describing expectations for students' entire educational experiences. For example, an institution may state that its students "write a range of texts to address different audiences and achieve different purposes." Collectively, then, programs and individual courses and services, such as those offered through writing centers, intentionally contribute to this larger institutional outcome. That is, they provide students with a plethora of writing experiences that develop students' ability to write different kinds of discourse. Outcome statements become more specific at the program or department level, reflecting the kinds of writing within a discipline, profession, or field of study. An outcome statement at a program level may state that students "write a range of representative documents in chemistry that solve problems for different audiences and purposes." Taken together, then, students' collective writing experiences during their undergraduate and graduate studies contribute to their flexibility as writers. That is, they become individuals who learn how to use the conventions and modes of discourse that represent how humans communicate generally and how they communicate in specific fields of work.

Figure 3.1 represents the relationship among levels of outcome statements; that is, it demonstrates the desired coherence that underlies students' educational journeys. A college or university's general education or core curriculum learning outcome statements, along with any other institution-specific outcomes reflected in a mission and vision statement, represent what an institution claims all of its students should be able to demonstrate by the time they graduate. In a cohesive curricular and co-curricular design, these institution-level outcomes are seeded into program- or department-level outcomes; in turn, institution- and program- or department-level outcomes are seeded into the courses and educational experiences that altogether contribute to students' major program of study and to their institution-wide learning. Institution- and program-or department-level outcomes become more specifically stated as they are adapted to the context of courses; modules; educational experiences, such as community service; or the range of services or programs in the co-curriculum. For example, among the learning outcomes a college or university would expect its students to demonstrate on graduation could be quantitative reasoning. Besides one or more courses in general education or a core curriculum course that specifically attends to this outcome, programs or departments also need to weave this outcome into their overarching disciplinary or professional outcomes. How is quantitative reasoning, for example, woven into the outcomes for a major in history, philosophy, or the humanities? Then, how is that particular outcome integrated and focused on in courses that contribute to that major? Individual courses and services, such as learning support services, library and information services and resources, and the range of programs and services offered in the co-curriculum, contribute to institution- and program-level learning outcomes. Recall that Figure 2.3 in chapter 2 illustrates how a student life division has aligned some of its outcomes with those of the institution.

Graduate schools or programs may state overarching expectations for all their master's and doctoral

Modules
Educational Experiences
Educational Opportunities
Courses

Program- or Department-Level Outcomes

(Including Programs and Services in the Co-Curriculum)

General Education/Institution-Wide Outcomes

FIGURE 3.1   Integration and Distribution of Campus-Wide Outcomes and Program- or Department-Level Outcomes Into the Curriculum and Co-Curriculum

programs—outcomes that define the attributes of graduates of the degree-granting institution. Additionally, each graduate school or program develops a specialized set of outcomes for the profession or discipline or interdisciplinary program of study that also states the overarching expectations for graduate-level programs.

TAXONOMIES

Useful in collaboratively developing outcome statements are taxonomies that help educators describe the design of the curriculum and co-curriculum and the sequencing of courses or modules or educational experiences that translate that design into educational experiences. Taxonomies also help educators identify the verbs that describe what students should chronologically represent or demonstrate. As described in chapter 2, pages 52–53, Bloom's Revised Taxonomy (Anderson et al., 2001) may anchor and guide agreement about what students should be able to demonstrate at the end of their undergraduate and graduate studies. Designing backward, then, educators determine how individual courses, modules, and sets of educational experiences chronologically foster those desired endpoint outcomes. Bloom's revised cognitive domain taxonomy extends across the following abilities: remembering, understanding, applying, analyzing, evaluating, and creating—abilities that can be simultaneously learned. Verbs such as *define, describe, enumerate,* and *reproduce* identify acts of knowing, for example. Verbs such as *criticize, defend,* and *interpret* identify acts of evaluation. The updated version of Bloom's Taxonomy covers learning, teaching, and assessing (Anderson et al., 2001). The "Additional Resources" at the end of this chapter list other kinds of taxonomies besides Bloom's Taxonomy that may better represent the underlying assumptions or design or philosophy of a program's or department's curricular and co-curricular design; see, for example, Shulman (2002). Focused initially on student engagement and motivation, this taxonomy of liberal and professional learning further identifies other learning outcomes that educators should aim to foster in undergraduates: (1) development of knowledge and understanding that lead to (2) student performance and actions, (3) interpretations, reflections, and critiques, (4) design and judgment, and eventually (5) student ownership of their learning through demonstration of their commitments and values.

Drawing on an existing taxonomy is not an arbitrary process; outcome statements should align with the de-

sign and sequence of the curriculum, co-curriculum, and complementary educational experiences. Some programs may structure course progression based on a developmental approach to Bloom's cognitive domain—from lower-order to higher-order cognitive complexity. Other programs may draw on Bloom's Taxonomy but not take a developmental approach to curricular design and sequencing—rather positioning students to develop simultaneously multiple cognitive levels. Course progressions in yet another program may be based on a different model, such as a problem-based curricular model that asks students to generate hypotheses earlier rather than later in their sequence of studies. Dialogue about the philosophy of teaching and learning and about how philosophies or sets of assumptions translate into educational practices should guide choices about which taxonomies to draw on or adapt. The verbs that anchor an outcome statement need to take into account students' chronology of learning, as well as their ways of learning, so that outcome statements align with educational practices.

Four examples, in Appendixes 3.1 through 3.4, illustrate how outcomes have been intentionally developed or adapted in relation to existing educational practices at an institution or in relationship to national organizations' work. Appendix 3.1 describes the process that geography faculty at the University of Washington used to develop their learning outcomes based on dialogue and peer questions about how and what faculty teach. Appendix 3.2 describes the process that members of the Student Affairs Division at the University of Maryland engaged in to agree on outcomes for the division, including integrating the university's general education outcomes and those nationally established in Keeling (2006) by their professional organization. As the appendix illustrates, representatives from each of the Student Affairs programs and services identified where they specifically offer students opportunities to develop agreed-upon learning outcomes. A portion of a program map in Appendix 3.3 represents how an accredited program at the University of West Florida has aligned its professional organization's outcomes (the Association to Advance Collegiate Schools of Business [AACSB]) with its master's degree program in accountancy. This map requires that faculty code their assessment practices in both core courses and upper-level courses so that students have multiple opportunities to demonstrate desired program outcomes—beginning with core courses. Appendix 3.4, an example of outcomes that align with the spiritual values of Azuza Pacific University as well as with professional nursing standards, takes a leveled approach to overarching outcomes to track students' chronological learning.

Bowling Green State University's (BGSU) Learning Outcomes, shown in Box 3.3, align with the majority of the Liberal Education and America's Promise (LEAP) learning domains developed at Association of American Colleges & Universities (AAC&U) and represent a thoughtful, integrated approach that reflects the mission of the institution. Departments and programs are developing or adapting their own general education learning outcome statements from AAC&U's learning domains originally developed under its LEAP Project (www.aacu.org/leap/vision.cfm). The domains under this project are as follows:

Intellectual and Practical Skills

- Inquiry and analysis
- Critical thinking
- Creative thinking
- Written communication
- Oral communication
- Reading
- Quantitative literacy
- Information literacy
- Teamwork
- Problem solving

Personal and Social Responsibility

- Civic knowledge and engagement—local and global
- Intercultural knowledge and competence
- Ethical reasoning
- Foundations and skills for lifelong learning

Integrative Learning

- Integrative learning

BOX 3.3   Bowling Green State University Learning Outcomes (approved 2009)

Each of the major areas of study at Bowling Green State University holds high and explicit expectations for student learning; these expectations are embodied in learning outcomes for each of the majors. Even though the learning outcomes are necessarily different from major to major—to accommodate the specialized knowledge of music to marketing; health to history; teacher preparation to technology—all our majors share fundamental educational values, which are described by the University Learning Outcomes. The University Learning Outcomes are also expectations of our general education program and of the many facets of student life, ranging from residence halls to student clubs and organizations. Thus, the University Learning Outcomes are a statement of our common responsibility for shared educational values, despite differences in the content of the many majors, disciplines, and activities offered at Bowling Green State University.

INTELLECTUAL AND PRACTICAL SKILLS

Critical and Constructive Thinking
- *Inquiry*—a close examination of an issue or situation in a search for information or truth; determining what questions should be asked; recognizing opportunities; formulating hypotheses; seeking information and evaluating claims; making discoveries and reaching new understandings; and making informed judgments.
- *Examining Values*—observing carefully and critically to identify the values, principles, standards, or qualities considered worthwhile or desirable in a dilemma, situation, problem, or decision.
- *Solving Problems Creatively*—generating a solution for a problem through original, imaginative, innovative, or artistic effort, including problems that are complex, ambiguous, and difficult to formulate.

Communication
- *Writing*—communicate clearly and effectively to an identified audience. To be effective, written communication should be informed by audience analysis, demonstrate reflection, employ critical thinking, and make appropriate use of supporting argument and citation.

BOX 3.3 *(continued)*

- *Presenting*—speak, show, demonstrate, exhibit, or perform for an individual or group. Effective presentation engages the intended audience, includes the use of non-verbal forms of communication, and may employ a variety of media.

Engaging Others in Action
- *Participating*—active engagement in some activity, including shared effort, understanding others' points of view, the lively exchange of ideas, compromise, and contributing to the group's product.
- *Leading*—guiding or influencing a group to achieve its goals. Leading does not require formal authority or power but rather is a matter of influence, integrity, spirit, and mutual respect.

GENERAL AND SPECIALIZED KNOWLEDGE

To be an effective and prepared citizen, capable of understanding and responding to the diverse challenges present in the modern world, students must be conversant with the core concepts of disciplines in the natural sciences, social sciences, and humanities and arts, along with knowledge related to human learning, interaction, and enterprise. Just as breadth of knowledge is a cornerstone of a liberal education, so too is expertise in a particular disciplinary area or major. Both breadth and depth are important concepts, not just in terms of acquired disciplinary knowledge, but also for development of the skills and methods necessary to explore issues that arise in day-to-day life.

PERSONAL AND SOCIAL RESPONSIBILITY

BGSU recognizes and intentionally fosters a learning environment in which students strive for excellence, cultivate personal and academic integrity, contribute to a larger community, take seriously the perspectives of others, and develop competence in ethical and moral reasoning, as shown by:

- Interacting with and understanding diverse perspectives.
- Engaging communities as a participant and leader using civic and professional knowledge as a basis for values-driven action.
- Giving full consideration to ethical integrity and actions consistent with one's principles as part of each individual's exploration of purpose. A balanced approach to questions of meaning also includes preparation for students' multiple and changing roles, including work, citizenship, family, and membership in multiple communities.

INTEGRATE, APPLY, AND REFLECT

Synthesis and advanced accomplishment across general and specialized studies as evidenced in project-based work systematically collected throughout the duration of the student's enrollment. Such projects draw on all of the skills and fields of knowledge described above. What has been learned from accumulated experiences is recorded in written reflections.

A BGSU education provides the foundation for a lifetime of continued learning, self-awareness, career success, contribution to community, and purposeful living. Evaluating the achievement of these University Learning Outcomes is critical and may take many forms, including the use of electronic portfolios and proposed national metarubrics (see www.bgsu.edu/offices/provost/value/index.html). Demonstrating quality performance on each of the learning outcomes is the hallmark of a BGSU graduate.

Source: Bowling Green State University. Used with permission from Milton Hakel.

COLLABORATION TO DEVELOP AND REVIEW OUTCOME STATEMENTS

Collaboration across a program or service, as well as across an institution, is key to creating learning outcome statements. They should be developed by the sorts of core working groups described in chapter 2. Not every course, service, or program addresses all program- or institution-level outcomes. However, mapping how and where outcomes are addressed at each level ensures that students have multiple and layered opportunities to develop the understanding, behaviors, habits of mind, ways of knowing, dispositions, and forms of expression and representation valued at both the institution and program levels. That is, there is an underlying coherence that contributes to students' enduring learning.

At a program level, for example, a core working group within a history program, consisting of faculty, staff, students, alumni, and local community members, for example, may work together to create an outcome statement or statements that describe how students demonstrate program-level quantitative reasoning. Similarly, an interdisciplinary core working group consisting of mathematicians, faculty from other disciplines, and representatives from academic support services may work together to develop an outcome statement or statements that describe how students should demonstrate institution-level quantitative reasoning. Other interdisciplinary core working groups may develop outcome statements for additional institution-level expectations focused on, for example, information literacy, lifelong learning, interdisciplinary perspectives, or spiritual development, depending on the institution's mission and purposes.

To build and achieve consensus across a department or program and across an institution, members of these larger communities need to agree on these outcomes. Whether that consensus building occurs informally in department or program meetings or formally as part of a campus-wide meeting or forum—often through discussion and debate translated into drafts—consensus is essential in building a sustainable institutional commitment. Without that consensus, faculty, staff, and administrators may easily become disconnected from the larger institutional priorities and from department-, program-, division-, or service-level priorities. Achieving consensus maintains institution- and program-level focus on educational priorities. These may, in fact, change over time depending on societal changes or new institutional commitments that emerge as an institution engages in strategic planning or undertakes a change in leadership or mission revision. For that reason, both institution- and program-level assessment plans must build in times for educators to review outcome statements as part of a cycle of inquiry into student learning to ensure that these statements remain current, relevant, and intentionally addressed through a coherent design of experiences and opportunities. To build in this important process, institutions and programs often limit the number of outcomes they assess at one time. Similar to the process at Rose-Hulman Institute of Technology, described in Box 2.2 in chapter 2, a cyclical review of outcome statements must begin by examining curricular integrity and coherence in relation to what institutions and their programs claim students are able to demonstrate.

STRATEGIES FOR DEVELOPING OUTCOME STATEMENTS

The following five strategies, often used interdependently, represent some ways institution- and program-level core working groups or task forces develop agreed-upon outcome statements.

Strategy 1: Mission Statements

Existing institution- and program-level mission statements provide one way to develop outcome statements. Representatives from across an institution and across a program develop outcome statements drawn from institution- or program-level mission statements.

What, specifically, do an institution and its programs and services believe students should be able to demonstrate based on these mission statements? If a mission statement asserts that students learn to "write effectively," "reason quantitatively," or become "responsible citizens," how do those descriptors translate into claims about what students should be able to do or demonstrate? The California State University example in Box 3.1 earlier in this chapter illustrates how that institution has translated general statements about ethics into specific outcomes it wishes its graduates to demonstrate. Reaching consensus about what students should be able to demonstrate or represent rests on verifying the relevance and accuracy of these statements within the context of the curriculum and co-curriculum.

Mapping those statements to the institution and

its programs or mapping program-level outcomes to courses and educational experiences that contribute to program learning develops that consensus.

Strategy 2: Professional Organizations

Another way to jump-start efforts to develop outcome statements is to use or adapt statements that disciplinary and professional organizations have developed. Institutions and programs may revise these statements to reflect their more specific intentions.

Increasingly, professional organizations are developing statements that describe what graduates should be able to demonstrate. The four organizations discussed in the following paragraphs are doing work that represents this trend. Responding to the question about what quantitative literacy requirements colleges and universities should establish for students who receive a bachelor's degree, the Commission on Undergraduate Programs in Mathematics of the Mathematics Association of America, in *Quantitative Reasoning for College Graduates: A Complement to the Standards* (1996), states that a quantitatively literate college graduate should be able to exhibit the following skills:

1. Interpret mathematical models such as formulas, graphs, tables, and schematics, and draw inferences from them

2. Represent mathematical information symbolically, visually, numerically, and verbally

3. Use arithmetical, algebraic, geometric, and statistical methods to solve problems

4. Estimate and check answers to mathematical problems in order to determine reasonableness, identify alternatives, and select optimal results

5. Recognize that mathematical and statistical methods have limits

Information literacy outcomes and statements of abilities for college and university graduates are comprehensively articulated in the work of the Association of College and Research Libraries (ACRL), a Division of the American Library Association, in *Information Literacy Competency Standards for Higher Education: Standards, Performance Indicators, and Outcomes* (2000) under five standards. The American Psychological Association provides a guide for setting undergraduate

goals and outcomes in the areas of science and application, liberal arts, and career and personal development (2007). Programs offering accredited programs align their courses to chronologically develop the sets of outcomes required by an accrediting body (as illustrated in Appendix 3.3).

The AAC&U has identified the 15 most common domains of general education learning (refer to page 92 in this chapter) that appear in college and university catalogs across the country. These domains, then, can either jump-start an institution's internal articulation of its general education learning outcomes or inspire institutions to revise or rethink their general education curriculum to address many of these 15 domains. (Chapter 6 illustrates how several of these outcomes are now assessed using nationally developed scoring rubrics.)

Strategy 3: Student Work

Deriving outcome statements based on collective examination of student work over time is a third strategy. That is, reviewing the kinds of work that students submit informs and even challenges consensus about what we expect them to be able to do over time. Selecting sample work that students produce at the midpoint and end of their studies provides direct evidence of their achievement. Examining this evidence becomes a reality-based strategy for achieving consensus about our students' learning. At the same time, this strategy may also unearth differences in opinion about what students should be able to demonstrate, thus promoting further dialogue about curricular and co-curricular coherence. For example, sampling students' midlevel work in a major; sampling representative work at a midpoint in students' general education; and sampling senior theses, research papers, collaborative projects, and performances become strategies for deriving outcomes. Faculty, librarians, and information resource professionals may examine, for example, a range of senior research papers across departments and programs to develop consensus about what senior-level research abilities students should be able to demonstrate by the time they graduate. This strategy develops a realistic context for developing outcomes based on reading actual work and the ways in which students represent their learning. This strategy also readies groups for the work described in chapter 6 that focuses on establishing standards for judging student work.

Strategy 4: An Epistemological and Ethnographic Process

Developing a "thick description" based on interviews and dialogue among colleagues in a program represents another strategy that yields outcome statements grounded in an epistemological approach to learning and curricular design (Ryle, 1971). Faculty in the geography department at the University of Washington engaged in a four-part ethnographic process to identify and negotiate learning outcomes in relationship to the courses they teach. A member of that program transcribed the results of this process. The thick description that recorded the collaborative work of program faculty became the means by which faculty achieved consensus about shared outcome statements within the context of different pedagogical strategies and intellectual foci. From this text, faculty gained a rich understanding of what and how students learn over time through the department's collective practices. The four-part process identified and then verified outcome statements embedded in the program curriculum. (See Appendix 3.1 at the end of this chapter.) In describing this process in correspondence to Peggy Maki in April and October 2003, Richard Roth, member of the advising staff in the geography department, concluded that this strategy was an effective way to achieve the following results:

- Generate substantive, engaged discussions of curricular restructuring because it exposes not only continuities but also overlaps, duplications, and gaps in the curriculum. It makes the curriculum a source of collective public ownership rather than a collection of private, individual curricular islands. The whole is truly greater than the sum of its parts.
- Engage faculty in talking about the logic and rationale of their courses: what material they have selected, why they have selected that material rather than other material, why they have sequenced this material in a particular way, and what the cumulative effects of a course are meant to be.
- Help faculty better appreciate the epistemological position of their students. In fact, the faculty themselves tend to recapitulate the epistemological progress of the students, going from general to specific (and back to general); from simple to complex; from being awash in disconnected bits of fact, information, data, and so on to learning how to make many dif-

ferent kinds of arguments; from merely becoming knowledgeable about a topic to learning the conditions and criteria for establishing and judging that knowing. The constructivist dimension of learning (category construction, canons of the validity of evidence, doctrine of cause and origin, versions of same and different, etc.) is thus revealed.

- Help students appreciate the ways that the various aspects of a course are contingent on one another.
- Develop ownership of the process of articulating outcome statements.
- Provide students with a way to articulate and situate their own intellectual and professional development.
- Link assessment (formative and summative), accountability, and epistemology.

For the final learning outcome statements that resulted from this epistemological and ethnographic process, go to http://depts.washington.edu/geog/courses_learning_goals.html.

Strategy 5: Deep and Surface Approaches to Learning

Exploring how courses and educational experiences position students as learners across their continuum of learning is yet another strategy for developing outcome statements. Of particular assistance in this strategy is the work of Marton and Saljo (1976a, 1976b). Curious to know why certain students developed a comprehensive understanding of academic texts and others did not, in the late 1970s Marton and Saljo interviewed students after reading academic texts. They concluded that students who took a surface approach to reading a text were externally motivated to recall bits of the text in response to questions they anticipated being asked and therefore failed to connect that information to other contexts. In contrast, students who took a deep approach to reading connected new information to previous learning to make meaning for themselves as they read. They were internally motivated to interpret information as they read, and thus to learn through the process of reading. Focusing on the relationship between deep and surface approaches to learning is helpful in identifying outcomes for student learning as well, raising questions about the kinds of learning that we value. To what degree do we promote and value surface approaches to learning? To what degree do we promote and value deep approaches to learning? Certainly, memorization and recognition become a part of students' ability to solve and analyze problems and construct responses. Yet how and when do curricular and other educational experiences position students to take a deep approach to their learning, promoting problem solving and self-reflection as ways of understanding? These broad brushstroke distinctions may help program- and institution-level groups collectively identify learning outcomes. Identifying transitional points in students' learning during which they shift from surface to deep learning may also contribute to achieving consensus about outcome statements. At what points in their continuum of learning do students construct and analyze solutions to problems? That is, when do we expect them to think divergently?

Box 3.4 illustrates how a program aims to foster students' deep approach to their learning by engaging students in thinking across multiple intellectual and personal dimensions. That is, it is designed to stimulate students to process and self-reflect on their learning, not solely to take in information. North Carolina State University's outcome statements for its service-learning program focus on students' abilities to address both the academic and personal dimensions of their learning. These outcome statements reflect the multidimensionality of learning and development. That is, learners construct meaning within the context of their academic learning. They also reflect on the significance of their learning on a personal level: how their learning shapes their commitments, behaviors, actions, and dispositions.

BOX 3.4   **North Carolina State University's Service-Learning Program-Wide Learning Outcomes**

Academic Dimension

1. **Identify and describe course-related concepts in the context of your service-learning related activities.**

   • Describe the course concept that relates to your service-learning experience.
   —AND—
   • Describe what happened in the service-learning experience that relates to that course concept.

2. **Apply course-related concepts in the context of your service-learning related activities.**

   • How does the course-related concept help you to better understand, or deal with, issues related to your service-learning experience?
   —AND/OR—
   • How does the service-learning related experience help you to better understand the course-related concept?

3. **Analyze course-related concepts in light of what you have experienced in the context of your service-learning related activities.**

   • In what specific ways are a course-related concept (or your prior understanding of it) and the experience the same and/or different?
   —AND—
   • What complexities do you see now in the course-related concept that you had not been aware of before?
   —AND/OR—
   • What additional questions need to be answered or evidence gathered in order to judge the adequacy/accuracy/appropriateness of course-related concepts when applied to the experience?

4. **Synthesize and evaluate course-related concepts in light of what you have experienced in the context of your service-learning related activities.**

   • Based on the analysis above, does the course-related concept (or your prior understanding of it) need to be revised and if so, in what specific ways? Provide evidence for your conclusion.
   —AND—

(continued)

BOX 3.4   *(continued)*

- If revision is necessary, what factors do you think have contributed to the inadequacy in the concept as presented or in your prior understanding of it? (E.g., bias/assumptions/agendas/lack of information on the part of the author/scientist or on your part.)
—AND—
- Based on the analysis above, what will/might you do differently in your service-learning or other academic-related activities in the future and what are the challenges you might face as you do so?
—OR—
- Based on the analysis above, what should/might your service organization do differently in the future and what are the challenges it might face as it does so?

Personal Dimension

1. **Identify and describe an awareness about a *personal* characteristic that has been enhanced by reflection on your service-learning related activities.**

   - What personal strength, weakness, assumption, belief, conviction, trait, etc. have you become aware of as a result of reflection on your service-learning related activities?

2. **Apply this awareness in the context of your service-learning related activities and to other areas of your life now or in the future.**

   - How does/might this characteristic affect your interactions with others associated with your service activities and in other areas of your life?
   —OR—
   - How does/might this characteristic affect your decisions/actions taken in your service activities and in other areas of your life?

3. **Analyze the sources of this characteristic and the steps necessary to use or improve on it in your service-learning related activities or other areas of your life.**

   - What are the possible sources of/reasons for this personal characteristic?
   —AND—
   - In what specific way(s) can you use this strength, improve upon this weakness, etc., in your service-learning related activities and other areas of your life?
   —AND—
   - What are the potential personal benefits *and* risks or challenges you might face as you do so?

4. **Develop and evaluate your strategies for personal growth.**

   - Based on the analysis above, what is an appropriate and significant way to use this new awareness in your service-learning related activities or other areas of your life?
   —AND—
   - How will you deal with any challenges or set-backs you might face?
   —AND—
   - How will you assess or monitor your progress or success?

Source: Sarah Ash and Patti Clayton, North Carolina State University.

COMMUNITY CONSENSUS ABOUT LEARNING OUTCOME STATEMENTS

Although previously mentioned core working groups of institution- and program-level committees develop learning outcome statements on behalf of their larger communities, achieving consensus within those larger communities is essential in building an institutional commitment to assessing for learning. Subjecting the final drafts of learning outcome statements to the representative or collective institution- and program-level approval processes is essential to build a shared commitment to assessing for student learning. The collaborative tasks and dialogue described in chapters 1 and 2 lead to learning outcome statement drafts that represent collective intentions translated into the life of the institution and its programs. Ensuring that members of an educational community have the final say in approving such statements through institution- or program-level governance and decision-making processes acknowledges and values the collective contribution of all stakeholders to students' learning. More important, achieving acceptance of learning outcome statements contributes to the early positioning of assessment as a core institutional process. Annually or periodically verifying where and how learning outcome statements are addressed across an institution or across a program or department is an essential collaborative process that (1) ensures underlying coherence, (2) identifies new learning priorities in light of professional developments in fields of study or in research, and (3) ensures that all constituencies have a shared understanding of how and where students learn.

DEVELOPMENT OF OUTCOMES-BASED SYLLABI TO PROMOTE ENDURING LEARNING

The three primary threads that chronologically connect students to institution-, program-, or department-level outcomes are the following:

1. Course or module syllabi
2. Methods of assessment (discussed in chapter 5)
3. Feedback based on criteria and standards of judgment (discussed in chapter 6)

An outcomes-based syllabus is an individual faculty member's means of translating agreed-upon institution-, program-, or department-level learning outcomes into his or her particular learning environment, pedagogy, forms or modes of instruction, or sets of educational experiences. In turn, syllabi become students' chronological maps of the curriculum and co-curriculum, identifying what and how they will learn across a wide range of teaching and learning methodologies and educational opportunities, including residential life, other co-curricular experiences, and online or face-to-face environments. Without consistent chronological exposure to learning outcomes, students can easily forget what they are responsible

for learning and also fail to make or see connections between, among, and across courses and educational experiences. Thus, along with the traditional "contractual" contents of syllabi, such as course description, meeting times, faculty office hours, chronological course topics and sequencing, and course policies, such as grading, attendance, submission of work, an outcomes-based syllabus also includes the following:

1. Learning outcomes for the course that align with department or program outcomes in addition to other course-specific outcomes that the faculty member will address
2. Learning outcomes for the course that align with general education or university-wide learning outcomes translated into program or department disciplinary or professional contexts, such as the development of information literacy across a program of study in music
3. Teaching/learning strategies that promote each learning outcome
4. Chronological assignments (methods of assessment) that students will submit to demonstrate their progress toward or achievement of outcomes
5. Distributed criteria and standards of judgment that faculty use to assess student assignments—usually appended to a syllabus, discussed and shared with an assignment, or available online

Figure 3.2 illustrates a table format that is frequently used in syllabi to communicate these kinds of outcomes-based information to students in paper-based or online syllabi. (Resources at the end of this chapter provide additional formats for outcomes-based syllabi, such as graphic formats.)

Syllabi for courses in a department identify outcomes that address department and general education outcomes so that students develop an understanding of (1) how disciplinary or professional courses chronologically contribute to both sets of learning outcomes and (2) how the range of educational opportunities students experience provides multiple yet different contexts for and modes of learning—lectures, labs, real-time simulations, learning communities, and so on. For example, along with stating course-level outcomes, to keep students focused on the institution's general education outcomes, faculty at Eastern Kentucky University are beginning to use a syllabus footer to focus students on how a particular department-

Outcomes	How You Will Learn	How I Will Assess Your Achievement of This Outcome	The Criteria and Standards of Judgment I Will Use to Assess Your Work
1. Design period costumes for two 18th-century plays	Online design modules; design simulations; critiques of your design exercises	E-portfolio of sketches, journal documentation of your research, final designs, and your statement of principles guiding your designs	Costume design criteria sheet available on course website
2.			
3.			
4.			
5.			
6.			

FIGURE 3.2   Possible Syllabus Format to Identify Outcomes, Pedagogy, Methods of Assessment, and Assessment Criteria

level course also fosters and integrates one or more general education outcomes. The first page of a syllabus from a course in psychology (Box 3.5) illustrates the use of the footer to connect learning in that course with several of the university's learning outcomes. Note also how the text of the syllabus effectively communicates to the learner and his or her experiences.

As described by Valencia College's assistant vice president of curriculum design and articulation, the

College has developed an "online course outline builder system that guides faculty as they create or revise a common course outline. The online system is designed not to seek conformity in pedagogy or content, but to provide students with common learning outcomes in multiple sections of each course. The institution also uses this information to prepare adjunct faculty for the courses they teach. Additionally, this system connects learning outcomes with the college's

BOX 3.5 First Page of an Information Literacy Course in Psychology

Psychology Syllabus
PSYCHOLOGY 250: Information Literacy in Psychology
3 credit hours CRN 12880 Fall 2009

Instructor: Dr. Rose Perrine (AKA Wilkins)   Email: rose.perrine@eku.edu
Phone: (859) 622–2378 (office & voicemail)   Office: Cammack 231
Office hours: TR: 9:30—11:30 & by appointment

Catalog Description: PSY 250: Information Literacy in PSY (3 hours)
Pre or Co-requisite: PSY 200. Prerequisite: Completion of developmental reading and writing requirements.
Course Description: Information literacy, reading, evaluating, summarizing scientific literature in psychology; scientific writing (APA format); basic research terminology.

Required Textbook: Mitchell, M. L., & Jolley, J. M. (2009). *Research design explained* (7th ed.). Belmont, CA: Thomson Wadsworth. Book is used again in PSY 309, 310, & 401.

Optional Textbook: *Publication Manual of the American Psychological Association* (5th ed.). Recommended for students who intend to pursue graduate work.

Instructor Goal for Course: It is my hope that by learning *how* psychologists develop ideas and test those ideas, you will become more excited about the field of psychology. "Research methods" is not the most interesting topic to most students, but the benefits of understanding research can be very exciting. For example, if you want to help people, research can show you the best ways to help. If you want to test your own ideas, knowing research methods allows you to do that. As you go through this course, I encourage you think about things that interest you. Why did you become interested in psychology? What topics are exciting to you? What would you like to know about those topics? How can you use what you learn in this class to better understand people (or animals)?

Student Learning Outcomes. By the end of the course you should be able to:

1. Understand general information literacy. How this outcome is evaluated: information-literacy skills items on Exam 3 & 4; self-reflection library assignments
   A. You will able to determine the nature and extent of information necessary for specific purposes.
   B. You will be able to access the information efficiently and accurately.
   C. You will be able to evaluate the information and its sources critically.
   D. You will be able to incorporate the information appropriately into the specific writing assignment.
   E. You will access and use information ethically and legally.

2. You will analyze the differences between commonsense, nonscientific approaches versus scientific approaches to knowledge. How this outcome is evaluated: exams

3. You will demonstrate the ability to read, analyze, and summarize scientific literature in the field of psychology.
   A. You will comprehend basic research terminology and content of entry-level journal articles in the discipline. How this outcome is evaluated: article summaries/analyses; research proposals (introduction sections)
   B. You will analyze and integrate information from research articles to create research questions/predictions for future research. How this outcome is evaluated: article summaries/analyses; research proposals (introduction sections)

4. You will evaluate research for internal, external, and construct validity issues. How this outcome is evaluated: exams

5. You will demonstrate the skill to write reports in the style, process, and format required by the discipline. How this outcome is evaluated: research proposals

6. You will demonstrate knowledge of career opportunities available in the field of psychology at the undergraduate and graduate levels. How this outcome is evaluated: question-answer sessions in class; reflective papers

PSY 250   Dr. Perrine/Fall 2009

Eastern Kentucky University WILL DEVELOP INFORMED, CRITICAL & CREATIVE THINKERS WHO COMMUNICATE EFFECTIVELY. (EKU Quality Enhancement Plan, 2009)

Source: Rose Perrine, professor of psychology, Eastern Kentucky University.

general education program outcomes, providing useful information about institutional effectiveness. Besides general course catalog information, the online system asks faculty to provide the following kinds of information:

- Major topics/concepts/skills/themes/issues addressed in a course
- Major learning outcomes of the course
- Evidence of student learning under each major outcome
- Indication of how major learning outcomes promote the college's core competencies for all students
- Indicators of student performance in each piece of evidence
- Connections to the general education program outcomes
- Indicators of how a major learning outcome connects to a general education program outcome
- College-wide assessments for general education outcomes" (Karen Borglum e-mail to author, Spring, 2010)

Without this transparency in syllabi we can only hope that students learn what we expect. By making our expectations chronologically explicit and public, we contribute to the understanding of several constituencies: fellow educators across the institution, our students, and external parties. Across the institution, then, we can build understanding among faculty and other educators about (1) the progression, content, topics, pedagogy and modes of delivery that individual faculty use to foster agreed-upon learning outcomes, and (2) the ways in which programs and departments foster institution-level outcomes, such as general education outcomes, that are desirable for graduates from any program of study. Public statements of our expectations also provide external parties, such as accreditors, parents, or transfer institutions (that want to know how comparable students' outcomes are to those they expect either for entry or for course equivalency), evidence of intentional curricular and co-curricular commitment to fostering levels of agreed-upon outcomes. Especially, explicit statement of our expectations helps students do the following:

- Understand over time how "things fit together" across learning experiences inside and outside the classroom

- Articulate their learning, including strengths and weaknesses
- Become chronologically accountable and responsible for demonstrating desired outcomes along their educational journey as well as at the end of their journey

Currently, however, helping students understand an institution's learning outcomes is not yet a common national practice among our colleges and universities. Based on a 48% response rate of chief academic officers or designated representatives among its 906 member institutions, the AAC&U's late 2008/early 2009 survey of its member institutions concluded:

> Despite higher education institutions' focus on outcomes and their communication of these outcomes in a variety of ways, administrators acknowledge a lack of understanding of these goals among many students. Slightly more than two in five (42%) administrators believe that the majority of students understand their institutions' goals or intended outcomes for undergraduate learning (April, 2009).

A college or university can easily adapt campus practices to introduce students to its institution-level learning outcomes by integrating institution-level outcomes into the following:

1. A freshman-year experience as part of that program's curriculum, including inviting upper-level students to discuss their own experiences learning about, building on, and demonstrating these outcomes in their chronological work
2. The content of periodic meetings with advisers

(Refer also to Miami Dade College's Covenant in chapter 1, page 21.)

STUDENTS' ACCOUNTABILITY FOR LEARNING

Situating students to take responsibility for their learning can occur once programs and institutions have developed and published outcome statements. Students may contribute to the dialogue that leads to outcome statements, and their work may help us verify the accuracy of our statements. However, how we position them within our assessment efforts is critical to their own learning over time. Either we can view them as recipients of our commitment to learn about their learning, or we can directly engage them in active reflection on and ownership of their learning. On one hand, assessment is an institution's means of learning about the efficacy and relevancy of its educational practices to improve student learning, and that is one tier of assessment. On the other hand, assessment is a means for students to learn about their own progression over time, and that is the second tier of assessment—a tier that holds students accountable for their own learning. Engaging students in their learning begins by providing them with outcome statements when they matriculate into the institution and into their programs of study. That is, students need to know what we expect them to be able to demonstrate along their continuum of learning. Without that knowledge, they may remain uncertain about our expectations; in fact, they may view much of what we expect as shrouded in mystery. Furthermore, students need to become acculturated to what outcome statements require them to demonstrate. For example, what does it mean to do the following?

- Critique a performance
- Evaluate different interpretations of the same phenomenon or event within a disciplinary context
- Take an interdisciplinary approach to solving a problem
- Make an argument in a field of study

Clarity about our expected learning outcomes grounds and guides students. Specifically, students:

- Become initiated into our educational cultures
- Develop an understanding of what institutions expect of them
- Learn to view themselves as responsible for their learning through multiple educational opportunities the institution offers accompanied with their analysis of and self-reflection on their chronological achievements
- Learn how to accomplish their individual learning goals by becoming familiar with institution- and program-level outcome statements that inform their educational choices or needs

Clarity about our intentions combined with intellectual curiosity about who learns what, when, where,

why, how, and how well underlies the work described in chapter 4 that drives a robust assessment process.

WORKS CITED

American Psychological Association. (2007). APA *guidelines for the undergraduate psychology major.* Washington, DC: Author.

Anderson, L., et al. (2001). A *taxonomy for learning, teaching, and assessing:* A *revision of Bloom's taxonomy of educational objectives.* New York: Addison Wesley Longman.

Association of American Colleges & Universities. (2009, April). *Learning and assessment: Trends in undergraduate education. www.aacu.org/ membership/documents/2009MemberSurvey_Part1 .pdf,p.1*

Association of College and Research Libraries. (2000). *www.ala.org/ala/acrl/acrlstandards/information literacycompetency.htm*

Keeling, R. P. (Ed.). (2006). *Learning reconsidered 2: Implementing a campus-wide focus on the student experience.* Washington, DC: NASPA.

Marton, F. (1998). Towards a theory of quality in higher education. In B. C. Dart & G. Boulton-Lewis (Eds.), *Teaching and learning in higher education* (p. 84). Melbourne, Australia: Australian Council for Educational Research.

Marton, F., & Saljo, R. (1976a). On qualitative differences in learning: I—Outcome and process. *British Journal of Educational Psychology, 46,* 4–11.

Marton, F., & Saljo, R. (1976b). On qualitative differences in learning: II—Outcome and process. *British Journal of Educational Psychology, 46,* 115–127.

Mathematics Association of America. *www.maa.org/ pubs/books/qrs.html*

Ryle, G. (1971). *The thinking of thoughts. Collected papers.* II. London: Hutchinson.

Shulman, L. (2002, November/December). Making Differences: A Table of Learning. *Change, 34*(6), 36–44.

ADDITIONAL RESOURCES

Developing Outcome Statements

Adelman, C. (Ed.). (1987). *Performance and judgment: Essays on principles and practice in the assessment of college student learning.* Washington, DC: U.S. Department of Education, Office of Research.

Astin, A. W. (1991). *Assessment for excellence: The philosophy and practice of assessment and evaluation in higher education.* New York: American Council on Education/ Macmillan.

Banta, T. W., et al. (1996). *Assessment in practice: Putting principles to work on college campuses.* San Francisco: Jossey-Bass.

Bloom, B. S., Engelhart, M. D., Furst, E. J., Hill, W. H., & Krathwohl, D. R. (1956). *The taxonomy of educational objectives, the classification of educational goals, Handbook I: Cognitive domain.* New York: McKay.

Chaffee, E. E., et al. (1997). *Assessing impact: Evidence and action.* Washington, DC: American Association for Higher Education.

Diamond, R. (1998). *Designing and assessing courses and curricula.* San Francisco: Jossey-Bass.

Dressel, P. L. (1976). *Handbook of academic evaluation.* San Francisco: Jossey-Bass.

Erwin, T. D. (1991). *Assessing student learning and development: A guide to the principles, goals, and methods of determining college outcomes.* San Francisco: Jossey-Bass.

Gronlund, N. E. (1970). *Stating behavioral objectives for classroom instruction.* New York: Macmillan.

————. (1998). *Assessment of student achievement.* Needham Heights, MA: Allyn & Bacon.

Harrow, A. (1972). *A taxonomy of the psychomotor domain: A guide for developing behavioral objectives.* New York: Macmillan.

Huba, M., & Freed, J. (2001). *Learner-centered assessment on college campuses: Shifting the focus from teaching to learning.* Needham Heights, MA: Allyn & Bacon.

Krathwohl, D. R., Bloom, B. J., & Masia, B. B. (1964). *The taxonomy of educational objectives: The classification of educational goals. Handbook II: Affective domain.* New York: McKay.

Leskes, A., & Wright, B. (2005). *The art and science of assessing general education outcomes: A practical guide.* Washington, DC: Association of American Colleges & Universities.

Mentkowski, M., & Loacker, G. (1985). Assessing and validating the outcomes of college. In P. T. Ewell (Ed.), *Assessing educational outcomes. New Directions for Institutional Research, 47,* (pp. 47–64). San Francisco: Jossey-Bass.

Mentkowski, M., Moeser, M., & Straight, M. J. (1981). *Using the Perry scheme of intellectual and ethical development as a college outcome measure: A process and criteria for assessing student performance.* Milwaukee, WI: Office of Research and Evaluation, Alverno College.

Mentkowski, M., & Rogers, G. P. (1988). *Establishing the validity of measures of college student outcomes.* Milwaukee, WI: Office of Research and Evaluation, Alverno College.

Palomba, C. A., & Banta, T. W. (1999). *Assessment essentials.* San Francisco: Jossey-Bass.

Rogers, G. P. (1988). *Validating college outcomes with institutionally developed instruments: Issues in maximizing contextual validity.* Milwaukee, WI: Office of Research and Evaluation, Alverno College.

Stark, J. S., & Lowther, M. (1986). *Designing the learning plan: A review of research and theory related to college curricula.* Ann Arbor: National Center on Postsecondary Teaching and Learning (NCRIPTAL), University of Michigan.

Stark, J. S., Shaw, K. M., & Lowther, M. A. (1989). *Student goals for college and courses* (Report No. 6). Washington, DC: School of Education and Human Development, George Washington University.

Walvoord, B. E., & Anderson, V. J. (1998). *Effective grading: A tool for learning and assessment.* San Francisco: Jossey-Bass.

Deep and Surface Approaches to Learning

Case, J., & Gunstone, R. (2002, October). Shift in approach to learning: An in-depth study. *Studies in Higher Education, 27*(4), 459–470.

Entwistle, N. (1998). Approaches to learning and forms of understanding. In B. C. Dart & G. Boulton-Lewis (Eds.), *Teaching and learning in higher education* (pp. 72–101). Melbourne, Australia: Australian Council for Educational Research.

Entwistle, N. J., & Ramsden, P. (1983). *Understanding student learning.* New York: Nichols.

Marton, F. (1975). *On non verbatim learning—II: The erosion of a task-induced learning algorithm.* Reports from the Institute of Education, University of Gothenburg, No. 40.

Marton, F. (1976). What does it take to learn? Some implications of an alternative view of learning. In N. J. Entwistle (Ed.), *Strategies for research and development in higher education.* Amsterdam: Swets & Zeitlinger.

Developing Outcomes-Based Syllabi

Fink, D. (2003). *Creating significant learning experiences: An integrated approach to designing college courses.* San Francisco: Jossey-Bass.

Nilson, L. B. (2007). *The graphic syllabus and the outcomes map: Communicating your course.* San Francisco: Jossey-Bass.

O'Brien, J. G., Millis, B. J., & Cohen, M. B. (2008). *The course syllabus: A learning-centered approach* (2nd ed.). San Francisco: Jossey-Bass.

Richlin, L. (2006). *Constructing college courses to facilitate, assess, and document learning.* Sterling, VA: Stylus. *http://stylus.styluspub.com/Books/BookDetail.aspx? productID=117 420*

Metasite on Student Affairs Outcomes and Outcomes Assessment Specific Sites on Taxonomies

The following sites list further references and Internet resources on taxonomies.

Indiana University-Purdue University Indianapoliswww.uni.edu/stdteach/TWS/Bloom RevisedTaxonomy_keywo rds-1–1.pdf

Provides a list of verbs that align with Krathwohl's renaming and reordering of Bloom's Taxonomy.

George Mason University http://assessment.gmu.edu/AcadProgEval/guide .shtml

Provides Internet resources for Bloom's taxonomy.

Bill Huitt's Home Page at Valdosta State University www.edpsycinteractive.org/topics/cogsys/bloom.html

Provides a chart of Bloom's Taxonomy for the cognitive domain.

Webb's Cognitive Complexity Taxonomy www.pac6org/images/upload/Exploring_Cognitive_ Demand_in_instruction

Provides a comparison between Bloom's Taxonomy and the four ways students interact with content according to Norman Webb.

WORKSHEETS, GUIDES, AND EXERCISES

1. *Developing Outcome Statements.* As an initial exercise with colleagues in a core working group established to develop learning outcome statements, focus discussion on students' continuum of learning at the program or institution level by exploring the value placed on surface and deep approaches to an expectation that the core group identified in chapter 2. Translate that discussion into outcome statements that reflect what students should be able to represent, demonstrate, or produce as a result of their learning chronology.

2. *Developing Outcome Statements.* As an initial exercise with colleagues in a core working group established to develop learning outcome statements at either the institution or program level, prepare drafts of outcome statements that build on the more general expectations agreed upon in chapter 2. As you draft institution- and program-level outcome statements, you may find some of the taxonomies listed under "Additional Resources" at the end of this chapter helpful.

Focusing on verbs that center your outcome statements will also promote dialogue about how the design of the curriculum and co-curriculum and other educational experiences contributes to the learning identified in your outcome statements. These discussions may cause members of your group to want to establish levels of outcome statements such as appear in Appendix 3.4 in this chapter. Or, members may decide to develop two sets of outcome statements:

1. One set that defines what students should be able to demonstrate or represent by the midpoint of their studies
2. A second set that defines what students should be able to demonstrate or represent at the end of their studies

3. *Developing Outcome Statements.* If you are beginning to develop outcome statements at the institution level, well before your initial meeting ask members of your core working group to use one or more of the five strategies described in this chapter to prepare a list of five or six outcome statements and discuss those outcomes. Pass each member's outcome statements to others in the group; then ask members to indicate if each statement fulfills criteria for an effective outcome statement and include comments about the effectiveness of each statement. Use the following chart to evaluate each outcome statement.

Checklist to Review an Institution- or Program-Level Draft of Learning Outcome Statements

	Describes what students should represent, demonstrate, or produce?	Relies on active verbs?	Aligns with collective intentions translated into the curriculum and co-curriculum?	Maps to curriculum, co-curriculum, and educational practices?	Is collaboratively authored and collectively accepted?	Incorporates or adapts professional organizations' outcome statements when they exist?	Can be assessed quantitatively and/or qualitatively?
Outcome:							
Outcome:							
Outcome:							
Outcome:							

After everyone has had a chance to evaluate each outcome, determine if there is consensus about these statements. That consensus may take more than one meeting. When you have reached consensus, circulate a draft of those statements in a faculty-staff forum that provides opportunity for further feedback before the statements are officially adopted through governance structures and processes; or, post these learning outcome statements on your institution's website, seeking further institution-wide responses before the statements move toward a final approval process at the institution level. The development of program-level learning outcome statements may also follow this same process to build consensus.

4. *Developing Learning Outcome Statements and Orienting Students.* To develop departmental learning outcome statements, the geography department at the University of Washington (described in Appendix 3.1 in this chapter) established the following time line to develop its outcomes, as well as make them public to students on the program's Careers website. This project focuses on assisting students in taking ownership of their learning as they develop a professional portfolio; that is, developing outcome statements educates them about program-level expectations and becomes the means for them to determine how they will build that portfolio. Use or adapt this timetable to develop learning outcome statements based on the epistemological and ethnographic process described on page 96 in this chapter.

Determine how you will publish these statements and orient students to them as a way to chart their educational journey. Or, building on the curricular or co-curricular map you developed in chapter 2, consider how you might develop a version of that to give your students when you orient them to their education. A graphic representation may well help them develop a more comprehensive understanding of what they will chronologically experience.

TIME LINE FOR THE DEVELOPMENT OF THE DEPARTMENT OF GEOGRAPHY'S OUTCOME STATEMENTS

Project Schedule

September 16, 1997—January 15, 2001

Task 1. Objectives and outcomes narrative synthesis

- Establish protocol for interviews.
- Conduct interviews.
- Create drafts of 35 individual course profiles.
- Negotiate and revise overviews of learning outcomes within concentrations.
- Coordinate with faculty to finalize learning goals and objectives for concentrations and entire curriculum.

January 16, 2001—September 15, 2001

Task 2. Objectives and outcomes analytical synthesis

- Create objectives and outcome matrices for each course.
- Synthesize matrices to concentration level.
- Synthesize matrices to department curriculum level.

September 16, 2000—August 15, 2002

Task 3. Objectives and outcomes career articulation

- Develop UW Geography Department Careers Web site.
- Develop alumni e-network.
- Develop alumni contact directory.
- Develop a searchable database designed to match current job qualifications and learning outcomes that helps students translate between learning outcomes and professional development. (Geography My Action Portfolio: G-MAP)

September 16, 2001—August 15, 2002

Task 4. Objectives and outcomes assessment

- Link instructor-graded assessments to anticipated outcomes and, hence, back to course objectives.
- Enable faculty to interview one another in a second, more iterative round of conversations.
- Assess a cross-section of portfolios of geography majors by faculty and outside professional panels.

September 16, 2000—August 15, 2002

Task 5. Geography My Action Portfolio (G-MAP)

- Agree on purposes and final architecture of the G-MAP site.
- Design user interface and navigation strategies for the site.
- Link existing documents conceptually and as hypertext documents.
- Test functionality of the site.
- Integrate the site into major requirements (required portfolio, etc.).

Source: Contributed by Richard Roth and members of the faculty, Department of Geography, University of Washington. Reproduced with permission.

5. *Integrating and Distributing Outcomes.* Having developed general education or institution-wide outcomes as well as program- or department-level outcomes—or after you have developed and agreed on them—use the following format to develop outcomes-based syllabi. Specifically, ask individuals who address a common set of outcomes to fill out the template to generate discussion about how students chronologically develop these outcomes and move to higher levels of performance or complexity. Alternatively, if colleagues have not recently revised their syllabi, ask them to use the template to develop an outcomes-based focus in those syllabi. Then use these revised syllabi to launch into discussion about how students chronologically develop these outcomes and move to higher levels of performance or complexity. This kind of discussion helps faculty identify student gaps in learning that they will need to address. More important, this discussion creates an opportunity for faculty to discuss patterns of weakness in students' chronological work that can be addressed through collaborative redesign of sequential courses.

This format is also useful when a program or department wants to learn more about how students learn in educational opportunities offered through academic and student affairs services, such as community service, support services, and library services. That is, members of a department or program, such as the general education program, could collaborate with educators in academic and student services to share results of this chart to deepen knowledge about where students have continued opportunities to learn outside of the curriculum and to encourage students to participate in those opportunities to complement and build on their learning:

Outcomes	How Students Learn	How I Assess Student Achievement of This Outcome	The Criteria and Standards of Judgment I Use to Assess Student Work
1.			
2.			
3.			
4.			
5.			

6. *Reviewing and Distributing Outcomes.* Building a sustainable institutional commitment to assessment occurs over time. Periodically, institution- and program-level committees and institutional leaders take stock of how this commitment is taking shape. The following checklist can be used in assessment committees, by leaders, during program-, department-, or division-level meetings, or during more public forums bringing together members of the academic community to track progress periodically. Asking members in these meetings to respond to each question by responding to a level of progress—"Some Progress," "Making Progress," or "Achieved"—as well as asking members to provide evidence for each response and summarizing those responses builds collective commitment over time. Collective responses identify progress that has been made as well as areas that need attention. Using this checklist, assessment committees can monitor progress toward an institutional commitment to assessment.

Tracking Progress Toward Developing and Disseminating Learning Outcome Statements

	Some Progress	Making Progress	Achieved	Evidence
Has your institution developed outcome statements that describe what all graduates should be able to represent, demonstrate, or produce?				
Has each program, division, school, department, and major educational service developed outcome statements that describe what students should represent, demonstrate, or produce?				
Are these statements published in the institution's catalog, on its website, and in other relevant publications?				
Are there ways in which students are oriented to institution-level outcomes upon matriculation, such as during first-year orientation or first-year programs or in the advising process?				
Are there ways in which students are oriented to program- or department-level outcomes when they enter their major program of study at the undergraduate and graduate levels?				
Do all course syllabi for a major program of study list learning outcome statements, identify how students will learn these outcomes, identify the assignments that will be used to assess student achievement, and attach or refer students to a list of criteria and standards of judgment that will be used to assess their performance?				
Do course outcomes in a department or major integrate relevant general education or core curricula outcomes?				
Is there alignment between agreed-upon department or program outcomes and specific course-based outcomes in syllabi?				
Besides discussing outcomes stated in syllabi, are there other department- or program-level practices that focus students on learning outcomes along their learning journey, such as asking upper-level students to talk about their educational journeys, inviting recent alumni to address students in a major, and using advising as a process to discuss with students how they are learning and demonstrating these outcomes?				
Do programs and services in the co-curriculum identify learning outcomes for participating students, including relevant general education or institution-level outcomes?				
Do academic support programs identify learning outcomes for participating students, including relevant general education or institution-level outcomes?				

APPENDIX 3.1 INSTITUTIONAL EXAMPLE: *University of Washington, Department of Geography Learning Outcome Project*

TOWARD "THICK DESCRIPTION": THE ITERATIVE INTERVIEWING PROCESS

To develop its learning outcome statements, the Department of Geography at the University of Washington, has, so far, gone through four distinct, cumulative phases, the first three of which were ethnographic, the final one collaborative and collective:

Phase I: An Initial Ten-Minute Exercise.
In a department meeting, faculty were asked to "state a specific learning objective for one course they teach in the Geography Program and to explain what indicators they use to assess students' achievement of this objective (content, topics, or methods, not just performance on an exam or paper)." One respondent's "course-specific learning objectives" were "critical thinking skills" and "writing skills." Her outcome indicators of the attainment of these skills included

1. application of theoretical approaches to empirical material in a clear, cogent, well-organized research or service learning project;

2. accurate and precise definition of concepts and approaches used and introduced in readings and lectures;

3. application of knowledge gained in the course to answer questions or solve problems.

Phase II: Follow-Up Faculty-to-Faculty Interviews. In each of the five concentrations within the major, faculty interviewed one another and asked for further elaboration of learning objectives leading to learning outcomes. The faculty member mentioned translated two of her objectives into outcome statements:

LEARNING OBJECTIVES: GEOG 371 (WORLD HUNGER AND RESOURCE DEVELOPMENT)

To understand the dimensions and causes of world poverty

To understand the dimensions and causes of world hunger

LEARNING OBJECTIVES: GEOG 371 (WORLD HUNGER AND RESOURCE DEVELOPMENT)

Diagnose and offer solutions for global food problems.
Critique arguments related to food and hunger.

Phase III: Second Interview: Supplying the Missing Links and Narrative Stitchery.
The second follow-up interview, with the transcriber, produced a more complex description of learning objectives and outcomes. The transcriber "played dumb" by asking "What do you mean by hunger? What do you mean by development? How are those two concepts linked?" etc. Basically, this iteration produced:

1. more complex causal thinking, including consideration of linkages and hierarchies ("understanding of how poverty and hunger are linked across geographic scales");

2. more of a sense of the narrative flow of a course ("having defined poverty as x, and hunger as y, and having seen how they are linked across various geographic scales, faculty could better frame their discussion of the world food system, agricultural modernization," etc.);

3. a better-defined sense of what kinds of arguments students should be able to make at the end of a course. For example, instead of just saying students should be able to "critique arguments related to food and hunger," the faculty member who teaches World Hunger and Resource Development now states students should be able to "critique concepts of agrarian development and reform";

4. a generated supplemental list of targeted "acquired skills" students would come away with from each course—an inventory.

**Phase IV: Negotiation of Learning Out-
come Statements.** The final phase entailed a
round-robin, consisting of a collaborative
process of writing the learning objectives and
outcomes for the entire development concentration within the major. This meant integrating six faculty members and about eighteen
courses. The developer of the thick text made a
first stab at consolidating and then circulated a
draft to members of the program. Learning
outcomes were negotiated over an intense
three-week period until consensus about learning outcomes was achieved. Results of this
process are available at the University of Washington's Web site: http://depts.washington.edu/
geog/courses.

Source: Richard Roth and members of the faculty,
Department of Geography, University of Washington.
Reproduced with permission.

APPENDIX 3.2 Developing Student Learning Outcomes for the Division of Student Affairs at the University of Maryland

The Student Affairs Learning Outcomes Group (LOG) developed a set of criteria for developing learning outcomes. It was determined that the outcomes adopted for review should:

1. Reflect whenever possible and appropriate the five institutional outcomes—critical reasoning and research skills, written and oral communication, science and quantitative reasoning, information literacy skills, and technology fluency.

2. Correspond to (i.e., development guided by) the outcome domains listed in the nationally recognized publication *Learning Reconsidered*.

3. Include areas that are found in multiple units in the Division.

4. Be readily adoptable at the current time.

Other principles adopted by LOG in the process of managing the Division's effort in developing learning outcomes included the following:

1. There should be both division-level and department-level learning outcomes.

2. Departments should not be charged with assessing all division-level outcomes.

3. Some of the department-level learning outcomes will reflect the division-level outcomes while others will be unique to the department's mission. Those that reflect the division-level outcomes will be part of the mapping process used across all units within Student Affairs.

4. The division should develop an appropriate number of learning outcomes over time, but will focus on a manageable number in the first year.

5. Members of LOG will serve as consultants to all departments to assist with the development of department-level learning outcomes.

6. There should be intentionality in the process of integrating learning outcomes into the management of the Division and its departments.

7. Input and concurrence will be sought from the leadership team (VP, AVPs, and Directors) of the Division in the process of developing division-level learning outcomes.

Seven learning outcomes were identified for which assessment plans were designed in the early spring of 2006. These were completed by the institutional deadline of March 15, 2006. The seven learning outcomes are presented here.

1. **Oral Communication:** Students who participate in the programs and services offered through the Division of Student Affairs (Health Center and Student Conduct) will develop practical competence in effective oral communication.

2. **Time Management:** Students enrolled in EDCP 108B, 108G, 108M, and 108R sponsored by the Learning Assistance Service will demonstrate competence in managing their time which will lead to continued persistence and academic achievement at the University. Students will demonstrate practical competence in effective time management strategies in order to balance their academic and co-curricular involvement.

3. **Ethical Development:** Students who are found responsible for violating the Code of Academic Integrity will develop interpersonal and intrapersonal competence and humanitarianism in ethical and principled reasoning, decision making, and actions though their participation in the discipline process and the Academic Integrity Seminar.

4. **Lifesaving Skills:** Students working in supervisory positions in the Department of Campus Recreation Services will demonstrate knowledge acquisition, integration, and application and practical competence in lifesaving skills.

5. **Resume Writing Skills:** Students who participate in the programs and services offered through the Career Center will develop knowledge acquisition, integration, and application and practical competence in resume writing skills as a factor in vocational competence and effective written communication.

6. **Group Process:** Students enrolled in Introduction to Leadership classes (e.g., EDCP 317) will demonstrate competence in civically engaged leadership in group processes that advance the iterests and purposes of the group.

7. **Dialogue Skills for Peer Dialogue Leaders:** As a result of participation in the Common Group Dialogue Peer Leader training program in Resident Life, Peer Dialogue Leaders will demonstrate an increased ability to see and understand multiple perspectives on multicultural societal dilemmas.

Following the initial submission of the seven learning outcomes, an internal auditing process was employed to evelute the assessment plans according to institutional criteria. These criteria included the following:

1. Each of the student learning outcomes measures assessed what students should be able to know, do, or appreciate.

2. Student learning outcomes were stated individually rather than aggregated within a single outcome.

3. The student learning outcomes and criteria were appropriately rigorous for a flagship university.

4. The student learning outcomes aligned with the program goals.

5. Assessments relied predominantly on individual student work rather than on final course grades.

6. The sampled student work was appropriate to the stated learning outcomes.

7. The method(s) of evaluating the sampled student work was (were) appropriate and sufficiently defined.

8. The assessment schedule was appropriate for the program.

Although following the internal audit there were alterations to the seven learning outcomes that addressed issues related to these eight criteria, all seven leaning outcomes were subsequently maintained and implemented during fall 2006.

Learning Outcomes for the Division of Student Affairs

Learning Reconsidered Categories	Division of Student Affairs Co-Curriculum. What do students learn from participation in our programs and services?[1]	Illustrative examples of where learning occurs[2]
Cognitive complexity	Critical thinking*	Judicial Board training
	Creativity—divergent thinking leading to novel outcomes	Visual arts programs
	Reflective thinking—making meaning of life experiences	Internship programs
Knowledge acquisition, integration and application	Knowledge—seeking, applying, and integrating knowledge; encouraging lifelong learning	Credit classes offered through Student Affairs units
	Career development—exploring, planning, and realizing career goals	Career Center programs
Humanitarianism	Diversity and multiculturalism—understanding and appreciating human differences	*Peer Dialogue Leader training*
		Cultural advocacy groups
Civic engagement	Leadership—participating in democracy, serving the community, and/or advocating for change	*Leadership classes*
		Leadership workshops and retreats
	Civic responsibility	Community service-learning
	Environmental stewardship	Recycling programs
Interpersonal and intrapersonal competence	Self awareness—realistic self-appraisal and self-understanding	Personal counseling
		Community living experiences
	Relationship with others—understanding of self in relation to others	Personal counseling
		Community living experiences
	Conflict resolution	Judicial hearing process
	Ethical development—understanding and applying an ethical decision-making process	*Academic integrity seminars*
	Spiritual awareness	Chaplaincy programs
Practical competence	Effective communication skills*	*Peer educator/volunteer training programs*
	Vocational competence—developing skills to enter and succeed in the workplace	*Resume writing programs*
		Lifesaving training programs
		Student employee training programs
	Wellness—understanding and applying healthy life choices	Health education programs
		Recreation programs
		Alcohol and drug programs
Persistence and academic achievement	Learning skills—acquiring skills for academic success	*Time management programs*
		Other learning assistance programs
	Involvement—engaging in the campus community	Community living experiences
		Student activities/programs
		Student organizations

[1] Items marked with an asterisk (*) are also one of the five campus-wide learning outcomes.
[2] Items in *italics* represent the seven areas where learning outcomes were identified in March 2006 for Middle States review.

Source: Division of Student Affairs, University of Maryland. Reproduced with permission.

APPENDIX 3.3 Master of Accountancy Curriculum

INSTRUCTION/ASSESSMENT CODES

I = instruction
UO = ungraded observaton
GO = graded observation
PE = problems-based examinations
EE = essay-based examinations
OE = objective-based examination;
    e.g., multiple choice, true-false,
    fill in the blank
GP = graded papers, presentations,
    other student work
O = other (please specify in a
    footnote)

ASSURANCE OF LEARNING (AoL) PLAN
LEARNING OUTCOME GROUPINGS
T&I = Theory and Issues
ACPS = Analytical, Communication,
    Presentation Skills
CPDR = Conduct and Present
    Descriptive Research
ER = Ethical Reasoning

MAcc AoL Plan & AACSB Standard 19

Course	Title	T&I: Identify Complex Accounting Issues and Problems — *AACSB Standard 19a, f	T&I: Evaluate Alternative Courses of Action — *AACSB Standard 19e, a, b, c, d, f	T&I: Integrate Knowledge Across Disciplines — *AACSB Standard 19a, b, c, d, e, f	T&I: Analyze Key Elements of Complex Accounting Issue or Problem — *AACSB Standard 19e, a, b, c, d, f	ACPS: Effectively Utilize Written Communication	ACPS: Effectively Use Presentation Technology	CDR: Plan Research Study, Conduct Research, Collect Data — *AACSB Standard 19, e, b, c, d, f	CDR: Prepare Oral Presentation	CDR: Prepare Written Report	ER: Apply Ethical Reasoning to Decisions — *AACSB Standard 19b, c, d, e, f	Diversity
MAcc Program Courses												
Core												
ACG 5658	Non-Profit Accounting & Auditing											
ACG 6308	Advanced Managerial Accounting											
ACG 6805	Seminar in Financial Accounting											
BUL 5831	Commercial Law											
FIN 6406*	Financial Management											
TAX 5105	Corporate Income Tax											
CoB Elective	(ACG 5807 or most MBA courses)											
Prof Acct												
ACG 5205	Advanced Financial Accounting											
ACG 6405	Accounting Information Systems											
ACG 6856	Advanced Auditing											
Taxation												
TAX 6065	Tax Data Bases, Res & Proced											
TAX 6405	Estate Gift & Trust Taxation											
TAX 6875	Special Topics in Taxation											

INSTRUCTION/ASSESSMENT CODES
I = instruction
UO = ungraded observaton
GO = graded observation
PE = problems-based examinations
EE = essay-based examinations
OE = objective-based examination; e.g., multiple choice, true-false, fill in the blank
GP = graded papers, presentations, other student work
O = other (please specify in a footnote)
ASSURANCE OF LEARNING (AoL) PLAN
LEARNING OUTCOME GROUPINGS
T&I = Theory and Issues
ACPS = Analytical, Communication, Presentation Skills
CPDR = Conduct and Present Descriptive Research
ER = Ethical Reasoning

Course	Title	Diversity	Identify Complex Accounting Issues and Problems *AACSB Standard 19a, f	Evaluate Alternative Courses of Action *AACSB Standard 19e, a, b, c, d, f	Integrate Knowledge Across Disciplines *AACSB Standard 19a, b, c, d, e, f	Analyze Key Elements of Complex Accounting Issue or Problem *AACSB Standard 19e, a, b, c, d, f	Effectively Utilize Written Communication	Effectively Use Presentation Technology	Plan Research Study, Conduct Research, Collect Data *AACSB Standard 19, e, b, c, d, f	Prepare Oral Presentation	Prepare Written Report	Apply Ethical Reasoning to Decisions *AACSB Standard 19b, c, d, e, f
Other Courses												
ACG 5807	Spec Topics in Acctg (also ACG 4174)											
ACG 5905	Directed Study											
BUL 5905	Directed Study											
Foundation Courses												
ACG 3101	Intermediate Financial Accounting I											
ACG 3111	Intermediate Financial Accounting II											
ACG 3343	Cost Accounting (or ACG 3351)											
ACG 3401	Accounting Information Systems											
ACG 4151	Accounting Theory											
BUL 3130	Legal Environment of Business											
FIN 3403	Managerial Finance											
TAX 4002	Tax Accounting											

***AACSB Standard 19 Master's Level Degree in Specialized Programs: Knowledge and Skills**

a. Knowledge of theories, models, and tools relevant to the speciality field
b. Apply appropriate theories, models, and tools to solve concrete business and managerial problems
c. Apply knowledge in new and unfamiliar circumstances through conceptual understanding of the specialty field
d. Adapt and innovate to solve problems
e. Critically analyze and question knowledge claims in the specialty field
f. Understand the specialty field from a global perspective

Source: Edward Ranelli, University of West Florida.

APPENDIX 3.4 Example of Leveled Outcome Statements
Undergraduate Program Outcomes for the School of Nursing
The University Mission to Level Competencies
Azusa Pacific University

UNIVERSITY MISSION STATEMENT:

Azusa Pacific University is an evangelical Christian community of disciples and scholars who seek to advance the work of God in the world through academic excellence in liberal arts and professional programs of higher education that encourage students to develop a Christian perspective of truth and life.

SCHOOL OF NURSING MISSION STATEMENT:

Consistent with the mission and purpose of the University, the School of Nursing is a Christian community of discipleship, scholarship, and practice. Its purpose is to advance the work of God in the world through nursing education, collaborative projects, and Church and community service that encourages those affiliated with the School of Nursing (whether faculty, staff, student, graduate, or colleague) to grow in faith and in the exercise of their gifts for service to God and humanity.

SCHOOL OF NURSING PROGRAM LEARNER OUTCOME:

The graduate of Azusa Pacific University's baccalaureate nursing program integrates faith and ethics as a skilled and knowledgeable practitioner, accountable professional, health care educator and advocate, and coordinator of care.

Program Competencies

I. Utilizes Christian worldview to integrate beliefs, values, ethics, and service in personal and professional life.

II. Provides nursing care utilizing professional knowledge and core competencies (critical thinking, communication, assessment, and technical skills) derived from a foundation of nursing science, general education, and religious studies.

III. Demonstrates initiative for continual personal and professional growth and development.

IV. Acts as a patient and family educator and advocate to promote optimal health and well-being.

V. Functions independently and collaboratively, both as a leader and/or member of a health care team to manage and coordinate care.

Level Competencies

Outcome I. Utilizes Christian worldview to integrate beliefs, values, ethics, and service in personal and professional life.

Level I
- Describes the beliefs, values, and ethics that influence personal behaviors and potentially impact professional behaviors.
- Describes the spiritual subsystem of self and patient.
- Defines what a worldview is and how it affects one's behavior.

Level II
- Integrates selected values and ethical principles in personal and professional interactions with patients, peers, faculty, and other health care professionals.
- Utilizes data from the assessment of the spiritual subsystem to develop a nursing plan of care.
- Continues to develop a structure and framework for a Christian worldview for selected nursing topics.

Level III
- Differentiates Christian worldview from other world views as applied to professional nursing practice.
- Integrates selected values and nursing Code of Ethics in personal and professional interactions.
- Implements spiritual care with the patient and the family based on identified strengths, challenges and resource.
- Articulates areas of personal spiritual growth.

Level IV

- Applies the Nurses Code of Ethics in professional nursing practice.
- Identifies how one's own Christian beliefs and spirituality are impacted when caring for vulnerable populations and patients/families facing acute health crises.
- Articulates a personal reflection on the concept of ministry as a Christian nurse.
- Evaluates the effectiveness of spiritual care interventions in professional nursing practice.

Outcome II. Provides nursing care utilizing professional knowledge and core competencies (critical thinking, communication, assessment and technical skills) derived from a foundation of nursing science, general education, and religious studies.

Level I

- Begins to utilize the elements of professional knowledge and core competencies (critical thinking, communication, assessment, and technical skills) to provide nursing care to well and selected ill adults.
- Identifies the relationship between general education, nursing science, and religious studies.

Level II

- Utilizes professional knowledge and core competencies (critical thinking, communication, assessment, and technical skills) to provide nursing care to individuals across the life span, including neonates and elderly.
- Applies selected concepts from general education and religious studies to nursing practice.

Level III

- Utilizes professional knowledge and core competencies (critical thinking, communication, assessment, and technical skills) to provide nursing care to individuals within a family context.
- Integrates concepts from general education and religious studies in provision of care to individual and families.

Level IV

- Utilizes professional knowledge and core competencies (critical thinking, communica-

tion, assessment, and technical skills) to provide nursing care in a diversity of settings with individuals, families, and community aggregates.
- Applies core knowledge of health promotion, risk reduction, and disease prevention in managing the care of vulnerable populations.
- Applies core knowledge of illness and disease management and health care technologies in managing the care of individuals and families facing acute health crises.
- Applies professional and clinical standards including evidence-based practice to guide professional decision making.
- Synthesizes concepts from general education and religious studies in the provision of individual comprehensive care to families and aggregates.

Outcome III. Demonstrates initiative for continual personal and professional growth and development.

Level I

- Identifies and reflects on experiences for personal and professional learning and growth.

Level II

- Identifies and chooses a variety of opportunities that will contribute to personal and professional growth.

Level III

- Demonstrates initiative for continual personal and professional growth and development.
- Selects personal and professional experiences for learning and growth.
- Participates in nursing opportunities that contribute to their personal and professional growth based upon identified needs.
- Examine the value of personal and professional experiences on growth and development.

Level IV

- Creates personal and professional experiences for continued learning and professional development.
- Analyzes own nursing practice, compares to professional practice standards, and determines areas for improvement.

Outcome IV. Acts as a patient and family educator and advocate to promote optimal health and well-being.

Level I

- Recognizes the basic role of patient educator and advocate based upon the identification of selected patient needs and rights within the health care system.

Level II

- Serves as a patient educator and advocate at a beginning level based on the identification of patient needs and rights.

Level III

- Assumes the role of health care educator and advocate for patients and their families.

Level IV

- Assumes the role of health care educator and advocate for patients, families, communities, and aggregates.

Outcome V. Functions independently and collaboratively, both as a leader and/or member of a health care team to manage and coordinate care.

Level I

- Identifies professional guidelines that define nursing roles and responsibilities.
- Makes beginning contributions to the health care team under supervision of the nursing clinical instructor.

Level II

- Defines independent and collaborative role of the nurse as a member of the health care team.
- Provides nursing care under the supervision of the RN team leader and the nursing clinical instructor.
- Utilizes professional guidelines to provide safe patient care.

Level III

- Implements independent and collaborative aspect of the nursing role.
- Provides nursing care and team leadership in collaboration and consultation with preceptor and nursing clinical instructor.
- Independently follows professional guidelines in all aspects of professional practice.

Level IV

- Functions in a leadership role in collaboration with preceptors and members of the health care team in coordinating services to patients, families, and aggregates.
- Demonstrates independence in clinical decision making based on comprehensive assessment and prioritization.
- Demonstrates professional accountability and clinical responsibility for outcomes of nursing care.

Source: Developed by the undergraduate nursing department at Azusa Pacific University under the leadership of Shila Wiebe, Program Director; D. Vicky Bowden, Curriculum Committee Chair; Professor Connie Austin, eportfolio Program Director; and Dr. Julia Jantzi, Director of Institutional Assessment Planning.

Chapter 4

RAISING AND PURSUING OPEN-ENDED RESEARCH OR STUDY QUESTIONS TO DEEPEN INQUIRY INTO AND IMPROVE STUDENT LEARNING

A measure of how differently teaching is regarded from traditional scholarship or research within the academy is what a difference it makes to have a "problem" in one versus the other. In scholarship and research, having a "problem" is at the heart of the investigative process; it is the compound of the generative questions around which all creative and productive activity revolves. But in one's teaching, a "problem" is something you don't want to have, and if you have one, you probably want to fix it. Asking a colleague about a problem in his or her research is an invitation; asking about a problem in one's teaching would probably seem like an accusation. Changing the status of the problem *in teaching from terminal remediation to ongoing* investigation *is precisely what the movement for a scholarship of teaching is all about. How might we make the problematization of teaching a matter of regular communal discourse? How might we think of teaching practice, and the evidence of student learning, as problems to be investigated, analyzed, represented, and debated?*

—Randy Bass, 1999

OVERVIEW: Unless educators initially connect professional curiosity about the teaching-learning process to the assessment process, they are not likely to learn more about how to improve teaching and learning than is currently possible. Chapter 4 positions educators to determine how they will drill down into the work students produce to learn more about students' patterns of performance represented in the tasks or work they produce. It also positions educators to determine how they will explore students' learning or meaning-making processes—processes that account for successful learning as well as not-so-successful learning. This chapter (1) provides a rationale for learning more about both students' learning products and the learning processes or strategies or approaches that underlie those products, including the typical challenges or obstacles students confront within the context of existing educational practices; (2) presents a problem-based approach to and framework for collaboratively raising and pursuing open-ended research or study questions about student learning; (3) presents case studies that demonstrate how deepening inquiry into patterns of student performance promotes collaborative discussions, reflection, and actions to improve or maximize student learning; and (4) identifies representative pedagogically based and learning-process-based questions to prime department-, program-, or institution-level identification of relevant research or study questions. The Worksheets, Guides, and Exercises at the end of this chapter position inquiry groups or communities of practice to engage in scholarly assessment as either a formal or an informal process that can lead to two by-products: actions to improve or maximize student learning, and inquiry-based findings and interpretations that contribute to or build on knowledge and practices in the teaching profession.

As a checkpoint, chapter 4 positions faculty and other educators to take a problem-based scholarly approach to the remaining assessment decisions and tasks detailed in succeeding chapters. Specifically, it encourages faculty and other educators to collaboratively identify and pursue student-focused learning problems or issues translated into open-ended research or study questions that educators care about. It encourages educators to identify the kinds of evidence or data that help explore answers to those questions. It encourages educators to pursue evidence of how well students initially learn and then transfer, apply, integrate, and build on their learning along the continuum of their learning. And, it encourages educators to focus on how students do or do not develop sustained or enduring learning—learning for the long haul as opposed to learning solely for the end of a course or a single educational experience. The problem-based approach to assessment presented in this chapter represents a scholarly commitment to assessment that shifts this commitment into an investigative role as opposed solely to an accountability role. This chapter extends the kinds of action research that some faculty may conduct in their individual courses to examine how well students chronologically transfer, apply, reapply, synthesize, connect, and integrate their learning over longer stretches of time.

BEYOND THE ACCOUNTABILITY FIXATION

The national pressure on institutions to demonstrate their students' learning to external stakeholders has conditioned most institutions to focus on reporting student achievement through numbers, percentages, national benchmarks, percentiles, and pass rates. That most educators probe more deeply into why students achieve or do not achieve in relation to pedagogy and educational practices is not currently a typical way of responding to assessment data. As Mach (2010) states, "We do not know the role of our curriculum or pedagogies in the failure or disappearance of our students" (p. 60). National pressures to produce scores translate into institutional pressures on educators "to get results" for external reporting purposes. That purpose usually slows down or cuts off further collaborative opportunities to learn more about and discuss the variables that account for students' different levels of performance or achievement. Without those kinds

of discussions, minimal attention is probably given to how variables such as students' different cognitive or conceptual levels, types of misunderstanding, and diverse ways of learning may be better addressed in the curriculum and complementary co-curricular programs and services.

Not surprisingly, one of the National Institute for Learning Outcomes Assessment's (NILOA) earliest reports on assessment practices at colleges (based on an 80% response from 2,800 campuses consisting of 2- and 4-year public, private, and for-profit colleges) flagged campuses' limited use of the data they collect to improve teaching and learning. The survey findings also highlight that the most common response to questions about how institutions use information about student learning was "to fulfill accreditation requirements." Encouraging campuses to use data to make improvements, Ikenberry cautions that "learning-outcome assessments can be an end in themselves" when they are used to fulfill accreditation requirements

("Many Colleges Assess Learning," 2009).). In the institute's final report, Kuh and Ikenberry (2009) precede the list of recommendations to improve assessment in higher education with the following challenge to colleges and universities:

> While considerable assessment activity is underway on college and university campuses, American higher education is far from where it needs to be in assessing student learning and in using the results to improve outcomes. Using assessment merely to check a box in an accreditation report will not in itself improve access, affordability, or accomplishment in American higher education. Overall, our findings suggest that the productive use of learning outcomes assessment information by campuses and programs to inform decisions and to improve teaching and learning remains the most important unattended challenge in this effort. (p. 28)

Often, however, the evidence and data do not lead educators to spend much time discussing patterns of student performance and the reasons behind those patterns that, in turn, lead to a focus on refining or developing new pedagogies and educational practices. For example, when faculty state that their major criterion for achievement is that 75% of graduating students in a major achieve a satisfactory or better score and that is what they find, then further discussion about pedagogy drops off. Who were the students who performed well and why? Who were the students who did not perform well and why? Delving into *how* students learn as well as *what* they learn extends the parameters of assessment to include a focus on exploring the ways in which students do or do not learn. Moving assessment beyond its current fixated accountability role into an investigative role, this chapter presents a scholarly problem-based framework for diving deeper into pedagogy and educational practices through raising and pursuing research or study questions at either the beginning or the end of the assessment process after educators have identified patterns of weakness in student performance.

A PROBLEM-BASED APPROACH TO ASSESSING STUDENT LEARNING

The following four case studies, further referenced in the problem-based framework on pages 138–141, illustrate how deeper inquiry into patterns of student learning and behaviors lead to new practices. Each case describes the context of a problem educators faced, the driving question they aimed to answer, and the ways in which they addressed those questions to improve student achievement.

Case 1: Making the Invisible Visible in Physics

Context of the Problem: To assess physics students' entering knowledge state of mathematics and physics concepts, as well as to continue to monitor students' future knowledge and understanding of these concepts, physics faculty often use concept inventories, tests designed to identify and classify errors in students' thinking. Typically, results of these concept inventories for matriculating students have documented that entering students do not have a coherent understanding of physics and mathematical concepts. According to Halloun and Hestenes (1985), students bring with them erroneous kinds of ideas about physics concepts such as force, weight, or buoyancy that interfere with their ability to correctly learn physics content. Specifically, students form their own "personal understanding "or "initial knowledge state" (p. 1043) that inhibits them from developing more complex knowledge as they move into subsequent courses. Initially, they carry qualitative, commonsense beliefs that form their own personal system of beliefs and intuitions. In turn, this system functions for them as a commonsense theory of the physical world through which they continue to interpret their past and new experiences. This belief system affects students' future performance in physics, often interfering with what students hear in a physics course and then deterring them from making progress in their future courses despite faculty efforts to position them to restructure their personal learning. Concept inventories predictably show the kinds of misconceptions and understanding that entering first-year students demonstrate. Historically, lectures, demonstrations, laboratories, exercises, and models have been ineffective in restructuring entering physics students' initial knowledge states and belief systems. For example, when presented with different scenarios that can be explained by the same underlying concept, students often apply different conceptual explanations, including some that have been proven historically incorrect.

What's the Driving Question? Recognizing that conventional teaching methods, laboratories, lectures, and demonstrations, for example, were not typically successful in correcting students' conceptual misunderstandings, Carl Wieman and his colleagues from the physics department at the University of Colorado asked: "How can we effectively restructure entering students' naïve understanding?" (April, 2008 and October, 2008).With initial support from the National Science Foundation (NSF), Wieman and his team turned to research on learning, specifically *How the Mind Works* (Bransford, 1999) and conducted student "think alouds" (see pages 177–178 in chapter 5) to learn more about the kinds of obstacles that impeded student learning, such as the inability to "see" what experts know. Wieman also recalled how consistently his diverse public lecture audiences learned the physics in his talks through the simulations he incorporated. He recalls:

> . . . [S]ims would be the primary thing people would remember from my talk, and based on their questions and comments, it appeared that they consistently learned the physics represented in the sims. What was particularly remarkable was that my audiences found the sims engaging and educationally productive whether the talk was a physics department collo-

quium, or a presentation to a middle school class. I had never seen an educational medium able to effectively address such a wide range of backgrounds, and so when I received support through the NSF Distinguished Teaching Scholars program in 2001, I used it to start the PhET project to systematically develop and research interactive sims for teaching physics. (personal communication, August 22, 2009)

What's the Solution? Drawing on these sources and his experiences with audiences in his talks, Wieman and his team designed initial sets of interactive computer simulations that positioned each student to engage with online scenarios as a strategy for them to learn concepts as well as restructure erroneous naïve understanding. Figure 4.1 represents an opening screen of one of many interactive computer simulations designed to promote students' learning of electricity principles and concepts under the Physics Education Technology (PhET) Project (phet.colorado.edu).

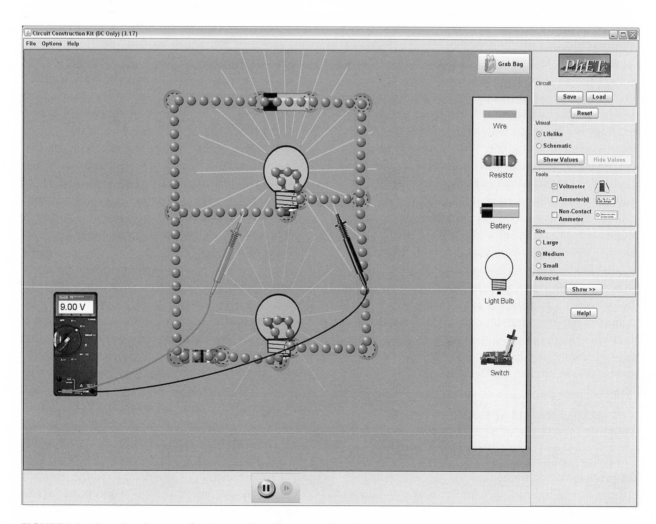

FIGURE 4.1 Opening Screen of an Interactive Computer Simulation

Interactive computer simulations, such as the one for electricity, position students to arrive at their own explanation and application of concepts, restructuring erroneous learning as well as reinforcing learning. Periodic use of concept inventories provides documentation about how well students carry their new restructured learning into future courses so that they build coherent conceptual knowledge. These inventories function as a way to diagnose students initially as well as to assess their future performance to ensure that they have corrected misconceptions or misbeliefs and are building on their restructured learning. Identifying obstacles in student learning, including students' inability to "see" what physics faculty know or understand, such as visualizing a standing wave on the string of a violin, and positioning students to become engaged in their learning through interaction with real-life phenomena and scientific concepts in real-time data sets has led to an alternative way to ground and advance students' conceptual learning in physics.

Over the years, PhET project teams have continued to design new simulations as well as update previous ones. How these remain current and effective has now become a driving force behind the ongoing testing model that involves students themselves as a way to determine the efficacy of revised or new online scenarios. As described in Box 4.1 and illustrated in Figure 4.2, a design process has now been established for each simulation that directly involves students, the learners, in the process as a way to ensure that students can interact with simulations to correctly learn concepts and principles. Additionally, this project has shaped how faculty teach, as described in Box 4.2.

BOX 4.1 Description of the Current Iterative PhET Process to Create and Evaluate the Efficacy of Online Interactive Physics Simulations to Anchor and Continue to Foster Students' Chronological Conceptual Development

The PhET development process for creating and evaluating a simulation begins with the selection of the simulation design team, consisting of three to five individuals including a professional software developer, at least one content expert (scientist), a teacher, and a student interface expert (education researcher). The design cycle starts with the content expert, teacher, and student interface expert creating specific learning goals for the simulation. These learning goals draw from the existing research literature on conceptual difficulties with the specific content and based on our and other teacher's experiences in the classroom.

A detailed initial layout for the simulation is created based on the learning goals and grade levels that are targeted. The simulation design follows the PhET Look and Feel,[1] which was originally created based on research on how students learn[2] and from our first year of simulation interviews, in which we went through many iterations of interface features until we could successfully build a simulation that engaged students in scientist-like exploration. A complete discussion is provided in the pair of papers by Adams and colleagues.[3] This PhET Look and Feel is a living document that slowly evolves based on new findings from our research on the simulations.

The next step is to show the initial layout to the developer to discuss feasibility, refine the interface, and acquire a cost-benefit analysis. Adjustments are made and the first version of the simulation is coded. The team members communicate regularly to make any needed adjustments as the simulation takes shape. The simulation can be posted to our website and is labeled as "under construction" after extensive use by the team members and all members feel it's clear, accurate, and engaging. Student interviews are conducted at this stage with students who have the same background and academic preparation as the target audience for the simulation. These interviews reveal interface weaknesses, resolve interface questions that were not agreed upon by the team, and often reveal pedagogically undesirable (and occasionally unexpected desirable) features and subtle programming bugs. Subsequent revisions are made, and if they are extensive, further interviews are conducted with a new set of students. More recent interview results are finding much smaller problems than the interviews conducted on

(continued)

BOX 4.1 *(continued)*

simulations that were written five years ago, indicating that our empirically developed design principles are working. After interviews establish that the desired engagement and learning is being achieved, the simulation is no longer marked as "under construction" on the website.

Each simulation is also used in the classroom by the teacher on the design team and often other teachers as well. Feedback from the teacher and any other observers is then used to identify possible issues that did not surface from the interviews, such as features that allow unproductive playing. Once a simulation is used in a classroom setting, where student use is observed and informally evaluated successfully, the simulation is considered complete and receives the "checkmark" label on the website. However, a simulation that has reached this stage is not set in stone forever.

Two to four times a year we engage in more formal, rigorous studies of simulations in the classroom or through a series of interviews.[4] These studies often reveal subtle changes that can improve student understanding of the concepts. In addition, we occasionally receive requests from users for new features or identification of subtle bugs that were missed during the preceding stages. Bugs are fixed and feature requests are logged and considered if the simulation is revisited.

Notes

1. *PhET Look and Feel.* http://phet.colorado.edu/phet-dist/publications/PhET Look and Feel.pdf
2. Bransford, J., Brown, A., & Cocking, R. (Eds.). (2004). *How people learn: Brain, mind, experience, and school.* Washington, DC: National Academies Press.
3. Adams, W. K., Reid, S., LeMaster, R., McKagan, S. B., Perkins, K. K., & Wieman, C. E. (2008). A study of educational simulations: Part I—engagement and learning. *Journal of Interactive Learning Research, 19*(3), 397–419.
4. Adams, W. K., Reid, S., LeMaster, R., McKagan, S. B., Perkins, K. K., & Wieman, C. E. (2008). A study of educational simulations: Part II—interface design. *Journal of Interactive Learning Research, 19*(4), 551–577.
5. *PhET: Interactive Simulations.* http://phet.colorado.edu/research/index.php

Source: Wendy Adams, co-director of PhET and director of research for CU SEI, University of Colorado, and Carl E. Wieman, director of CWSEI, University of British Columbia; Distinguished Professor of Physics and director of CU SEI, University of Colorado.

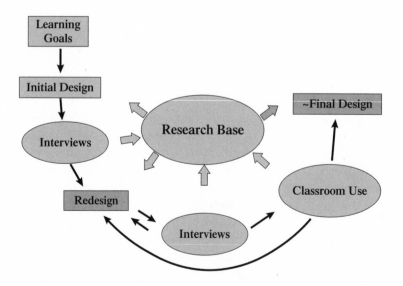

FIGURE 4.2 The PhET Design Process
Source: Wendy Adams, co-director of PhET and director of research for CU SEI, University of Colorado, and Carl E. Wieman, director of CWSEI, University of British Columbia; Distinguished Professor of Physics and director of CU SEI, University of Colorado.

BOX 4.2   How the PhET Project Has Shaped the Science Education Initiative (SEI) Model

The Science Education Initiatives (SEI) at the University of Colorado (CU) and the University of British Columbia (UBC) are a model for institutional transformation to achieve widespread sustained improvement in science education at the university level. The model is targeting change at large research universities. There are significant indications of success. After 3 years we have three large science departments at Colorado in which more than 60% of the faculty have made significant changes, adopting more effective evidence-based methods in their teaching and assessment of learning.

A basic element of the SEI model is the investment of significant onetime resources at the departmental level to achieve long-lasting improvement in the effectiveness of teaching while making it more rewarding and less time-consuming for faculty.

Funding (US$1 million at CU, Cn$1.3–2 million at UBC, to be spent over 6 years) is distributed to departments on the basis of competitive proposals. The heart of the SEI work is a course-by-course transformation effort driven by research on teaching and learning, learning goals, and rigorous assessment. Successful proposals lay out a process for establishing the SEI "holy trinity" for all undergraduate courses regularly offered by the department: (1) What should students learn? (establishing the desired learning goals or outcomes); (2) what are they learning? (identifying good assessment of the learning); and (3) how can teaching be changed to improve student learning? (implementing and testing research-based best practices). The proposal must also lay out a system by which the information learned and the improved materials and assessment for each course are to be disseminated and reused.

Departments have flexibility in how they spend the money, but all have used the funds primarily to hire "science education specialists" (SESs), a rather novel position that has worked well to both support the introduction of new educational practices and assessment and help educate faculty. The SESs work collaboratively with faculty members to implement the SEI trinity. To be an SES requires mastery of the discipline, knowledge of educational research and proven effective teaching methods, and diplomatic skills. SESs typically come with the first and third qualifications as new Ph.D.s in the science discipline, but with a strong interest in education. They then receive on-the-job training from central SEI staff to master the second.

We are learning a great deal about barriers and drivers of change in science education at research universities, but preliminary indications are encouraging.

Source: Wendy Adams, co-director of PhET and director of research for CU SEI, University of Colorado, and Carl E. Wieman, director of CWSEI, University of British Columbia, Distinguished Professor of Physics, and director of CU SEI, University of Colorado.

Case 2: Shifting to a New Paradigm

Context of the Problem: In the engineering program at Northwestern University, one of the universities participating in the VaNTH (Vanderbilt-Northwestern-Texas-Harvard/MIT) Engineering Research Centers' learning projects (see pages 37–38 in chapter 1), faculty continued to find that students were unable to transfer writing principles fostered in required writing courses to writing assignments in engineering courses. Originally, students were required to take a standalone course in writing offered by communication experts outside the program. A curricular development

in succeeding years required students to take writing-intensive courses in the university's writing-across-the-curriculum program. Yet, despite these requirements, faculty continually documented that students were unable to transfer writing principles in these courses to the kinds of required writing in engineering courses.

What's the Driving Question? Recognizing this chronologically consistent pattern, faculty asked: "How, then, can we effectively develop students' writing abilities?" Reading about how students learn to write, they were struck by Turner and Thomas's (1996) claim that writing skills are most successfully taught when they are integrated with genuine (rather than contrived) activities that build on past learning, create a real need for the new skills, and offer an opportunity to learn those skills. "Intellectual activities," Turner and Thomas claim, "lead to skills, but skills do not generate intellectual activities" (p. 4).

What's the Solution? Coming to terms with this claim led faculty to shift to a new paradigm—one that integrated writing and other modes of communication important for students to develop over time, such as visual and oral communication, into students' first engineering course, Engineering Design and Communication (EDC). Inviting communication faculty to work with them, engineering faculty designed students' first EDC course to integrate writing, speaking, and visual communication into engineering content. Seeing the positive results of students' writing in their first course—that students grounded their writing in what they were learning and that writing itself strengthened and clarified students' professional thinking, such as in explaining an engineering process or concept design to a real client—prompted faculty to integrate writing in all other engineering courses leading to the capstone project. That is, faculty found that intellectual immersion in a discipline or field of study not only fosters disciplinary knowledge and ways of thinking and knowing, but also necessary communication skills. Reflecting on this new model, the Northwestern University report concludes:

> Students in EDC—and faculty too—see that communication in engineering is a multifaceted activity. Engineering communication combines written, oral, interpersonal, graphical, and mathematical communication. Like engineers in industry, students in EDC talk, write, and sketch to share ideas, and they use new communication technologies and tools, such as Visio and SolidWorks, as part of the communication enterprise. This approach to communication is vastly different from students' experience in stand-alone writing courses or the writing intensive courses that came out of WAC. It is a new, integrated paradigm for communication instruction. (Hirsch, Kelso, Shwom, Troy, & Walsh, 2001)

This case was developed based on Hirsch, Kelso, Shwom, Troy, and Walsh (2001).

Case 3: Changing Multiple Practices

Context of the Problem: To assess students' exit writing abilities at a community college, faculty agreed to embed a common writing prompt into their second-year courses; identified cohorts of their student body; developed a scoring rubric that focused on four criteria (purpose and audience, organization, development, and language); used four proficiency levels (superior, proficient, essential, in progress) as their standards of judgment; and assembled the following kinds of institutional data about their students to see what bearing any of these data might have on student performance:

- Accuplacer scores in reading and writing
- Number of college credits completed
- Program affiliation
- Grades in courses related to the assessment outcome
- GPA
- History of enrollment in a Learning Community or First Year Experience class
- Student survey results that requested students identify other courses they had taken that required them to write

Analysis of students' persuasive writing at the end of their two years, based on embedding a common writing assignment in students' final courses, showed the following results:

- Thirty percent of the second-year students were writing at the proficient level (holistic score of 3 or higher represented in a graph).
- The median and mode holistic score (2.5) and the mean holistic score (2.34) were not quite at the proficient level, so the distribution curve lumped to the left of center.
- Students were closer to proficiency in the skills relating to *purpose and audience* and *organization* than they were in skills relating to *development* (support of ideas with evidence, examples, elaboration of topics) and *language* (effective use of sentence structures, word choices, and mechanics of standard written English).

Drilling deeper into the institutional data that faculty requested, as well as into students' performance levels, faculty identified the following patterns:

- Developmental students consistently scored below all other students; however, developmental students enrolled in learning communities performed higher under all criteria than developmental students who did not enroll in a learning community.

- Students enrolled in learning communities overall scored at or above the proficient level.
- Developmental students who did not immediately take English 101 after their developmental writing course represented another cohort of students who scored below the proficient level.
- Students who reported having written essays in classes other than English 006 and 101 demonstrated greater levels of writing skill and were more likely to have reached the proficient level.
- Scores indicated steady increases in students' writing at the proficient level in three sequential categories of writing-intensive courses: English 006, English 101, and writing beyond English 101. However, across these three stages, a significant number of sampled students continued to write below the essential level.

What's the Driving Question? Based on the patterns faculty saw, faculty raised the following question: How can we improve students' writing and aim to increase the percentage of students writing proficiently by one third from 30% to 40% over the next academic year using the same common writing assignment to assess progress toward this goal?

What's the Solution? Final review of the results of students' writing and related relevant data, such as course-taking patterns, led faculty to propose a four-pronged approach for some immediate changes as well as some longer-term changes in educational practice:

- *Advising:* Because students had not consistently taken writing courses in sequence—that is, the college's policy had not been enforced—academic advisers, counselors, and support staff needed to be reminded to follow the college's policy, which stated that English 099 students should immediately complete English 101 and that all other students should complete English 101 within their first 15 credits.
- *Professional Development:* Because students who reported having written essays in classes other than English 006 and 101 demonstrated greater levels of writing skills and were more likely to have reached the proficient level, faculty recommended that the

college should offer professional development for faculty in the disciplines to develop writing-intensive courses with assigned tutors to provide supplemental instruction in writing.

- *Expansion of Learning Communities:* Because students enrolled in learning communities, including developmental students, scored higher in all categories of their writing, the college should continue to develop learning communities that pair writing courses with introductory courses in the disciplines.
- *Benchmarks for Writing Courses:* Because scores indicated steady increases in students' writing at the proficient level in three sequential categories of writing-intensive courses (English 006, English 101, and writing beyond English 101) the college should establish milestones for student performance in English 006 and English 101 to increase the percentage of students writing at or above the essential level building on this year's baselines.

Case 4: Changing Pedagogy to Address Levels of and Obstacles to Learning

Context of the Problem: In their assessment of students' learning in basic mathematics courses, mathematics professors at a community college became concerned that typically only one-third of students taking periodic exams could perform all or most of the mathematics problems. After exams, faculty would review terms, concepts, principles, and strategies with students; go over assignments; identify problem sets students were having difficulties with; and do repeat exercises with the class. As much as faculty would review material, repeat practice examples, and even recommend that students take advantage of the support center, predictably, two-thirds of the students simply could not demonstrate that they could perform basic mathematics. As faculty reviewed test scores more closely, they discovered the following performance patterns: About one-third of the students did not even attempt to solve most problems; another third tried to solve the problems but made some kind of mistake in one of the subtasks of the problems; and the final third could solve most of the problems perfectly.

What's the Driving Question? What barriers were preventing students from successfully solving mathematical problem sets? Armed with students' results—one form of evidence about students' achievement levels—faculty turned toward students themselves to learn more about why two-thirds of their students consistently underperformed. Faculty agreed to ask students the following kinds of questions to probe more deeply into explanations for students' behaviors on the tests:

- Listing mathematical terms from the recently administered test, faculty asked students to self-identify whether they could define these terms. A handful of students who could indeed define the terms raised their hands; these students had received a B or better.
- Drawing on mathematical problems in the test, faculty asked students: What are these problems asking you to do? A handful of students answered for each kind of problem; these students had received a B or better.
- Following up on the previous question, faculty asked for more detailed responses about each set of problems: How do you actually perform the process for this kind of problem? An even smaller handful of students answered; these students had received a high B or an A.

Going back to students' test results and reviewing responses to the preceding sample questions, faculty identified three levels of learners in the mathematics courses:

1. Those who were still unable to comprehend mathematics terminology and thus were spending test time struggling to figure out what terms meant
2. Those who comprehended the terminology, had developed conceptual understanding, and understood how to solve representative problems, but missed a step in the problem-solving process
3. Those who comprehended terminology, had developed conceptual understanding, understood how to solve problems, and accurately performed the problem-solving process

What's the Solution? Recognizing that students in mathematics courses were at different learning levels, faculty decided to break from their traditional approach of lecturing and repeatedly going over exercises and past exams as a daily practice. Instead, to address students' learning levels in the courses, mathematics faculty decided to develop differentiated teaching ap-

proaches in their courses. After introducing new terms, processes, and practice exercises, they now spend most of their class time moving among the three groups to advance each learning group's ability and at the same time address challenges. For one-third of students, that means initially helping them comprehend and understand terms and operations; for another third, that means helping students identify missed steps in operations and recognize why they missed those steps; and for the final third, that means providing more complex problems for them to solve to extend their learning.

What drives these case studies is initial identification of a problem leading to an open-ended question that educators are invested in answering. The pages that follow describe how a problem-based approach to assessment, as demonstrated in these case studies, is established and carried out.

THE SEEDS OF A PROBLEM-BASED APPROACH TO ASSESSMENT

As the previous cases illustrate, a problem-based approach to assessment positions educators to deepen inquiry into the complexities or layers of the teaching and learning processes. This inquiry leads to new understanding of the reasons that underlie performance patterns of successful and not-as-successful students. In turn, new understanding leads to discussion about and reflection on how alternative pedagogies or modes of delivery and other educational practices can more effectively address patterns of weakness in student achievement. Within the context of a problem-based approach to assessment, educators become problem identifiers, then problem solvers, committed to solving the questions they raise about the efficacy of existing educational practices and about the ways in which students learn—best represented in the words of Laurillard (1993):

> It is always possible to defend the inspirational lecturer, the importance of academic individuality, the value of pressuring students to work independently, but we cannot defend a mode of operation that actively undermines a professional approach to teaching. Teachers need to know more than just their subject. They need to know the ways it can come to be understood, the ways it can be misunderstood, what counts as understanding; they need to know how individuals experience the subject. But they are neither required nor enabled to know these things. (p. 6)

Between teaching and students' demonstration of learning are the various ways in which students make meaning or fail to make meaning, as the physics case demonstrates. Rarely do two students learn precisely the same way or at the same time. Individuals' learning strategies, learning histories, cognitive and conceptual levels of development, life experiences, mindsets, and reliance on individualized life experiences are some of the variables that condition what students bring to a learning context. One or more of these variables promotes or inhibits learning. Often students' ways of problem solving are based on incorrect constructs drawn from highly personalized experiences, misunderstandings, or misconceptions that block them from making progress in their studies. As the physics illustration demonstrates, entering physics students rely on their "commonsense" interpretation of the world that accounts for the misconceptions they carry around with them and carry along with them in their physics studies. Frustrations in learning often occur when students persistently use an incorrect strategy repeatedly without opening themselves to or being exposed to alternative strategies.

Deepened knowledge about students' patterns of performance and their ways of making meaning enables educators to monitor students' chronological learning and effect changes in educational practices. Typical kinds of patterns may include the following: incorrect assumptions, misunderstandings, misconceptions (such as those identified in the physics case study on pages 125–126), missing steps in a process or approach, overgeneralizations, miscalculations, faulty search strategies or reasoning, incorrect performance of operations, or weaknesses in conventions of writing.

Developing a taxonomy or classification of student weaknesses or errors becomes a useful assessment practice. As illustrated in Figure 4.3, a taxonomy of student weaknesses, errors, or fuzzy thinking helps focus and direct discussions among educators about how they will improve student performance and in what areas. In addition, a taxonomy specifically documents what educators will closely assess once they have implemented changes to improve those patterns of weakness.

Conversations across institutions are often peppered with educators' frustration about students' abilities, such as, "When students come into my course, even after they have taken the writing 101–102 sequence, they can't write well," or, " Students should know the concepts I build on in my upper-level courses when they enter my classroom; I should not have to teach them what they should already know,"

Types of Weaknesses, Errors, or Fuzzy Thinking	Identify Context of Weaknesses, Errors, or Fuzzy Thinking	Identify Possible Causes With the Assistance of Students
1. For example, *conceptual, mathematical, analytical, computational, grammatical, fuzzy recall, procedural, linguistic, pattern discernment, interpretive reasoning, inability to apply to new or unfamiliar contexts, etc.*		
2.		
3.		
4.		

FIGURE 4.3 Taxonomy of Student Weaknesses, Errors, or Fuzzy Thinking

or, "They can't recall, let alone apply, concepts or principles they are supposed to have learned in their lower-level courses." The senior reference librarian at Princeton University Library frets about her decades of experience with students conducting research for assignments, stating that "most students simply do not retain the concepts and logic involved in discovering information sources—never mind the principles for evaluating the sources they do turn up." She questions whether there is a disconnect between faculty pedagogical intent and students' actual research behaviors and wonders what professors think students are doing to come up with the resources they need for their research paper. Among the most troubling annual student confessions she hears is students' confusion about the difference between primary and secondary resources (George, 2009).

Across these kinds of institutional examples are the collective seeds of inquiry that can lead to advancing assessment from a "counting" activity—how many students passed, how many achieved a norm—to a problem-based exploration of students' learning products and processes that leads to innovations or changes in educational practices. The anchor for this problem-based exploration of student achievement rests in educators' ability, as Bass (1999) declares in the opening quotation of this chapter, to identify problems in the teaching-learning process and then resolve to address those problems. Among the range of learning problems educators often identify are their students' inabilities to do the following:

- Transition from practicing mathematical formulas to applying those formulas to solve word problems
- Apply quantitative reasoning skills in contexts outside quantitatively focused courses
- Transfer previous learning in prerequisite or required courses to higher-level courses in a program of study
- Advance beyond recall and recognition to higher levels of cognition in sequences of courses
- Develop coherent conceptual understanding
- Synthesize rather than summarize

A SCHOLARLY PROBLEM-BASED APPROACH TO ASSESSMENT

To make informed decisions about the efficacy of pedagogy and educational practices, we need to reposition how we approach the assessment process. Disconnects, disjunctures, gaps in learning, misunderstanding, misconceptions, and miscalculations; inabilities to extend or apply learning of a process, procedure, concept, theory, or principles to a new context; partial or incomplete understanding; studying, reading, and note-taking strategies; long-held beliefs based on individuals' life experiences; and overgeneralizations or oversimplifications—identifying these kinds of learning issues establishes the problem-based context within which educators collaboratively agree on a research or study question. Educators pursue these kinds of questions either at the outset of a chronologically focused assessment process—one that seeks evidence of student learning along the continuum of students' learning—or at the end of the process, when patterns of student performance lead to "why" or "how" questions, such as the physics case, the engineering case, and the basic mathematics case illustrate.

Because institutions may not have the resources to launch and sustain formal empirical studies, collaboratively based action research, similar to the action research that faculty conduct in individual classes, can become an alternative scholarly practice that aims to answer questions about the teaching-learning process, such as the efficacy of certain educational practices in promoting enduring learning. Action research is "not about learning why we do certain things, but rather how we can do things better. It is about how we can change our instruction to impact students" (Ferrance, 2000, p. 3). Either an informal or formal process of investigation, this problem-based scholarly approach to assessment folds in and pursues research or study questions about students' learning processes and products to discover patterns of thinking, behaving, problem solving, meaning making, or misunderstandings or gaps in learning that prohibit students from progressing. This approach takes assessment beyond an accountability role of documenting how many or what percentage of students reached a certain performance level to an investigative role. Investigation leads to raising questions about how and why students learn or are unable to learn within the context of curricular content, delivery options, pedagogical and instructional approaches, and complementary educational opportunities offered by those in student affairs, student services, and library and information resources.

Fulfilling Robert Diamond's (2002) scholarly research principles, a problem-based approach to assessment does the following:

a. Requires a high level of expertise and is pursued with adequate preparation

b. Is conducted in a scholarly manner with clear goals

c. Uses methodology appropriate to the research questions

d. Answers significant questions

e. Clearly communicates the research methodology and findings

f. Is innovative

g. Can be replicated or elaborated on (pp. 73–80)

The problem-based assessment framework represented in Figure 4.4 requires that experts and educators (1) raise significant open-ended questions about learning within the context of their fields and within current related literature (a, b); (2) identify the kinds of evidence and data they will use to answer the significant question they have raised (c, d); (3) disseminate the results of their research (e); and (4) replicate the problem-based assessment process to ascertain how proposed changes or innovations improve student learning (f, g).

COLLABORATIVE TASKS IN A PROBLEM-BASED ASSESSMENT FRAMEWORK

1. Create an Inquiry Group, Team, or Community of Practice

Developing inquiry groups, teams, or communities of practice, consisting of individuals invested in answering

FIGURE 4.4 A Problem-based Assessment Framework

a question—faculty, student affairs professionals, library and information resource professionals, learning support professionals, and students themselves—is key to firing up the tasks described in Figure 4.4. This framework identifies the nine tasks in a problem-based assessment process that engage inquiry teams to seek evidence of student learning and learning processes at chronologically identified times along the continuum of students' learning. A highly collaborative investigative process, problem-based assessment brings individuals together to raise and pursue answers to research or study questions. Educators should be invested in answering these questions within the context of current educational practices. Moreover, they should be open to change based on the results of their inquiry.

An observation or generalization about student learning often becomes the lightning rod drawing others into further discussion that leads to a research or study question. An observation may arise in one department, program, or service, such as the library, yet create an opportunity to connect with other professionals at the institution. For example, the observation the head reference librarian made on page 134 about students' inability to apply research skills would involve initial communication with faculty in a department or departments, professionals in learning support centers, and students to learn more about what and how they are or are not learning. Connecting individuals across these constituencies could become the basis of an inquiry group or community of practice.

This inquiry group could develop a plan to investigate why students cannot develop sustainable research skills in relation to existing pedagogy and educational practices. It may decide to investigate why students seem to practice these skills when they first learn them but chronologically decline in their ability to practice them. Librarians' assessment of students' chronological abilities and learning processes could be brought together with faculty assessment of students' chronological abilities and processes, demonstrated in assigned projects and interviews with students about their research behaviors. For example, if a team's inquiry into pedagogy and curricular design reveals that there is inconsistent attention to developing students' research abilities or that faculty think students are learning research skills in other courses when, in fact, they are not, then these findings can prompt discussion about new approaches to developing students' research abilities. If students continue to be confused about the differences between primary and secondary resources, then that piece of knowledge

should also figure into discussions about how to anchor and sustain students' abilities to research and interpret different kinds of resources. Integrating different levels and kinds of research into all courses in students' majors—with the assistance of librarians—could represent a shift in current practices that would necessitate both course content changes and instructional changes to chronologically improve students' lingering patterns of weakness.

2. Identify Learning Outcome Statement(s) You Will Assess

Selecting one or more department-, program-, or institution-level outcomes represents the focus of Task 2. For example, writing faculty may want to track how well students apply the principles and conventions of writing taught in first-year required writing courses to subsequent courses, including capstone projects. A biology department may want to track how well students develop more complex problem-solving abilities as they transition from lower-level courses to upper-level courses. Or, graduate school faculty in chemistry may want to track students' chronological abilities to document and write about their research for representative disciplinary or interdisciplinary publications—a focus that requires assessing multiple learning outcomes, such as scientific habits of mind, ways of thinking and knowing, and students' abilities to represent the results of research according to conventions of the discipline and a specific publication.

3. Couple Outcomes With an Open-Ended Research or Study Question

Having agreed on one or more department-, program-, or institution-level outcomes to assess, in Task 3 representatives from one of these levels then identify a problem they wish to solve in the assessment process or a problem that has arisen from previous repeated assessments of student learning, such as students' inability to transfer conceptual learning into upper-level coursework. They then convert these problems into open-ended research or study questions. These questions should be "higher-order questions," as opposed to yes/no questions, an essential criterion of the action research model of the Brown Alliance (Ferrance, 2000, p. 10). That is, they should be questions that educators do not already have answers to but are curious to answer.

Where do these problems turned into research or study questions originate? They may be drawn from the stockpile of observations, complaints, or laments that faculty and other educators raise in informal contexts at lunch, around the water cooler, or at the end of an exhausting semester. One of those laments may be: "Few students can apply early coursework in the discipline to upper-level courses." Converting that statement into a research or study question may result in the following questions: "Typically, why are so many students unable to apply early coursework in the discipline to upper-level courses?" "Why do students struggle with analysis of higher-level complex problems in our discipline?" "What kinds of strategies are students using to read historical texts, and how do these strategies either promote or inhibit their ability to interpret historical texts?" "What assumptions are we making about our current pedagogies or about how students are learning that may be impeding students' abilities to develop conceptual understanding?" "What problems or obstacles underlie the patterns of weakness that show up in students' work?" "When, how early, or how persistently do these patterns emerge in student work?" Representative kinds of learning-based or pedagogically based research questions are listed in Appendix 4.1—questions that can prime collaborative development of a research or study question.

Asking the question, "Typically, why are so many students unable to apply early coursework in the discipline to upper-level courses?" could well prompt initial discussion between upper- and lower-level course faculty about what students are required to learn in lower-level courses; how well students demonstrate that learning; and where else they continue to build on that learning before they enter upper-level courses. It could be that lower-level courses' focus on knowledge building under the pressure to "cover" content provides minimum time for students to demonstrate more than recall and recognition. Or, it could be that the primary means of assessment in lower-level courses has typically valued recall and recognition of vocabulary, terms, concepts, and principles, with minimum value placed on requiring students to explain, apply, or use memorized learning. Predictably, then, students' memory of terminology wanes quickly unless there are chronological opportunities to move students toward applying or using early-learned terminology. Under this scenario, if upper-level courses expect students not only to recall but also to apply previous learning, the likelihood of

that is chronologically slim. Further, cognitive psychologists would say, students typically learn new material concretely—based on the example or examples from which they learned (Willingham, 2002). Unless students have multiple other opportunities to practice and apply that learning in other contexts, they remain tethered to that initial example and struggle with extending or applying that learning to other contexts. An illustration of this difficulty is often apparent when students are asked to shift from performing exercises or drills, such as calculations, to solving word problems or case studies that require students to extend that initial learning into a new context.

4. Identify Others Invested in Answering the Question

Having raised a research or study question, a team then identifies the mix of other individuals who may be invested in answering the question or are willing to contribute evidence and sources of data to answer that question. Those individuals may include the following people:

- Faculty invested in answering the question
- Other educators in student affairs and student services, such as learning support centers, who have knowledge about how students learn, maintain data about student learning, or undertake studies to learn about students' learning
- Teaching assistants or graduate assistants, who teach or work directly with students in discussion groups or laboratories, for example, and witness students' successful and unsuccessful learning strategies
- External contributors to student learning such as internship advisors or community-service coordinators, who also witness students' abilities
- Students themselves, who provide not only evidence of their learning through the work they produce, but also useful firsthand accounts of the successful or unsuccessful strategies or processes they use to learn and the kinds of challenges or obstacles they face as learners
- Institutional research professionals, who often have a storehouse of student data

Developing a mix of invested people leads to a more robust analysis of students' learning and moves assessment findings beyond a report on the percentage of students who "passed" to a report that elaborates on the results of digging into multiple sources of evidence.

5. Read Relevant Current Educational Literature or Research

Before actually designing the assessment process, team members in Task 5 identify and read relevant current educational literature or research on learning or the science of learning (as documented in the physics case study on page 126) related to the agreed-upon research or study question. This task positions teams to become knowledgeable about current work; to determine the significance of the proposed research or study question; and to add, build on, advance, or even challenge current knowledge and practices, fulfilling Diamond's scholarly principle of "innovation" in research. This task educates the team about related current literature that informs members about how others have answered a similar kind of question or have developed pedagogy or educational practices to improve student learning.

Alternatively, you may decide to localize your research based on data that already exist about your students, such as entering test scores, grade point averages, or baseline assessment data in writing, reading, quantitative reasoning, results of surveys such as the National Survey of Student Engagement or the Community College Survey of Student Engagement, or data kept by support services and advisers. Even then, what you learn may be relevant to colleagues in other institutions who have, for example, the same kind of demographic spread as your institution has. Kuh (2008) is one kind of source that may prove useful for a team to read, providing a basis for thinking about ways to develop alternative teaching and learning strategies to address a collaboratively agreed-upon set of outcomes. Bransford, Brown, and Cocking (1999) and Pellegrino, Chudowsky, and Glaser (2001) represent excellent research-based publications that provide overviews of cognitive science that educators can draw on to inform or shape pedagogy. The *Cambridge Handbook of the Learning Sciences* provides examples of how educators are drawing on the learning sciences to improve or change pedagogy and educational practices, including with the use of technology (Sawyer, 2006).

6. Identify Relevant Sources of Student Evidence and Institutional or National Data

Central to Task 6 is identifying the kinds of student evidence and institutional or national data you will need to bring together to answer your guiding question. Shulman (2006) asserts that "the first lesson regarding an assessment is to take responsibility for locating its unavoidable insufficiencies in relation to what it claims it can measure . . . We do not seek one perfect measurement instrument, but an array of indicators that can be understood in relation to one another." Span across your institution, program, or department to identify sources of evidence or data that may be relevant to answering the question you have raised. The kinds of evidence and data you may identify include the following:

- Direct evidence of student learning: work that students produce and their learning documentation, such as results of "think alouds"; journal entries that identify how students solved a problem; online discussion boards that document the kinds of obstacles students faced in working on a project (described in chapter 5, pages 164–178)
- Indirect evidence of student learning, such as learning gains surveys, results of small group instructional diagnosis, or interviews (described in chapter 5, pages 178–179)
- Institutional, departmental, program, or national data focused on entry-level readiness, placement, or performance levels; course-taking patterns; level of participation in learning support services or programs; educational practices used, such as learning communities or problem-based approaches to learning

Student data that already exist at your institution may be useful in your final analysis and interpretation of evidence. For example, the director of a university learning center has been surveying 249 students in science, technology, engineering, mathematics, the humanities, and the social sciences about their learning practices. Among his preliminary findings are that high-achieving students across these disciplines use "active, metacognitive, and peer learning strategies" in note-taking, reading, and studying (personal communication, October 25, 2009). Identifying data that exist on campus, such as data from this survey, as shown in Box 4.3, is an early important component in this sixth task of a problem-based approach to assessment.

Local data can take on significance in the discussions that surround improving pedagogy and other educational practices. For example, learning about study or reading strategies successful students use

> **BOX 4.3**   Learning Strategies Characteristic of Successful Students
>
> Among some of the strategies successful students have identified are the following:
>
> - Writing beyond what is visually presented during a lecture
> - Identifying clues to help organize information during a lecture
> - Evaluating notes after class
> - Reorganizing notes after class
> - Monitoring the effectiveness of note-taking practices
> - Comparing note-taking methods with peers
> - Using one's own words while reading to make notes
> - Evaluating one's understanding while reading
> - Consolidating reading and lecture notes
> - Sharing practices on how to organize, think, and memorize content
> - Evaluating one's own understanding

Source: Calvin Y. Yu, director of Cook/Douglass Learning Center, Rutgers University.

may lead faculty to incorporate these strategies into introductory disciplinary courses to seed successful study habits for all students, not just high-performing ones. Identifying and incorporating learning strategies of high-achieving students, such as their note-taking habits or their ways of developing mental models, into the content of typically challenging courses may help less successful students adopt or adapt new approaches to studying difficult content. Identifying learning strategies of low-achieving students may also help educators develop strategies to help those students overcome typical obstacles they face, such as consistently highlighting everything they read as opposed to learning to become more selective and strategic in their reading habits.

7. Design an Assessment Plan

Agreeing on the assessment plan design and the timetable of subtasks in that plan takes place in Task 7. Those subtasks include the following:

- Identifying baseline data or evidence that you will use to assess students' achievement over time, such as a first-year writing sample, a first-year response to a case study, or a taxonomy of student weaknesses, errors, or fuzzy thinking that will assist in gauging the efficacy of changed educational practices.
- Identifying cohorts of students you will track over time based on the demographics of your institution or program or based on the use of different modes of delivery or pedagogies.

Addressing this second sub-task requires comparing student performance across different kinds of pedagogy and sections of courses, defining a control group to compare cohorts studying under different kinds of learning environments (online versus face-to-face, for example), as well as creating opportunities to interview and learn directly from students themselves about how and what they have learned. (See more about including students in the assessment process on pages 20–21 and 25–26 in chapter 1 and page 161 in chapter 5.)

- Identifying the direct and indirect assessment methods you will use to answer the agreed-upon research or study question, discussed in chapter 5.
- Identifying the criteria and standards of judgment you will use to assess students' chronological performance, discussed in chapter 6.
- Identifying department, program, institution, or national data that you believe will be helpful in answering the question you have raised.
- Determining who is responsible for collecting and analyzing student work.
- Determining who is responsible for collecting relevant institution, national, program, or department student data.
- Identifying a time or times to triangulate results of assessed student work and relevant data to promote informed discussion about and reflections on results that lead to implementing changed practices, such as alternative

ways of teaching and learning, use of different pedagogies or instructional styles, or use of different modes of delivery.

8. Develop a Time Line to Implement and Reassess Agreed-Upon Changes

Task 8 involves developing a time line (1) to implement agreed-upon changed practices and (2) to assess how these changes are affecting students' achievement. Previously collected data and evidence of student work serve as benchmarks for determining the efficacy of new practices. Continuing to draw on direct and indirect evidence and relevant data within the context of new educational practices will document the efficacy of new practices.

9. Disseminate Findings and Resulting Changes Within and Outside the Institution

The final task, Task 9, in this problem-based assessment process involves disseminating the results of inquiry. Initially these results should be disseminated across the institution through symposia; through centers for teaching, learning, and assessment; through local publications; and through the institution's assessment website. To inform institutional decision making, planning, and allocation of resources and even faculty development programs, these results should also be channeled into decision-making bodies and to decision-making leaders so that efficacious new practices can be integrated more widely across a department, a program, or the institution itself. (See also pages 23–24 in chapter 1.)

Disseminating information beyond a program, a department, or the institution is a principle of scholarly practice that contributes knowledge about the efficacy of educational practices to a range of professional communities in higher education. As lifelong learners, professionals continue to learn about developments in their fields or disciplines and immerse themselves in the debates that arise about research findings, new strategies, or new methods—particularly in light of developments in technology. Engaging in a problem-based assessment process provides a rich professional opportunity to (1) engage in lifelong learning about teaching and learning and (2) contribute to national and international dialogue about how students learn. Specifically, through publications, presentations, and workshops, the PhET Project, for example, has contributed and is contributing exten-

sively to national and international dialogue on teaching physics and other sciences. It serves as a model, then, for how institutions or programs can contribute to and improve teaching and learning.

Publishing; presenting at regional, professional, or national conferences; or sharing results of inquiry into students' learning through the current technologies becomes the wider professional context for our assessment work. Iiyoshi and Kumar (2008) make a compelling call to educators to take advantage of new knowledge-sharing tools to make their "own learning visible, enhancing the collective understanding of how best to use these same tools in the classroom" (p. 2). See also "The Scholarship of Teaching and Learning" in chapter 1. In 2009, a nonprofit think tank, the Committee for Economic Development, also continued the call for more openness in the sharing of information about teaching and learning across higher-education institutions—particularly research on the effectiveness of digital education ("Think Tank Stresses Importance of Information Sharing"). The efficiencies of the digital age now provide educators with opportunities to contribute to and advance knowledge about the efficacies of educational practices documented through assessment.

FLEXIBLE APPROACHES TO THE PROBLEM-BASED ASSESSMENT PROCESS

The framework represented in Figure 4.4 illustrates a chronological approach to assessment—a robust and useful approach to diving deeply into student learning that provides ongoing learning results that can be periodically shared across a department or program. A chronological approach to assessment also builds in opportunity to learn more from current students about their learning processes, usually a powerful source of evidence, as the mathematics case study shows on pages 131–132 in this chapter. Chronologically designed assessment provides documentation of levels or kinds of misunderstanding or inabilities that, left unaddressed, continue to impede students' progression. As the context of the physics case study reveals in this chapter on pages 125–126, before the interactive simulations were developed, concept inventories documented that first-year students typically held on to incorrect concepts as they progressed through their studies. Knowing that this pattern typically exists when students matriculate drove faculty to address this weakness in students' first-year courses so that students would develop a coherent foundation for future courses. Continued use of concept inventories provides chronological evidence about how well students continue to build on that foundation.

Chronologically assessing student learning within the context of existing educational practices is the approach that faculty and administrators are taking at the University of Minnesota Rochester campus. A newly designed health sciences program has built-in assessment, beginning with students' first-year courses, to monitor students' chronological patterns of strength and weakness in relation to its problem-based approach to teaching and learning ("Learning Goes Under a New Microscope," 2009).

Alternatively, the framework in Figure 4.4 can be adapted at the end of an assessment cycle when results of student achievement have been analyzed. Under this scenario, team members may need to explore those results in greater detail to identify patterns that account for students' unsuccessful work. Documenting these patterns in a taxonomy of student weaknesses, errors, or fuzzy thinking then raises questions about how to address those patterns in the teaching-learning process. Recall that the physics case on pages 125–129 was anchored in concept inventory results that identified the kinds of misunderstanding and misconceptions that first-year students carry with them.

A project among history faculty at Indiana University Bloomington, the History Learning Project, is another example of using results to change educational practices. Identifying typical "bottlenecks"—tasks or concepts that history students find difficult along their program of study, such as using "pieces of evidence to support a historical argument"—faculty have changed their instructional design. They have broken down those tasks or concepts into smaller instructional units; that is, they have "decoded" the discipline. In these units, faculty repeatedly engage students in exercises such as online assignments that focus on specific steps involved in analyzing historical evidence. By breaking down instruction into smaller units, faculty can also identify where students are continuing to have difficulties (Glenn, 2009).

THREE REPRESENTATIVE TECHNOLOGY-FOCUSED DISSEMINATION PROJECTS

Three technology-focused projects deserve recognition as models for opening new doors to our understanding of what and how students learn in technology environments and for identifying new sources of evidence to assess student learning as well as new criteria to apply to students' work.

1. The Visible Knowledge Project (VKP)

The Visible Knowledge Project (https://digitalcommons.georgetown.edu/blogs/vkp/), a 6-year project engaging almost 70 faculty from 22 different institutions across higher education, emerged in 2000 as the scholarship of teaching and learning took hold and networked digital technologies began to appear in higher education. The VKP dedicated itself to examining and documenting how new media shape teaching and students' learning patterns often documented over periods longer than one course. Among the kinds of work that faculty studied and students produced were digital stories, narratives that combine images and video from digital archives, voice-overs, music, and texts in short multimedia movies. This project allowed VKP faculty to study the impact of new technologies on learning and teaching. It also helped frame questions about learning problems in relation to teaching practices, with particular focus on technological innovation and change.

Several VKP projects have reported their student outcomes assessment results. A multimedia project undertaken at the University of Southern California compared students' final research projects in new media learning environments in the humanities and social science courses with students' final research projects in more traditionally taught humanities and social science courses. First-round assessment results, as reported by Kahn (2009), documented that multimedia deepened students' abilities to (1) prioritize and dramatize main points in research projects, in contrast to student research developed in more traditional settings that buried their main points; (2) assume multiple perspectives; (3) engage in layered analysis (that is, students explore issues in greater depth); and (4) experiment with interactive analyses through the use of media. Research findings such as these expand knowledge about how different learning environments or opportunities promote student learning outcomes—even deepen them; offer new ways for students to demonstrate their learning; and also point the way toward identifying new ways to assess student learning.

Currently, the VKP has received Teagle Foundation funding to explore the learning that students document in e-portfolios, often making visible what heretofore has been invisible about students' patterns or ways of learning.

2. The Carnegie Foundation for the Advancement of Teaching's KEEP Toolkit (Now Hosted by MERLOT)

Originally designed and implemented at the Carnegie Foundation for the Advancement of Teaching and now hosted at www.merlot.org, the KEEP Toolkit is a set of tools that "enable faculty and students to create succinct Web-based representations of aspects of teaching and learning so they can be shared with others" (www.cfkeep.org/static/about/about.html). Designed to facilitate "knowledge exchange and dissemination," the KEEP Toolkit also provides links to faculty presentations on teaching, learning, and assessment. For example, several case studies on this site demonstrate how students document learning outcomes in e-portfolios or how faculty are integrating technology into teaching to deepen students' learning of outcomes.

3. Academic Commons

Academic Commons (www.academiccommons.org; sponsored by the Center of Inquiry in the Liberal Arts at Wabash College and NERCOMP, the Northeast Regional Computing Program) brings together faculty, academic technologists, librarians, administrators, and other academic professionals in an online community focused on exploring how new technology and networked information are shaping teaching and learning in the liberal arts. Among the postings on this site are ones from faculty and other educational professionals who are researching teaching and learning with technology or in technology-based environments and also reporting their assessment results and the ways in which they are rethinking both how they will assess in the future and how their criteria for assessing may change.

EDUCATORS AS LIFELONG LEARNERS ABOUT THEIR EDUCATIONAL PRACTICES

To view assessment as solely an accountability act is to forgo our responsibility to become lifelong learners curious about the efficacy of our practices in fostering our students' enduring learning. Creating a collaborative framework, then, for raising research or study questions about our students' learning positions educators to look beyond students' achievement in a single course to achievement along the continuum of their studies at both the undergraduate and graduate levels. What pedagogies or learning contexts foster or enable students to sustain, build on, transfer, or draw on previous learning or reposition their understanding to meet an institution's or a program's exit expectations? Problem-based assessment serves as the following:

- A means of identifying major patterns of strength and weakness in students' learning, exhibited through the work they produce
- A means of concurrently gaining knowledge about the kinds of processes and approaches students draw on to demonstrate their learning, including the kinds of obstacles, challenges, or even fixations they face as they chronologically learn within the context of pedagogies and educational practices

We can learn about our students' patterns of and approaches to learning to gain knowledge and develop perspectives that lead to refinements, improvements, or innovations in educational practices. We can become learners about the efficacy of our practices by exploring how students do or do not make meaning. In words that echo Bass's introductory passage to this chapter, Laurillard (2008) states, "Teaching must become problematized, innovative, and professional, taking research as its model" (p. 328). Now is that time in higher education.

WORKS CITED

Bass, R. (1999, February). The scholarship of teaching: What's the problem? *Inventio*, (1), 1. *http://doit.gmu.edu//archives/feb98/rbass.htm*

Bransford, J. D., Brown, A. L., & Cocking, R. R. (Eds.). (1999). *How people learn: Brain, mind, experience, and school*. Washington, DC: National Research Council.

Diamond, R. (2002). Defining scholarship for the 21st century. In K. J. Zahorski (Ed.), *Scholarship in the Postmodern Era: New Venues, New Values, New Visions. New Directions in Teaching and Learning*, 90 (pp. 73–80). San Francisco: Jossey-Bass.

Ferrance, E. (2000). Themes in education: Action research. Northeast and Islands Regional Educational Laboratory at Brown University. *www .alliance.brown.edu/pubs/themes_ed/act_research.pdf*

George, M. W. (2009, April 13). Admissions of another sort. *Inside Higher Education. www.insidehighered.com/views/2009/04/13/george*

Glenn, D. (2009, November 15). A teaching experiment shows students how to grasp big concepts.

The Chronicle of Higher Education. *http://chronicle.com/article/Teaching-Experiment-Decodes-a/49140/?sid=at&utm_source=at&utm_medium=en*

Halloun, I. A., & Hestenes, D. (1985, November). The initial knowledge state of college physics students. *American Journal of Physics*, 1043–1048.

Hirsch, P., Kelso, D., Shwom, B., Troy, J., & Walsh, J. (2001). Redefining communication education for engineers: How the NSF/VaNTH ERC is experimenting with a new approach. *Proceedings of the American Society for Engineering Education*. Session 2261. *www.vanth.com/docs/016_2001.pdf*

Iiyoshi, T., & Kumar, M. S. V. (2008). (Eds.). *Opening up education: The collective advancement of education through open technology, open content, and open knowledge*. Cambridge, MA: MIT Press.

Kahn, M. E. (2009, February 9). Multimedia in the classroom at USC: A ten year perspective. *www.academiccommons.org/commons/essay/multimedia-classroom*

Kuh, G. (2008). *High-impact educational practices: What they are, who has access to them, and why they matter*. Washington, DC: AAC&U.

Kuh, G., & Ikenberry, S. (2009, October). *More than you think, less than we need: Learning outcomes assessment in American higher education*. Report from the National Institute of Learning Outcomes Assessment. *www.learningoutcomeassessment.org/documents/niloafullreportfina12.pdf*

Laurillard, D. (1993). *Rethinking university thinking: A framework for the effective use of educational technology*. London: Routledge.

Laurillard, D. (2008). Open teaching: The key to sustainable and effective open education. In T. Iiyoshi & M. S. V. Kumar (Eds.). *Opening up education: The collective advancement of education through open technology, open content, and open knowledge* (pp. 319–336). Cambridge, MA: MIT Press.

Learning goes under a new microscope: Health-sciences major at U. of Minnesota tests models for teaching and tenure. (2009, November 1). *http://chronicle.com/article/Putting-Learning-under-a/48997/?sid=at&utm_source=at&utm_medium=en*

Mach, J. (2010). Wanted: Nutrient-rich environments for genuine assessment. In P. Maki (Ed.). *Coming to terms with assessment: Faculty and administrators' journeys to integrating assessment in their work and institutional culture*. Sterling, VA: Stylus. *http://stylus.styluspub.com/Books/BookDetail.aspx?productID=218787*

Many colleges assess learning but may not use data to improve, survey finds. (2009, July). *http://chronicle.com/article/Many-Colleges-Assess-Learni/47892/*

Pellegrino, J. W., Chudowsky, N., & Glaser, R. (Eds.). (2001). *Knowing what students know: The science and design of educational assessment*. Washington, DC: National Academies Press.

Sawyer, K. (Ed.). (2006). *The Cambridge handbook of the learning sciences*. Cambridge, MA: Cambridge University Press.

Shulman, L. (2006). Principles for the uses of assessment in policy and practice. *www.teaglefoundation.org/learning/pdf/2006_shulman_assessment.pdf*

Think tank stresses importance of information sharing in research and teaching. (2009, November). *http://chronicle.com/blogPost/Think-Tank-Stresses-Importance/8753/?sid=at&utm_source=at&utm_medium=en*

Turner, M., & Thomas, F. (1996). *Clear and simple as the truth: Writing classic prose*. Princeton, NJ: Princeton University Press.

Wieman, C. E., Adams, W. K., & Perkins, K. K. (2008, October). PhET simulations that enhance learning. *Science*, (322), 682–683.

Wieman, C. E., Perkins, K. K., & Adams, W. K. (2008, April). Oersted Medal Lecture 2007: Interactive simulations for teaching physics: What works, what doesn't and why. *American Journal of Physics*, (76)4, 393–399.

Willingham, D. T. (2002, Winter). Inflexible knowledge: The first step to expertise. *American Educator*, 26(4), 31–33.

ADDITIONAL RESOURCES

Action Research

Craig, D. V. (2009). *Action research essentials*. San Francisco: Jossey-Bass.

Gilmer, P. (2010). *Transforming university science teaching using collaborative learning and technology: Ready, set, action research!* New York: Springer.

Gordon, S. P. (2008). *Collaborative action research: Developing professional learning communities*. New York, NY: Teachers College Press.

Hinchey, P. H. (2008). *Action research primer*. New York: Lang.

Kemmis, S. (2009, September). Action research as a practice-based practice. *Educational Action Research*, (17)3, 463–474.

Joshy, V. (2005). *Action research for improving practice: A practical guide*. Thousand Oaks, CA: Sage.

Levin, M., & Greenwood, D. (2001). Pragmatic action research and the struggle to transform universities into learning communities. In P. Reason & H. Bradbury (Eds.), *Handbook of action research: Participative inquiry and practice.* Thousand Oaks, CA: Sage.

McIntyre, A. (2008). *Participatory action research.* Thousand Oaks, CA: Sage.

McKernan, J. (1996). *Curriculum action research: A handbook of methods and resources for the reflective practitioner* (2nd ed.). Abingdon, UK: Kogan Page.

Mills, G. (2010). *Action research: A guide for the teacher researcher* (4th ed.). Upper Saddle River, NJ: Prentice Hall.

Norton, L. S. (2009). *Action research in teaching and learning: A practical guide to conducting pedagogical research in universities.* London: Routledge.

Somekh, B., & Zeichner, K. (2009, March). Action research for educational reform: Remodeling action research. Theories and Practices in Local Contexts. *Educational Action Research, 17*(1), 5–21.

Stringer, E. T. (Ed.). (2007). *Action research* (3rd ed.). Thousand Oaks, CA: Sage.

Assessment Case Studies

Teagle Foundation. Resources. *www.teaglefoundation.org/learning/resources.aspx.* Among the resources on this site are institutional examples of assessing liberal arts.

WPA Assessment Gallery: Assessment Models. Council of Writing Program Administrators. *http://wpacouncil.org/assessment-models.* Narratives discuss how institutions have used results of writing assessment to improve students' writing.

Basic Principles and Methods of Educational Research

Ary, D., Jacobs, L. C., Razavieh, A., & Sorenson, C. K. (2010). *Introduction to research in education* (8th ed.). Belmont, CA: Wadsworth.

Daponte, B. O. (2009). *Methods for conducting sound research.* San Francisco: Jossey-Bass.

Hamrick, F. A., Evans, N. J., & Schuh, J. (2002). *Foundations of student affairs practice: How philosophy, theory and research strengthen educational outcomes.* San Francisco: Jossey-Bass.

Lapan, S. D., & Quartaroli, M. T. (Eds.). (2009). *Research essentials: An introduction to designs and practices.* San Francisco: Jossey-Bass.

Lodico, M. G., Spaulding, D. T., & Voegtle, K. H. (2010). *Methods in educational research: From theory to practice* (2nd ed.). San Francisco: Jossey-Bass.:

Moss, P. (Ed.). (2007). *Evidence and decision-making.* San Francisco: Jossey-Bass.

Smart, J. C. (2005). *Higher education: Handbook of theory and research.* Vol. 20. New York, NY: Springer.

Some Essential Resources on How Humans Learn

Bransford, J. D., Brown, A. L., & Cocking, R. P. (Eds.). 2000. *How people learn: Brain, mind, experience, and school.* Washington, DC: National Academies Press.

Kaufman, J. C., & Grigorenko, E. (Eds.). (2008). *The essential Sternberg: Essays on intelligence, psychology, and education.* New York, NY: Springer.

Pascarella, E. T., & Tenenzini, P. T. (2005). *How college affects students.* Vol. 2. San Francisco: Jossey-Bass.

Pellegrino, J. W., Chudowsky, N., & Glaser, R. (2001). *Knowing what students know: The science and design of educational assessment.* Washington, DC: National Academies Press.

Zull, J. (2002). *The art of changing the brain.* Sterling, VA: Stylus. *http://stylus.styluspub.com/Books/BookDetail.aspx?productID=44780*

Some Resources, Including Metasites, on Effective Educational Practices

Angelo, T. A., & Cross, K. P. (1993). *Classroom assessment techniques* (2nd ed.). San Francisco: Jossey-Bass.

Association of American Colleges and Universities. *www.aacu.org* (click on "Publications" or go to a subset of online publications under "Web Publications")

Bamburg, J. D. (1994). *Raising expectations to improve learning. www.ncrel.org/sdrs/areas/issues/educatrs/leadrshp/le0bam.htm*

Carnegie Foundation for the Advancement of Teaching. Publications and online readings about teaching and learning at both the undergraduate and graduate level. *www.carnegiefoundation.org/resources*

Carnegie Mellon University. Enhancing Education. *www.cmu.edu/teaching/solveproblem/index.html*

Carnegie Mellon University. The Open Learning Initiative, an open educational resource that includes learning effectiveness studies. *http://oli.web.cmu.edu/openlearning/publications/71*

Education Resources Information Center. (ERIC). Conduct a search of publications related to your research or study question at this site. *www.eric.ed.gov*

Faculty Inquiry Network. Consisting of contributions from community college faculty across California, this site is dedicated to learning more about how students learn to improve their learning of basic skills. Contents include a toolkit for ways to advance students' learning. *http://facultyinquiry.net/about-fin/*

Gardiner, L. F. (1994). *Redesigning higher education. Producing dramatic gains in student learning.* Washington, DC: George Washington University.

Lesson Study Project at the University of Wisconsin—La Crosse. A teaching improvement site focused on developing lessons based on how students learn. *www.uwlax.edu/sotl/lsp/*

Shulman, L. (2006). *Principles for the uses of assessment in policy and practice. www.teaglefoundation.org/learning/pdf/2006_shulman_assessment.pdf*

Visible Knowledge Project. *https://digitalcommons.georgetown.edu/blogs/vkp/*

Wahlberg, H. J., & Paik, S. J. (2000). *Effective educational practices. www.ibe.unesco.org/publications/practices.htm*

WORKSHEETS, GUIDES, AND EXERCISES

The following worksheets, guides, and exercises anchor assessment of student learning into scholarly research leading to actionable results—changes, refinements, adaptations in educational practices.

1. Use the following tasks as a way to move through your problem-based assessment plan:

   a. **Create an Inquiry Group.** Based on initial discussion of problems or issues in student learning, create an inquiry group, team, or community of practice that includes members of your program, department, or general education team and other professionals who would be invested in pursuing answers to identified problems or issues and/or able to provide evidence or data to help solve the problem. Individuals who would be invested in pursuing answers to your initial problem might be upper- and lower-division faculty, student affairs professionals, support service professionals, undergraduate or graduate students, or cohorts among those constituencies such as first-generation students or non-traditional-age students:

   _____

   _____

   _____

   _____

   _____

   _____

   _____

   b. **Identify Learning Outcome Statements.** In your department or program, or with representatives from your general education program, identify one or more outcomes that you intend to assess in your next assessment cycle.

   Outcome(s) to be addressed in an assessment cycle:

   _____

   _____

   _____

   _____

   c. **Couple Outcome with a Research or Study Question.** Collaboratively agree on an observation or generalization that you will convert into an open-ended research or study question you will pursue in your next assessment cycle. Use one or more of the following strategies to generate an open-ended research or study question:

   i. Refer to those listed in Appendix 4.1 to prompt discussion.
   ii. With your inquiry group, make a list of generalizations or observations or issues that have arisen around students' learning of these outcomes, such as librarians' observations about student research behaviors or faculty comments about students' weak quantitative abilities.
   iii. If used to track weaknesses in student learning, base your research or study question on a Taxonomy of Student Weaknesses, Errors, or Fuzzy Thinking that documents patterns of

student difficulties, such as cognitive weaknesses, conceptual weaknesses, quantitative weaknesses, and misunderstandings. (Use the empty Taxonomy under 2 on page 150.)

_____

_____

_____

_____

_____

_____

_____

d. Identify Others Invested in Answering the Question. Identify educators, staff, and administrators who have access to evidence or data that may help to answer the question you have raised: Individuals who can provide evidence or data to help answer the question, such as the registrar, institutional research professionals, teaching assistants, advisers, or support service professionals:

_____

_____

_____

_____

_____

e. Read Relevant Current Educational Literature or Research. Based on your research or study question, determine who among your inquiry group will identify current related educational literature or research on learning that relates to your question. Refer to the "Additional Resources" in chapters 1–4 to help you begin to identify relevant resources. Then determine how to divide relevant readings among the group and when you will come together to synthesize those readings and draw relevant knowledge from them into a possible restatement of your problem or into the design of your assessment plan. Answer the following questions:

  i. How does current educational literature shape or refine our research or study question?
  ii. How does current research on learning shape or refine our research or study question?

f. Identify Relevant Sources of Student Evidence and Institutional and National Data. Within your inquiry group, identify the direct and indirect methods you will use to answer your research or study question as well as institutional data or national data that may shed light on the answer to your question.

Relevant sources of evidence:

_____

_____

_____

_____

_____

g. Design an Assessment Plan. Keeping in mind what you learned from relevant readings, such as how others may have tackled a similar problem or how research on learning may have helped you restate your question or prompted you to consider the various kinds of evidence or data you may need to build into your action plan, develop a draft action plan consisting of the following elements:

• Baseline data or evidence that you will use to assess students' achievement over time, such as a first-year writing sample or responses to a case study
• Cohorts of students you will track over time based on the demographics of your institution or program or based on the use of different modes of delivery or pedagogies

- Chronological direct and indirect assessment methods you will use to answer the agreed-upon research or study question
- Criteria and standards of judgment you will use to assess students' chronological performance
- Department, program, institution, or national data that you believe will be helpful in answering the question you have raised
- Those who are responsible for collecting and analyzing student work
- If relevant or available, a taxonomy of student weaknesses, errors, or fuzzy thinking
- Those who are responsible for collecting relevant institution, national, program, or department student data
- Times to triangulate results of assessed student work and relevant data to promote informed discussion about and reflections on results that lead to implementing changed practices, such as alternative ways of teaching and learning, use of different pedagogies or instructional styles, and use of different modes of delivery
- Ask each member of the inquiry group to review that draft and return to a follow-up meeting to share comments, additions, or revisions to the plan to ensure that you have addressed all the tasks as well as identified the kinds of evidence and data you believe you will need to collect, analyze, and interpret
- Collaboratively agree on the final plan that you will implement and agree that each member of the team will keep notes about how well the plan works so that you can evaluate the success of your plan for future assessment efforts
- Once you have collected, analyzed, and interpreted data and student work and agreed on actions to improve patterns of weakness in students' work, identify the kinds of changes that will be implemented when and by whom. For example, in the case study on pages 130–131, several kinds of changes are recommended for different constituencies—faculty, advisers, and the faculty development office. Use the following chart to document how you will go about implementing proposed changes in pedagogy, curricular design, or educational practices:

List of Changes	Timetable for Implementation	Individuals Responsible for Implementing Changes

h. Develop a Time Line to Implement and Re-assess the Efficacy of Agreed-upon Changes.

    i. If you are implementing changes based on assessment results you already have, such as results of norm-based tests or results of applying criteria and standards of judgment to student work, compare student performance under implemented changes with those results.

    ii. If you raised a research or study question to chronologically document students' learning over time:

        1. Develop a baseline of student performance against which to chronologically assess students' chronological achievement.

        2. Determine points along the continuum of learning when you will assess students' achievement.

        3. Develop criteria and standards of judgment to consistently assess students' work along the continuum of their learning or identify other performance benchmarks, such as scores.

i. Disseminate Findings and Resulting Changes Within and Outside of the Institution.

- For internal audiences:
    a. Provide a narrative summary of your project and findings accompanied with a visual representation.
    b. Discuss how implemented changes in educational practice could be used in programs, departments, or services other than the contexts of the study.
    c. If relevant, address how implementing proposed changes may affect others at the institution not directly involved in the project.
    d. If relevant, address how proposed changes can be scaled up to effectively educate more students.
    e. Address the need for faculty and staff development to implement changes more broadly.
    f. Address human, technological, and financial resources that will be required to implement changes more broadly.
- For external audiences:
    a. Place your project within the context of current educational literature and research.
    b. Describe how it contributes to that current literature and research—builds on, challenges, or extends research or existing practices.
    c. Describe major elements of your assessment plan, with particular focus on the forms of evidence and data you used to assess the efficacy of implemented changes.
    d. Provide a narrative summary of your findings, accompanied with a visual representation.
    e. Explain how others outside your project context may be able to implement what you found or build on what you found to continue to build knowledge and expand new or adapted educational practices.

2. Use the following format to classify patterns of student weaknesses, errors, or fuzzy thinking.

Taxonomy of Student Weaknesses, Errors, or Fuzzy Thinking

Types of Weaknesses, Errors, or Fuzzy Thinking	Identify Context of Weaknesses, Errors, or Fuzzy Thinking	Identify Possible Causes With the Assistance of Students
1. Conceptual, mathematical, analytical, computational, grammatical, fuzzy recall, procedural, pattern discernment, interpretive reasoning, inability to apply to new or unfamiliar situations, etc.		
2.		
3.		
4.		

3. Use the following template to monitor your problem-based approach to assessment:

Problem-Based Assessment Template

Action:	Individual(s) Responsible:	Date for Action:
1. Create an inquiry group, team, or community of practice		
2. Identify learning outcome statement(s) you will assess		
3. Couple outcomes with a research or study question		
4. Identify others invested in answering the question		
5. Read current relevant educational literature or research		
6. Identify relevant sources of student evidence and institutional and national data		
7. Design an assessment plan		
8. Develop a time line to implement and reassess agreed-upon changes		
9. Disseminate project findings and resulting changes within and outside the institution		

APPENDIX 4.1   Some Representative Research or Study Questions That Promote Department-, Program-, or Institution-Level Identification of Related Research or Study Questions

I. LEARNER-FOCUSED QUESTIONS

What . . .

- approaches to learning do students take as they shift from one disciplinary course to another or from introductory courses to higher-level courses in their program of study?
- gaps in skill level occur as students transition into subsequent courses or learning experiences?
- kinds of erroneous ideas, concepts, or misunderstandings predictably interfere with students' abilities to learn new content?
- approaches do successful and unsuccessful learners take to solve representative disciplinary problems?
- patterns of weakness continue to surface or persist in students' work, such as weak reading abilities, analytical abilities, or computational skills?
- kinds of processes, problems, and tasks typically stump students?
- strategies do successful and unsuccessful students draw up to read and interpret different kinds of visual or written texts in different media?
- kinds of overgeneralizations or oversimplifications do learners carry with them as they move to higher-level courses?
- kinds of misunderstandings, misinterpretations, missing steps, or underdeveloped concepts manifest themselves in the work students produce?
- strategies do students use to restructure naïve or intuitive theories?
- conceptual or computational obstacles inhibit students from shifting from one form of reasoning to another form, such as from arithmetic reasoning to algebraic reasoning?
- successful alternative ways of understanding do learners use or develop to learn a new concept or principle or complex content?

- kinds of mental or visual models do successful learners develop to achieve enduring learning?
- kinds of changes in thinking are taking place when students reposition their understanding—belief revision, conceptual change, restructured knowledge?
- kinds of learning obstacles, such as lack of understanding of vocabulary or lack of appropriate reading strategies (for reading texts or visual material) prohibit students from interpreting, analyzing, or summarizing written or visual texts?

How or how well do . . .

- students represent new learning to themselves?
- students' representation or demonstration of learning in lower-level, prerequisite, or general education courses prepare them to develop increasingly more complex conceptual understanding or cognitive development that is expected in consecutive or upper-level courses?
- skills-based courses prepare students for consecutive or higher-level courses that require students to build on or integrate those skills
- students chronologically build layers of complexity across the curriculum and co-curriculum, such as cognitive complexity?
- students reposition, modify, or change altogether long-held misconceptions, misunderstanding, or beliefs?
- students integrate new learning into previous learning, draw on previous learning in the progression of their studies, or apply previous learning to new contexts?
- students' professional or disciplinary dispositions develop along the chronology of their studies?
- students' beliefs affect conceptual development?
- students' levels of cognition affect their conceptual development?

- students transfer learning from their general education program of study into their major program of study?
- students transfer their general education or core curricular learning or major program learning into the life outside the class, such as in community service?
- students build their own knowledge based on the use of instructional multimedia designs?
- students initially construct meaning in a field or discipline that enables them to continue to succeed?

II. TEACHER-FOCUSED QUESTIONS

How do . . .

- time restrictions or demands for increased program "coverage" inhibit students' abilities to develop deep sustained learning?
- various kinds of pedagogy (e.g., problem-based, experiential, or didactic) promote complex problem solving?
- various modes of instruction promote complex problem solving?
- experiential learning opportunities offered in the curriculum and co-curriculum promote or deepen learning?

What . . .

- kinds of representational models develop complex conceptual understanding?
- forms of animation or nonverbal communication enable students to overcome learning barriers?
- kinds of visual representations are conducive to learning in a particular discipline?
- strategies enable students to transition from thinking arithmetically to thinking algebraically?

- kinds of out-of-course assistance, such as online tutorials or software, promote desired student outcomes?
- kinds of approaches to teaching enable students to overcome typical learning barriers or obstacles?
- kinds of abilities are students developing under current experiential learning opportunities?
- kinds of contexts or content promote creativity?
- kinds of mental images in disciplinary learning do students transfer?
- chronological educational practices promote the following abilities?
  - recall and recognition
  - comprehension
  - application
  - synthesis
  - analysis
  - evaluation
  - habits of mind
  - ways of knowing
  - ways of seeing and interpreting
  - transfer
  - integration
  - creativity

How or how well do . . .

- stand-alone skills based courses, such as mathematics or writing courses, prepare students to integrate or apply those skills into disciplinary or professional courses?
- digital dialogue games or other forms of interactive technology foster students' reasoning or conceptual abilities?
- hypermedia technologies foster complex problem solving?
- online interactive discussions help students construct knowledge?

Chapter 5

IDENTIFYING OR DESIGNING TASKS TO ASSESS THE DIMENSIONS OF LEARNING

Assessments do not function in isolation; an assessment's effectiveness in improving learning depends on its relationships to curriculum and instruction. Ideally, instruction is faithful and effective in relation to curriculum, and assessment reflects curriculum in such a way that it reinforces the best practices in instruction. In actuality, however, the relationships among assessment, curriculum, and instruction are not always ideal. Often assessment taps only a subset of curriculum and without regard to instruction, and can narrow and distort instruction in unintended ways.

—National Research Council, 2001

OVERVIEW: Dialogue about teaching, philosophies of teaching, models of learning, and articulation of outcomes companioned with research or study questions lead to dialogue about the assessment methods or tasks that prompt students to represent the dimensions of their institution- and program-level learning. Focused on engaging core working groups in identifying or designing formative and summative assessment methods, this chapter identifies the considerations that surround the choices we make, including how well a method aligns with what and how students learn and receive feedback on that learning and how well a method "fits" its purpose. The Worksheets, Guides, and Exercises at the end of this chapter, together with the Inventory of Traditional and Technology-Enabled Direct and Indirect Assessment Methods in Appendix 5.4, are designed to deepen discussions leading to decisions about methods by focusing on (1) the parameters of decision making that lead to choices; (2) the properties of methods that make them fit for use; and (3) the range of conventional and technology-based direct and indirect methods that capture the dimensions of learning.

THE RANGE OF TEXTS THAT DEMONSTRATE OR REPRESENT LEARNING

"Will this be on the test?" "What will the test cover?" and "Do we have to know this for the test?" are frequent questions students raise as they gear up for an examination. These queries represent a surface student approach to learning—an approach that focuses on memorizing or rehearsing in response to an external motivator, passing the test itself, "getting it out of the way," as opposed to an internal motivator, constructing meaning over time. That is, the test becomes a container, a receptacle, into which they deposit what they have rehearsed or hope that they have rehearsed well enough. Often what students store in their short-term memories and then deposit on a test vaporizes after they have completed the test—unless, of course, they have future opportunities to build on that learning. If students are historically conditioned to learn this way, they become facile in recall and recognition, banking their short-term memories in response to what "the test," viewed as an end point, will require them to know.

This chapter identifies the parameters of decision making that lead to selecting or designing assessment methods that extend or build on recall and recognition and reveal the multidimensions of institution- and program-level learning. Robust developments in educational technology and technological tools have expanded the ways in which students represent their learning: wikis, blogs, podcasts, and threaded online discussions; handheld electronic wireless devices; online simulations and lab reports; written, spoken, visual, and interactive multimedia texts; and learning products that emerge from engagement or data mining in virtual environments, such as in Second Life or microworlds. Facilitated by or created with technology, students generate evidence of their abilities to:

- Integrate and transfer learning over time
- Apply knowledge and understanding into new contexts
- Analyze and explore representative professional, disciplinary, and interdisciplinary problems
- Interpret, construct, express, and create meaning
- Represent or express thinking and problem solving in different forms of discourse, within different kinds of contexts, for different audiences

At the institution and program levels, assessment committees establish core working groups to select or design methods to assess the learning described in collectively agreed-upon learning outcome statements, described in chapter 3, that are coupled with research or study questions, discussed in chapter 4. A collaborative process based on multiple perspectives, this decision-making process draws on the experience and expertise of a range of individuals. For example, in a graduate-level program, faculty, representative graduate students, members of a professional advisory board, a librarian, and a representative from the institution's office of research and planning may work together to identify assessment methods. Their collective expertise and experience bring multiple perspectives to the underlying dialogue that eventually narrows the pool of appropriate possibilities. For example:

- A member of a professional advisory board contributes information about current external needs or demands.
- Faculty contribute information about how pedagogy, curricular design, and the design of course-based assessment methods develop intended learning outcomes.
- A representative graduate student or students contribute learner-centered information about their sets of learning experiences and the ways in which they have represented their learning over time.
- A librarian contributes knowledge about the demands or dimensions of a method in relationship to expectations for graduate-level research.
- A representative from institutional research and planning deepens understanding about the logistics of using, collecting, analyzing, and interpreting results of methods. (See also chapter 7, pages 257–258).

MULTIPLE METHODS OF ASSESSMENT

Capturing the complexity of our students' learning calls for identifying or designing multiple methods of assessment. A method that prompts students to define disciplinary terms supports inferences about what students know; it does not support inferences about how well they use that knowledge to solve representative disciplinary problems. The limitations of one method stimulate the design or selection of other methods that altogether capture the dimensions of learning. Relying on one method to assess the learning described in outcome statements restricts interpretations of student achievement within the universe of that method. Using multiple methods to assess the learning expressed in an outcome statement is advantageous in several ways:

- Reduces straitjacket interpretations of student achievement based on the limitations inherent in one method
- Provides students with opportunities to demonstrate learning that they may not have been able to demonstrate within the context of another method, such as timed tests
- Contributes to comprehensive interpretations of student achievement at both institution and program levels
- Values the dimensionality of learning
- Values the diverse ways in which humans learn and represent their learning

Combinations of quantitative and qualitative assessment methods add depth and breadth to interpretations of student learning. *Quantitative methods* place interpretative value on numbers—the number of right versus wrong answers, for example. *Qualitative methods* place interpretative value on the observer—observations of group interaction or an individual's performance in a simulation. Qualitative methods also enable an observer to assess concurrently broader dimensions of learning, such as how individuals translate understanding into behaviors, dispositions, reactions, and interactions. Behaviors, attitudes, and beliefs resist easy quantification and lend themselves to narrative interpretation, as, for example, in assessing group interactions through videotaping. In their research on learning, Entwhistle and Ramsden (1982) argue that

> . . . [I]n our experience, neither qualitative nor quantitative methods of research taken separately can provide a full and a convincing explanation of student learning. . . . it seems essential that an understanding of student learning should be built up from an appropriate alternation of evidence and insights derived from both qualitative and quantitative approaches to research. In our view the strength of our evidence on

student learning is the direct result of this interplay of contrasting methodologies, and has led to a realistic and useful description of approaches and contexts of learning in higher education. (p. 219)

The institutional example in Box 5.1 illustrates how a qualitative method, enhanced through technology, provides a means to capture robust learning.

The National Board of Medical Examiners' decision to observe medical students' clinical skills with standardized patients acknowledges the value of relying on more than one method to assess student learning. Historically, medical students have represented their professional knowledge and understanding in standardized medical examinations. This method, however, limits drawing inferences about students' actual behaviors with and dispositions toward different patients, including their communicative styles. Written responses restrict such inference drawing. Now, observers assess medical students with a range of standardized patients to draw inferences about how medical students translate knowledge and understanding into professional practices across a range of representative patients ("Clinical Skills Assessment in the USMLE," 2002).

As alternatives or complements to commercially developed standardized instruments, educators may well decide to design or develop their own assessment methods. Locally developed methods enable us to translate educational practices into tasks that specifically capture our intentions. As designers, we gain the advantage of developing methods that fit with what and how students learn over time within our institution- and program-level contexts. More important, we have the opportunity to track students' complex ways of understanding, thinking, and behaving. Further, as designers we can explore how our students understand and integrate learning from various experiences, as well as apply and build on it. Designing

---

BOX 5.1 INSTITUTIONAL EXAMPLE: *Stanford University*

Stanford University's Virtual Labs Project uses web technology, media-rich images, and interactive multimedia to track physiology students' understanding and behaviors in simulations during which they examine, diagnose, and treat virtual patients. These patients are accompanied with information about their medical history and current complaints (virtuallabs.stanford.edu/demo/). Importantly, the simulation aligns with the simulation-based curriculum modules delivered through the web. These modules promote learning through visual and conceptual understanding of temporal and causal relationships. (To view current projects, viewers need to install Shockwave and QuickTime.)

our own methods provides us with high-powered lenses to observe the multidimensionality of our students' progress in relation to our intentions.

The institutional examples in Box 5.2 and Box 5.3 illustrate how locally designed methods capture the dimensions of learning.

Direct Methods

Developing a comprehensive understanding of the dimensions of student learning involves the selection or design of direct and indirect methods. *Direct methods* prompt students to represent or demonstrate their learning or produce work so that observers can assess how well students' work or responses fit institution- or program-level expectations. Performances, creations, results of research or exploration, interactions within group problem solving, or responses to questions or prompts represent examples of direct methods. Observers draw inferences based on what students produce, how they perform, or what they select in response to a universe of questions or stimuli designed to assess dimensions of their learning.

How two direct methods complement each other is also important to explore. For example, identifying patterns of weakness in calculus students' abilities to solve increasingly complex problems may not lead faculty to determine why those patterns exist. Gath-

---

BOX 5.2   INSTITUTIONAL EXAMPLE: *University of Michigan*

To assess students' emerging definitions of spirituality across individuals representing different worldviews, at the University of Michigan, Matthew Mayhew, while earning his doctorate in higher education, relied on three methods to assess his students' definitions of spirituality: students' visual representation, written text, and semistructured interviews. He provided students with digital/disposable cameras to take pictures or images that reflected their working meanings of *spirituality*. Students wrote full-sentence captions for each of the final 10 pictures they selected and then entered into an album, along with a rationale for including each of the 10 photographs. These mini-albums became the basis of a 30- to 45-minute semistructured interview. During these interviews, Mayhew questioned students about their images and choice of words, thus providing him with a rich data set from which to make inferences about students' definition of spirituality.

Source: Matthew Mayhew, Assistant Professor of Higher Education, New York University.

BOX 5.3   INSTITUTIONAL EXAMPLE: *North Carolina State University*

Students in North Carolina State University's Service-Learning Program produce written products multiple times throughout the semester as the concluding step for reflective activities. Through these documents, called Articulated Learnings, students describe what and how they have learned in their service-related experiences, as well as how these experiences shaped their future thinking, actions, or commitments. The writings capture the dimensions of their knowing, thinking, and reflection. Four questions prompt these final documents:

1. What did I learn?
2. How, specifically, did I learn it?
3. Why does this learning matter, or why is it important?
4. In what ways will I use this learning, or what goals shall I set in accordance with what I have learned in order to improve myself and/or the quality of my learning and/or the quality of my future experiences/service?

Source: Sarah Ash and Patti Clayton, North Carolina State University. Based on the Integrative Processing Model developed by Pamela Kiser at Elon University (Kiser, 1998).

ering descriptive data about their problem-solving processes through a *think aloud,* a direct method of assessment that probes into students' ways of thinking and problem solving, will help faculty identify procedural errors or gaps or incorrect conceptual understanding that prohibit students from correctly solving those problems. (See pages 177 to 178 in this chapter for a more in-depth description of think alouds.)

Indirect Methods

Indirect methods, such as inventories, surveys, questionnaires, interviews, and focus group meetings, capture students' perceptions of their learning and the efficacy of educational practices and the educational environment that supports that learning, such as the array of services, programs, and educational opportunities offered in the co-curriculum. By themselves, indirect methods provide insufficient evidence about students' actual performance levels: students' may underestimate or overestimate their actual performance levels. Yet patterns of students' perceptions, interpretations, and responses are important to analyze and interpret along with results of direct methods; they expand the boundaries of discussion among colleagues that lead to identifying ways to improve the teaching-learning process.

For example, the Global Perspectives Inventory (GPI) gauges the extent to which students shift or change attitudes, values, or perspectives after engaging with individuals in other cultures. An online survey, the Student Assessment of their Learning Gains (SALG), provides students with the opportunity to identify the components of learning they found effective or ineffective in their coursework or a specific educational opportunity. Conducted by an experienced outsider, focus group interviews, such as those used in Small Group Instructional Diagnosis (SGID), can elicit detail from students about their learning challenges in a course. If they accompany direct methods, these kinds of indirect methods yield data that help explain students' performance levels—explanations that educators would not otherwise be privy to. Additionally, building in opportunities for students to describe firsthand how they experienced sequenced courses or educational opportunities centers them on taking ownership of their learning. Programs and departments should also consider using both the SALG and SGID at significant points along the continuum of students' learning, providing students with multiple opportunities to identify the chronological practices they believe contribute to their enduring learning or identify remaining learning obstacles.

METHODS ALONG THE CONTINUUM OF LEARNING: FORMATIVE AND SUMMATIVE

Seeking evidence of learning along the progression of students' studies, *formative assessment,* as well as at the end of their studies, *summative assessment,* records students' progress toward and achievement of institution- and program-level learning. After a certain number of courses/credits and educational experiences, or at points that index when students should be able to master certain abilities or ways of behaving, assessment methods provide evidence of how well students are learning.

Results of formative assessment provide useful information about program- and institution-level learning that can stimulate immediate change in pedagogy, design of instruction, curriculum, co-curriculum, and services that support learning. Although all students do not have to be assessed to learn about the efficacy of educational practices, if all students are assessed and they receive results of their performance, this information can also dramatically change the advising process, positioning students and advisers to talk about and reflect on how students can improve their performance. Typically, formative assessment methods are built into the performing and visual arts curricula: faculty provide continuous feedback to students as emerging professionals. That is, formative assessment becomes a way for students to learn; it also becomes a way for faculty to learn about the efficacy of their practices. The institutional example in Box 5.4 illustrates how formative assessment methods capture students' integrated learning. Student work and patterns of feedback provide programs with evidence of student learning in relation to expected learning outcomes.

Patterns of students' performance identify students' strengths as well as weaknesses. Collectively, faculty and others who contribute to student learning determine how to address patterns of weakness in students' remaining coursework and sets of learning experiences. They may consider, for example, one or more of the following ways to improve patterns of weakness in student work:

• Increase opportunities for students to transfer learning or rehearse or practice learning along the continuum of students' studies.

BOX 5.4   INSTITUTIONAL EXAMPLE: *Alverno College*

Alverno College's practice of using multiple methods of assessment both formatively and summatively is illustrated in chemistry students' third-year assessment. Multiple methods capture these majors' learning as they collaboratively and individually solve a problem. For example, a group of three to four students may be asked to provide input to an advisory committee for the Milwaukee Estuary Remediation Action Plan regarding contamination in the Milwaukee harbor. Each student is given approximately 2 weeks to research the situation in advance of the actual assessment. For the assessment, each student prepares a position paper on an issue, specifically assigned to her, related to contaminated sediment. She also prepares a procedural document for monitoring a contaminant in the harbor. At the time of each student's individual assessment, each member of the group defends her own position and recommended procedures for treating, preventing, or disposing of contamination in the harbor.

Working collaboratively, using the information provided by each student, the group then drafts a long-term plan for the management of contaminated sediment in Milwaukee Harbor. The meeting is videotaped for two audiences: (1) the chemistry faculty, who assess the students' performance, and (2) the students, who will assess their own performance.

Source: Georgine Loacker, senior assessment scholar and professor of English, Alverno College.

- Diversify teaching and learning practices to expand opportunities for students to deepen their learning.
- Examine the efficacy of prerequisites or curricular sequencing, including students' ability to navigate the curricular sequence to avoid enrolling in certain kinds of courses that would contribute to their learning.
- Provide more focused practice with technological tools.
- Review advising practices.
- Adapt new pedagogies.
- Adapt high-impact educational practices. (Kuh, 2008)

Summative assessment methods provide evidence of students' final mastery levels. They prompt students to represent the cumulative learning of their education and ask the question, "How well do our students achieve our institution and program-level expectations?" Again, results of summative methods are useful to improve the curriculum, co-curriculum, pedagogy, and the design of instruction, program, and services. If they are used along with formative assessment methods, they provide students with a final perspective on their work as it has emerged over time. If an institution and its programs use only summative assessment methods, there is no opportunity to revise, adapt, or innovate practices that will improve the achievement of a current graduating class. Results are useful to improve educa-

tional practices for future classes but not for a class about to graduate. Thus, an institutional commitment to assessing for learning builds in formative as well as summative assessment to respond to patterns of weakness along students' learning progression. In this commitment, educators become flexible designers who adapt, revise, or develop new practices in response to what they learn along students' educational journey.

POINTS OF LEARNING

Where and how we choose to position ourselves as observers of our students' work to answer a research or study question and where and how we position our students in relation to institution- and program-level assessment also contribute to the selection or design of assessment methods. We can dip down and take snapshots of our students' learning by embedding these methods into required courses and also by asking students in a focus group scheduled outside class time to identify what they believe they are achieving and what they are having difficulty achieving and why. Based on inferences from these snapshots and results of focus group discussions, we derive a composite picture of learning and generalize about students' achievement against our collective expectations. Rising junior examinations, for example, represent this approach; sometimes these examinations also serve a gatekeeping function to identify students who are unable to achieve expected levels of achievement and, consequently, need to demonstrate that learning before they graduate.

A collaborative approach to assessment involving faculty and students may take other forms, such as ongoing review of student work from course to course in a major so that students receive feedback about their abilities to build on, apply, and integrate learning. Practiced in the arts, ongoing review of student work, based on public and shared criteria, promotes integration of learning and students' self-reflection about their achievement. Appendixes 5.1 and 5.2 (also discussed on pages 170 to 172 in this chapter) describe Goddard College's formative assessment portfolio model requiring faculty and students to reflect chronologically on students' accomplishments. This review also enables faculty to identify patterns of student weaknesses along the continuum of their learning. These findings then become the focus of routine program-level dialogue during which colleagues determine ways to implement changes to address those patterns in sequences of courses, pedagogy, or other educational practices. In this approach, students' ongoing work or culminating projects represent chronological evidence of their achievement. This chronological approach to assessment values student-generated texts that emerge from specific educational contexts as opposed to externally designed contexts such as in standardized tests. In the institutional examples in Box 5.5 and Box 5.6, students are positioned to generate work within their contexts for learning. That is, assessment practices are closely aligned with what and how students learn.

ISSUES OF ALIGNMENT: OUTCOMES, INFERENCES, AND STUDENTS' LEARNING HISTORIES

The learning described in outcomes statements, along with accompanying research or study questions, guides the selection or design of assessment methods. *Alignment* refers to the degree to which a method captures

---

BOX 5.5 INSTITUTIONAL EXAMPLE: *Marian College*

As a culminating project in the curriculum and assessment class of the graduate educational leadership program at Marian College, students build a shared online faculty development program for creating effective methods to assess student learning based on the texts and documents they have read and discussed over time. In this paperless project, each student creates two PowerPoint assessment workshops with follow-up materials and URLs for classroom teachers to use. The completed workshops are placed in a common folder in an online platform for the culminating course in the program. All class members assess their peers' work electronically based on professional criteria. As part of their practicum, students select a workshop from this common folder that best fits the needs of their particular school and field-test that workshop as a staff development training opportunity. Practitioners, in turn, assess students' workshops against agreed-upon criteria. Students are positioned in this culminating project as contributors to the wider educational community that draws on their work to enhance professional practices. In turn, they receive feedback from professionals in their field.

Source: Carleen Vande Zande, Marian College.

BOX 5.6 INSTITUTIONAL EXAMPLE: *Keystone College*

In the fine arts department at Keystone College, one of the department's formative assessment methods involves (1) visual recording of students as they work on key projects and (2) before-and-after digital photography of students' works of art. Assessment of students' behaviors provides program-level evidence of students' progress toward professional practices in relation to the design of curriculum and educational practices. "Before and after" pictures of student creations provide the comparative basis for faculty, peer, and self-assessment along the continuum of students' evolution as artists.

Source: Digital images from David Porter, Judith L. Keats, and William Tersteeg, Keystone College.

that learning. Just as exploring students' learning histories and educational practices leads to collective articulation of learning outcome statements, exploring the relationship between learning outcome statements and proposed assessment methods leads to consensus about relevant and effective ways to prompt students to represent the dimensions of that learning. Maps of the curriculum and co-curriculum described in chapter 2 provide a visual representation of students' opportunities to practice the learning described in outcome statements. Recall that the curriculum map at Rose-Hulman Institute of Technology, presented in chapter 2, Figure 2.4, documents (1) where students have opportunities to learn what a program or institution values and (2) where students receive feedback about their achievement.

Categorizing the kinds of feedback students receive contributes to determining how well assessment methods align with students' learning histories. For example, suppose students' predominant form of feedback in a major program of study consists of receiving scores on objective tests that value selecting correct answers. Yet if a program-level outcome statement values students' ability to identify and then evaluate the feasibility of several solutions to a problem, there will be a disconnect between students' dominant ways of performing and receiving feedback and the ways of performing necessary to fulfill this program-level outcome statement. That is, there is lack of alignment between values—between those practiced in a program and those expected. The design or selection of an assessment method, then, takes into consideration collective intentions translated into educational practices. According to the Mathematics Association of America, selecting a method to assess quantitative literacy is based on clarity about the type of learning a program or an institution values:

> Assessment should fit the nature of a quantitative literacy program using methods which reflect the type of learning to be measured, rather than methods which are most easily constructed or scored. For example, if students are to learn how to respond to open-ended problem settings, they must be asked to do so in the assessment procedure. Facing them with a multiple-choice test for the measurement of such a goal would be inappropriate. (1998)

Typically, it is unlikely that students accustomed to receiving feedback on objective tests will perform well on open-ended methods or tasks designed to assess students' generative abilities, such as interpreting evidence from multiple perspectives. Case and Gunstone's (2002) research on the difficulties students experience in developing a conceptual approach to solving quantitatively based chemistry problems illustrates this point. Their study of chemistry students' approaches to learning reveals that students who initially take a recall-and-recognition approach to quantitative reasoning in chemistry—that is, they memorize algorithms or take solely an information approach to learning—have difficulty shifting later on in their studies to a conceptual approach to quantitative problem solving. That is, students' conditioned ways of knowing impede their ability to move toward conceptual understanding (Case & Gunstone, 2002, pp. 459–470).

Ascertaining whether students' chronology includes opportunities for them to self-reflect and receive feedback on the learning described in outcome statements deepens discussions about alignment. *Self-reflection* reinforces learning by engaging learners in focused thinking about their understanding and misunderstanding. In addition, feedback from multiple individuals—faculty, staff, peers, internship advisers, outside reviewers, or representatives from a profession—provides students with realistic responses to their work, causing them to continue to reflect on their achievement. Limited feedback, coupled with little opportunity for students to self-reflect on their development or understanding, may well contribute to some students' inability or low ability to represent the learning described in outcome statements, especially given that humans learn differently over time.

Asking members of core working groups to address the following alignment questions identifies a pool of methods for assessing students at points along the continuum of their learning, some of which have proven value based on their historical use within a program or across the campus:

- What kinds of methods or tasks prompt students to represent the learning described in outcome statements?
- Do students' learning histories include multiple opportunities for them to demonstrate, receive feedback on, and reflect on the learning they are expected to represent in an assessment method? That is, how frequently have students represented the dimensions of that learning in numerous and varied kinds of tasks?

- What dimension or dimensions of learning is a method or task designed to capture?
- What dimension or dimensions of learning is a method or task not designed to capture?
- What inferences will observers or raters be able to draw from students' responses to each method? What inferences will they not be able to draw?
- What inferences will observers or raters be able to draw from students' responses that will help answer our research or study question? What inferences will they not be able to draw?

Beyond identifying methods that assess students' abilities to select "right" answers, dialogue about identifying aligned methods of assessment should also focus on methods that represent institution- and program-level learning outcomes that emerge or develop across the progression of students' learning. Open-ended methods provide students with opportunities to construct responses, solve problems, identify problems, and create, interpret, design, perform, translate, and integrate their learning over time into various kinds of contexts.

PROPERTIES OF A METHOD: VALIDITY AND RELIABILITY

Collecting and reporting assessment results often translates into charts and graphs that provide a summary of student achievement. However, assessing for learning dives beneath reporting percentages to interpret the relationship between students' achievement and the practices that contribute to that achievement. Those who teach and educate students, members of the programs and services that contribute to students' learning, become the interpreters of assessment results. The relevance of those interpretations depends on the usefulness of collected results. If results do not lead to interpretations about student learning, interpretations that are based on patterns of strength and weakness in relation to expectations for learning, then methods have minimal usefulness in an organization committed to learning about the efficacy of its practices. (Chapter 6 focuses on developing criteria and standards of judgment, or scoring rubrics, that provide useful institution- and program-level results with which to identify patterns of student performance.)

The process of selecting or designing assessment methods, then, involves analyzing properties of each proposed assessment method to determine (1) how well a method prompts students to represent the learning described in outcome statements and (2) how consistently raters score students' responses or work to provide patterns of students' strength and weaknesses that are, in turn, useful in stimulating dialogue about the efficacy of educational practices. With the support and expertise of representatives from institutional research or other individuals knowledgeable about statistical measures and processes, core working groups narrow down the pool of possible summative and formative methods by testing the *validity* and *reliability* of a proposed method.

Validity

The property of *validity* refers to the extent to which a method prompts students to represent the dimensions of learning desired. A valid method enables direct and accurate assessment of the learning described in outcome statements. If a program is based on a problem-based model of learning that values students' abilities to articulate and justify solutions to problems, resorting to a multiple-choice method to assess students' learning will not prompt students to represent the valued learning they have practiced. This method will provide evidence of students' ability to select answers without evidence of the thinking that justifies a selection. It will not provide evidence of their ability to construct or create responses, including unanticipated ones. The discussions that surround learning outcome statements, curricular and co-curricular design, pedagogy, models of teaching and learning, and philosophies of teaching provide the necessary institution- and program-level context within which to analyze the validity of methods. Given the complex institution- and program-level outcomes of higher education, these discussions are increasingly leading working groups to design methods that emerge from institution- and program-level teaching and learning processes to assure a method's validity.

Reliability

The property of *reliability* refers to the extent to which trial tests of a method with representative student populations fairly and consistently assess the expected traits or dimensions of student learning within the construct of that method. In addition, it measures how consistently scorers or scoring systems grade student responses. Inquiry into the reliability of a method is prompted by the following kinds of questions:

- How well do trial tests yield the same results after multiple administrations?
- More specifically, how well do representative populations respond to levels or types of questions or stimuli?
- Does the language of questions or instructions or the sequence or format of questions or tasks disadvantage certain populations?
- How well do scores across observers, graders, or automated grading systems agree?

Interrater reliability—the degree to which different individual observers or graders agree in their scoring—develops through multiple trials of scoring sample student work or responses to achieve common calibrations among graders. Calibrating graders or observers so that they respond similarly to what students produce is a component of pilot-testing a designed method. An example of how an institution weaves tests of validity and reliability into its commitment to assessment is illustrated in the institutional example in Box 5.7.

AN OVERVIEW OF STANDARDIZED INSTRUMENTS

Historically, standardized instruments have served as a primary method to assess student learning. Often required for placing students in appropriate-level courses in colleges and universities, for certifying achievement in a major or profession, or for gate-keeping purposes to identify students who are unable to perform according to institution- or program-level expectations, standardized instruments are accompanied with large-scale validity and reliability studies conducted over years of administration with representative populations. T. Dary Irwin's definitions and comparison of validity and reliability properties and their subcomponents across frequently used standardized tests provide valuable information about these properties. In addition, his analysis of what each test aims to assess contributes to campus discussions about how well standardized tests align with program- and institution-level outcome statements or provide results that complement alternative assessment methods developed within an institution (U.S. Department of Education, 2000). A similar sourcebook focusing on definitions and assessment methods for communication, leadership, information literacy, quantitative reasoning, and quantitative skills is currently under review. (Appendix 5.3 lists strategies for reviewing and selecting standardized instruments.)

Although backed by validity and reliability studies, traditional standardized instruments have been historically designed to report on students' discrete abilities as a "measure" of their understanding, often through multiple-choice or closed-ended questions. Writing about the majority of traditional standardized methods to assess students' writing, Murphy and Grant (1996) describe the paradigm that has anchored traditional testing:

> Most traditional assessment measures are anchored in a positivist paradigm, a paradigm that is dominant in education in general and to some degree in the field of writing assessment. Positivism treats knowledge as skills, as information that can be divided into testable bits, or as formulaic routines. With positivism there is a truth, a correct interpretation, a right answer that exists independently of the learner. . . . Within a positivist framework, there is no room for the idea that several equally valid interpretations might be possible. (p. 285)

Stating institution- and program-level outcomes, exploring how well methods align with those statements and students' learning histories, and exploring how well standardized instruments capture the multidimensions of learning drive dialogue focused on designing local methods. These locally designed methods serve as alternatives or complements to standardized tests. They value students' abilities to perform authentic tasks that parallel or replicate real-world tasks and prompt students to represent the dimensions of their learning (Wiggins & McTighe, 1998). In addition, these methods provide opportunity for feedback from faculty, staff, administrators, peers, and others who contribute to student learning; they also provide opportunity for students' self-reflection on their achievement. If not to replace standardized tests, alternative methods complement evidence of learning assessed through standardized tests. Indeed, they provide rich evidence of institution- and program-level outcomes, thereby representing higher education's complex expectations for student learning.

AN OVERVIEW OF LOCALLY DESIGNED AUTHENTIC, PERFORMANCE-BASED METHODS

Representing student learning through commercially and nationally normed methods, such as standardized tests, satisfies external audiences focused on making budgetary decisions or decisions aimed at comparing institutions' performance. How well externally validated

BOX 5.7   INSTITUTIONAL EXAMPLE: *Alverno College*

At Alverno College, validation of methods includes a set of questions closely aligned with the values of the institution. These questions are designed to foster faculty inquiry into the validity of the assessments that they use to foster and credential each student's learning outcomes (Alverno College Faculty, 1979/1994, p. 121). Because the questions are about the validity of the college's curriculum-embedded assessments, which are a regular part of how students learn, they reflect not only what and how students have learned, but also the expectation that these student learning outcomes transfer to postcollege settings. In this context, the alignment of assessment methods with outcome expectations is doubly important. Some of the alignment questions include the following: "Is the mode of assessment appropriate to the outcome(s)?" "Does the instrument assess both content and ability?" "Do the criteria taken collectively sufficiently measure the outcomes?" Other questions call attention to additional validity concerns.

"Can the instrument elicit performance with sufficient data to provide for diagnostic, structured feedback to the student on his or her strengths and weaknesses?" The validity of an educational assessment includes its learning consequences, which is why the presence and nature of feedback is fundamental to the validity of assessment-as-learning at Alverno. When assessments have embedded learning and credentialing consequences, they also motivate students to do their best and so avoid the kind of low motivation that often threatens the validity of judgments drawn from add-on assessments.

"Does the instrument integrate previous levels of competence?" Increased curricular coherence heightens the role that local context plays in assessment validity. This question assumes that assessments need to developmentally build on a particular kind of integration of prior learning because Alverno educators require that students demonstrate higher levels of the curriculum's abilities in more advanced coursework.

"Can the instrument elicit the fullest expression of student ability at a level appropriate to context?" Performance-based assessments are often updated with new stimuli or are intentionally revised in other ways, and so faculty observation of change in student performance becomes a key source of validity evidence. For assessments that occur outside the classroom, Alverno faculty design teams review performance to determine implications for improvement of the assessment and curriculum.

For purposes such as accreditation, more formal processes for aggregating and documenting evidence from curriculum-embedded assessments are increasingly necessary. An assessment that senior education majors and minors complete as part of their student teaching requirements provides an example of how curriculum-embedded assessments can serve both accountability and improvement needs. Research staff from Educational Research and Evaluation thematically analyzed 40 performance assessments, which included the student teachers' lesson plans, the assessments they used, and how well they analyzed their pupils' learning. The researchers also coded the student teachers' self-assessments against curriculum-based and research-validated criteria. The report included estimates of interrater reliability and examples of the thematic categories, representing typical performance as well as the range observed. A visiting site team from the U.S. Department of Education used the report as summative evidence of the quality of the education program.

Across the college, collective review by faculty of student performance has been the strongest support to improving curriculum and the validity of assessment judgments. For example, in a follow-up study, 13 education department faculty rated and discussed the performance of 11 preservice teachers on the student teaching assessment. Because each preservice teacher provided extensive evidence of his or her performance, including examples of pupils' performance on an assessment he or she designed, the review process was tightly scripted to make it feasible. Each individual faculty reviewed only three or four performances, one of which they all had in common. Their small- and large-group discussions led to affirmations of prior faculty judgments of these student teaching assessments, which had indicated that these students were ready to teach based on criteria that integrated departmental criteria and state standards. But these discussions also yielded concerns about the quality of the student teachers' analyses of their pupils' performance that have guided specific changes in the assessment and preparation for it in prior field experiences. Such collaborative inquiry by faculty into the validity of assessments is supported by broadly conceptualizing the scholarship of teaching (Mentkowski & Associates, 2000).

Source: Glen Rogers, senior research associate, Educational Research and Evaluation, and Kathy Lake, professor of education, Alverno College.

methods align with institution- and program-level outcomes, pedagogy, curricular and instructional design, and educational practices is another matter. Many institutions and programs resort to narrowing the curriculum and students' approaches to learning to more greatly ensure that students will achieve passing scores on these standardized methods. Pressures of external mandates or efficient reporting of results conditions pedagogy and curriculum to prepare students to perform on these standardized instruments.

Locally designed and validated authentic performance-based assessment methods offer a complementary interpretation of student achievement that may refute or challenge externally validated results. To demonstrate the complexity of our intentions and the dimensions of student learning, the results of internally developed and validated methods need to be presented alongside externally validated methods. Furthermore, the results of internally designed assessment methods provide us with the richest information about the efficacy of our own educational practices. Maps and inventories provide an early opportunity to validate formative and summative locally designed assessment methods because they illustrate how well these methods align with what and how students learn. Because educators assess students' learning in courses and after educational experiences—that is, they develop methods that align with their teaching—establishing a pool of these practices is helpful in identifying program- or institution-level formative and assessment methods. That is, there may already be locally designed methods that can be used to track student learning over time, such as a case study or problem that community members agree would best stimulate students to represent their learning. The following questions underlie approaches to validating locally designed methods:

- Does the method align with what and how students have learned?
- Have students practiced and received feedback on what the method will assess?
- Have students had multiple and varied opportunities to learn?
- Are students aware that they are responsible for demonstrating this learning?
- Have there been opportunities to pilot-test the method across student populations to ensure that the method does not bias certain populations?

Aligning, pilot-testing, and administering designed methods over semesters has been the hallmark of Alverno College's pioneering efforts to develop and model practices that ensure the validity and reliability of its designed methods. The work of Mentkowski and colleagues provides direction and models for institutional processes that assure the validity and reliability of designed methods (Mentkowski & Associates, 2000; Mentkowski & Doherty, 1980, 1984; Mentkowski & Loacker, 1985; Mentkowski & Rogers, 1988). The institutional example in Box 5.7 summarizes the processes that underlie the college's internally developed validation process. The process of designing assessment methods is yet another example of the collaboration that underlies an institutional commitment. This collaboration leads to consensus about the appropriateness of a method in relationship to learning outcome statements, the intentional design of educational experiences, and the degree to which methods are valid, reliable, and useful in providing results that identify patterns of student performance.

AN OVERVIEW OF TECHNOLOGY-ENABLED DIRECT ASSESSMENT METHODS

The possible ways to assess student learning are burgeoning given the revolutionizing power of web technology (Bonk, 2009). Developments in educational technology and technological tools offer new opportunities to learn not only what students are learning, but also how they are learning. Many of these new and emerging possibilities enable us to deepen our understanding of the ways in which students construct meaning, as well as provide occasions for students to individualize their learning in ways that move well beyond the boundaries of traditional assessment methods. Often, a method of instruction—blogs, wikis, podcasts, or videos posted on YouTube—becomes a method students use to demonstrate their learning as well. Further, given the developments in educational technology, traditional methods of assessment are now possible in online environments, as shown later in this chapter. The following ways in which students learn through technology and technological tools also represent opportunities to assess with technology:

- Students who learn online through online delivery systems, such as distance education programs, consistently demonstrate their learning in that online context. In this scenario, assessment methods are built into the online programs and scored within that environment, often with integrated scoring technology.

- Students who learn in traditional face-to-face or hybrid programs practice and/or demonstrate their learning in online environments. That is, they may be assigned to perform in a virtual simulation or they may be assigned a project that requires them to use the web, web-based resources, software packages, or technological tools, such as with Web Quests, inquiry-based assignments that require students' interaction with Internet resources.

- Students who maintain an e-portfolio not only store their work but also create a *personal learning environment* in which they chronologically represent their learning and learning processes (see pages 174–175 in this chapter).

Standardized Instruments

Representing a shift from the traditional standardized test is the Collegiate Learning Assessment (CLA), an online standardized test of undergraduate students' abilities to think critically, reason analytically, and communicate. A sample of freshmen and seniors at an institution takes the online test. Besides identifying fallacies in reasoning, unlike most closed-ended standardized tests, the CLA requires students to write an analytical essay to make or break an argument, performing the following tasks: analyzing a series of documents, synthesizing written information and quantitative data, arriving at conclusions, and recommending actions. Although still focused on presenting results of how well students perform according to the universe of that test, this shift in practice positions students to perform authentic tasks—a focus that is characteristic of the authentic performance-based direct methods identified in the inventory in Appendix 5.4.

Current developments in technology-enabled tests now used primarily to assess learning in healthcare education, the military, and K–12 will probably take hold in higher education as the costs of the following options come down: (1) standardized online tests that track and diagnose learners' decisions and thinking strategies by breaking down students' performance patterns into diagnostic units and (2) computer adaptive tests that present students with questions based on their initial performance level (from beginner to mastery level, for example) and

thereby report the actual achievement results at that level, rather than immersing students in levels of questions that they are not yet able to answer (Tucker, 2009, pp. 2–3). The kinds of descriptive data available from the two previous examples, in turn, inform pedagogy. Writing about the future of technology-based assessment, Tucker (2009) states that the future will provide heretofore unknown information about student actions and decisions:

> These new technology-enabled assessments offer the potential to understand more than whether a student answered a test question right or wrong. Using multiple forms of media that allow for both visual and graphical representations, we can present complex, multi-step problems for students to solve, and we can collect detailed information about an individual student's approach to problem solving. This information may allow educators to better comprehend how students arrive at their answers and learn what those pathways reveal about students' grasp of underlying concepts, as well as to discover how they can alter their instruction to help move students forward. Most importantly, the new research projects have produced assessments that reflect what cognitive research tells us about how people learn, providing an opportunity to greatly strengthen the quality of instruction in the nation's classrooms. (p. 1).

Closed-ended questions have entered the mainstream of online learning systems, such as in *learning management systems*. Learning management systems (LMSs) such as Blackboard, Moodle, or Sakai, distribute educational courses and programs over the Internet. *Course management systems* (CMSs) provide content and organizational formats for educators to develop online courses. *Software authoring programs* help educators develop their own web-based courses or modules from scratch, and *open online learning* sites provide an opportunity for individuals to design and offer courses through that site using a standard authoring system. All of these systems have the capacity to randomly generate closed-ended questions from a pool of questions. Authors of courses or programs can also add or revise questions to ensure alignment between the sets of questions and the outcomes of a course. These online systems track and report student results, providing data about which questions pose the greatest challenge to students or about patterns of weakness in student work that extend over periods of time, such as through sequences of courses. Many of the courses offered through MIT's OpenCourse-Ware Consortium (www.ocwconsortium.org) include closed-ended tests as a way to assess student learning. The institutional example in Box 5.8 illustrates how a mathematics and computer science department has incorporated a software program to assess majors' readiness to progress to higher-level calculus courses.

The MySpaceOnline learning site (www.spaced.com), a website launched in 2009, was designed based on research on medical students' learning conducted by an associate professor of surgery at Harvard Medical School, Price Kerfoot. Learners, he concluded, are "more likely to retain information when they see it periodically and are tested on their knowledge, rather than simply provided with reading material." In the online courses offered at MySpaceOnline, students receive a set of questions as frequently as once a day, via e-mail or RSS feed (text messaging and instant messaging are in the works). All the teaching is done through a trial-and-error testing method: "Answer a question wrong and it repeats; get it right and it repeats less often; get it right multiple times and it disappears."

An algorithm adjusts for the student's level and content knowledge, based on his or her score as it develops" ("Learning Online, at a Pace," August, 2009). Based on Kerfoot's research, information that is presented over spaced intervals and repeated constantly is assimilated much better than information that must be ingested in one sitting ("Online Learning Radically Simplified," n.d.).

Authoring software offers educators the possibility to design their own web-based courses from scratch that include closed-ended types of questions. SpacedEd offers that option so that new course designers can create and launch their courses on that site. Authoring software made it possible for a team of science faculty, technologists, and instructional designers from Maricopa Community Colleges to develop an online teaching module about different research methods ("Research Methods in the Social and Natural Sciences: The Laboratory, 1995). Each of the five research methods ends with a posttest consisting of standardized closed-ended questions.

Besides providing results of closed-ended questions

BOX 5.8   INSTITUTIONAL EXAMPLE: *Eastern Connecticut State University, Department of Mathematics and Computer Science*

Frustrated that mathematics majors could not transfer prerequisite course content into increasingly more advanced courses, mathematicians in the Department of Mathematics and Computer Science at Eastern Connecticut State University selected a powerful technology tool, Maple T.A., a computer-based mathematics assessment program. In conjunction with this decision, because students enrolled in the calculus sequence courses were identified for initial assessment, a Calculus Committee of the Mathematics Department identified basic chronological topics that students needed to retain from prerequisite courses to Calculus I, II, and III. These topics served as the basis for the initial calculus assessment system; at the beginning of each semester, students take an online readiness exam. Those who do not perform well on this computer-based exam are immediately enrolled in online tutorials that ready them for the next level of calculus. Currently, students are assessed on their retention of prerequisite course materials in a much broader and diverse list of mathematics courses that includes courses in the calculus sequence.

Maple T.A. provides statistical information at both the course level and the individual student level. For example, on the entry exams, in addition to a list of students' final scores, faculty can access the dates on which students took the exam and the amount of time they spent on the exam. The percentage of students who answered each question correctly as well as an individual student's answers can be determined. This type of information is useful in identifying weaknesses in the calculus sequence as well as an individual student's content weaknesses. As Keating and Davis (2006) state, "Access to such data brought a great deal of ownership not only to instructors, but to students as well. With this information, changes in the curriculum have been made to ensure that courses are better suited to address student needs and their deficiencies. Thus, deciding to use an online assessment system has unified the efforts of the entire department."

Source: Salvatrice Keating, Ph.D., and Marsha Davis, Ph.D., professors of mathematics, Department of Mathematics and Computer Science, Eastern Connecticut State University.

for a course, learning management systems and online courses may also integrate institution-, program-, and department-level questions geared toward finding out how well students transfer, integrate, and apply prior knowledge. The sequence of calculus courses that the mathematics department tracked in Box 5.8 represents an example of how this might work; over three courses faculty determined gaps in skill or knowledge levels as students moved to more complex mathematical courses.

Capstone Projects

Demonstrated in traditional or online contexts, capstone projects represent the culmination of students' learning in their major program of study, often demonstrating students' abilities to integrate general education outcomes and self-reflection on their chronological learning. Box 5.9 describes the capstone project for law enforcement majors at the Community College of Rhode Island, a project developed in a three-credit course, which focuses on students' abilities to integrate their chronological learning by solving representative case studies. Additionally, and importantly, the project also focuses on learners themselves, asking them to reflect on the significance of their program of study as a component of their personal and professional lives and future decisions. Thus, students' capstone project also becomes a means through which

---

BOX 5.9 Integrative Capstone Course for Law Enforcement Majors at the Community College of Rhode Island, Criminal Justice and Legal Studies Department

Title: Case Studies in Criminal Law (3 credits)

Integration of Prior Courses: This course will integrate the five areas of study in the law enforcement major: the substantive criminal law (Criminal Law—Law 1010); criminal procedural law (Administration of Justice—Laws 1020); crime scene investigation (Criminalistics I—Laws 1030); evidentiary law (Law of Evidence—Laws 2010); and constitutional law related to law enforcement (Criminal Law & the Constitution—Laws 2030).

Method Used for Integration: This capstone course will accomplish its objective of integrating these five areas through the use of two case studies. One of the case studies will involve a murder case, and the second, another crime such as robbery, larceny, arson, or assault and battery. The instructor may vary the crimes used in a particular semester. These case files will include documents that would be involved in an actual criminal case such as bills of indictment, felony information, misdemeanor criminal complaints, police reports, witness statements, forensic reports, search warrant affidavits and inventories, transcripts of court hearings involving the case, motions to suppress evidence or confessions, and the substantive criminal laws that may apply to the facts of the case.

Written Case Reports: Students will be expected to prepare a written report on each case study used in the course which will show their grasp of the five areas being integrated in the program: substantive law, procedural law, forensics, evidence, and constitutional law. These written case reports shall be a minimum of 1500 words each (six word-processed pages, double spaced, with one inch margin, and a font size between 10 and 12 points). These written case reports will demonstrate their critical thinking skills and their ability to integrate the material studies and communicate clearly and effectively in conventional English using the proper professional terminology.

Career Reflection Piece: Each student shall also be required to make a thoughtful considered "career reflection" as a requirement of the course. This shall be in writing and a minimum of 750 words (three word-processed pages, double spaced, with one inch margin, and a font size between 10 and 12 points). The student will reflect on his or her experiences and courses at CCRI in the Law Enforcement major including: (1) reasons for choosing the major, (2) views of the major that may have changed or not changed while the student was enrolled in the program, (3) plans for the future, including further education or work or both, or (4) plans to remain in the legal field or not, along with reasons for those plans.

Prerequisites: This course will have as prerequisites the five courses mentioned above, namely, Laws 1010, 1020, 1030, 2010, and 2030. Thus, students will take this course near the end of their time at the Community College of Rhode Island.

Source: Daniel J. Donovan, Criminal Justice and Legal Studies Department, Community College of Rhode Island.

students internalize their learning in terms of their life's work.

Portfolios and E-Portfolios

E-portfolios

Conventional paper-based portfolios—collections of student work—have been replaced with e-portfolios, electronically stored collections that provide a chronological account of students' learning through the range of work they produce in traditional or online environments to demonstrate progress toward or achievement of one or more learning outcome statements (see Batson, 2010). Box 5.10 is an online page from a graduating University of Florida music education student's e-portfolio. The page categorizes and provides links to work she produced that aligned with her program's learning outcomes statements.

Goddard College's Learning Portfolio reflects the philosophical and pedagogical philosophy of the institution, illustrated in Appendix 5–1. In the Learning Portfolio students include work that demonstrates how they have used knowledge and how they have changed as a result of learning. This work is reviewed as part of a progress review (PR) at two points in students' undergraduate studies. A progress review group (PRG) of cross-program undergraduate faculty members reviews the portfolio and offers feedback and recommendations regarding degree criteria fulfillment. The worksheet for preparing the learning portfolio, shown in Appendix 5–2, identifies the kinds of artifacts students are required to enter. It also asks students to select additional work that documents their learning—a learner-centered practice that acknowledges and values students' ways of constructing meaning in a wide range of contexts. Two examples of Goddard College e-portfolio entries and faculty responses to student entries appear in Box 5.11.

BOX 5.10   Student's Opening E-portfolio Page

UNIVERSITY OF FLORIDA
SCHOOL OF MUSIC

Sandee Rose Katz
Florida Accomplished Practices

Below are links to illustrations which demonstrate my competency in the twelve Florida Accomplished Practices of Successful Teachers. For a detailed description of each practice, click the title of each section.

Accomplished Practice #1 - Assessment
Assesses student learning in music.
Second Grade- Steady Beat Assessment
Sixth Grade- Scales
Severely Disabled Students Lesson and Recognition of International Music

Accomplished Practice #2 - Communication
Communicates effectively with students, parents, and other educators.
Private Horn Instruction
Sixth Grade- Dotted Quarter Eighth Note Rhythms
8th Grade Lesson Plan, Tempo Changes

Accomplished Practice #3 - Continuous Improvement
Continually seeks to improve teaching.
Horn Tutor at Howard Bishop Middle School
Attendance of Conferences
Student Teaching Notebook

Accomplished Practice #4 - Critical Thinking
Encourages critical and creative thinking by the students.
Second Grade- Counting System
Micro Teaching- Hakuna Matata Fi Kenya
Middle School Lesson Plan, The Matrix

Accomplished Practice #5 - Diversity
Uses teaching methods that reflect the culture, learning styles, and special needs of all students.
Fourth Grade- Signing "This Land is Your Land"
Micro Teaching: Hakuna Matata Fi Kenya
Internship at Sidney Lanier School for Students with Disabilities

Accomplished Practice #6 - Ethics
Adheres to the Code of Ethics for music educators and the Principles of Professional Conduct of the Education Profession in Florida.
P.K. Yonge Teaching Experience
Buchholz High School: Wind Ensemble Horn Sectional
Student Teaching Internship Experience

Accomplished Practice #7 - Human Development and Learning
Applies knowledge of human growth and development in teaching music.
Lesson Plan: Second Grade
Lesson Plan: Sixth Grade- Beginning Band
Lesson Plan: Moderately Disabled Students

Accomplished Practice #8 - Knowledge of Subject Matter
Demonstrates knowledge and skill in music.
Private Instruction
Junior Recital
Lesson Plan, Sixth Grade: Introduction to Eighth Notes
Horn Tutor at Howard Bishop Middle School
Attendance of Conferences
Student Teaching Notebook

Accomplished Practice #9 - Learning Environments
Creates and maintains a positive learning environment.
Horn Tutor at Howard Bishop Middle School
Buchholz High School: Wind Ensemble Horn Sectional
Rehearsal Etiquitte: Sawgrass Springs Middle School

Accomplished Practice #10 - Planning
Plans effective music instruction in a variety of musical settings.
Fourth Grade Lesson Plan
Dotted Quarter-Eighth Note Rhythm Lesson Plans
Musical Alphabet and Accomodation

Accomplished Practice #11 - Role of the Teacher
Demonstrates understanding of the role of the teacher as guide and leader.
Fourth Grade: Signing "This Land is Your Land"
Sixth Grade: Standard of Excellence
Student Teaching Internship, Sawgrass Springs Middle School

Accomplished Practice #12 - Technology
Uses appropriate technology in teaching.
Web Portfolio
Use of Pyware Technology
Smartboard Technology

Click here to return to home page.

BOX 5.11   Goddard College Progress Review (Portfolio Assessment)

CASE STUDIES

Students develop portfolios of approximately 70 pages, demonstrating their learning across Goddard's progressive, liberal arts degree requirements. These portfolios typically include transcripts from other colleges, samples of critical writing, and reflections on learning as a holistic endeavor. At particular moments in their Goddard career, they submit these portfolios to review committees.

The review committee is made up of three undergraduate faculty. Faculty from all undergraduate programs are asked to volunteer for review committee work. A progress review group, consisting of three faculty members, will read and respond to approximately 20 portfolios together over the course of a semester.

Faculty on review committees receive student portfolios electronically and discuss them at length. The substance of these conversations engages the nuances of Goddard pedagogy: What does it mean to respond to degree requirements in the context of student-centered learning? Each committee member offers his or her input as to the strengths and growing challenges of each student's development across a breadth of liberal arts domains, critical thinking and writing, and Goddard's unique degree requirements previously described. Following this conversation, a committee member composes a letter to the student on behalf of the committee, responding to the progress and development of each individual student's learning.

This is a time-consuming process, taking approximately 2–4 hours per portfolio, longer for the member who is responsible for authoring progress review response.

Student Portfolio Sample 1

One student has sent a portfolio that includes the following:

The worksheet (13 pages), poetry annotation (18 single-spaced pages), ecological economics (6 single-spaced pages), transcripts from prior colleges, evaluations from prior Goddard advisers, a 3-page paper on a philosopher, a memoir of educational experiences as an example of engaged critical writing (15 pages) with an annotated bibliography of 5 books cited, 4 photos of sculptures, and 3 sketches, and a website for a contra dance group.

The PRG responded to this student as follows:

> You have taken an inspiring approach, reflecting on your educational experiences and weaving in critical reading and ideas. You may realize that you probably have four papers embedded in this one! For future endeavors we recommend fine-tuning your focus; maintain your wonderful enthusiasm and take the reader into the depths of wonder and ideas on a smaller scale. Powerful writing happens when you talk about your experience and the quote from Eleanor Duckworth about how some learners just can't integrate information at such a fast pace. You've got a lot to talk about to "deepen" this section, for instance special education and gifted and talented education assessment, differentiated learning/teaching, and Duckworth's theories. Outdoor education offers yet another paper worthy of full focus. Perhaps you have a series of essays in mind for a final project that weave personal experience with the literature.

Goddard fully supports this student, who brings transfer credits fulfilling the mainstream disciplines as well as engagement in community through study groups, contra dancing, and a public conversation about economics. The student is developing engaged critical-thinking and writing skills with every packet (five each semester) and with every semester of independent/interdependent learning at Goddard.

(continued)

BOX 5.11   *(continued)*

The student has two semesters to design, research, and construct a final project. Chances are it will be multimedia, carefully revised during both semesters in order to bring the full integrity of the student and his learning to the page.

Student Portfolio Sample 2

As another example, a student whose interest was in music chose to fulfill requirements through historical and cultural studies of diverse musical genres, explorations into the mathematical under-pinnings of music theory, and a scientific study of the anatomy and physiology of voice.

The student's review committee was impressed with the depth and breadth of her learning and encouraged her to push herself further.

We are pleased to see that you're engaging in studies at Goddard that are new to you, yet that build upon your mastery in music. We encourage you to continue to extend yourself in this way—letting your inquiry reach out beyond the bounds of what you already know. How might music be engaged through literature, poetry or social and ecological activism?

Source: Shelley Vermilya, Ed.D., IBA faculty, and Sarah Van Hoy, MA, MA, MTCM, Goddard College.

The portfolio for majors in paralegal studies at the Community College of Rhode Island (Box 5.12) chronicles representative student work that faculty score at the end of students' studies. Presented as a powerful way for students to represent themselves when they apply for jobs, it includes a career reflection piece that pauses students to connect themselves to their professional studies and to speculate about their individual futures.

Currently, there are several options for launching an e-portfolio system at an institution or in a program. The software for e-portfolios is now built into many *assessment management systems,* such as those represented in chapter 8. Open source software, another option for launching e-portfolios, was made available through the Open Source Portfolio (OSP), a nonproprietary organization that in 2003 made the University of Minnesota's e-portfolio system available to the world (www.rsmart.com/assets/understandingOSP_Dec2005.pdf). Barrett describes how it is also possible to build an e-portfolio platform using off-the-shelf software (Barrett, 2009). For assessment purposes, student work in an e-portfolio should be accompanied with *scoring rubrics,* described in chapter 6, that document student achievement levels along ranges of performance. Some *assessment management systems,* described in chapter 8, now provide the possibility for student work to be assessed by external scorers once student work samples are uploaded and sent to

them from students' e-portfolios; others have the capacity to score student work.

Web 2.0 technology has now morphed e-portfolios into interactive sites so that in their newest form e-portfolios incorporate (1) social networking, the possibility of allowing users to interact, build, or create content, such as through wikis; (2) multimedia formats to represent learning; and (3) documentation of the progress or process of completing a task using numerous resources, including human resources through social networks such as nings, blogs, Twitter, podcasts, video interaction, webinars, and Facebook (a list of Web 2.0 technology tools that can be incorporated into e-portfolios is available at www.go2web20.net; see also Batson, 2010). Box 5.13 represents the way in which a writer has organized her work—managed her content—in an e-portfolio to prepare a professional writing project. Included among her resources are professionals she maintains connections with through social networking to keep her work current. With Web 2.0 applications, students' e-portfolios are becoming their *personal learning environments,* not just storing a wide range of work—written work; live performances such as online videos of a dance; and multimedia projects that combine text, still images, audio, video, animated graphics, and sometimes even interactivity with audiences—but also representing themselves and connecting themselves to peers, professionals, friends, and interest groups. An undergraduate student discusses

---

BOX 5.12   **Student Assessment Portfolio for Paralegal Studies Majors**

Introduction: In order to assess the student learning outcomes developed for students matriculating in the Paralegal Studies Program at the Community College of Rhode Island, a portfolio of various pieces of course work as outlined below shall be submitted to the Criminal Justice & Legal Studies Department near the end of the student's course of study for evaluation.

Instructions: The portfolio shall be submitted in a hardcover three-ring binder. Students may also be required to submit their portfolio material electronically to an e-portfolio system established by the college. The portfolio shall contain:

(1) a title page with the student's name, campus, semester and year submitted, and e-mail address;

(2) a table of contents page listing the individual pieces of work included in the portfolio, together with a designation of the course name and number (including section number) for which each item was done, the name of the instructor for that particular course, and the semester and year the course was taken;

(3) a selection of eight (8) samples of the student's work as detailed below placed into the three-ring binder with numbered index tabs separating the pieces of work included; and

(4) a career reflection piece as outlined below regarding his or her college career at CCRI and his or her future plans, whether within or outside of the area of the course of study in which the student matriculated at the college.

Course Work to Be Included in the Portfolio: The heart of the portfolio should consist of eight (8) samples of the student's work taken from course work done during the student's time at the Community College of Rhode Island. The eight items to be included in the portfolio shall come from the following six categories of course work:

(1) The original research conducted for the class on Legal Research & Writing (Laws 2090) including copies of all statutes, court decisions, administrative regulations, and secondary legal materials located and actually used in completing the research project. The research materials in this section shall have a table of contents listing all of the items included with proper legal citations to the material.

(2) The research memorandum written as part of the research project for the course on Legal Research and Writing (Laws 2090). The memorandum shall properly quote from and cite the statutes, court decisions, and other materials used in the research project. It shall be a minimum of 1,000 words (four word-processed pages, double-spaced, with one inch margins and a font size between 10 and 12 points).

(3) The litigation documents (complaints, discovery documents, etc.) prepared as part of the drafting project completed for the course on Basic Civil Procedure for Paralegals (Laws 2020). Each document shall be in the proper court format, including (where appropriate) the proper case caption, document designation, prayer for relief, signature clause, and certificate of service.

(4) Two case briefs (summaries of reported and published appellate court decisions) completed in a format prescribed by the Criminal Justice & Legal Studies Department that clearly identifies the legal issue or issues in the case, the legal holdings of the appellate court, and reasoning given by the court for its holding. The case briefs may have been prepared for any one or more of the following courses: Constitutional Law (Laws 2000); Law of Evidence (Laws 2010); Law of Torts (Laws 2100); or Legal Research & Writing (Laws 2090).

(5) One Critical Thinking Exercise using a template approved by the department on the eight elements of thought (question, purpose, information, concepts, assumptions, inferences, implications, and point of view) prepared for either Introduction to Paralegal Studies (Laws 1080) or Law of Contracts (Laws 2050).

(continued)

BOX 5.12   *(continued)*

(6) Two written assignments from other law courses in the curriculum including Administration of Justice (Laws 1010); Law of Property (Laws 2060); Law of Business Organizations (Laws 2070) or elective courses such as Criminal Law (Laws 1020) and Law & Society (Laws 2040). Each written assignment shall be a minimum of 750 words (three word-processed pages, double-spaced, with one inch margins, and a font size between 10 and 12 points).

Career Reflection Piece: Each student shall include a "reflection" piece in the portfolio. This reflection shall be a minimum of 750 words (three word-processed pages, double-spaced, with one inch margin, and a font size between 10 and 12 points). The student will reflect on his or her experiences and courses at CCRI in the Paralegal Studies major including: (1) reasons for choosing the major; (2) views on how the major may have changed (or not changed) while the student was enrolled in the program; (3) future plans, including whether those plans involve further education or work or both; and (4) plans to stay in this legal field of work or move to some other field, along with the reasons for the decision.

Time of Submission: The student's portfolio shall be submitted at the end of the semester in which the student will have completed both of the skills courses in the paralegal program: Laws 2020 (Basic Civil Procedure) and Laws 2090 (Legal Research & Writing). The instructor of the last of these courses that the student takes will be the faculty member to whom the portfolio shall be submitted and who will evaluate the portfolio. The evaluation will be based upon the six student learning outcomes established for the program, and will be scored through a rubric established by the department. The rubric shall contain a scale of six points for each of the six program student learning outcomes with a maximum score of 36 points. Students receiving 24 or more points on the rubric shall be deemed to demonstrate competency in their major area of study. Students who receive fewer than 24 points on the portfolio will be given one semester to revise and resubmit the portfolio to the original instructor who evaluated it. Students completing the portfolio with a score of 24 or higher shall receive a Certificate of Portfolio Completion signed by the faculty evaluator attesting that the student has demonstrated "competency" in the field of study.

Students should know that the portfolio is a powerful tool for procuring employment in the field; that the portfolio will be the basis for any recommendation that the faculty evaluator may be asked to provide for students; and that the Certificate of Portfolio Completion can enhance students' resume in any employment search.

Source: Daniel J. Donovan, Criminal Justice and Legal Studies Department, Community College of Rhode Island.

and illustrates her own learning environment by illustrating the various groups she is a part of and contributes to in a YouTube presentation available at www.youtube.com/watch?v=hLxq6CM9Sk8. The contents in Box 5.13 illustrate how a graduate student has organized a semester writing project in her personal learning environment.

Web 2.0 e-portfolios represent learning as layered, connected, and changing based on interactions with others and deeper chronological engagement with that learning. Margo Tamez's social science Calaboz e-portfolio dissertation (https://mysite.wsu.edu/personal/mtamez/calaboz/default.aspx) has received significant national and international attention because

of its real-world application and interactive content in chronicling the conflict between indigenous women living in the Lower Rio Grande Valley and federal agencies over attempts to build a border wall through ancestral land (cited in Schaffhauser, 2009, p. 26).

As Web 2.0 e-portfolios become more common across higher education, we have the opportunity to rethink how we view and assess learning. No longer solely a means to store learning products, Web 2.0 e-portfolios represent learning as a narrative composed of various episodes of meaning making, including students' own reflection on how they think about their learning. Thus, we will have a new source of direct evidence of learning—descriptive data from students' chronological re-

BOX 5.13   Contents of a Graduate Student's 2.0 E-portfolioThat Illustrate How She Organized and Managed a Writing Project in Her Personal Learning Environment

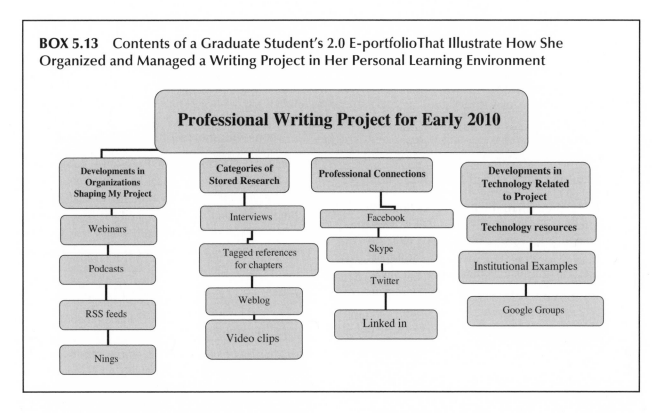

flections or online postings. We can see how students probe an issue or problem, change their perspective as they learn more or dive more deeply into different kinds of resources, and then present their answer or solution or perspective through multiple means of representation. We can see them chronologically build on their learning and connect new learning to their personal and professional lives. According to Barrett and Wilkerson (2006), Web 2.0 e-portfolios have the potential to provide insight into the ways in which students think, make meaning, gather evidence—a constructivist's approach to learning. In the words of Yancey, Cambridge and Cambridge (2009), e-portfolios are "an antidote to the inadequacies of testing," providing multiple stakeholders with evi-

dence of student learning that can inform pedagogy and curricular design. "If foundation and governmental funding were channeled to support e-portfolio system development in the same way that such funding has supported test development and implementation, e-portfolios would emerge as essential complements to tests" (Yancey et al., 2009). Projecting about the future of e-portfolios, Trent Batson, president of the recently founded Association for Authentic, Experiential and Evidence-Based Learning (AAEEBL), offers cautionary words about how a "fulfilling future" for this medium can be achieved through fundamental changes in teaching, learning, and the development of assignments in Box 5.14.

BOX 5.14   The Future of E-Portfolios

Because "ePortfolios are in the trough" (Gartner, Inc., 2008) and used clumsily and with little understanding, and most especially because, for e-portfolios to be recognized as valuable, a big change in how faculty construct their assignments is necessary, e-portfolios may never have the impact on education that many of us believe they can have. But, surprisingly, they have become widespread because people do accept the fact that once work is in digital format it *should* be saved or reused in some way and, secondly, because accrediting agencies in the United States have recognized an opportunity for additional data points from institutions and because federal governments in other parts of the world have realized the same and have pushed e-portfolios.

(continued)

BOX 5.14 *(continued)*

So we are now in the position of premature deployment—like the dark fiber still lingering from the premature deployment of too much fiber by telecoms in the 1990s; institutions are committing to doing e-portfolios without a full, or, in many cases, even a partial understanding of why they are doing them.

E-portfolios will have a fulfilled future only if higher education sees them as a learning opportunity—learning to change teaching and learning in fundamental ways. Otherwise, they will be another management tool to support the status quo and no different from course management systems, except that they manage artifacts in ways that course management systems don't.

No matter what, then, there will be e-portfolios because they fill a need, a storage and sorting and presenting function that persists over time. They do have a future. But do they have a future where more than 2% of their potential is realized? That is the real question.

In normal times, the answer would be "no" because to realize full potential requires a deeper co-operation and more extreme risk taking, not to mention just plain work, than faculty in general across all institutions have ever given to any initiative. But the times are not normal because technology of all kinds is setting the bar higher for change, because education and lifelong learning is a growth market with imaginative competitors, and because faculty members themselves are discovering the value for their own research using new technologies.

We in the field of e-portfolios would believe education had achieved an amazing turnaround if just some percentage—say, 15%—of K–12 and higher education institutions throughout the world found a way to restructure the relationship between teachers and students through imaginative and brave use of electronic portfolios in the next 5 years. This is doable but only through extensive cooperation. Change this profound cannot be achieved by institutions acting on their own.

Source: Trent Batson, AAEEBL.

High-Tech Tools and Software

Technology tools, such as clickers, digital cameras, flip cameras, iPhones and camcorders, along with software packages such as iMovie and Inspiration and data presentation software such as Pasco's DataStudio (data collection and software analysis) have advanced the ways in which students represent their work—well beyond traditional formats. As the research in chapter 4 (page 141) documents, these nontraditional ways of representing or demonstrating learning offer new pathways for students to research and analyze layers of a problem—such as locating and judging the relevance of resources, monitoring how they will use or organize the results of their research, and determining how they will communicate their results or interpretations. New ways of representing learning will spawn new criteria and standards of judgment to assess that learning.

Viewed by some educators as little more than technological gimmicks, handheld electronic devices, or clickers, have typically been used to survey students' responses to closed-ended questions that faculty raise

in a course to determine how well students learn content. Each student purchases a clicker or is provided with one to respond to questions listed on a screen at the front of the room. Anonymous student responses to questions (each clicker is numbered and corresponds to a student name in a faculty's roll book) are immediately tallied and graphed on a screen at the front of the room so that the faculty member and all students can see results. Patterns of weakness prompt faculty to consider how they should address incorrect or weak responses or to ask students to form groups to further share and correct responses with each other. Bruff (2009) describes developments in clickers that will enable faculty to ask open-ended questions. Faculty could also chronologically embed sequences of questions across a program of study to assess how well students retain and apply previous learning. These results could be shared with other program faculty to identify chronological patterns of weakness in student learning.

Flip cameras are another technological tool to document student work, such as teamwork or group problem solving in curricular or co-curricular settings.

Replay of the contents not only serves as evidence of learning for educators but also enables students to reflect on their processes and behaviors.

Wikis, Blogs, Podcasts, and Other Online Postings

Web-based tools offer yet another means for students to generate direct evidence of their learning when these options are connected to assignments. That is, students' creations of wikis, blogs, podcasts, or exchanges on online discussion boards, authored through web-based tools, can provide evidence of what and how they are learning or even how they are conducting research—information that can help faculty intervene when they see that students are not moving in the right directions or are limiting their research sources. Research at Stanford University for Innovations in Learning is currently examining the various ways in which students can demonstrate their learning through a wiki. In her research on students' wikis, Helen Chen, research scientist at the university, is focusing on the ways in which wikis are creating "connections among learners within an environment . . . and capturing evidence of learning and interaction that would not otherwise be visible" (Chen, Gilbert, & Sabol, 2006). Given the option to design their own senior-level culminating exam, students in a humanities major may decide, for example, to establish a wiki to collaboratively design that exam. Date- and time-stamped, this wiki would provide evidence of who contributed what and when. Contributing to professional discussions among chemists focused on developing new scientific communication models, Bradley (2006), a chemistry professor at Drexel University, describes how web-based communication options can become the ways scientists and students present their learning and research. These, he asserts, are more accessible ways to share knowledge publicly.

Educational Online Gaming

Evidence of student learning is also available in the analysis, decision making, and actions students undertake in educational online gaming. Holbert (2008), a chemistry teacher, convincingly argues that educational online gaming promotes numerous thinking and decision-making strategies, not the least of which are abilities to "probe" an environment to form a hypothesis and to adapt to changing circumstances. Herz (n.d.), a member of the National Research Council's committee on creativity and information technology and creator of a documentary on the history of video games, describes ways in which multiplayers in complex game environments (environments that continue to function even when players are logged off) demonstrate different ways of thinking and quantitative reasoning that can be assessed (pp. 186–188).

Online Performances, Creations, and Disciplinary Practices

Traditional methods of program-, department-, and institution-level assessment are now occurring in online environments—such as students' performance in online case studies and their performance in virtual environments, such as laboratories, microworld projects, and virtual realities such as Second Life (SL). Practica, internships, lab reports, research projects, performances, recitals, exhibitions, and simulations represent some of the disciplinary practices that document evidence of student learning. These options typically align well with program content and are often interspersed across a program of study so that there is more than one opportunity to assess students' progress toward and achievement of expected outcomes. That is, baseline assessment of students' early performances can be used as a way to track how well students learn and build on their learning over time. Some disciplinary practices can be performed online, such as lab reports or research projects that include hyperlinks to the kinds of research that led to the current project. Some disciplinary practices can be performed in virtual environments. Utah's online virtual lab, for example, has the capacity not only to provide data about the work students produce, but also about the kinds of actions or decisions students make—data that helps faculty pinpoint erroneous patterns of thinking and thus improve pedagogy (www.psych.utah.edu/learn/statsampler.html#Utahvirtuallab). Developments in assessment of medical students now include performances in Second Life ("Virtual Medical Training Comes to Second Life," Lafsky, 2009). Virtual space in Second Life became the environment in which a master's-degree student in art education temporarily displayed his thesis exhibit and enabled viewers to participate in it as he narrated (Batson, 2008).

Think Alouds

Helping to probe more deeply into students' ways of thinking and problem solving is the practice of *think alouds,* a direct method of assessment that prompts students to say what they are thinking or doing as they solve a problem or perform a process. Results of this method provide important descriptive data about students' learning-thinking processes. Asking students to verbalize what they are reading was the original use of this strategy to assist development of comprehension. This strategy has also been used to learn more about expert thinking and problem solving in physics and mathematics. Collected ideally in video, think alouds can be a source of identifying the kinds of obstacles that students encounter as they perform a task or solve a problem ("Think-Aloud Method," 2009). That is, the strategy surfaces what educators would otherwise not see in students' work—it represents a firsthand accounting.

In her work with history students, Levy adapted the think-aloud strategy to help her and her students better understand why students were having difficulty interpreting historical texts. Using the comment feature in Word as a think-aloud strategy, she asked students to mark the troublesome places in historical texts they were reading (for example, a letter from an important figure, such as George Washington) as falling "into one of three categories of difficulty: words students did not know; words or terms that seemed confusing as used; and concepts that seemed enigmatic or particularly complex." She reports that students could better address their overall difficulty interpreting texts by differentiating between decoding challenges and interpreting challenges (Bass & Eynon, 2009).

In a 3-year research project led by the Carnegie Foundation for the Advancement of Teaching, involving 11 California community colleges focused on improving teaching and learning in basic mathematics and English, faculty were encouraged to move beyond traditional assessment methods. As senior scholar Bond reports, "to determine what students lack and need, participating faculty were encouraged to use think alouds to go beneath and beyond" traditional indices of learning to uncover new ways to improve pedagogy (Bond, 2009, p. 3). In this report, Bond references the video of a student think aloud that Pasadena City College mathematics faculty have created ("How Jay Got His Groove Back," n.d.).

Online Team or Solo Projects

Individual and group problem-based assignments such as the group project in accounting at the University of Maryland's Virtual Resource Site for Teach-

ing with Technology (www.umuc.edu/virtualteaching/module1/authentic.html); chronological use of case studies to determine how well students have progressed in their problem-solving abilities; projects that position students to mine data in real or virtual contexts such as Second Life; labs such as Carnegie Mellon University's one on causal and statistical reasoning (www.cmu.edu/CSR/); and interactive multimedia projects represent some of the online options to assess students' problem-solving abilities.

OVERVIEW OF TRADITIONAL AND TECHNOLOGY-ENABLED INDIRECT METHODS

Indirect methods capture students' or others' perceptions or interpretations. By themselves, indirect methods lack sufficient evidence about how well students perform. Students' self-evaluations of how well they achieved a specific outcome may be either overestimations or underestimations of their actual performance. Yet patterns of students' perceptions, interpretations, and responses are important to analyze and interpret—along with results of direct methods—because they expand the boundaries of discussion among colleagues about ways to improve the teaching-learning process. In assessment, multiple sources of evidence lead to more robust discussions. Among the kinds of indirect methods that provide useful data about students' learning experiences are the following:

- The online Global Perspectives Inventory (GPI; https://gpi.central.edu/index.cfm), which gauges the extent to which students shift or change attitudes, values, or perspectives based on educational experiences
- The online Student Assessment of Their Learning Gains (SALG; www.salgsite.org), which asks students to identify components of learning that they believe are effective
- Small Group Instructional Diagnosis (SGID; www.miracosta.edu/home/gfloren/sgid.htm), a facilitated small-group interview process that elicits detail from students about their learning challenges

The overview of assessment methods in this chapter, the Inventory of Traditional and Technology-Enabled Direct and Indirect Assessment Methods in Appendix 5.4, and the "Additional Resources" at the end of this chapter contribute to collective dialogue and decision making focused on selecting or designing assessment methods. The selection process should also involve discussing the following:

- How well methods align with institution-, program-, or department-level educational practices and chronological feedback to students
- How well selected methods altogether contribute to answering agreed-upon research or study questions.

Agreement about methods of assessment leads working groups to develop standards and criteria of judgment, or scoring rubrics, the focus of chapter 6.

WORKS CITED

Alverno College Faculty. (1994). *Student assessment-as-learning at Alverno College.* Milwaukee, WI: Alverno College Institute. (Original work published 1979)

Barrett, H. (2009). Eportfolio learning. EduTechwiki. *http://edutechwiki.unige.ch/en/Learning_e-portfolio*

Barrett, H., & Wilkerson, J. (2006, March). Conflicting paradigms in electronic portfolio approaches: Choosing an electronic portfolio strategy that matches your conceptual framework. *http://electronicportfolios.com/systems/paradigms.html*

Bass, R., & Eynon, B. (2009, January 7). *Capturing the visible evidence of invisible learning* (Part II). *www.academiccommons.org/commons/essay/capturing-visible-evidence-invisible-learning-2*

Batson, T. (2008, March 19). *Second Life—A libertarian paradise where there are no zoning laws. http://campustechnology.com/articles/2008/03/second-life--a-libertarian-paradise-where-there-are-no-zoning-laws.aspx*

Batson, T. (2010, January 6). ePortfolios: Let me count the ways. *Campus Technology. http://campus technology.com/articles/2010/01/06/eportfolios-let-me-count-the-ways.aspx*

Bond, L. (2009, April). *Toward informative assessment and a culture of evidence.* A report from Strengthening Pre-collegiate Education in Community Colleges (SPECC). Stanford, CA: Carnegie Foundation for the Advancement of Teaching. *www.carnegie foundation.org/sites/default/files/publications/elibrary_pdf)778.pdf*

Bonk, C. J. (2009). *The world is open: How web technology is revolutionizing education.* San Francisco: Jossey-Bass.

Bradley, J. C. (2006). *Open notebook science using blogs and wikis.* Presented at the American Chemical Society Symposium on Communicating Chemistry. *http://precedings.nature.com/documents/39/version/1.*

Bruff, D. (2009). *Teaching with classroom response systems: Creating active learning environments.* San Francisco: Jossey-Bass.

Case, J., & Gunstone, R. (2002, October). Shift in approach to learning: An in-depth study. *Studies in Higher Education, 27*(4), 459–470.

Chen, H., Gilbert, D., & Sabol, J. (2006). *Using wikis to build learning communities: Successes, failures, and next steps* Poster Presentation at the Educause Learning Initiative in San Diego, CA. *http://scil.stanford.edu/news/wiki4-06.htm*

Clinical Skills Assessment in the USMLE. (2002, Fall/Winter). *law.gsu.edu/Communication/NBME-Examiner-Fall02.htm*

Entwhistle, N. J., & Ramsden, P. (1982). *Understanding student learning.* New York, NY: Nichols Publishing.

Gartner, Inc. (2008). *Inside Gartner research. http://imagesrv.gartner.com/research/methodologies/inside_gartner_research.pdf*

Herz, J. C. (n.d.). *Gaming the system: What higher education can learn from multiplayer online worlds* (pp. 169–191). *http://net.educause.edu/ir/library/pdf/ffpiu019.pdf*

Holbert, N. (2008, February). Shooting aliens: The gamer's guide to thinking. *Educational Leadership,* (65)5.

How Jay got his groove back. (n.d.) *www.cfkeep.org/html/stitch.php?s=13143081975303&id=18946594390037*

Keating, S., & Davis, M. (2006). *Calculus readiness assessment and remediation using Maple T.A.: A model for creating and implementing computer-based assessment and remediation.* Connecticut State University System Assessment of Learning for Educational Improvement Grant Program Reports for Projects Conducted in the 2005–2006 Academic Year. Hartford, CT: Department of Education.

Kiser, P. M. (1998). The Integrative Processing Model: A framework for learning in the field experience. *Human Service Education, 18,* 3–13.

Kuh, G. (2008). *High-impact educational practices: What they are, who has access to them, and why they matter.* Washington, DC: AAC&U.

Lafsky, M. (2009, July–August). Can training in Second Life teach doctors to save real lives? *Discover. http://discovermagazine.com/2009/jul-aug/15-can-*

medical-students-learn-to-save-real-lives-in-second-life/article_view?b_start:int=0&-C

Mathematics Association of American. (1998). *Quantitative reasoning for undergraduate students: A complement to the standards. http://www.maa.org/past/ql/ql_toc.html*

Mentkowski, M., & Associates. (2000). *Learning that lasts: Integrating learning, development, and performance in college and beyond.* San Francisco: Jossey-Bass.

Mentkowski, M., & Doherty, A. (1980). *Validating assessment techniques in an outcome-centered liberal arts curriculum: Insights from the evaluation and revisions process.* Milwaukee, WI: Office of Research and Evaluation, Alverno College.

Mentkowski, M., & Doherty, A. (1984). *Careering after college: Establishing the validity of abilities learned in college for later careering and performance.* Milwaukee, WI: Alverno Publications.

Mentkowski, M., & Loacker, G. (1985). Assessing and validating the outcomes of college. In P. Ewell (Ed.), *Assessing educational outcomes*, 47 (pp. 47–64). *New Directions for Institutional Research.* San Francisco: Jossey-Bass.

Mentkowski, M., & Rogers, G. P. (1988). *Establishing the validity of measures of college student outcomes.* Milwaukee, WI: Office of Research and Evaluation, Alverno College.

Murphy, S., & Grant, B. (1996). Portfolio approaches to assessment: Breakthrough or more of the same? In E. White, S. Lutz, & S. Kamusikiris, *Assessment of writing: Politics, policies, practices* (pp. 285–300). New York: Modern Language Association.

National Research Council. (2001). *Knowing what students know: The science and design of educational assessment* (pp. 206–212, 221). Washington, DC: National Academies Press.

Online Learning, at a Pace. (2009, August 5). *Inside Higher Education. www.insidehighered.com/news/2009/08/05/spaceded*

Online Learning Radically Simplified. (n.d.). *SpacedED. http://www.spaceded.com/info/spacing_effect*

Research methods in the social and natural sciences: The laboratory. (1995). *http://www.mcli.dist.maricopa.edu/proj/res_meth/*

Schaffhauser, D. (2009, November). Here, there, and everywhere. *Campus Technology*, (23)3, 25–30.

Think-aloud method. (2009). *www.tiresias.org/tools/think_aloud.htm*

Tucker, B. (2009, February). Beyond the bubble: Technology and the future of assessment. *Education Sector Reports*, pp. 1–16. *www.educationsector.org/usr_doc/Beyond_the_Bubble.pdf*

U.S. Department of Education, National Center for Educational Statistics. (2000). *The NPEC sourcebook on assessment, Vol. 1: Definitions and assessment methods for critical thinking, problem solving, and writing.* NCES 2000—172. Washington, DC: U.S. Government Printing Office. *http://nces.ed.gov/pubsearch/pubsinfo.asp?pubid=2000195*

Virtual medical training comes to Second Life. (2009, July 20). *http://chronicle.com/blogPost/Virtual-Medical-Training-Comes/7277*

Wiggins, G., & McTighe, J. (1998). *The understanding by design handbook.* Alexandria, VA: Association for Supervision and Curriculum Development.

Yancey, K., Cambridge, B., & Cambridge, D. (2009, January 7). *Making common cause: Electronic portfolios, learning, and the power of community. www.academiccommons.org/commons/essay/making-common-cause-electronic-portfolios*

ADDITIONAL RESOURCES

Areas of Assessment Focus
Advising

Miller, M. A., & Alberts, B. M. (2003). Assessing and evaluating the impact of your advisor training and development program. In National Academic Advising Association. *Advisor training: Exemplary practices in the development of advisor skills.* Monograph Series, 9. Manhattan, KS: Author.

Disciplinary Assessment

Banta, T. W., & Palomba, C. A. (2003). *Assessing student competence in accredited disciplines.* Sterling, VA: Stylus.

Business

Martel, K., with Calderon, T. (2005). *Assessment of student learning in business schools: Best practices each step of the way.* Tallahassee, FL: Association for Institutional Research.

Engineering

Kelly, W. E. (Ed.). (2008). *Assessment in engineering programs: Evolving best practices.* Tallahassee, FL: Association for Institutional Research.

Spurlin, J. (2008). *Designing better engineering education through assessment: A practical resource for faculty and department chairs on using assessment and ABET criteria to improve student learning.* Sterling, VA: Stylus.

History

American Historical Association. (2008). *Assessment in history: A guide to best practices.* Washington, D.C., Author.

Mathematics

Gold, B., Keith, S., & Marion, W. (Eds.). (1999). *Assessment practices in undergraduate mathematics.* Washington, DC: Mathematics Association of America.

Madison, B. (2006). *Assessment of student learning in college mathematics: Towards improving programs and courses.* Tallahassee, FL: Association for Institutional Research.

Psychology

American Psychological Association. *The assessment cyberguide for learning goals & outcomes in the undergraduate psychology major. www.apa.org/ed/governance .bea/assess.aspxl*

Dunn, D. S., Mehrotra, C. M., & Halonen, J. S. (Eds.). (2004). *Measuring up: Educational Assessment challenges and practices for psychology.* Washington, DC: American Psychological Association.

Sciences, Technology, Engineering, Mathematics

Committee on Undergraduate Science Education, Center for Science, Mathematics, and Engineering, and Technology, National Research Council. (1999). *Transforming undergraduate education in science, mathematics, engineering, and technology.* Washington, DC: National Academies Press.

Field-Tested Learning Assessment Guide (FLAG). A good source of assessment methods in science, technology, engineering, and mathematics. *www.wcer.wisc.edu/archive/cl1/flag/*

Hake, R. R. (1998). *Research, development, and change in undergraduate biology education* (REDCUBE): A *web guide for non-biologists. www.physics.indiana.edu/ ~redcube.*
Hake has assembled an impressive number of resources on teaching, learning, and assessing in the sciences. *www.physics.indiana.edu/~hake*

Mathieu, R. (2000). Assessment tools to drive learning: FLAG, SALG, and other proven assessments available online. In *Targeting curricular change: Reform in undergraduate education in science, math, engineering, and technology* (pp. 26–31). Washington, DC: American Association for Higher Education.

Mintzes, J. J., Wandersee, J. H., & Novak, J. D. (Eds.). (2000). *Assessing science understanding: A human constructivist view.* San Diego: Academic Press.

North Carolina State University. *www2.acs.ncsu.edu/ UPA/assmt/resource.htm#hbooks*

Project Kaleidoscope. See especially sites focused on use of portfolios. *www.pkal.org/*

Seymour, E., Wiese, D., & Hunter, A. (n.d). *Report on a panel testing of the student assessment of their learning gains instrument by faculty using modular methods to teach undergraduate* chemistry. University of Colorado at Boulder. *www.wcer.wisc.edu/archive/cl1/flag/cat/salg/salg5.htm*

Wright, J. C., Millar, S. B., Kosciuk, S. A., Penberthy, D. L., Williams, P. H., & Wampold, B. E. (1998, August). A novel strategy for assessing the effects of curriculum reform on student competence. *Journal of Chemical Education, 75,* 986–992.

First College Year

Cutright, M. (Ed.). (2003). *Annotated bibliography on assessment of the first college year.* Columbia, South Carolina: Policy Center on the First Year of College University of South Carolina.

Gardner, J. N., Barefoot, B. O., & Swing, R. L. (2001). *Guidelines for evaluating the first-year experience at four-year colleges.* Columbia, South Carolina: National Resource Center, University of South Carolina.

Gardner, J. N., Barefoot, B. O., & Swing, R. L. (2001). *Guidelines for evaluating the first-year experience at two-year colleges.* Columbia, South Carolina: National Resource Center, University of South Carolina.

Siegel, M. J. (2003). *Primer on assessment of the first college year.* Columbia, South Carolina: Policy Center on the First Year of College, University of South Carolina.

Swing, R. L. (Ed.). (2001). *Proving and improving: Strategies for assessing the first college year.* Monograph 33. Columbia, South Carolina: National Resource Center, University of South Carolina.

General Education

Allen, M. J. (2006). *Assessing general education programs.* Boston: Anker Press.

Association of American Colleges and Universities. Lists resources and AAC&U publications for assessing general education on its website. *www.aacu.edu*

Association of American Colleges and Universities. (2002). *Greater expectations: A new vision for learning as a nation goes to college.* National Panel Report. Washington, DC: Author

Banta, T. W. (Ed.). (2007). *Assessing student achievement in general education: Assessment update collections*. San Francisco: Jossey-Bass.

Bauer, K. W., & Frawley, W. J. (2002). *General education curriculum revisions and assessment at a research university*. Paper presented at the Association of Institutional Research (AIR) conference, Toronto, Canada.

Gaff, J. G., & Ratcliff, J. L. (Eds.). (1997). *Handbook of the undergraduate curriculum: A comprehensive guide to purposes, structures, strategies, and change*. San Francisco: Jossey-Bass.

General Education Assessment Sites and Information. *www.spsu.edu/irpa/Assessment/General%20Education%20Assessment%20sites-1.doc*

League for Innovation in the Community Colleges. 21st Century Learning Outcomes Colleges. *www.league.org/leagueprojects/pew/*

Lopez, C. L. (1998). How campuses are assessing general education. *Liberal Education, 84*(3), 36–43.

Lopez, C. L. (1999). General education: Regional accreditation standards and expectations. *Liberal Education, 85*(3), 46–51.

Ratcliff, J. L. (1993). *Linking assessment and general education*. University Park, PA: NCTLA.

Stone, J., & Friedman, S. (2002). A case study in the integration of assessment and general education: Lessons learned from a complex process. *Assessment and Evaluation in Higher Education, 22*(2), 199–210.

Suskie, L. (2009). *Assessing student learning: A common sense approach* (2nd ed.). San Francisco: Jossey-Bass.

Walvoord, B. E. (2010). *Assessment clear and simple: A practical guide for institutions, departments, and general education* (2nd ed.). San Francisco: Jossey-Bass.

Information Literacy

Association of College and Research Libraries. *www.ala.org/ala/professional resources/atoz/profresources infolit/informationliteracy_cfm*

Dunn, K. (2002, January–March). Assessing information literacy skills in the California State University: A progress report. *Journal of Academic Librarianship, 28*(12), 26–35.

Hernon, P., & Dugan, R. E. (2002). *An action plan for outcomes assessment in your library*. Chicago: American Library Association.

Middle States Commission on Higher Education. (2003). *Developing research and communication skills: Guidelines for information literacy in the curriculum*. Philadelphia: Author.

Interdisciplinary Assessment

Innovative Higher Education. Lists abstracts as far back as 1989, some of which relate to assessment. *www.uga.edu/ihe/ihe.html*

Stowe, D. E. (2002, May–June). Assessing interdisciplinary programs. *Assessment Update, 14*(3), 3–4.

Vess, D. (2000). *Exploration in interdisciplinary teaching and learning*. *www.faculty.de.gcsu.edu/~dvess/ids/courseportfolios/front.htm*.

Learning Communities

MacGregor, J., et al. (2003). *Doing learning community assessment: Five campus stories*. National Learning Communities Project Monograph Series. Olympia, WA: Evergreen State College, Washington Center for Improving the Quality of Undergraduate Education, in cooperation with the American Association for Higher Education.

Taylor, K., Moore, W. S., MacGregor, J., & Lindblad, J. (2003). *What we know now about learning community research and assessment*. National Learning Communities Project Monograph Series. Olympia, WA: Evergreen State College, Washington Center for Improving the Quality of Undergraduate Education, in cooperation with the American Association for Higher Education.

Senior Year

Gardner, J. N., Van der Veer, G., & Associates. (1997). *The senior year experience: Facilitating integration, reflection, closure, and transition*. San Francisco: Jossey-Bass.

Service Learning and Civic Engagement

American Political Science Association. Bibliography of books and articles. *www.apsanet.org/content_7594.cfm*

Bonner Program. Meta site that lists assessment methods. *www.bonner.org/resources/assessment/assessing%20service.html*

Bonthron, S. (Ed.) (1999). *Service learning and assessment: A field guide for teachers*. Developed by the National Service-Learning and Assessment Study Group. *www.vermontcommunityworks.org/cwpublications/slassessguide/slassessguide.html*

National Service-Learning Clearinghouse. (2008). *Assessment, evaluation, and performance measurement: Selected resources bibliography*. Scotts Valley, CA: Author. *www.servicelearning.org/instant_info/bibs/he_bibs/assess_eval/*

Student Affairs

Bresciani, M. (2003). *Identifying projects that deliver outcomes and provide a means of assessment: A concept mapping checklist.* Washington, DC: NASPA.

Bresciani, M., Gardner, M. M., & Hickmott, J. (2009). *A practical guide to outcomes based assessment of learning and development in student affairs.* Sterling, VA: Stylus.

Bresciani, M., Zelna, C., & Anderson, J. (2004). *Assessing student learning and development: A handbook for practitioners.* Washington, DC: NASPA.

Garis, J. W., & Dalton, J. C. (2007, September). E*portfolios: Emerging opportunities for student affairs. New Directions for Student Services,* 119. San Francisco: Jossey-Bass.

Kuh, G. D., Gonyea, R. M., & Rodriguez, D. P. (2002). The scholarly assessment of student development. In T. W. Banta & Associates, *Building a scholarship of assessment* (pp. 100–127). San Francisco: Jossey-Bass.

Pascarella, E. T. (2001). Identifying excellence in undergraduate education: Are we even close? *Change,* 33(3), 19–23.

Pascarella, E. T., & Terenzini, P. T. (1991). *How college affects students: Findings and insights from twenty years of research.* San Francisco: Jossey-Bass.

Schroeder, C., et al. (1994). *The student learning imperative: Implications for student affairs.* Washington, DC: American College Personnel Association.

Schuh, J. H., & Associates. (2009). *Assessment methods for student affairs.* San Francisco: Jossey-Bass.

Schuh, J. H., & Upcraft, M. L. (1996). *Assessment in student affairs: A guide for practitioners.* San Francisco: Jossey-Bass.

Schuh, J. H., Upcraft, M. L., & Associates. (2000). *Assessment practice in student affairs: An applications manual.* San Francisco: Jossey-Bass.

Stage, F. K. (Ed.). (1992). *Diverse methods for research and assessment of college students.* Washington, DC: American College Personnel Association.

Upcraft, M. L., & Schuh, J. H. (1996). *Assessment in student affairs: A guide for practitioners.* San Francisco: Jossey-Bass.

Winston, R. B., Jr., Creamer, D. G., Miller, T. K., & Associates. (2001). *The professional student affairs administrator: Educator, leader, and manager.* Philadelphia: Taylor & Francis.

Writing

Conference on College Composition and Communication. *www.ncte.org/cccc/*

Council of Writing Program Administrators. *www.wpacouncil./wpa-l*

Ericsson, P. F., & Haswell, R. (Eds.). (2006). *Machine scoring of student essays: Truth and consequences.* Logan, Utah: Utah State University Press.

Haswell, R. H. (Ed.). (2001). Beyond outcomes: Assessment and instruction within a university writing program. *Perspectives on Writing: Theory, Research, Practice,* 5. Westport, CT: Ablex.

Huot, B. (2002). *(Re)articulating writing assessment in teaching and learning.* Logan, Utah: Utah State University Press.

Huot, B., & O'Neill, P. (2008). *Assessing writing: A critical source book.* Boston, MA: Bedford/St. Martin's Press.

O'Neill, P., Moore, C., & Huot, B. (2009). *A guide to college writing assessment.* Logan, Utah: Utah State University Press.

White, E. M. (1994). *Teaching and assessing writing: Recent advances in understanding, evaluating, and improving student performance* (2nd ed.). San Francisco: Jossey-Bass.

White, E. M., Lutz, W. D., & Kamusikiri, S. (1996). *Assessment of writing: Politics, policies, practices.* New York: Modern Language Association.

Considerations Affecting the Design and Selection of Assessment Methods

Allen, M. J. (2004). *Assessing academic programs in higher education.* Boston: Anker Press.

Association of American Colleges & Universities. Website consisting of AAC&U publications, resources, annual meetings, initiatives, institutes, resources, and campus practices on assessment in general education and in disciplines. *www.aacu.org/resources/assessment/index.cfm*

Banta, T. W., Jones, E. A., & Black, K. E. (2009). *Designing effective assessments: Principles and profiles of good practice.* San Francisco: Jossey-Bass.

Bresciani, M. J., Zelna, C. L., & Anderson, J. (2004). *Assessing student learning and development: A handbook for practitioners.* Washington, DC: NASPA.

Brown, S., & Glasner, A. (1999). *Assessment matters in higher education: Choosing and using diverse approaches.* Philadelphia: SRHE and Open University Press.

Clarke, M., & Gregory, K. (Eds.). (2003, Winter). The impact of high stakes testing. *Theory Into Practice,* 42, 1.

Driscoll, A., & Wood, S. (2007). *Developing outcomes-based assessment for learner-centered education: A faculty introduction.* Sterling, VA: Stylus. *http://stylus.stylus pub.com/Books/BookDetail.aspx?productID=130091*

Erwin, D. T., & Wise, S. E. (2002). A scholarly-practitioner model for assessment. In T. W. Banta & Associates, *Building a scholarship of assessment* (pp. 67–81). San Francisco: Jossey-Bass.

Ewell, P. (1991). To capture the ineffable: New forms of assessment in higher education. In G. Grant (Ed.), *Review of research in education* (pp. 75–125). Washington, DC: American Educational Research Association.

Ewell, P. T. (1987, Fall). Establishing a campus-based assessment program. In D. F. Halpern (Ed.), *Student outcomes assessment: What institutions stand to gain* (pp. 9–24). *New Directions for Higher Education,* 59. San Francisco: Jossey-Bass.

Ewell, P. T., & Jones, D. P. (1985). The costs of assessment. In C. P. Adelman (Ed.), *Assessment in American higher education: Issues and contexts.* Washington, DC: Office of Educational Research and Improvement, U.S. Department of Education.

Grant, G. (Ed.). 1991. *Review of research in education,* 17. Washington, DC: American Educational Research Association.

Herman, J., Aschbacher, P., & Winters, L. (1992). *A practical guide to alternative assessment.* Alexandria, VA: Association for Supervision and Curriculum Development.

Jacobs, L. D., & Chase, C. I. (1992). *Developing and using tests effectively.* San Francisco: Jossey-Bass.

Kohn, A. (2000). *The case against standardized tests.* Portsmouth, NH: Heinemann.

Maki, P. (2001, March-April). From standardized tests to alternative methods: Some current resources on methods to assess learning in general education. *Change,* 33(20), 29–31.

Maki, P. (2009, Winter). Moving beyond a national habit in the call for accountability. *Peer Review,* 11(1), 13–17.

Mezeske, R. J., & Mezeske, B. A. (Eds.). (2008). *Beyond tests and quizzes: Creative assessments in the college classroom.* San Francisco: Jossey-Bass.

Pike, G. R. (2002). Measurement issues in outcomes assessment. In T. W. Banta & Associates, *Building a scholarship of assessment* (pp. 131–147). San Francisco: Jossey-Bass.

Sacks, P. (1999). *Standardized minds: The high price of America's testing culture and what we can do to change it.* Cambridge, MA: Perseus Books.

Suskie, L. (2009). *Assessing student learning: A common sense guide* (2nd ed.). San Francisco: Jossey-Bass.

Wehlburg, C. M. (2008). *Promoting integrated and transformative assessment: A deeper focus on student learning.* San Francisco: Jossey-Bass.

Wiggins, G. (1989). Teaching to the (authentic) test. *Educational leadership,* 46, 45.

Wiggins, G. (1990). The case for authentic assessment. *Practical Assessment, Research and Evaluation,* 2(2). *http://PAREonline.net/getvn.asp?v=2&n=2*

Assessments for Diverse Learners

Graduate Record Examinations. (1999). *New directions in assessment: Fairness, access, multiculturalism and equity.* The GRE, FAME Report Series. 3. Princeton, NJ: Educational Testing Service.

Michelson, E. (1997, Fall). Multicultural approaches to portfolio development. In *Assessing adult learning in diverse settings: Current issues and approaches. New Directions for Adult and Continuing Education,* 75 (pp. 41–54). San Francisco: Jossey-Bass.

Moran, J. J. (1997). *Assessing adult learning: A guide for practitioners.* Malabar, FL: Krieger.

Rose, A. D., & Leahy, M. A. (Eds.). (1997, Fall). *Assessing adult learning in diverse settings: Current issues and approaches. New Directions for Adult and Continuing Education,* 75. San Francisco: Jossey-Bass.

Sheckley, B. G., & Keeton, M. T. (1997). *A review of the research on learning: Implications for the instruction of adult learners.* College Park: Institute for Research on Adults in Higher Education, University of Maryland.

Vella, J., Berardinelli, P., & Burrow, J. (1998). *How do they know? Evaluating adult learning.* San Francisco: Jossey-Bass.

E-Portfolios and Portfolios

Banta, T. W. (Ed). (2003). *Portfolio assessment: Uses, cases, scoring, and impact.* San Francisco: Jossey-Bass.

Barrett, H. (2005). *Electronic portfolio handbook.* *http://electronicportfolios.com/handbook/index.html*

Barrett, H. (2009). *Using technology to support alternative assessment and electronic portfolios. http://electronic portfolios.com/portfolios.html*

Batson, T. (2002, November). *The electronic portfolio boom: What's it all about. http://campustechnology.com/ articles/2002/11/*

Becta. (2007). Impact of e-portfolio on learning (pp. 1–118). *http://emergingtechnologies.becta.org.uk/ upload-dir/downloads/pag e_documents/research/ impact_study_eportfolios.pdf*

Cambridge, B., Yancey, K., & Cambridge, D. (2009). *Electronic portfolios 2.0: Emergent research on implementation and impact.* Sterling, VA: Stylus.

http://stylus.styluspub.com/Books/BookDetail.aspx? productID=183 392

Ittelson, J. (2008, Summer). Know your ePortfolio. *Converge.* (pp. 32–35). *http://media.centerdigitaled .com/Converge_Mag/pdfs/issues/Conve rgeSum08_72.pdf*

Jafari, A. (2004, July–August). The sticky e-portfolio system: Tackling challenges and identifying attributes. *Educause*, 38–48.

Jafari, A., & Kaufman, C. (2006). *Handbook of research on electronic portfolios*. Hershey, PA: IGI Global.

Joint Information Systems Committee. (2009). *Effective practices with e-portfolios. www.jisc.ac.uk/media/documents/ publications/effectivepracticeeportfolios.pdf*

Miles, K. (2003). *Web portfolio guide: Creating electronic portfolios for the web.* Upper Saddle River, NJ: Pearson.

Regis University. (n.d.) *E-portfolio basics. http://academic .regis.edu/LAAP/eportfolio/basics.htm*

Waters, J. K. (2007, October 1). ePortfolios meet social software. *Campus Technology. http://campus technology.com/Articles/2007/10/ePortfolios-Meet-Social-Software. aspx?Page=1*

Wolf, D. (1989, April). Portfolio assessment: Sampling student work. *Educational Leadership*, 46(7), 35–39.

Zubizarreta, J. (2009). *The learning portfolio: Reflective practice for improving student learning* (2nd ed.). San Francisco: Jossey-Bass.

E-Portfolio and Portfolio Bibliographies and Resources

Association for Authentic, Experiential and Evidence-Based Learning. *www.aaeebl.org/page/ePortfolio+ Resources*

Aurbach & Associates. (1996). *Portfolio assessment bibliography. www.aurbach.com/files/bibliography.pdf*

Barrett, H. Dr. Helen Barrett's favorite links on alternative assessment and electronic portfolios. Includes higher education and professional examples as well as a bibliography on portfolios. *http://electronicportfolios.org/portfolios/bookmarks.html*

Glendale Community College. *www.gc.maricopa.edu/ English/assessment/resources_portfolio.html*

Three Rivers Community College. *www.trcc.commnet .edu/Ed_Resources/ePortfolio/PDFs/ePortfolio% 20Bibliography.pdf*

University of Minnesota. Useful for resources to construct an e-portfolio or to identify vendors who offer templates for e-portfolios. *www.tc.umn.edu/ ~rozai001/workshops/eportfolio/eportfolio_bib.pdf*

National Organizations Focused on E-Portfolios

Association for Authentic, Experiential and Evidence-Based Learning (AAEEBL). A global academic association of 80 educational institutions established in 2009, AAEEBL focuses on developing new designs in learning and assessment for the future and increasing connections among the portfolio community. *www.aaeebl.org*

Educause Learning Initiative (ELI). *www.educause.edu/ search?quick_query=eportfolios&Image1.x=47& Image1.y=7*

Electronic Portfolio Action and Communication (EPAC). Up-to-date site for resources and examples of e-portfolios, including ways to construct them and the most recent Barrett resources. *http://epac.pbworks.com/ePortfolio-Compilations-of-ResourcesInter/*

National Coalition for Electronic Portfolio Research. An organization that convenes research/ practitioners to study the impact of electronic portfolios on student learning and educational outcomes. Each year a cohort of 10 institutions investigates a common educational question or theme issue over three years. *http://ncepr.org*

Open Source Portfolio Initiative (OSPI). An evolving group of individuals and organizations interested in collaborating on the development of the best nonproprietary, open source electronic portfolios. *www.theospi.org*

Project Kaleidoscope. Examples of portfolios in psychology, physics, biology, chemistry, and neuroscience, some of which focus on assessment of student learning. *www.pkal.org/documents/ WhatIsLearned.cfm*

Graduate-Level Assessment

Council of Graduate Schools. (2005). *Assessment and review of graduate programs. A policy statement.* Washington, DC: Author.

DeVaney, T. A., Adams, N. B., & Elliott, C. B. (2008, Winter). Assessment of online learning environments: Using the OCLES (20) with graduate level online classes. *Journal of Interactive Online Learning*, 7(3), 165–174. *www.ncolr.org/jiol/issues/*

Haworth, J. G. (Ed.). (1996, Winter). *Assessing graduate and professional education: Current realities, future prospects. New Directions for Institutional Research.* San Francisco: Jossey-Bass.

Lovitts, B. (2007). *Making the implicit explicit: Creating performance expectations for the dissertation.* Sterling, VA: Stylus. *http://stylus.styluspub.com/Books/ BookDetail.aspx?productID=128088*

Lovitts, B., & Wert, E. (2008). *Developing quality dissertations in the humanities: A graduate student's' guide to*

achieving excellence. Sterling, VA: Stylus. *http://stylus
.styluspub.com/Books/BookDetail.aspx?productID=
163103*

Lovitts, B., & Wert, E. (2008). *Developing quality dissertations in the sciences: A graduate student's' guide to achieving excellence.* Sterling, VA: Stylus. *http://stylus.stylus
pub.com/Books/BookDetail.aspx?productID=163105*

Lovitts, B., & Wert, E. (2008). *Developing quality dissertations in the social sciences. A graduate student's' guide
to achieving excellence.* Sterling, VA: Stylus.
*http://stylus.styluspub.com/Books/BookDetail.aspx?
productID=163104*

Maki, P., & Borkowski, N. (Eds.). (2006). *The assessment of doctoral education: Emerging criteria and new
models for improving outcomes.* Sterling, VA: Stylus.
*http://stylus.styluspub.com/Books/BookDetail.aspx?
productID=128082*

Fairness in Assessment Methods

Fair Test Examiner. *www.fairtest.org*

Joint Committee on Testing Practices. (n.d.) *Code of fair
testing practices in education. http://ericae.net/code.txt*

Jorgensen, S., Fichten, C. S., Havel, A., Lamb, D.,
James, C., & Barile, M. (2003). *Students with disabilities at Dawson College: Successes and outcomes.*
Adaptech Research Network. *http://adaptech.
dawsoncollege.qc.ca*

Sedlacek, W. E. (1993). *Issues in advancing diversity
through assessment.* Research Report 45–93. College
Park: Counseling Center, University of Maryland.
*www.inform.umd.edu/EdRes/Topic/diversity/General/
Reading/Sedlacek/issues.htm*

Suskie, L. (2000, May). *Fair assessment practices.*
*www.elcamino.edu/administration/vpsca/docs/assessment/
FairAssessmentPractices_Suskie.pdf*

Validity and Reliability

Lissitz, R. W. (2009).*The concept of validity: Revisions, applications, and new directions.* Charlotte, North Carolina:
Information Age.

National Postsecondary Educational Cooperative
(NPEC) of the National Center for Educational
Statistics. (2002). *Defining and assessing learning:
Exploring competency-based initiatives.* Pages 10–12
are especially helpful in defining validity and
reliability and its component measures.
*http://nces.ed.gov/pubsearch/pubsinfo.asp?pubid=
2002159*

Palomba, C. A., & Banta, T. W. (1999). *Assessment essentials: Planning, implementing, and improving assessment
in higher education.* San Francisco: Jossey-Bass.

Pike, G. R. (2002). Measurement issues in outcomes
assessment. In T. W. Banta & Associates, *Building
a scholarship of assessment* (pp. 131–147). San Francisco: Jossey-Bass.

Some Direct and Indirect Assessment Methods
Visual Representations

Generic Centre. Learning and Teaching Support Network. Lists articles on concept maps and their
usefulness in assessing learning. *http://dbweb
.liv.ac.uk/ltsnpsc/AB/AB-html/node12.html*

Shmaefsky, B. (2007, January–February). E-concept
mapping. *Journal of College Science Teaching,* 36(4),
14–15.

Focus Groups

Krueger, R. A., & Casey, M. A. (2000). *Focus groups:
A practical guide for applied research.* London: Sage.

Morgan, D. L. (1998). *Focus groups as qualitative research*
(2nd ed.). London: Sage.

Schreiner, C. (2009). *Handbook of research on assessment
technologies, methods and applications in higher education.* Hershey, PA: Information Science
Reference.

Steward, D., & Shamdasani, P. (1990). *Focus groups:
Theory and practice.* University Paper series on
quantitative applications in the social sciences.
Newbury, CA: Sage.

Wilson, V. (1997, April). Focus groups: A useful
qualitative method for educational research?
British Educational Research Journal, 23(2),
209–225.

Interviews

Merton, R. K., Fiske, M., & Kendall, L. (1990).
The focused interview (2nd ed.). Glencoe, IL: Free
Press.

Seidman, I. (1998). *Interviewing as qualitative research*
(2nd ed.). New York: Teachers College Press.

Inventories in Student Affairs

Jerry Rudman, Coastline College. Inventories and assessment methods used in student services.
*virtual2.yosemite.cc.ca.us/.../Learning%20Outcomes%
20Assessment%20in%20Student%20Services*

Sietar. Lists instruments that assess intercultural
competencies and sensitivities. *www.sietar.de/
SIETARproject/Assessments&instruments.html#
Topic26*

Locally Designed Methods

Banta, T. W., & Schneider, J. A. (1986, April). *Using locally developed comprehensive exams for majors to assess and improve academic program quality.* Paper presented at the annual meeting of the American Educational Research Association, San Francisco, CA.

Haladyna, T. M. (1999). *Developing and validating multiple choice test items.* Mahwah, NJ: Erlbaum.

Lopez, C. L. (1998, Summer). Assessment of student learning. *Liberal Education, 36–43.*

Sanders, W., & Horn, S. (1995, March). Educational assessment reassessed: The usefulness of standardized and alternative measures of student achievement as indicators for the assessment of educational outcomes. *Education Policy Analysis Archives, 3*(6), 1–15. *http://epaa.asu.edu/epaa/v3n6.html*

Questionnaires and Surveys

Borden, V., & Owens, J. (2001). *Measuring quality: Choosing among surveys and other assessments of college quality.* Washington, DC: ACE.

Ewell, P. T. (1983). *Student outcomes questionnaires: An implementation handbook* (2nd ed.). Boulder, CO: National Center for Higher Education Management Systems.

Sudman, S., & Bradburn, N. (1982). *Asking questions: A practical guide to questionnaire design.* San Francisco: Jossey-Bass.

Suskie, L. (1996). *Questionnaire survey research: What works* (2nd ed.). Tallahassee, FL: Association for Institutional Research.

Technology-Enabled Assessment Other Than E-Portfolios

Aldrich, A. (2004). *Simulations and the future of learning.* San Francisco, CA: Pfeiffer.

Aldrich, C. (2009). *Learning online with games, simulations, and virtual worlds.* San Francisco: Jossey-Bass.

Anderson, R. S., Bauer, B. W., & Speck, B. W. (Eds.). (2002, Fall). *Assessment strategies for the on-line class: From theory to practice. New Directions for Teaching and Learning, 91.* San Francisco: Jossey-Bass.

Bender, T. (2003). *Discussion-based online teaching to enhance student learning: Theory, practice and assessment.* Sterling, VA: Stylus. *http://stylus.styluspub.com/Books/BookDetail.aspx?productID=64994*

Brown, S., Race, P., & Bull, J. (Eds.). (1999). *Computer assisted assessment in higher education.* Oxon, England: Routledge

Comeaux, P. (2005). *Assessing online learning.* San Francisco: Jossey-Bass.

Conrad, R., & Donaldson, J. A. (2004). *Engaging the online learner: Activities and resources for creative instruction.* San Francisco: Jossey-Bass.

Finkelstein, J. (2006). *Learning in real time: Synchronous teaching and learning.* Online Teaching and Learning Series. San Francisco: Jossey-Bass.

Halloran, M. E. (2002, April). Selecting course management software to meet requirements of faculty and students. *Educause, 8,* 1–16.

Jolliffe, A., Ritter, J., & Stevens, D. (2001). *The online learning handbook: Developing and using web-based learning.* Times Higher Education Supplement. New York: NY: Routledge.

Meyer, K. A. (2002). *Quality in distance education: Focus on on-line learning.* ASHE-ERIC *Higher Education Report,* 29, 4. San Francisco: Jossey-Bass.

Morgan, C., & O'Reilly, M. (1999). *Assessing open and distance learners.* Sterling, VA: Stylus.

Palfrey, J., & Gasser, U. (2008). *Born digital: Understanding the first generation of digital natives.* New York: Basic Books.

Palloff, R. M. (2009). *Assessing the online learner. Resources and strategies for faculty.* Online Teaching and Learning Series. San Francisco: Jossey-Bass.

Palloff, R. M., & Pratt, K. (2005). *Collaborating online: Learning together in community.* Online Teaching and Learning Series. San Francisco: Jossey-Bass.

Palloff, R. M., & Pratt, K. (2007). *Building online learning communities: Effective strategies for the virtual classroom.* Online Teaching and Learning Series. San Francisco: Jossey-Bass.

Pitler, H., Hubbell, E. R., Kuhn, M., & Malenoski, K. 2007. *Using technology with classroom instruction that works: Effective strategies for the virtual classroom.* Alexandria, VA: Association for Supervision and Curriculum Development.

Richardson, W. (2009). *Blogs, wikis, podcasts, and other powerful web tools for classrooms* (2nd ed.). Thousand Oaks, CA: Corwin Press.

Solomon, G., & Schrum, L. (2007). *Web 2.0: New tools, new schools.* Washington, DC: International Society for Technology in Education.

Tapscott, D. (2009). *Growing up digital: How the next generation is changing your world.* New York: McGraw-Hill.

Warlick, D. F. (2007). *Classroom blogging* (2nd ed.). Lulu.com.

West, J. A., & West, M. L. (2009). *Using wikis for online collaboration: The power of the read-write web.* Online Teaching and Learning Series. San Francisco: Jossey-Bass.

Web Resources Focused on Assessing the Impact of Technology on Student Learning. *www2.acs.ncsu.edu/UPA/assmt/litre/resources/web_resources.htm*

Websites to Help Launch or Evaluate Technology-Enabled Assessments

Bristol University. Assessment guidelines. *www.bris.ac.uk/esu/elearning/tools/perception/resources.html*

Directory of Educational Software. *www.educational-software-directory.net/organizations*

Educause. Resources that evaluate educational technology options. *www.educause.edu/resources*

EvaluTech. Evaluation of educational software with primary focus on K–12. *www.evalutech.sreb.org/about/index.asp*

Open Courseware Directory. Open courseware in higher education. *http://iberry.com/cms/OCW.htm*

Respondus. Development of assessment software for course management systems. *www.respondus.com/about/index.shtml.*

Websites to Help Develop or Use Online Projects

University of Maryland University College. Virtual resource site for teaching with technology. *www.umuc.edu/virtualteaching/vt_home.html*

University of Oregon. Web-based testing and student assessment. *www.uoregon.edu/~jqj/edtech/testing.html*

Publication That Includes Articles on Recent Developments in Educational Technology

Campus Technology. It also maintains a website that includes case studies, recent updates, and research. *http://campustechnology.com/pages/about.aspx*

Qualitative and Quantitative Methods

Banta, T. W., Lund, J. P., Black, K. E., & Oblander, F. W. (1996). *Assessment in practice: Putting principles to work on college campuses.* San Francisco: Jossey-Bass.

Cresswell, J. W. (1998). *Qualitative inquiry and research design: Choosing among five traditions.* Thousand Oaks, CA: Sage.

Denzin, N. K., & Lincoln, Y. S. (Eds). (1994). *Handbook of qualitative research.* Thousand Oaks, CA: Sage.

DeVellis, R. F. (1991). *Scale development.* Thousand Oaks, CA: Sage.

Erwin, D. T., & Wise, S. E. (2006). A scholarly-practitioner model for assessment. In T. W. Banta & Associates, *Building a scholarship of assessment* (pp. 72–77). San Francisco: Jossey-Bass.

Kvale, S. (1996). *Interviews: An introduction to qualitative research interviewing.* Thousand Oaks, CA: Sage.

LeCompte, M. D., Millroy, W. L., & Preissle, J. (Eds.). (1992). *The handbook of qualitative research in education.* San Diego: Academic Press.

Lofland, J., & Lofland, L. H. (1995). *Analyzing social settings: A guide to qualitative observation and analysis.* Belmont, CA: Wadsworth.

Maxwell, J. A. A. (1996). *Qualitative research design: An interactive approach.* London: Sage.

Merriam, S. B. (1997). *Qualitative research and case study applications in education.* San Francisco: Jossey-Bass.

Merriam, S. B. (Ed.). (2002). *Qualitative research in practice.* San Francisco: Jossey-Bass.

Miles, M. B., & Huberman, A. M. (1994). *Qualitative data analysis* (2nd ed.). Newbury Park, CA: Sage.

Morse, J. M. (Ed.). (1993). *Critical issues in qualitative research methods.* Thousand Oaks, CA: Sage.

Morse, J. M., & Field, P. A. (1995). *Qualitative research methods* (2nd ed.). Thousand Oaks, CA: Sage Publications.

Palomba, C. A., & Banta, T. W. (1999). *Assessment essentials: Planning, implementing, and improving assessment in higher education* (pp. 337–342). San Francisco: Jossey-Bass.

Patton, M. Q. (1990). *Qualitative evaluation and research methods* (2nd ed.). Newbury Park, CA: Sage.

Silverman, D. (1993). *Interpreting qualitative data: Methods for analyzing talk, text, and interaction.* Thousand Oaks, CA: Sage.

Smith, M. L. (1986). The whole is greater: Combining qualitative and quantitative approaches in evaluation studies. In D. Williams (Ed.), *Naturalistic evaluation. New Directions for Program Evaluation, 30.* San Francisco: Jossey-Bass.

Wolcott, H. F. (1994). *Transforming qualitative data: Description, analysis, and interpretation.* Thousand Oaks, CA: Sage.

Standardized Tests

Buros Institute. The Mental Measurements Yearbook Test Reviews Online. *http://buros.unl.edu/buros/jsp/search.jsp*

ERIC/AE Test Locator. *http://ericae.net/testcol.htm*

Factors Effecting Test Outcomes. Generic Centre. Learning and Teaching Support Network. Source of articles on tests and alternative to tests. *http://dbweb.liv.ac.uk/ltsnpsc/AB/AB-html/node6.html.*

Representative Institutional Sites Featuring Assessment Methods

American University. *http://www.american.edu/provost/assessment/index.cfm*

Bowling Green State University.
   http://www.bgsu.edu/offices/assessment/page31436.html
California State University—Monterey Bay.
   http://catalog.csumb.edu/site/x4344.xml
Doña Ana Community College.
   *http://dabcc-www.nmsu.edu/fs/iep/assessment/plans_
   reports.shtm*
Ferris State University.
   *www.ferris.edu/htmls/administration/academicaffairs/
   assessment/programs/htm*
Kings College.
   www.kings.edu/Academics/capprogram.htm
Marquette University.
   http://www.marquette.edu/assessment/ap_cas.shtml

Miami University.
   *www.units.muohio.edu/celt/assessment/student_success/
   majors_assessment.php*
Sinclair Community College.
   *http://www.sinclair.edu/about/learning/assessment/
   assessscc/policies/*
University of Colorado at Boulder.
   *http://www.colorado.edu/pba/outcomes/ovview/
   mwithin.htm*
University of Illinois at Urbana-Champaign.
   http://cte.illinois.edu/outcomes/outcome.html

WORKSHEETS, GUIDES, AND EXERCISES

1. *Strategies for Identifying Formative and Summative Program-, Department, or Institution-Level Assessment Methods.* The following strategies may be useful to identify existing assessment practices in courses and educational experiences, such as service-learning, that can be used to track students' progress toward and achievement of program-, department-, and institution-level outcomes.

   a. *Developing a chronological documentation of assessment methods.* Use the following guides to inventory existing assessment practices at the course or educational experience level to identify chronologically formative and summative methods currently used to assess students' progress toward and achievement of department-, program-, and institution-level learning outcomes as well as to provide evidence to answer your research or study question. Refer to this inventory to identify chronological evidence of learning that you will assess at the institution or program level during a cycle of assessment of one or more outcomes. Or, during a cycle of inquiry into one or more outcomes at the department, program, or institution level, ask colleagues to provide results of their assessment of that outcome or outcomes to develop a chronological perspective on students' progress toward or achievement of those outcomes. For example, beyond students' foundation-level mathematics courses, what evidence does an institution or program have that students continue to know how to use or apply mathematical processes and concepts in their major programs of study? In many cases an institution-level learning outcome and a program- or department-level outcome are the same, such as an outcome on critical thinking. In that case, then, a core inquiry group would be interested in tracking how well students demonstrate this outcome in their general education courses and then how well they continue to apply, transfer, or build on this general education outcome in their disciplinary or professional programs of study.

Institution Level

Institution-level learning outcome(s) for a cycle of inquiry	Coupled research or study question	Identify a course or courses or an educational experience you offer that provides evidence of students' performance of this outcome(s) and identify when this course or experience typically occurs in students' undergraduate or graduate program of study	Describe or provide a copy of your assessment method and criteria and standards of judgment	List the kinds of inferences you can draw about students' performance of this outcome through this method that may contribute to our understanding of how well students are making progress toward or achieving an outcome as well as contribute to our research or study question

Program or Department Level

Program- or department-level outcome for a cycle of inquiry	Coupled research or study question	Identify a course or courses or an educational experience you offer that provides evidence of students' performance of this outcome(s) and identify when this course or experience typically occurs in students' undergraduate or graduate program of study	Describe or provide a copy of your assessment method and criteria and standards of judgment	List the kinds of inferences you can draw about students' performance of this outcome through this method that may contribute to our understanding of how well students are making progress toward or achieving an outcome as well as contribute to our research or study question

b. *Using an agreed-upon set of scoring rubrics.* Alternatively, if the institution and its programs and services are using a common scoring rubric (chapter 6), then the preceding chart would be a means of identifying relevant chronological student work that would be scored using a shared set of criteria and standards of judgment. For example, if an institution were to use the AAC&U scoring rubrics developed for 15 general education domains (chapter 6), then individuals would use them in various contexts to develop baseline evidence and then chronological evidence thereafter in multiple contexts.

2. *Criteria to Identify or Create Aligned Direct and Indirect Assessment Methods.* To successfully answer your research or study question—perhaps based on a Taxonomy of Student Weaknesses, Errors, or Fuzzy Thinking (chapter 4)—and identify or create an assessment method that aligns with your outcome, use the following chart to guide your decision:

Identifying or Creating Valid Direct and Indirect Assessment Methods

Department-, Program-, or Institution-Level Direct and Indirect Methods Under Consideration to Assess Outcome:	Source of Evidence to Answer Research or Study Question— Explain	Alignment With Students' Learning Histories, Previous Assessments, and Feedback	Inferences That Can Be Drawn About Student Achievement of Outcome	Inferences That Cannot Be Drawn About Student Achievement of Outcome	Use for Baseline, Formative, and/or Summative Evidence of Learning	Reliability of Scoring Method
Direct Method 1:						
Direct Method 2:						
Direct Method 3:						
Indirect Method 1:						
Indirect Method 2:						
Indirect Method 3:						

3. *Schedule for Formative and Summative Assessment.* In collaboration with offices of institutional research and planning, core working groups focused on identifying and selecting methods of assessment also develop a timetable to assess students along the continuum of their learning. Use the following worksheet to develop a timetable to assess students' learning along the continuum of their studies. The resulting timetable provides an overall chronology of assessment efforts at either the institution or program level. Cycles of inquiry into how well students make progress toward and eventually achieve institution- and program-level outcomes occur over time. Each year or every couple of years, the institution and its individual programs focus on assessing one or two outcomes at a time to sustain ongoing inquiry.

If you have developed a Taxonomy of Student Weaknesses, Errors, or Fuzzy Thinking (chapter 4) and have made pedagogical or instructional changes to improve a pattern of weakness, then consider how methods of assessment will chronologically enable you to determine how well these changes are improving students' performance.

List Each Agreed-Upon Institution-, Program-, or Department-Level Outcome for a Cycle	Identify Method(s) to Assess Each Outcome	Identify Formative Assessment Schedule (for Example, After Each Course, After a Certain Number of Credits or Sequences of Courses or Educational Experiences)	Identify Summative Assessment Schedule (for Example, in a Senior Capstone Project or Internship; at the Time of Graduation, etc.)
1.			
2.			
3.			
4.			

4. *Development of Assessment Methods Within the Design of Curricula and Educational Experiences.* Reconceptualizing or creating a new program is an opportunity to develop an organic relationship among educational philosophy, learning outcomes, curricular and co-curricular design, sequence of educational experiences, and methods of assessment. Consider the following kinds of questions as you design your program and integrate assessment of student learning into it:

a. What will you expect students to demonstrate, represent, or produce because of their studies in this program (learning outcome statements)?

b. What is the shared philosophy or set of assumptions about teaching and learning that underlie your proposed program?

c. How are you designing your curriculum and sets of complementary educational experiences—based on your shared philosophy or set of assumptions to foster desired learning—to foster agreed upon learning outcome statements?

d. What kinds of research or study questions will you couple with your learning outcome statements?

e. At what points along the continuum of students' learning will you assess students' learning outcomes as well as pursue answers to your research or study questions?

f. What collaboratively agreed-upon times will you routinely establish to bring colleagues together to discuss assessment results and improve patterns of weakness?

5. *Developing Assessment Methods.* The example in Box A represents a way in which different constituencies of an institution—librarians and faculty—have worked together to develop assessment methods that provide evidence of student learning from multiple lenses. This example also illustrates the importance of institutional context in the collective identification of questions of curiosity that members of an educational community wish to pursue. In the design of assessment methods, consider how cross-disciplinary members of core working groups or other established groups might work together to develop complementary methods of assessment that explore students' knowledge, understanding, habits of mind, ways of knowing, attitudes, and values.

BOX A   Academic Librarians and Faculty: Information Literacy

Academic libraries, like the institutions of which they are a part, are exploring the type of contribution that they can make to outcomes assessment. The broad area of library evaluation and assessment has historically focused on the "user in the life of the library" (i.e., input, output, and performance measures), but, more recently, attention has centered on the "library in the life of the user" (e.g., customer satisfaction). Now, there is even a different perspective: the "user and library in the life of the institution"—the accomplishment of the institutional mission (i.e., outcomes assessment). Each of the three perspectives has value and, to date, researchers have not sufficiently explored interconnections.

As shown in *An Action Plan for Outcomes Assessment in Your Library,*[1] professional associations (Association of College and Research Libraries [ACRL] and the Wisconsin Association of Academic Librarians), the Florida State Library (with its outcomes workbook), the Citadel (Daniel Library), and the California State Library system have viewed information literacy as the link between outcomes assessment and libraries; outcomes focus on the ways in which library users have changed (how they know, think, and are able to do) as a result of their contract with the library's resources and programs. This is not to say that librarians cannot work with others in other areas of outcomes assessment.

ACRL has developed Information Literacy Competency Standards for Higher Education (reprinted as Appendix H in *An Action Plan for Outcomes Assessment in Your Library*). In our book, we take the information literacy competency standards and performance indicators and convert them into measurable student learning outcomes (chapter 6).

The Mildred F. Sawyer Library at Suffolk University in Boston has taken that framework and included student learning outcomes as part of an assessment plan, part of which relates to student ability to retrieve, evaluate, and use electronic information. The learning outcomes that were sought have a lifelong effect on students and, although that effect would be difficult to measure, there should be an effort to do so. Although faculty involvement was essential, the staff wanted to identify and design learning modules that were in concert with carefully chosen learning objectives and known library strengths and within the limits of available resources.

This report describes two methods of assessment related to achievement of the assessment plan. The first relies on the type of data that libraries can gather from electronic databases supplied by commercial vendors, and the second involves cooperation with teaching faculty.

USE OF BOOLEAN SEARCH OPERATORS

Librarians advocate the teaching of information search skills. Along with other searching skills, Boolean operators (AND, OR, and NOT) are used to reduce or refine the number of "hits" (retrievals) per search of almost every electronic database. This skill, once learned and applied, will save students time by increasing the effectiveness of the search process; their retrievals will be more "on target," resulting in less information overload and less time reading through abstracts of articles or sources that

(continued)

BOX A   *(continued)*

do not meet their needs. Librarians at Sawyer Library gather data about the knowledge and application of Boolean searching by conducting a pretest and posttest of students receiving formal searching instruction and by retrieving the statistics from vendors supplying the databases to track the number of retrievals per search for each month of the academic term.

They retrieve monthly statistics for "number of searches" and "number of hits," and then calculate the number of hits per search. The Boolean operator AND is emphasized during the instructional sessions because it is used to combine two or more keywords, thereby reducing the number of results. If the number has dropped, the library may claim that its efforts in instructing students on this specific Boolean operator have reduced the number of retrievals per search. Adding to the validity of the claim is that the library received such statistics before implementing the instruction program, and there was no observable/measurable change during the school term.

The library staff compiles and reviews the pretest and posttest from the instruction sessions and the monthly vendor statistics. Analysis of the test scores is used to improve the content and methods employed during the instruction sessions; analysis of the vendor statistics verifies whether the instructional sessions changed student searching processes to include Boolean operators.

TECHNOLOGY SKILLS

The Accounting Department at Suffolk University recognized the importance of technology-related competencies to accountants if they are to access and assimilate electronic information, and to solve unstructured problems found in different consulting and strategic decision-making situations. Using pretests and posttests, student ability to incorporate traditional and nontraditional sources of information into company analysis projects was measured. There was even a multiple-choice Internet quiz.

Although developing skills provides students with the competencies to access technology, improving their perceived abilities is vital to ensure successful use of computers in the workplace. Combining strong skills and highly perceived abilities should allow students to access, synthesize, and analyze timely information from various information sources when working on an appropriate independent assignment, the very competencies that accounting recruiters expect.

The development of effective pedagogical tools must recognize that the benefits of technology may depend on the learning situation and the psychological and other characteristics of the students. Librarians can partner with classroom faculty to meet the learning objectives for the course, especially those related to the use of technology to navigate the Internet and to retrieve, download, and evaluate information for the completion of classroom assignments. In doing so, libraries ensure that their outcomes are key to the instructional programs of the college or university.

CONCLUSION

The same toolkit of methods that teaching faculty use to assess outcomes applies to libraries and their measurement of student learning. Both faculty and librarians can gather direct and indirect evidence of the changes that occurred in student learning during a course or program of study. What are librarians trying to do in their instructional programs? Why are they doing it the way they are? How well do those approaches work to accomplish the assessment plan? The assessment plan, a planning document, guides whatever course of action the library takes (see http://www.suffolk.edu/files/SawLib/05annualreport.pdf for a sample plan). At the same time, it is critical that information literacy be related to the broader concept of critical thinking and competencies such as "formulate and state a research question, problem, or issue . . ."; "organize information in a manner that permits analysis, evaluation, synthesis, and understanding"; "create and communicate information effectively using various media"; and "understand the ethical, legal, and sociopolitical issues surrounding information."[2]

Notes

1. Hernon, P., & Dugan, R. E. (2002). *An action plan for outcomes assessment in your library.* Chicago: American Library Association. For other examples of the use of outcomes assessment in academic libraries, see *The Journal of Academic Librarianship* (2002, January–March.
2. Dunn, K. (2002, January–March). Assessing information literacy skills in the California State University: A progress report. *Journal of Academic Librarianship, 28*(12), 26–35.

Source: Peter Hernon, Professor, Simmons College, Graduate School of Library and Information Science, and Robert E. Dugan, Director, Mildred F. Sawyer Library, Suffolk University.

APPENDIX 5.1   INSTITUTIONAL EXAMPLE: The Educational Context for Goddard College's Learning Portfolio and Progress Review

GODDARD COLLEGE

Mission and Pedagogy

Founded in 1863, Goddard College is recognized for innovation in education. Its mission is to advance the theory and practice of learning based on the ideals of democracy and the principles asserted by John Dewey and furthered by the work of Paulo Freire, Elizabeth Minnich, bell hooks, and others.

The Goddard liberal arts undergraduate curriculum is student centered, beginning with students' passions and questions. The curriculum is progressive in intentionally preparing students to address the problems of the world and fosters change and transformation in its students. It is intended to free students from cultural and other biases in their worldview and facilitate their ability to participate in positive social change, based on "an earnest concern for others and the welfare of the earth" (from the college's mission statement).

Students are all in low-residency programs with a residency on campus each semester. Individual Bachelor of Arts, BFA in Creative Writing, Education and Health Arts and Science are among the undergraduate programs.

Integration of Degree Requirements

Goddard's undergraduate curriculum is particular to each student. At a traditional college or university, students graduate when they have successfully completed a required series of courses and tasks. At Goddard, students and faculty build individual studies into broader understandings while attending a residency in a program-based framework. Students plan a course of study that begins with their own interests, passions, and questions and leads to their ability to demonstrate competence in each of the undergraduate degree requirements.

Students have the responsibility to document how they have changed, what they have learned, and how that learning has affected their life and practices in the world. They assemble documentation that demonstrates their learning and change in a *learning portfolio,* which becomes part of a progress review (PR) at two points in the undergraduate program. A progress review

group (PRG) of cross-program undergraduate faculty members reviews the portfolio and offers feedback and recommendations regarding degree criteria fulfillment.

The culmination of the Goddard College undergraduate degree is an intense, yearlong final product and presentation at the residency.

From the Undergraduate Curriculum Guide (2009)

Degree Requirements—they're all connected
Goddard degree requirements are interrelated aspects of a holistic model of learning rather than discrete entities. Therefore, in order to understand these degree requirements, it is helpful to understand how they fit together.

At the core of Goddard's undergraduate curriculum are Knowing, Being, and Doing: core requirements known as **Wide Knowledge, Positive Self-Development, and Thoughtful Action.** They form the basis of Goddard's progressive education. For Goddard students, Knowing, Doing, and Being *overlap;* they influence each other.

The **Social and Ecological Context** degree requirement is the emancipatory *background* for Wide Knowledge, Positive Self-Development, and Thoughtful Action. You are invited to understand and articulate your relationship to the social and ecological worlds in which you live. In this way, you embody Goddard's mission statement, as you become "creative, passionate, lifelong learners, working and living with an earnest concern for others and for the welfare of the earth."

Critically engaged thinking and writing are skills that help deepen learning across all degree guidelines. Through critical thinking and writing you learn to question ideas and engage conversations from multiple viewpoints.

Assessment Tool: The Progress Review Portfolio

Students in the review process are encouraged to **Show the process and articulate** *how* they work with knowledge, and not simply *that* they worked with knowledge. For instance:

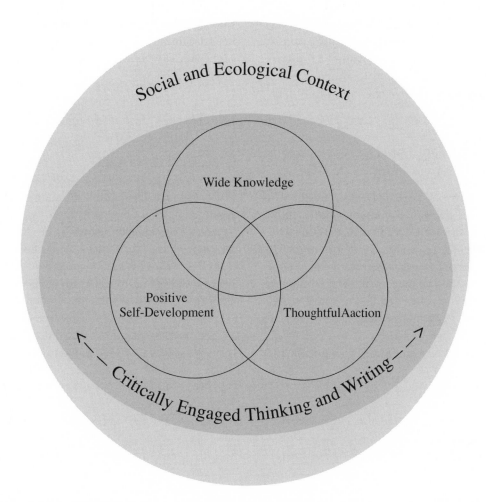

Educational Context at Goddard College

If a student wants to demonstrate learning in math by building a chair, he or she cannot simply send a picture of the chair and say, "I used geometry." We want to know *how* geometry was used to create that chair.

Similarly, if a student wants to demonstrate learning in science by working with herbal medicine, he or she cannot simply assert that medicine is science. We want to know how specific scientific learning promoted understanding in some aspect of the practice of herbal medicine.

Students are encouraged to **Teach us.** What are the vectors of force on a chair when someone sits in it? What do we need to understand about physics to answer this question and to build a solid chair? Why does a particular herb treat a particular condition? What do we need to know about pathophysiology and pharmacology in order to understand the effect of herbs on the body?

Students must **Be aware of their lens and biases.**

Wide knowledge areas can be seen as lenses for looking at a particular topic in different ways. Keep in mind that it is possible to look at a natural science topic, such as chemical toxins, through a social science lens, such as public policy. This would demonstrate learning in social sciences. In order to demonstrate learning in natural sciences, that lens is used. Students are asked to articulate their perspectives, examine their assumptions and stereotypes, and understand the biases and methodologies of authors/sources.

Students are encouraged to **Be aware of their audience.** The review committee is in search of students' success in the review process. We need explanations and clarity regarding the work. A preface indicating how a sample of work addresses specific degree criteria is extremely helpful as well as filling in the worksheet clearly and concisely.

Students are frequently asked to resubmit evidence or articulate something further. Faculty are often assisted in their own work with students by the progress review process, which is meant to be a constructive learning experience for both. The consequences of not successfully completing the review may occur when a student is not permitted to enroll in the final semester until he or she successfully completes the process.

Validity and Reliability and Administration of Assessment

Currently we have an administrative coordinator who collects the portfolios and distributes them among the committees. After the review of the portfolio is complete, the responses are then sent to students and advisers. The progress review committee chair coordinates the committees, facilitates biweekly phone conferences with the chairs, problem-solves when necessary with chairs, and hears student appeals.

Assessments are also completed by students and their advisors (faculty) at midsemester and at the end of each semester. The assessments validate the content of the students' semester work as well as fulfilling degree requirements.

Benefits

It is a truly authentic assessment that matches the pedagogy of the college.

Students acknowledge their own learning and know they are accountable to address all degree requirements for the liberal arts.

Faculty work together across programs, which offers insight into the college as a whole and creative thinking regarding their own practice. The process offers professional development and collegial relationships in the low-residency model.

Source: Shelley Vermilya, Ed.D., IBA faculty, and Sarah Van Hoy, MA, MA, MTCM, Goddard College.

APPENDIX 5.2   Goddard College Undergraduate Programs Curriculum Guide: 2009/10

PROGRESS REVIEW PORTFOLIO WORKSHEET

Name:

Present level:

Present advisor:

Progress Review: I ☐   II ☐

Program: IBA ☐   HAS ☐   EDU ☐   BFA ☐

PART I: SUMMARY OF YOUR STUDIES

A very brief list. See related examples on FirstClass. (Please refer to your word processing software user's manual or on-line help for inserting rows in a table.)

Year	Semester or Level	Institution	Course Title or Subject of Study	Degree Requirement Addressed

Please note: The PRG members **do not** have access to your transcripts or Advisor End of Semester Evaluations on SIS. Please include copies of transcripts and advisor evaluations as attachments to this worksheet. Transcripts and advisor evaluations can be downloaded from your SIS account. Please contact the Records Office for assistance.

If you have petitioned for APL Credits, include your petition in your PR II portfolio, and list proposed credits here:

Course Title or Subject of Study	Degree Requirement to be Addressed

PART II: DESCRIPTION OF YOUR LEARNING BY DEGREE REQUIREMENTS

Please reflect on your summary of studies, and sort your work into the degree requirement areas listed below. Briefly explain how you are addressing or have met degree requirements in each area. Remember, you are asked to describe your learning in a clear, concrete way. Do not assume what is implicit in your portfolio will be obvious to your readers.

In pointing your committee to your learning evidence, you are welcome to reference your summary of studies, reflective essay, or attached documentation **You are not asked to include a separate piece of evidence for each degree requirement.**

> *For each degree requirement, please briefly describe your learning as shown in your summary of studies (transcripts from prior colleges or Goddard evaluations) or in your attached portfolio evidence (see part IV).*

1. Wide Knowledge

Arts & Creative Expression:

Humanities

Mathematics as a Lived Experience:

Natural and Life Sciences:

Social Sciences:

2. Thoughtful Action:

Please briefly write about your engagement with Thoughtful Action here. You may also provide additional evidence as shown in Reflective Essay, APL, and/or the additional evidence section of your portfolio. (see part IV):

3. Positive Self-Development

Please briefly write about your studies and experiences of Positive Self-Development here. You may also provide additional evidence as shown in Reflective Essay, APL, and/or the additional evidence section of your portfolio. (see part IV):

4. Social and Ecological Context:

Please briefly reflect here on an aspect of the social and ecological context of your work. How do you understand yourself or your learning in relationship to issues of social justice and ecological sustainability? You may also provide additional evidence as shown in Reflective Essay, APL, and/or the additional evidence section of your portfolio. (see part IV):

5. Engaged Critical Thinking:

Evidence included in PR Portfolio must include at least one Engaged Critical Paper. Please list the title(s) of that paper here.

PART III: REFLECTIVE ESSAY (MINIMUM OF 3 PAGES, MAXIMUM OF 5):

   a. Highlight your main areas of inquiry and your learning and growth in those areas. How has this learning changed you?

   b. For PR II only: Briefly discuss your (even tentative) plans for a senior study

Part IV: Additional Evidence (Samples of Studies)

Attach evidence of your learning, including an engaged critical paper and 2-3 other samples of your work. Choose the additional samples carefully to document learning in degree requirements areas not addressed in transcripts or Goddard evaluations. *Please do not include more than three additional samples.*

	What degree requirements does your chosen evidence address? Samples often highlight several degree requirements as listed below. *(Please highlight all that apply)*
Sample # 1 **Engaged Critical Paper** PR I: 6-10 pages, and bibliography 　　Title: PR II: 10-15 pages, and bibliography 　　Title:	• Arts and Creative Expression • Humanities • Mathematics as a lived experience • Natural and Life Sciences • Social Sciences • Positive Self Development • Thoughtful Action • Social and Ecological Context • Critical Thinking
Sample #2 Title or description:	• Arts and Creative Expression • Humanities • Mathematics as a lived experience • Natural and Life Sciences • Social Sciences • Positive Self Development • Thoughtful Action • Social and Ecological Context • Critical Thinking
Sample # 3 Title or description:	• Arts and Creative Expression • Humanities • Mathematics as a lived experience • Natural and Life Sciences • Social Sciences • Positive Self Development • Thoughtful Action • Social and Ecological Context • Critical Thinking
OPTIONAL Sample # 4 Title or description:	• Arts and Creative Expression • Humanities • Mathematics as a lived experience • Natural and Life Sciences • Social Sciences • Positive Self Development • Thoughtful Action • Social and Ecological Context • Critical Thinking
Please do not include more than three additional samples.	

PART V: CHECKLIST

Use this Checklist to ensure your Progress Review portfolio is complete and all necessary materials are included.

PR PORTFOLIO COMPLETE—CHECKLIST:

☐ Completed Progress Review Worksheet

☐ Reflective Essay

☐ Engaged Critical Writing sample (*PR I: 6 – 10 pp or PR II 10 – 15 pp*)

☐ Sample #2

☐ Sample #3

☐ Sample #4 (Optional)

☐ Transcripts (transfer credits accepted by Goddard College from other institutions)

☐ Advisor End of Semester Evaluations

☐ PRG response to PR I *(if applicable)*

☐ APL petition *(if applicable)*

Contributed by Shelley Vermilya, Ed.D., IBA Faculty, and Sarah Van Hoy, MA, MA, MTCM, Goddard College

APPENDIX 5.3   Strategies for Reviewing and Selecting Standardized Instruments

- Review a sample of the instrument to determine how well it aligns with collective program- or institution-level outcome statements, the educational practices that foster the learning described in those statements, and the assessment methods students have responded to along the continuum of their learning. Particularly helpful is Buros Institute's *Mental Measurements Yearbook Test Reviews Online* (http://buros.unl.edu/buros/jsp/search.jsp), which contains information on more than 4,000 commercially designed tests.

- Review a sample of the instrument and its accompanying literature to determine its validity (how well it assesses what it claims to assess) and its reliability (how well scores correlate across groups tested and across test versions; how well items and parts of a test correlate; and how well different raters' scores agree based on scoring the same test).

- Identify the kinds of inferences that can be drawn from the test and the kinds of inferences that cannot be drawn in relation to your outcome statements.

- Determine how fair the test is for your representative student populations and their learning chronologies. Specifically, identify the multiple and varied ways students have had opportunities to learn and receive feedback about what the test is assessing. The following resource is especially helpful in addressing issues of fairness: National Council on Measurement in Education, Code of Fair Testing Practices in Education (http://ericae.net/code.txt).

- Determine restrictions inherent in administering the instrument in relation to using the results to improve student learning and providing feedback to students. Are results available in a reasonable amount of time to inform educators and students about their performance and inform institution- and program-level dialogue about how to improve students' learning experiences? Or are tests restricted primarily for summative administration and, therefore, unable to inform educational practices along the continuum of students' learning?

- Identify alternative direct methods that you might use to assess other dimensions of what you expect students to demonstrate based on your learning outcome statements and the design of educational practices that contribute to that valued learning.

APPENDIX 5.4   An Inventory of Traditional and Technology-Enabled Direct and Indirect Assessment Methods

DIRECT METHODS

Standardized Tests and Learning Inventories

Standardized Instruments. Historically, *standardized instruments,* such as objective tests, have served as the primary direct method to assess student learning. Content or disciplinary experts identify the standard content, knowledge, and tasks that students should know and be able to perform. In addition, they determine what constitutes levels of achievement based on the construction, design, and sequencing of questions or prompts. Students' achievement is referenced against other student groups' achievement on the same instrument, referred to as *norm referencing.* Primarily designed to make decisions about students, standardized instruments perform a gatekeeping role. They certify competence in a profession or field, such as in the case of licensure examinations for nursing students, or program-level knowledge or skills, such as in the case of general education tests. Results are also used to place students in appropriate courses or to identify level of achievement at points in students' studies, such as in the case of rising junior examinations.

What Standardized Instruments Provide

- Content and tasks developed by external experts within fields or programs of study
- A psychometric approach to assessment that values quantitative methods of interpreting student achievement
- Evidence of what students know or can do within the universe and framework of questions, prompts, and tasks of an instrument
- Evidence to make gatekeeping decisions such as professional certification or end-of-study achievement or to meet external mandates that value standardized instruments as a way to evaluate or rank institution- or program-level educational effectiveness
- Evidence to track student learning if the instrument can be used formatively and if results have utility for programs and the institution
- Quick and easy adoption and efficient objective scoring
- History of validity and reliability studies

- One possible source of evidence within an institutional commitment to assessing student learning through multiple lenses

What Standardized Instruments Do Not Provide

- Evidence of the strategies, processes, and ways of knowing, understanding, and behaving that students draw on or apply to represent learning
- Evidence of the complex and diverse ways in which humans construct and generate meaning
- Alignment with institution- and program-level learning outcome statements and students' learning histories
- Realistic time frames or contexts that reflect how humans solve problems, seek additional information or resources, correct mistakes, or reposition their thinking; students respond within a time frame that may affect their decisions or actions, such as deciding to make a last-minute guess among options in a question
- Highly useful results that directly relate to pedagogy and educational practices

Results relate to the construct of the instrument itself and what it is designed to measure. Patterns of student performance reported in scales or scores identify discrete areas of performance, such as a skill level, that identify strengths and weaknesses in curricular or co-curricular attention. However, these patterns do not assist in learning about why students responded in the ways they did, or whether they learned successful strategies for selecting or making "good guesses."

Examples of Standardized Instruments

Instruments that test general education knowledge and abilities include the following:

- Collegiate Assessment of Academic Proficiency (CAAP): www.act.org/caap/index.html
- Collegiate Learning Assessment (CLA): www.cic.org/projects_services/coops/cla.asp
- ETS Proficiency Profile: http://www.ets.org/proficiencyprofile/aboutwww.ets.org

Instruments dedicated to measuring specific skills include the following:

- ACCUPLACER
- California Critical Thinking Skills Test
- Tasks in Critical Thinking
- Reflective Judgment Inventory
- Measure of Intellectual Development
- e-Write, a component of ACT's COMPASS/ESL system

Examples of achievement tests in a particular field of study or profession include the following:

- Graduate Record Examinations' Subject Tests: www.greguide.com/GRE-Subject-Test.html
- Major field tests in undergraduate and MBA programs: www.ets.org
- The PRAXIS Series: Professional Assessment for Beginning Teachers: http://www.ets.org/praxis
- Area Concentration Achievement Tests: www.collegeoutcomes.com
- Graduate Management Admission Test: www.mba.com/mba

Online Question Banks and Tests. Pools of questions across disciplines and professions now exist online. Course management systems, described on page 167 have integrated online question banks that faculty can use, adapt, or add to. Alternatively, commercial vendors, such as Scantron, have developed software packages to help educators create their own question banks and analyze results (see www.scantron.com/higher education/ and www.scantron.com/classroomtesting/).

Learning Inventories. Multiple-choice questions are used primarily in the sciences to diagnose students' initial knowledge about concepts and then to monitor students' achievement based on pedagogy and educational practices (see Libarkin, 2008).

Locally Designed Tests

In a collective and shared commitment to assessing student learning, core working groups may well determine that no appropriate standardized instruments exist that align with institution- and program-level outcomes. That decision generates the design of local tests or inventories or use of existing instruments that have an institutional history of providing useful results. Within the parameters of software programs, educators can develop their own online tests or inventories as discussed on page 168.

What Locally Designed Tests and Learning Inventories Provide

- Strong alignment of content and format with learning outcome statements and course-based assessment methods that students have experienced along their learning histories
- Useful results that can be interpreted within the local contexts of teaching and learning and then used to improve student learning
- An opportunity to establish local instrument criteria that reflect what an institution and its programs value in educational practices
- An opportunity for faculty, staff, administrators, students, teaching assistants, tutors, intern advisors, advisory board members, and institutional researchers, for example, to contribute their perspectives on what should be assessed and how it should be assessed

What Locally Designed Tests Do Not Provide

- Immediate reliability and validity results that verify content, construct, format, and consistency in scoring, unless instruments have been pilot-tested and evaluated over several semesters; thus, time to pilot-test an instrument for an institution's representative student populations is a necessary component of an institutional commitment to assessing for learning

Knowledge Surveys. These instruments, consisting of closed-ended questions or short-answer questions, are designed to ascertain how well students retain learning over a period of time—at the end of a course, after a sequence of courses, or at the end of a program of study (Nuhfer & Knipp, 2003).

Milestone Examinations. A more extensive version of a knowledge survey, this kind of locally designed test assesses learning over longer time periods to ascertain students' mastery of learning, often before students engage in their final year of study or before beginning a thesis, dissertation, internship, or final project.

Conventional or Technology-Enabled Authentic Performance-Based Methods

Authentic performance-based methods prompt students to represent their learning in response to assignments and projects that are woven into their educational experiences. These methods value divergent thinking and responding, as opposed to convergent thinking, most typically represented in standardized tests. Focusing on how students think, problem-solve, react, interpret, or express themselves becomes the focus of these kinds of direct methods. Further, these methods can easily be embedded into students' continuum of learning, providing evidence of their growth over time, often demonstrated in self-reflective writing and responses to feedback from those who contribute to their education, such as peers, internship advisers, external reviewers or evaluators, faculty, and staff.

What Authentic Performance-Based Methods Provide

- Representation of integrated learning
- Direct alignment with students' learning experiences
- Opportunities for students to reflect on and receive formative feedback about their learning and development
- Student-generated opportunities to demonstrate learning, as opposed to test-generated occasions
- Opportunities for students to create new or unexpected responses to an assessment task
- Opportunities for students to represent their learning in alternative ways, such as web-based interactive multimedia presentations

What Authentic Performance-Based Methods Do Not Provide

- Easily quantifiable evidence given the complexity they capture
- Efficient scoring opportunities

The following list represents some authentic performance-based methods of assessment:

- *Authorship of online products*—student-generated products online such as on wikis, podcasts, YouTube videos or documentaries, blogs, or other established sites, such as virtual environments. Among the projects at the Digital Scholarship Lab at Richmond University is the History Engine (http://historyengine.richmond.edu/search/basic), a repository of student-generated episodes from U.S. history that also can be chronologically tracked on a map of the United States. Students' end-of-semester exhibition for Art 101 in Second Life is available at http://blogs.bgsu.edu/secondlife/2009/08/04/art-101-final-exhibition-in-second-life/ (see also "Team-Based or Collaborative Projects" on page 178).

- *Capstone or other culminating projects such as a thesis or dissertation*—an independent or collaborative research project or professional project at the end of students' undergraduate or graduate careers that provides evidence of how students solve representative higher-order disciplinary, professional, or interdisciplinary problems often represented in more than one kind of text—in writing as well as in speaking or in visual texts, such as poster presentations. These projects provide evidence of how well students integrate, synthesize, and transfer learning; they also can provide evidence of how well students integrate institution-level outcomes. Undergraduate senior theses or senior research projects are also examples of capstone projects that provide opportunity for faculty and other experts to assess students' mastery level within a field of study, discipline, or profession.

- *Case study, critical incident, or event analysis*—methods that position students to analyze, draw inferences, solve problems, deconstruct, and offer alternative solutions or responses to a problem or issue. Used over time, as well as at the end of students' studies, case studies, often used in business programs, provide opportunity to assess students' problem-solving abilities within a major program of study or along students' continuum of studies to determine how well they are integrating knowledge, perspectives, abilities, values, attitudes, and habits of mind. Parallel case studies used over time provide evidence of students' abilities to solve representative disciplinary, professional, or more general problems drawing on students' general education learning. In addition, they provide evidence of students' writing abilities. Online cases with multimedia components provide a rich way for students to become engaged in analyzing different sources of evidence, such as in Harvard University's online case of the space shuttle *Columbia* (http://hbr.org/product/columbia-s-final-mission-multimedia-case/an/30503/html_bundle). The Digital Scholarship Lab at the University of Richmond (http://digitalscholarship.richmond.edu) develops innovative digital humanities projects that contribute to research and teaching at and beyond the university. It develops online projects that integrate interpretation in the humanities and social sciences with innovations in new media. For example, through progressive chronological visualizations in one program, students can track U.S. voter turnout across each of the states in elections from 1840 to 1996.

- *Chronological reexamination of a problem or case study*—a method to assess how well individuals or teams are integrating and applying their chronological learning. This method periodically asks students to reexamine a problem or case study. In particular, teams revisiting complex muddy problems over time demonstrate how well they are becoming more sophisticated or more expert in addressing the multiple layers and dimensions of those kinds of problems—environmental, political, economic, scientific, and ethical dimensions, for example. A particularly fascinating extension of this approach to assessment is that described by the Federation of American Scientists, who are interested in how experts in different fields or disciplines approach *conceptual collisions,* situations in which experts who have heretofore not worked together confront a concept from their various disciplinary or professional perspectives for the first time (www.fas.org/programs/ltp/emerging_technologies/arts_and_humanities.html). In their virtual simulations, the Federation of American Scientists has created environments for experts to bring "previously disconnected knowledge sources into contact for the first time."

- *Conversion*—a method that asks students to convert one form of representation into another form of representation, such as a written text into a visual, audio, or artistic form of representation.

- *Data mining*—tasks that require students to gather and analyze data to test or form their own conclusions or hypotheses. An assignment may require that they visit learning online repositories, such as those at Merlot, or digital collections or sites in a virtual reality, such as Second Life, to collect, analyze, and interpret their findings.

- *Embedded assignments*—tasks that educators integrate into their courses or modules or educational experience to provide chronological evidence of student learning for program-, department-, or institution-level assessment. Here are several approaches to embedding assignments: (1) inserting a collaboratively agreed-upon question or case study into students' final examination that is designed to learn about students' enduring learning in a department or program; (2) reserving time in a designated course or experience to have students respond to a collaboratively agreed-upon case study or question; or (3) asking students to hand in two copies of an assignment in a designated course so that department- or program-level assessors can score this work without reference to the remarks and grades a faculty member or other person gives students on that assignment. An overarching program- or department-level assessment plan may consist of assessing representative student work extracted from lower-level, midlevel, and higher-level courses to track students' emerging abilities.

- *Identification of the significance of an artifact*—a method particularly useful in determining how well students have developed a sense of historical developments in a field of study and the concurrent events or conditions that led to the production of a specific artifact, such as a legal document, a painting, or a codified set of beliefs or behaviors. Key to this method is deleting the name of the artifact, its date, and its author or authors so that students demonstrate their abilities to draw inferences from the artifact itself that, in turn, contribute to their ability to identify and discuss the context that led to the development of the artifact—such as political, social, and economic forces or beliefs. This particular method demonstrates inference drawing as well as chronological understanding.

- *Learning Record Online (LRO)*—a running record of students' learning originally developed for K–12 and now developed for higher education. The LRO (www.cwrl.utexas.edu/~syverson/olr/) provides formative and summative evidence of students' learning within their curricula and against agreed-upon criteria and standards of judgment. Similar to the portfolio (described on pages 170–176), the LRO provides ongoing evidence of students' emerging learning within contexts for learning, including evidence of their reflective process, their metacognition. Facilitated by online technology, educators and others interested in learning about students' development are able to aggregate or disaggregate groups to draw inferences and make decisions about students' progress and eventual levels of achievement.

- *Log books or journals*—documents, often maintained online, that provide firsthand evidence of students' research, processes of conducting research or an experiment, or self-reflections as they explore a problem or possible solutions to a problem. (See also *self-reflection* on page 212).

- *Observation*—a real-time method of assessing actual individual or group behaviors, mannerisms, interactions, or integration of abilities that also may be videotaped, such as a videotaped student senate meeting or a team project. Videotapes are useful not only for educators but also for students promoting peer-to-peer assessment opportunities. Cell phones may be used to videotape group or individual work.

- *Online educational gaming or multiplayer gaming in online worlds*—virtual environments that position students to engage in higher-order thinking abilities to strategize, make decisions, and anticipate results of actions. A source for identifying online educational software games for higher education is Open Courseware in Higher Education (http://iberry.com/cms/OCW.htm). Educause's resources contain research articles on the efficacy of online gaming in promoting learning. Of particular value in this method

of assessment is students' ability to consider the consequences or results of their actions and to anticipate actions of others.

- *Oral examination*—a method often used at the end of a professional program or a graduate program, as in an oral doctoral defense (University of Arizona, Graduate College: http://grad.arizona.edu/academics/program-requirements/doctor-of-philosophy/final-oral-defense-examination) to provide opportunities for students to represent how well they integrate learning and apply it to solving a case study or problem, responding to guided questions, or presenting a product they created. Measurement Research Associates provides some guidelines for conducting effective oral examinations (www.measurementresearch.com/media/standardizedoral.pdf).

- *Performances, products, creations, exhibits*—required over time as well as at the end of students' studies, creative or created products represent how learners interpret, express, and construct meaning. Traditionally, arts faculty have formatively assessed students' performances to provide learners with immediate feedback that shapes their future performances. This approach provides not only students with immediate feedback but also faculty and others who contribute to students' learning. Either internal or external scorers, such as professional artists, writers, and dancers, may be called on to score students' creative work. The advent of technology now offers the possibility of students authoring simulations, games, or a web page as evidence of how they apply their learning.

- *Portfolio or e-portfolio*—a collection of multiple kinds of student-generated texts stored electronically or in paper form. Developments in technology now make it possible for students to create digital portfolios. This method of storage and collection provides a longitudinal representation of learning that demonstrates how students make chronological meaning within their contexts of learning through assignments, projects, narrative self-analyses, and social networking sites. It provides an opportunity for students to demonstrate how they integrate learning over time from multiple learning experiences and opportunities within the curriculum, the co-curriculum, and occasions that extend beyond their formal educational experiences. It provides a valuable source of evidence for institution- and program-level learning by documenting a range of texts that represent student learning. *Webfolios, digital learning records,* and *electronic learning records* are other current terms for this method. The development of Web 2.0 electronic portfolios offers students a context in which to demonstrate their learning processes as well as learning products. Two major national resources that focus on technological developments in electronic portfolios are the following: (1) the newly founded global academic organization Association for Authentic, Experiential and Evidence-Based Learning (AAEEBL: www.aaeebl.org) and (2) the community of practice Electronic Portfolio Action and Communication (EPAC: http://epac.pbworks.com). Cambridge, Cambridge, and Yancey (2009) provide a taxonomy of electronic portfolios and describe the potential of Web 2.0 electronic portfolios. For information about Alverno College's Diagnostic Digital Portfolio, go to www.ddp.alverno.edu.

- *Professional or disciplinary practices*—methods that place students in a representative range of professional or disciplinary situations to assess how well they integrate their learning to react and respond to those situations. These situations can also prepare students for the kinds of problems, activities, or situations individuals address not only in their fields of study but also as contributors to society and local communities. The Harrell Professional Development Center in the University of Florida's College of Medicine (http://simulation.med.ufl.edu/harrell-center/about/) has created an environment that permits observation of medical students interacting with patients. Audiovisual equipment captures, records, and displays these interactions. Replaying these interactions provides opportunities for faculty and students to assess students' knowledge, understanding, behaviors, and dispositions. Authentic experiences such as internships and practica are a subset of professional or disciplinary practices often assessed by internship and practica advisors. That is, au-

thentic experiences become a direct method of assessment, providing opportunity for students to demonstrate the dimensions of their learning within the context of a real environment. A step beyond simulations, these direct methods assess how well students translate their cumulative learning into actual practice.

- *Questioning a solution*—a method to ascertain how deeply students probe a problem or issue and draw on their stored problem-solving abilities. This method consists of presenting students with a problem and the solution and then asking them the following question: "Is that the only solution?"

- *Self-reflection*—students' thoughts about or analysis of their work or the effects of a learning experience represent another source of evidence of learning. Self-reflections can accompany any work students hand in, such as a capstone project (see Box 5.9) and often chronologically accompany portfolio or e-portfolio entries (see Box 5.12 and Appendixes 5.1 and 5.2). They may also occur in online postings, such as blogs, or in journals or notebooks. Self-reflections serve as a chronological documentary of students' learning or discovery—a means of slowing students down to take stock of what and how they have learned and changed.

- *Simulation*—an actual or online program or environment, such as Second Life, that imitates real situations or interactions providing a context for students to demonstrate their learning. Students can now perform experiments in virtual labs or diagnose virtual patients. Student can draw inferences from simulations such as the one on global warming at http://zebu.uoregon.edu/nsf/gh.html#BB. Students can mine data in virtual simulation sites such as Second Life or in open resource sites such as Merlot (www.fas.org/programs/ltp/emerging_technologies/arts_and_humanities.html).

- *Team-based or collaborative projects*—methods that enable assessment of individuals' knowledge, understanding, behaviors and attitudes as well as their ability to work together to create a product or solve a problem. These projects are often videotaped, and groups of faculty, staff, and students themselves have access to immediate results that inform students as well as educators. Alverno College's institutional example on page 160 illustrates assessment that focuses on individual students as well as their collective achievement. Community service projects provide another source of evidence of how well students apply or transfer or integrate learning to solve a problem as well as an opportunity for students to self-reflect on how they contributed and what and how they learned from the experience. Teamwork is now possible and can be represented across media (digital media and interfaces) and modes of communication. Wikis and podcasts are technology-based methods that provide evidence of teamwork that is both time- and date-stamped to identify each contributor's work. For example, at the end of a program of study, teams of students might collaborate to create a culminating assignment on a wiki site, designed to assess how well majors integrate knowledge, abilities, habits of mind, and ways of thinking and knowing.

- *Think alouds*—written, audio, or visual transcripts of students verbalizing how they are solving a problem or performing a process, such as solving a complex chemistry problem. This direct method is useful in identifying the kinds of difficulties students are experiencing as they try to solve a problem or perform a process—difficulties that are invisible to us otherwise (www.tiresias.org/tools/think_aloud.htm).

- *Visual representation*—a method that provides evidence of how well students connect ideas or concepts. Representing learning visually through charting, graphing, or mapping, for example, provides students with alternative ways to represent their learning, often a practice within disciplines such as mathematics and the sciences. Mathematicians often represent developments in their thinking in mind maps (http://jonathan.mueller.faculty.noctrl .edu/toolbox/examples/seaver/mindmappin gtask.htm). Visual representations extend students' repertoire of making meaning, developing versatility in forms of representation that respond to the different needs of audiences, contexts, and the purposes of communication. The Biology Teaching Home Page provides examples of different kinds of con-

ceptual maps, as well as procedures for incorporating them into students' learning (www.fed .cuhk.edu.hk/~johnson/misconceptions/ concept_map/cmap guid.html). Designs for Thinking (www.mapthemind.com/) provides research on and examples of "thinking maps." Examples of graphic organizers are available at www.eed.state.ak.us/tls/Frameworks/mathsci/ ms5_2as1.htm#graphicorganizers.

- *WebQuest*—an inquiry-focused task that requires students to interact with Internet resources. Dodge, the originator of this method, distinguishes between two kinds of WebQuests: short-term, helping students acquire and integrate knowledge, and long-term, leading students to create a product to which others can respond. Faculty can design their own WebQuests or use existing WebQuests, such as those at http://webquest .org/index-resources.php. The University of Maryland's Virtual Resource Site for Teaching with Technologyy (http://www.umuc.edu/ virtualteaching/module1/media.html) offers online examples of assignments that promote problem solving, object and document analysis, data gathering and synthesis, case studies, virtual labs and field trips, and collaborative learning and inquiry.

A women's studies history project for undergraduate and graduate students, involving data gathering and synthesis, from online texts, images, and repositories is also on the university's online teaching and technology site (www.umuc.edu/virtualteaching/module1/ research.html#women).

Tom Pfaff's assignment for calculus students (www.ithaca.edu/tpfaff/sustainability.htm) is an example of a WebQuest that provides resources for students to consult in responding to a sustainability question.

INDIRECT METHODS

Conventional and Technology-Enabled Indirect Methods

Helpful in deepening interpretations of student learning are indirect methods, which focus on perceptions of student learning by asking students or others to respond to a set or series of questions. Indirect methods complement direct methods rather than substitute for them.

What Indirect Methods Provide

- Evidence of students' attitudes, perceptions, and experiences
- Evidence that may help explain student performance levels

What Indirect Methods Do Not Provide

- Work that represents evidence of student learning unless an instrument asks students to produce a text as evidence

Examples of Indirect Methods

- *Focus groups*—formation of demographically representative student groups to probe a specific issue that may have been identified in a survey or identified in patterns of student performance as a result of formative or summative assessments. Van Aken and collaborators (1999) describe the successful design of a focus group to obtain perceptions of historically underrepresented students enrolled in an engineering program.
- *Interviews*—formation of demographically representative groups to gain knowledge about students' perceptions of their learning experiences. Small Group Instructional Diagnosis (SGID; www.miracosta.edu/home/gfloren/sgid.htm) is a facilitated group interview process conducted by a trained interviewer who asks students to identify what and how they have learned and what kinds of learning obstacles they are facing or have faced. Used initially at the midpoint in a course to provide feedback to a faculty member about how well students are or are not learning, this method can also provide useful formative assessment data at the program, department, or institution level, providing students chronological opportunities to describe their experiences learning.
- *Student, alumni, employer, faculty, and staff surveys and questionnaires*—provide information about students' or others' perceptions of students' learning. Alumni questionnaires and surveys provide a retrospective view of graduates' educational experience and create an opportunity for them to recommend improvements in education based on what is relevant to their current employment, profession, or graduate education. Faculty-staff surveys or questionnaires provide perceptions of student learning and their learning environment. Several sources that are useful in designing surveys are the following:

The Teaching, Learning, and Technology Group's (TLT) design matrix to tailor a survey for different respondents (www.tltgroup.org/Flashlight/flashlightonline.htm)

Software survey design programs such as Survey Monkey (www.surveymonkey.com) or Scantron's survey software (www.scantron.com/surveysolutions/software/)

Software survey services integrated into assessment management systems described in the appendixes in chapter 8

The following list represents some frequently used surveys in higher education:

- ACT's surveys for adult learners, alumni, entering students, withdrawing students, and for institutional services (www.act.org)
- The Cooperative Institutional Research Program (CIRP), a survey given to first-year students before they take classes (www.heri.ucla.edu/cirpoverview.php)
- College Student Experiences Questionnaire (CSEQ; http://cseq.iub.edu)
- Community College Survey of Student Engagement (CCSSE; www.ccsse.org/aboutccsse/aboutccsse.html)
- Community College Student Experiences Questionnaire (CCSEQ; http://www.memphis.edu/cshe/ccseq.php)
- Diverse Learning Environment Survey (http://heri.ucla.edu/dle/?c=survey)
- Faculty Survey of Student Engagement (FSSE; http://fsse.iub.edu)
- The National Center for Higher Education Management Systems' Comprehensive Alumni Assessment Survey (www.nchems.org)
- National Survey of Student Engagement (NSSE; http://nsse.iub.edu/)
- Noel-Levitz Student Satisfaction Inventory https://www.noellevitz.com/Our+Services/Retention/Tools/Student+Satisfaction+Inventory

- Your First College Year (YFCY) for first-year students in their second semester (www.heri.ucla.edu/yfcyoverview.php)
- Student Assessment of their Learning Gains (SALG)—a customizable online end-of-course survey that asks students to rate the components of a course, such as lab work or discussion groups, and the degree to which these components contributed to their learning (www.salgsite.org). This survey could well be used for program-, department-, or institution-level assessment if a sample of students were asked chronologically to rate how well and why the components of learning they experienced contributed to stated learning outcomes. Given that the survey is customizable, institutions can add additional questions that probe students' perceptions of their learning.
- *Self-perception inventories*—methods that assess the extent to which students have shifted or changed attitudes, values, or perspectives based on learning experiences. These kinds of inventories are frequently used before and after an educational experience or experiences to chart patterns of change. Examples include the following:

  Global Perspective Inventory (GPI)—a 46-item online inventory designed to assess the effect of cultural experiences on learners' global perspectives through three dimensions: cognitive, intrapersonal and interpersonal (https://gpi.central.edu)

  Intercultural Development Inventory (IDI)—a 44-item inventory-based paper and pencil instrument designed to assess the extent of an individual's intercultural sensitivity along a continuum that ranges from ethnocentrism to ethnorelativism, identifying a person's ability to shift from denial of difference to integration of difference (www.intercultural.org)

A list of inventories frequently used in student services is contained in Scott (2009).

REFERENCES

Cambridge, D., Cambridge, B., & Yancey, K. (2009). *Electronic portfolios 2.0: Emergent research on implementation and impact.* Sterling VA: Stylus.

Dodge, B. (1997). *Some thoughts about webquests.* http://webquest.sdsu.edu/about_webquests.html

Libarkin, J. (2008, October). Concept inventories in higher education science. A manuscript prepared for the National Research Council Promising Practices in Undergraduate STEM Education Workshop 2. Washington, D.C.: www7.nationalacademies.org/bose/Libarkin_CommissionedPaper.pdf

Nuhfer, E., & Knipp, D. (2003). The knowledge survey: A tool for all reasons. To *improve the Academy.* 21, 59–78.

Scott, J.H. (2009). *Factors to consider before choosing an assessment instrument.* Retrieved August, 2010 at: www.uga.edu/studentaffairs/assess/ateam/sessions/200708/Skill%20Session_3/Creating%20a%20Focus%20Group%20(p%2012–13).pdf

Van Aken, E. M., Watford, B., & Mdeina, B. A. (1999, July). The use of focus groups for minority engineering program assessment. *Journal of Engineering Education,* 88(3), 333–342.

Chapter 6

REACHING CONSENSUS
ABOUT CRITERIA AND
STANDARDS OF JUDGMENT

If students are expected to develop a degree of independence in pursuit of learning, reach a satisfactory level of skill in communication, demonstrate sensitivity to their own values and those of their associates, become capable of collaborating with peers in defining and resolving problems, be able to recognize the relevance of their increasing knowledge to the current scene, and seek continually for insightful understanding and organization of the total educational experience, these outcomes must be specifically stated. In addition they must be made explicit in relation to learning experiences and by providing opportunities for demonstration of the developing behavior and for evaluation of it. Content, subject matter, and behavior are interrelated and must be construed by teachers, students and evaluators. This requires an interrelated trinity of conceptual statements defining the objectives of operational statements, including how the behavior is to be evoked and appraised, and providing standards for deciding whether progress is evident and whether accomplishment is finally satisfactory.

—P. L. Dressel, 1976

OVERVIEW: How observers or raters interpret the work, projects, and creations that students generate in response to a method of assessment is the subject of this chapter. Developing criteria and standards of judgment provides a means to document and examine patterns of student achievement: the intellectual complexity, creativity, application of disciplinary logic, behaviors, and dispositions that provide evidence of integrated learning. Specifically, core working groups that design or develop methods of assessment also work with representative constituencies at their institution to collaboratively develop scoring rubrics. Consisting of criteria and levels of achievement for each criterion, scoring rubrics are public grading sheets that scorers apply to the work students produce in response to an assessment method. These sheets enable scorers to assess the dimensions of student work, that is, how well a particular project or creation meets collaboratively agreed-upon criteria. The Worksheets, Guides, and Exercises at the end of this chapter are designed to guide core working groups as they (1) develop scoring rubrics that enable scorers to rate student work against criteria and standards for judgment, (2) pilot-test these scoring rubrics to ascertain how well they capture the dimensions of students' learning, and (3) develop interrater reliability among scorers as they apply scoring rubrics to samples of student work.

INTERPRETATIONS OF STUDENT ACHIEVEMENT

How well do students progress toward institution- and program-level learning outcomes? How well do they achieve institution- and program-level expectations by the time they graduate? Interpreting students' achievement along the progression of their learning marks the next phase of the assessment process, that is, deciding how to interpret what students say, do, or prepare in response to an assessment method. Identifying the criteria and standards of judgment that an institution and its programs choose to apply to student work raises the following questions:

- Will criteria and standards of judgment be externally or internally established?
- What kind of results do externally and internally developed criteria and standards of judgment provide?
- How useful are results in promoting collective and targeted interpretations of student achievement within the context of educational practices?

Two approaches, norm referencing and criteria referencing, provide results that lead to different levels of community conversations.

Norm Referencing

A *norm-referenced approach* to assessing student learning primarily aims to compare a student's achievement against the achievement of other students who have performed the same task. Based on the achievement levels of a broader population, an individual student's performance is compared against the achievement of that broader population—referred to as a norm. A student's score, then, places that student within the context of others' performance. Unless developed within an institution based on shared criteria and standards of judgment, standardized instruments, such as tests of students' general education knowledge, are norm-referenced to certify levels of attainment against externally established criteria and standards of judgment. In this gatekeeping role, standardized tests focus on categorizing students. Interpretations of student performance, for example, serve as predictors of future achievement, such as students' attainment in graduate school, law school, or medical school. Or they certify entry into a profession, such

as in national licensure examinations in nursing, law, or medicine. Categories of performance also enable institutions to benchmark the achievement of their students against students at comparative institutions or in comparable programs. Frequently, policy makers, legislators, and other public audiences aim to rank states or institutions based on results of standardized norm-referenced instruments, believing that a onetime "measure" of students' performance reflects an institution's or a program's effectiveness within the defined universe of a standardized instrument.

When institutions develop standardized instruments themselves, normed within an institutional context, institutions and programs may use these results to place or identify students—those who pass and those who fail, or those who can write at a certain level and those who cannot—such as in rising junior year examinations. Collective interpretations of norm-referenced standardized instrument results based on students' scores may also identify areas of weakness in student learning, such as determining that students need more opportunities to learn how to identify assumptions that underlie an argument. Interpreting why students can or cannot achieve within the scope of a norm-referenced method is the most important question in an institutional commitment to assessing student learning. Unless a norm-referenced method provides students with opportunities to explain their responses or unless a method is specifically constructed to track problem-solving abilities, such as in the "generalized graded unfolding models" designed to assess students' cognitive complexity described by Erwin and Wise (2002), norm-referenced results provide limited information about students' behaviors, attitudes, habits of mind, problem-solving processes or strategies, and the interplay between understanding and action.

Criterion Referencing

Standardized norm-referenced approaches to assessment build in criteria and standards based on the collective expertise of those who develop, design, and test them. Students' results are reported in terms of numerical scores that place them in an achievement level based on these externally developed and tested criteria and standards of judgment. A *criterion-referenced approach* to assessment, on the other hand, deepens context-specific collective interpretations about student achievement based on criteria and standards of judgment developed within an institution and its programs.

Criterion-referenced results report on students' performance against the multiple dimensions and possible performance levels of a task—an exhibit, a presentation, a performance, or interaction in a group project. Results relate to the construct of a direct or indirect method that aligns with institution- or program-level outcomes and students' learning histories. Students learn about their achievement in relation to these criteria and achievement levels; institutions and programs learn about students' learning in the same way. Institution- and program-level value is placed on students' achievement against criteria. How well students meet specific performance criteria along a continuum of achievement, as opposed to how well they compare with other students, becomes the focus of collective interpretation. Developed to align with institution- and program-level outcome statements, assessment methods, and students' learning chronologies, criterion-referenced results lead to dialogue about the relationship among pedagogy; curricular, co-curricular, and instructional design; and educational opportunities. How well do students' work, projects, and responses fit institution- and program-level criteria and standards for learning?

Some standardized instruments, such as the Graduate Record Examination in writing, provide results of student performance along criteria that identify areas of students' strengths and weaknesses (www.gre.org/descriptor.html). Again, these results may foster interpretation about what students have learned, but probably do not promote interpretations about how they have learned or why they performed as they did on one particular testing day. Further, whereas most commercially designed standardized instruments value reporting numerical results, locally designed assessment methods value both quantitatively and qualitatively stated results. These results support institution- and program-level inquiry into the efficacy of educational practices that promote integration, synthesis, and transference. The complexity of institution- and program-level outcomes cannot be solely reflected in numerical results; the power of observation captures complexity. Intellectual processes and the confluence of understanding, behaving, and responding, for example, are difficult to measure in simplistic ways. Over time, criterion-based results may lead to reporting percentages of student performance against an institution- or program-level norm. However, within those percentages is robust evidence about the dimensions of learning that foster collective interpretation within the context of educational practices.

SCORING RUBRICS

Scoring rubrics, a set of criteria that identify the expected dimensions of a text and the levels of achievement along those dimensions, are criterion-referenced, providing a means to assess the multiple dimensions of student learning represented in students' projects, work, products, and performances. Raters assess student work based on these criteria to derive inferences about students' learning represented in various kinds of texts. In effect, rubrics translate outcome statements into criteria, also referred to as *primary traits* or *performance indicators.* These criteria publicly identify the significant dimensions that raters apply to texts students generate in response to an assessment method. Results of applying these criteria provide evidence of learning patterns. At both the institution and program levels, these patterns identify students' areas of strength as well as weakness. Interpreting patterns of weakness leads to adjustments or modifications in pedagogy; curricular, co-curricular, and instructional design; and educational practices and opportunities.

Scoring rubrics consist of two kinds of descriptors:

1. *Criteria descriptors*—descriptions of the criteria or traits manifested in a project, performance, or text students produce in response to an assessment method. Criteria identify the ways of thinking, knowing, or behaving represented in what students produce, such as the following:
   - Creativity
   - Self-reflection
   - Originality
   - Integration
   - Analysis
   - Synthesis
   - Disciplinary logic

   Criteria descriptors may also identify characteristics of the text itself, such as the following:
   - Coherence
   - Accuracy or precision
   - Clarity
   - Structure

2. *Performance descriptors*—descriptions of how well students execute each criterion or trait along an achievement continuum—score levels. This continuum, then, describes representative ways that students perform or execute each criterion, reflecting mastery

levels, national or professional levels, or levels established through the collective expertise of faculty, staff, and others who contribute to students' education based on their observation of students' progression over time or the typical developmental process. Achievement along a continuum may be expressed numerically, such as through a 1–5 scale, or expressed verbally to identify levels of excellence, expertise, or proficiency, as illustrated in the following examples:

Exemplary	Commendable	Satisfactory	Unsatisfactory
Excellent	Good	Needs Improvement	Unacceptable
Exceptional	Acceptable	Marginal	Unacceptable
Expert	Practitioner	Apprentice	Novice

The following scoring rubrics identify the criteria and standards of judgment for texts that students produce as evidence of either institution- or program-level learning. In all of the examples, note that criteria are described under each level of achievement, providing students with specific feedback about their work and providing educators with specific patterns of evidence on which to base collective interpretation.

Figure 6.1 represents a scoring rubric designed to assess nursing students' abilities to integrate personal as well as professional experiences into the early stages of their emerging professional lives. Scorers grade reflective writings over the course of nursing students' studies against levels of achievement they expect students to demonstrate that correlate with the design of the curriculum and related educational experiences. This particular scoring rubric also asks

Level II Competency Paper

Students write a 1–2 page paper reflecting on how well they meet the Level II expectation in their journey toward becoming an "Accountable Professional." It is scored by the following rubric.

Scoring Rubric

Criteria	Beginning ✓−	On Target ✓	Exceeds Expectation ✓+	SCORE
Personal and professional learning and growth	Reflection does not connect to personal needs and experiences and/or does not reflect an effort to seek out growth experiences.	Reflection identifies self-initiative in seeking experiences for personal and professional growth beyond course requirements.	Reflection analyzes areas for personal and professional learning and growth that exceed the course requirements and shows evidence of collaboration with others in at least a beginning effort to obtain additional experiences.	
Personal and professional accountability	Reflection demonstrates nursing actions without necessary thought for personal and professional actions.	Reflection identifies and applies personal and professional accountability.	Reflection demonstrates the foundation for consistent personal accountability and responsibility. Provides at least 2 examples.	

FIGURE 6.1 INSTITUTIONAL EXAMPLE: Azusa Pacific University

Source: The undergraduate nursing department at Azusa Pacific University under the leadership of Professor Shila Wiebe, Director; Dr. Vicky Bowden, Curriculum Committee Chair; Professor Connie Austin, ePortfolio Program Director; and Dr. Julie Jantzi, Director of Institutional Assessment Planning.

graders to indicate the level of achievement translated into a numerical score.

Appendix 6.1 illustrates an example of a scoring rubric for a final project in psychology, a thesis. Assessing the level at which students meet the criteria that describe the professional components of a thesis in psychology, scorers apply these criteria to each component of the document to determine how well students demonstrate professional conventions and practices, disciplinary logic, and conformity to the standards of written English. Scoring may also involve *weighting* certain criteria, that is, placing increased value on certain ones. The summary sheet that records scorers' responses to students' theses (page 237) shows that students' literature review and the quality of their writing, for example, have increased weight assigned to them. As this summary sheet also demonstrates, it is possible to convert students' scores into grades.

Analytic and Holistic Rubrics

Scorers may grade student work using an *analytic scoring rubric* that lists each criterion scorers rate as they read or observe students' work, as illustrated in Appendix 6.1. Analytic scoring rubrics provide detailed results about patterns of student achievement. Viewing the results of analytic scoring rubrics promotes targeted interpretation and decision making. For example, results that identify students' weak abilities to solve certain kinds of problems or take multiple perspectives on an issue lead to discussions about how to modify or change pedagogy; the design of curriculum, co-curriculum, and instruction; and other educational opportunities to improve these thinking processes. These analytic scoring rubric patterns become fertile evidence on which to base focused interpretations about students' strengths or weaknesses.

Scorers may also grade student work using a *holistic scoring rubric* that lists features of a work that scorers use to make more global judgments. Figure 6.2 is an example of a holistic scoring rubric that graders use to place students' portfolios in one of four achievement levels. Each portfolio receives one numerical score based on scorers' assessment of the qualities of a portfolio. Holistic scoring rubrics are useful for categorizing student work to determine overall performance levels

1.	Incomplete and poorly organized portfolio that does not contain artifacts that demonstrate achievement of program outcomes.
	No accompanying summary or self-reflective sheets that describe the significance of the artifacts to the learner.
	Submissions overall do not conform with conventions of English—spelling, grammatical, punctuation, word usage errors.
2.	Incomplete portfolio that contains some artifacts that demonstrate achievement of program outcomes.
	No or a few summary or self-reflective sheets that describe the significance of the artifacts to the learner.
	Submissions overall do not conform to conventions of English—spelling, grammatical, punctuation, word usage errors.
3.	Complete portfolio that includes artifacts that demonstrate achievement of program outcomes.
	Each artifact is accompanied with summary and reflective sheets that describe the significance of the artifact to the learner.
	Submissions overall conform to conventions of English—spelling, grammatical, punctuation, word usage.
4.	Complete portfolio that includes artifacts that demonstrate achievement of program outcomes.
	Each artifact is accompanied with summary and reflective sheets that chronologically describe the significance of the artifact to the learner.
	Submissions conform to conventions of English with only minor mistakes in spelling, grammar, punctuation, word usage.

FIGURE 6.2   Holistic Scoring Rubric for a Program-Level Portfolio

in response to a task, such as how many students developed portfolios under each numerical level.

One of the rubrics that the service-learning program asks raters to use as they read students' Articulated Learnings (ALs), illustrated in chapter 3, Box 3.4 is a holistic critical thinking rubric applied to students' responses to both the academic and personal dimensions of their responses (adapted from Paul, 1993). Raters use a scale of 1–4 to assess students' critical thinking as represented in students' writing. Raters award a 4 to students' writing if, overall, it meets the criteria listed in the institutional example in Box 6.2.

Strategies to Develop Scoring Rubrics

Developing internal scoring rubrics is another line of collaborative work that draws on multiple levels of expertise inside and outside an institution and its programs. How are they developed? Who develops them? What are the standards against which student work is applied? How do we ensure that they represent standards of quality? Quality in Undergraduate Education (QUE), a national project, supported by the Education Trust and the National Association of System Heads (NASA) in association with Georgia State University, defines quality standards as "high, achievable, and credible to policymakers, students, families, and employers" (www2.gsu.edu/~wwwque/). This 7-year project developed standards and criteria to assess student work in six disciplines—biology, chemistry, English, history, mathematics, and physics (www2.gsu.edu/~wwwque/standards/discipline.html). In his 2006 publication, *Faculty Development for Student Achievement: The QUE Project*, Henry presents the final set of standards and criteria of judgment that faculty in these six disciplines can use or adapt.

The core working groups that select or design direct methods may also be the same core working groups that develop scoring rubrics because these two processes are interdependent. To develop standards of quality, institutions and programs invite additional external members into this group: internship advisers, professionals within the local community, representatives from business advisory groups, representatives from professional organizations, representative organizations that employ students, colleagues from surrounding 2- and 4-year institutions, and colleagues from K–12 whose knowledge and expertise is useful in developing criteria that contribute to students' successful entrance and progression in learning.

In addition, this group draws on (1) emerging work in professional and disciplinary organizations focused on establishing criteria and standards for judgment, and (2) available research on learning in a

---

BOX 6.2   INSTITUTIONAL EXAMPLE: *North Carolina State University*

- Consistently avoids typographical, spelling, and grammatical errors
- Makes clear the connection(s) between the service-related experience and the dimension being discussed
- Makes statements of fact that are accurate, supported with evidence (**Accuracy**)

For ALs:

- Accurately identifies, describes, and applies appropriate academic principles
- Consistently expands on ideas, expresses ideas in another way, and provides examples/illustrations (**Clarity**)
- Describes learning that is relevant to AL category and keeps the discussion specific to the learning being articulated (**Relevance**)
- Addresses the complexity of the problem, answers important question(s) that are raised, and avoids oversimplifying when making connections (**Depth**)
- Gives meaningful consideration to alternative points of view and interpretations (**Breadth**)
- Demonstrates a line of reasoning that is logical, with conclusions or goals that follow clearly from it (**Logic**)
- Draws conclusions and sets goals that address any major issue(s) raised by the experience (**Significance**)

Source: Sarah Ash and Patti Clayton, North Carolina State University.

particular field of study focused on identifying abilities, traits, and ways of knowing and problem solving that mark progression of learning in that field of study. Understanding the progression of learning contributes to developing scoring rubrics that capture learning over time against agreed-upon criteria and standards of judgment.

Development of Scoring Rubrics

The following process guides core working groups to develop scoring rubrics. Specific strategies under each major step of the process are helpful in reaching consensus about the criteria and levels of achievement of a scoring rubric.

1. After agreement on a direct assessment method, have each member of a core working group independently list the criteria to apply to students' work and then describe each criterion.
   Specific strategies that produce a pool of responses include the following:

   a. Ask a member to research disciplinary or professional organizations' current work focused on student learning.
      Example: The Valid Assessment of Learning in Undergraduate Education (VALUE) Project discussed on pages 225–226, which has developed 15 scoring rubrics to assess general education outcomes
      Example: Lovitts and Wert's (2008a, b,c) publications on scoring rubrics for humanities, science, and social science dissertations, also discussed on page 226 in this chapter
      Example: The QUE standards and criteria of judgment that have been published in *Faculty Development for Student Achievement: The QUE Project* (Henry, 2006)
   b. Adapt or use existing rubrics such as those provided in Stevens and Levi (2005) or those listed under "Additional Resources" at the end of this chapter.
   c. Ask a member of a core working group to research literature on learning in a discipline or field of study to ascertain what that current research reveals about how students learn. The National Research Council (2001) provides a rich resource

on this kind of research, such as criteria that distinguish between novice and expert ways of thinking and behaving.
   d. Derive rubrics from work that students have submitted previously in response to a similar task, such as case studies, research projects, or problems. That is, reviewing representative student work identifies the traits that distinguish exemplary from less successful work. Review representative student work graded from A through F to determine criteria and levels of achievement that identify the continuum of learning and its markers along the way.
   e. Interview students to find out what they believe they have mastered over time; that is, let their experiences inform your rubric. Developing student interview protocols similar to those developed by Marton and Saljo (1976a, 1976b) to learn about students' approaches to reading (see chapter 3, page 96) may also provide valuable information about what students can accomplish over time that can inform development of a scoring rubric. Interviews with tutors and graduate teaching assistants also provide an opportunity to explore and identify criteria that they experience in their educative roles.
   f. Ask members to describe what they have observed about student learning as students progress in their learning. Incorporate agreed-upon abilities or attributes students need to improve over time, such as those identified in the Taxonomy of Student Weaknesses, Errors, or Fuzzy Thinking (page 133 in chapter 4), so that you can track how well students improve. The scoring rubrics developed at Association of American Colleges & Universities (AAC&U) have been designed to identify the salient attributes that characterize beginning-level to accomplished-level student work for 15 general education scoring rubrics.

2. In a group meeting, identify overlap among the pooled criteria descriptors to identify consensus about the criteria. Review contributions that do not overlap and discuss the necessity of including them in the scoring

rubric. As a group, identify levels of achievement and write descriptions of each criterion within the context of a level of achievement. If it is not possible to achieve consensus about a criterion or its level of achievement, the following process provides the opportunity to test a draft that may have questionable criteria or unclear descriptions of achievement levels.

3. Pilot-test the scoring rubric by applying it to samples of student work that have been previously handed in. Revise the rubric based on these pilot tests and continue to apply it to samples of student work until the group has reached consensus that it clearly describes each criterion along levels of achievement. If, during these pilot tests, student texts do not represent a dimension or attain a level, that finding may identify lack of sufficient feedback, practice, or gaps in students' learning opportunities.

STRATEGIES TO ENSURE INTERRATER RELIABILITY

Once a scoring rubric has been refined based on the preceding strategies and before it is applied for institution- and program-level assessment, establishing *interrater reliability* as raters apply a rubric is essential. This process ensures that individuals' ratings are reliable across different samples and samples from representative student populations. Raters may consist of faculty and staff within the institution or external reviewers such as internship advisers, alumni, professionals within the community, and faculty from other institutions. Developments in assessment management systems, discussed in chapter 8, pages 315–323, have made it possible for experts outside an institution to assess student work. In an agreement with colleagues at another institution, for example, a humanities department may upload sample senior papers, accompanied with scoring rubrics, to peers at another institution and then derive patterns of student performance from externally scored reviewers—a practice that could become a national one to ensure objectivity in the scoring process.

Calibration, the process of establishing interrater reliability in scoring student texts, is developed over successive applications of a scoring rubric to student work, semester after semester and sometimes over several years, to ensure that rater responses are con-

sistent across representative student populations. Specifically, do raters score students' work the same way? Do major discrepancies exist? The following steps establish interrater reliability:

1. Ask raters to independently score a set of student samples that reflects the range of texts students produce in response to a direct method.
2. Bring raters together to review their responses to identify patterns of consistent and inconsistent responses.
3. Discuss and then reconcile inconsistent responses.
4. Repeat the process of independent scoring on a new set of student samples.
5. Again, bring all scorers together to review their responses to identify patterns of consistent and inconsistent responses.
6. Discuss and then reconcile inconsistent responses.

This process is repeated until raters reach consensus about applying the scoring rubric. Ordinarily, two to three of these sessions calibrate raters' responses. In actual practice, two raters score student work; a third rater may be called upon if there is a disagreement between the two scorers' responses.

To calibrate scorers' responses to the critical thinking criteria illustrated on page 222, Ash and Clayton ask each member of a team of scorers to independently evaluate students' work. Scorers report their individual evaluations, and the team meets as a whole to compare the results, discuss discrepancies, and reconcile the differences through a process of reaching consensus on each score. This sharing of evaluative judgments supports an iterative process of revising the learning materials themselves to increase their ability to produce the desired student outcomes. In addition, repetition of this process over time and with an ever-widening set of scorers assists instructors in their own use of the articulated learning process and also establishes interrater reliability to ensure consistent scoring of student texts. (Contributed by Sarah Ash and Patti Clayton, North Carolina State University.)

THREADED OPPORTUNITIES FOR INSTITUTIONAL AND STUDENT LEARNING

Internally developed, scoring rubrics become a way to position teachers and learners together to track students' learning over time against institution- and program-level criteria and standards of judgment. Members of the institutional community learn about students' achievement against which to target program- and institution-level dialogue focused on pedagogy and educational practices. In addition, threaded throughout students' undergraduate and graduate education, scoring rubrics provide students and educators with a running record of students' development and achievement. Scoring rubrics used in individual courses and services also promote learning as integrative, as opposed to an aggregation of courses or experiences. Students begin to see connections between and among courses—how educational experiences contribute to their learning and development.

Integration is what institution- and program-level rubrics capture. They focus on and value the whole of students' texts—their performances, interactions, creations, written and oral presentations, research projects—through viewing the parts that contribute to a whole text. Strength in one criterion does not guarantee a final high score—a score that may be affected by weaker performance under other criteria. Scoring rubrics focus on both the content of a text as well as its execution—that is, the qualities that help or impede others in interpreting that text, such as structure, use of design principles, coherence within a text, use of disciplinary logic, precision and accuracy, and depth of analysis. Whereas individual courses or educational experiences may focus on components of learning, such as how to write or how to solve certain kinds of problems, at the institutional and program level value is placed on how students connect components to solve a new problem, create a work of art, treat a patient, or address a social issue.

Just as sharing outcomes with students on matriculation into an institution or its major helps orient them to their education, sharing institution- and program-level scoring rubrics with them also orients them to viewing learning as a process. Sharing outcomes and scoring rubrics encourages student responsibility for learning. Together, outcome statements and scoring rubrics create a context against which students, as well as institutions and their programs, chart progress and achievement.

Along with fostering a student work ethic built on practice, chronological use of scoring rubrics in a program, in a service, or across an institution fosters the following:

- Students' capacity to chronologically self-reflect on the dimensions of learning in their work
- Students' commitment to improve specific dimensions in their work
- Students' understanding that the process of learning is ongoing—a disposition of lifelong learning that higher education aspires to instill in its students

CURRENT PRACTICE ACROSS HIGHER EDUCATION

The use of scoring rubrics has now become a common practice in undergraduate education, as well as in the programs and services that contribute to student learning in the co-curriculum. In addition, graduate and professional education programs are beginning to warm to this practice as evidenced in the following kinds of developments.

The product of AAC&U's multiyear national VALUE Project (Valid Assessment of Learning in Undergraduate Education) is the set of 15 scoring rubrics that institutions are now using to assess general education outcomes related to students' intellectual and practical skills, personal and social responsibility, and integrative learning (Rhodes, 2010). (For a list of the 15 general education learning outcome domains, see page 92 in chapter 3.) These rubrics were developed by teams of faculty experts, representing 2- and 4-year colleges and universities, who reviewed existing campus rubrics across colleges and universities to establish a national version. Rubric drafts were refined based on feedback from other higher education educators who offered recommended changes or provided feedback based on pilot-testing a rubric draft on their campuses. The VALUE rubrics have been developed to track students' chronological achievement of general education outcomes at both 2-year and 4-year institutions or to establish baseline data for incoming students in order to track their achievement over time. Further, these scoring rubrics are not wedded to a specific assessment method; rather, they have been designed to assess the broad ways in which students authentically represent their general education outcomes—not only in their general education program of studies but also in their major programs of study to capture more sophisticated levels of attainment that would be present in a senior project, for example. Four of these scoring rubrics appear in the appendixes at the end of this chapter: Appendix 6.2, Creative Thinking VALUE Rubric, and

Appendix 6.3, Quantitative Literacy VALUE Rubric, are two of many rubrics educators use to assess a range of intellectual and practical skills, listed on page 92 in chapter 3. Appendix 6.4, Civic Engagement VALUE Rubric, is one of the rubrics that educators use to assess students' personal and social responsibility. Appendix 6.5 is the rubric educators use to assess integrative learning.

In contrast to current standardized instruments that restrict how students represent a limited number of "easier to measure" general education outcomes, the range of chronological work that undergraduate students realistically and authentically author represents students' achievement of an institution's multiple general education outcomes. Higher education prepares students to draw on their repertoire of learning so that projects they produce demonstrate, for example, how well they might integrate quantitative reason, creative thinking, and writing in a task. Thus, educators can apply more than one VALUE scoring rubric to rate students' authentic work, such as a capstone or culminating project or the range of work in an e-portfolio. Not tethered to a specific way of representing learning, the VALUE rubrics are intended for educators to apply to conventional methods of assessment as well as emerging technology-enabled methods—written texts, live or videotaped performances, or products created online involving multimedia tools (as described in chapter 5). As represented in Appendixes 6.2, 6.3, 6.4, and 6.5, a cover sheet that accompanies each rubric provides the definition of a learning outcome, framing language that describes the context for applying a rubric, and definitions of terms used in the rubrics.

Huba and Freed (2000) provided groundbreaking examples of scoring rubrics used in doctoral programs such as for teamwork and oral communication (pp. 151–200, 201–232) to enable faculty to learn more about patterns of student weakness and to help students understand doctoral level expectations for learning. Advancing the practice of using scoring rubrics to help doctoral students understand faculty expectations for dissertations have been Lovitts's research and publications (2002, 2007) and Lovitts and Wert's publications of scoring rubrics for dissertations in the social sciences, sciences, and humanities (2008a, 2008b, 2008c). Professional programs at the doctoral level have also developed scoring rubrics, such as the small-group problem-based rubric developed at Loma Linda University (2008) to assess medical students.

Co-curricular programs and services are also using scoring rubrics to reinforce students' learning of general education outcomes and outcomes specific to co-curricular programs, services, or educational opportunities. Two of many scoring rubrics from the University of Maryland's Division of Student Affairs illustrate this practice. Professionals in the Division of Student Affairs have aligned many of their professional organization's outcomes with those of the institution and then identified and developed scoring rubrics to apply to student work and behaviors in the range of programs, services, and opportunities they offer. Appendix 6.6, for example, a scoring rubric for ethical development, is chronologically used to assess students who have violated the university's code of academic integrity as they go through a disciplinary process and a required seminar. The time management rubric in Appendix 6.7 is used to assess students in the university's learning assistance programs.

The Student Affairs Assessment Committee at the University of Rhode Island has developed a scoring rubric (Appendix 6.8) that serves two purposes: (1) to clarify expectations for students who work on campus and (2) to give students feedback about their performance. This comprehensive rubric integrates criteria for several of the university's general education outcomes, such as under communication, information literacy, and cultural awareness, and criteria for workplace skills and behaviors, such as the ability to work independently. Thus, students develop an understanding of the relevance and usefulness of curricular and co-curricular learning in their personal contexts. Moreover, students have a record of their work performance to provide a future employer.

Developing scoring rubrics that align with learning outcome statements, coupled with research or study questions, is the task that precedes the processes of collecting, analyzing, and interpreting student work—the subject of chapter 7.

WORKS CITED

Dressel, P. L. (1976). *Handbook of academic evaluation.* San Francisco: Jossey-Bass.

Erwin, T. D., & Wise, S. L. (2002). A scholar-practitioner model of assessment. In T. W. Banta & Associates, *Building a scholarship of assessment* (p. 75). San Francisco: Jossey-Bass.

Henry, D. L. (Ed.). (2006). *Faculty development for student achievement: The QUE project.* San Francisco: Jossey-Bass.

Huba, M. E., & Freed, J. E. (2000). *Learner-centered assessment on college campuses: Shifting the focus from teaching to learning.* Boston: Allyn & Bacon.

Loma Linda University. (2008). *Small-group problem-based learning rubric*. *www.llu.edu/pages/medicine/ education/documents/analytic_scoring_rubric.pdf*

Lovitts, B. (2002, November). *Making the implicit explicit: A conceptual approach for assessing the outcomes of doctoral education*. Paper presented at the 2002 ASHE meeting, Sacramento, CA. *www.carnegie foundation.org/CID/ashe?lovitts.pdf*

Lovitts, B. (2007). *Making the implicit explicit: Creating performance expectations for the dissertation*. Sterling, VA: Stylus. *http://stylus.styluspub.com/Books/Book Detail.aspx?productID=128088*

Lovitts, B., & Wert, E. (2008a). *Developing quality dissertations in the humanities: A graduate student's guide to achieving excellence*. Sterling, VA: Stylus. *http://stylus. styluspub.com/Books/BookDetail.aspx?productID= 163103*

———. (2008b). *Developing quality dissertations in the sciences: A graduate student's guide to achieving excellence*. Sterling, VA: Stylus. *http://stylus.styluspub.com/ Books/BookDetail.aspx?productID=163105*

———. (2008c). *Developing quality dissertations in the social sciences: A graduate student's guide to achieving excellence*. Sterling, VA: Stylus. *http://stylus.styluspub .com/Books/BookDetail.aspx?productID=163104*

Marton, F. & Saljo, R. (1978a). *On qualitative differences in learning: I—Outcome and Process. British Journal of Educational Psychology*. 46, 4–11.

Marton, F. & Saljo, R. (1978b). *On qualitative differences in learning: II—Outcome and Process. British Journal of Educational Psychology*.46, 115–127.

National Research Council. (2001). *Knowing what students know: The science and design of educational assessment*. Washington, DC: National Academies Press.

Paul, R. (1993). *Critical thinking: What every person needs to survive in a rapidly changing world*. Santa Rosa, CA: Foundation for Critical Thinking.

Rhodes, T. L. (Ed.). (2010). *Assessing outcomes and improving achievement: Tips and tools for using rubrics*. Washington, D.C.: Association of American Colleges and Universities.

Stevens, D. D., & Levi, A. J. (2005). *Introduction to rubrics: An assessment tool to save grading time, convey effective feedback, and promote student learning*. Sterling, VA: Stylus.

ADDITIONAL RESOURCES

Arter, J. A., & McTighe, J. (2001). *Scoring rubrics in the classroom: Using performance criteria for assessing and improving student performance*. Thousand Oaks, CA: Corwin Press.

Bond, L. (1996). Norm and criterion-referenced testing. *Practical Assessment, Research and Evaluation*, 5, 2.

Hanson, G. R. (Ed.). (2003). *Let's do assessment*. Assessment in Student Affairs; Interactive CD-ROM Series 1. Washington, DC: NASPA.

Hanson, G. R. (Ed.). (2003). *Let's talk assessment*. Assessment in Student Affairs; Interactive CD-ROM Series 2. Washington, DC: NASPA.

Hanson, G. R. (Ed.). (2003). *Let's use assessment*. Assessment in Student Affairs; Interactive CD-ROM Series 3. Washington, DC: NASPA.

Linn, R. (2000). Assessments and accountability. *ER Online*, 29(2), 4–14.

Marzano, R. J., Pickering, D., & McTighe, J. (1993). *Assessing student outcomes: Performance assessment using the dimensions of learning model*. Alexandria, VA: Association for Supervision and Curriculum Development.

Moskal, B. M. (2000). Scoring rubrics: What, when and how? *Practical Assessment, Research and Evaluation*, 7(3). *http://PAREonline.net/getvn.asp?v=7&n=3*

Murphy, P. D., & Gerst, J. (1996, May). *Assessment of student learning in graduate programs*. Paper presented at the Annual Forum of the Association of Institutional Research, Albuquerque, NM. *http://www.eric.ed.gov/PDFS/ED409765.pdf*

Sanders, W., & Horn, S. (1995, March). Educational assessment reassessed: The usefulness of standardized and alternative measures of student achievement as indicators for the assessment of educational outcomes. *Education Policy Analysis Archives*, 3(6). *http://epaa.asu.edu/epaa/ v3n6.html*

Tierney, R., & Simon, M. (2004). What's still wrong with rubrics: Focusing on the consistency of performance criteria across scale levels. *Practical Assessment, Research and Evaluation*, 9(2). *http://PAREonline .net/getvn.asp?v=9&n=2*

TLT Group. Guide to rubric development and resources based on work by Bonnie Mullinix. *www.tltgroup.org/resources/rubrics.htm*

Walvoord, B. E., & Anderson, V. J. (1998). *Effective grading: A tool for learning and assessment*. San Francisco: Jossey-Bass.

Wiggins, G. (1989, May). A true test: Toward more authentic and equitable assessment. *Phi Delta Kappan*, 703–713.

Wiggins, G. (1997). Feedback: How learning occurs. In *Assessing impact: evidence and action* (pp. 31–39). Washington, DC: American Association for Higher Education.

Wiggins, G. (1998). *Educative assessment: Designing assessments to inform and improve student performance.* San Francisco: Jossey-Bass.

Scoring Rubrics in Graduate Education

Maki, P., and Borkowski, N. (2006). *The assessment of doctoral education: Emerging criteria and new models for improving outcomes.* Sterling, VA: Stylus. *http://stylus.styluspub.com/Books/BookDetail.aspx?productID= 128082*

Scoring Rubrics for Online Learning

Albalooshi, F. (2003). *Virtual education: Cases in learning and teaching technologies.* Hershey, PA: IRM Press.

Howell, S. L., & Hricko, M. (2006). *Online assessment and measurement: Case studies from higher education, K–12, and corporate.* Hershey, PA: Information Science.

O'Donnell, A., Smith, J., Gigliotti, G., & Young, J. W. (Eds.). (in press). *Evaluating online learning in higher education: What are students learning and how can we measure it?* Sterling, VA: Stylus. *http://stylus.styluspub.com/Books/BookDetail.aspx?productID= 66214*

Palloff, R. M., & Pratt, K. (2009). *Assessing the online learner: Resources and strategies for faculty.* San Francisco: Jossey Bass.

Scoring Rubrics in Student Affairs

Zelna, C. (n.d.). *Rubrics in student affairs.* PowerPoint presentation. *http://studentaffairs.uncg.edu/ assessment/wp-content/uploads/rubrics_for_student_ affairs.pdf*

Metasites for Examples of Scoring Rubrics in Higher Education

California State University. Links to examples of scoring rubrics including disciplinary rubrics. *http://www.calstate.edu/itl/sloa/links/rubrics.shtml*

California State University, Fresno. Rubric Library. *www.csufresno.edu/irap/assessment/rubric.shtml*

DePaul University. *http://condor.depaul.edu/~tla/ Assessment/ModifyRubrics.html*

Kathy Schrock's Guide for Educators. Assessment rubrics. *http://school.discovery.com/schrockguide/ assess.html*

The Technology Applications Center for Educator Development. *http://www.tcet.unt.edu/START/ instruct/general/rubrics.htm*

WORKSHEETS, GUIDES, AND EXERCISES

1. *Development of a Scoring Rubric:* In conjunction with designing a direct method of assessment, the same or a separate core working group will develop an accompanying scoring rubric. If you are a member of that group, consider how the group might use one or more of the following strategies to develop a scoring rubric for an agreed-upon method.

STRATEGIES FOR DEVELOPING A SCORING RUBRIC

- Research disciplinary or professional organizations' current work on developing scoring rubrics, such as AAC&U's VALUE scoring rubrics for assessing general education outcomes or QUE's scoring rubrics.
- Research current literature on learning in a discipline or field of study to ascertain what that research reveals about indicators of learning.
- Adapt or use existing rubrics, such as those provided in Stevens and Levi (2005) or those listed under "Additional Resources" at the end of this chapter.
- Derive rubrics from work that students have submitted previously in response to a similar task, such as case studies, research projects, or disciplinary problems. Similar to the AAC&U rubrics, you may then create a rubric that educators can use to chronologically track students' progress toward and then final achievement of agreed-upon outcomes.
- Refer to a completed Taxonomy of Student Weaknesses, Errors, or Fuzzy Thinking (chapter 4, page 133) to identify criteria that you want to track chronologically in student work that will enable you either to see whether students are improving based on changes in pedagogy or to identify where and when students demonstrate patterns of weakness in a first cycle of assessment.
- Interview students to find out what they believe they have mastered over time.
- Interview colleagues or graduate teaching assistants about students' learning progression based on their observations of students.

2. Use the following format to ask members of a core working group or a wider group of individuals who contribute to students' learning to fill in descriptors for both the achievement levels and criteria that raters will use to assess student work in response to an agreed-upon assessment method:

	Achievement Level	Achievement Level	Achievement Level	Achievement Level	Achievement Level
1. Criterion Descriptor	Performance Descriptor				
2. Criterion Descriptor	Performance Descriptor				
3. Criterion Descriptor	Performance Descriptor				
4. Criterion Descriptor	Performance Descriptor				
5. Criterion Descriptor	Performance Descriptor				

3. From the individually designed rubrics, develop a composite rubric and ask members of a core working group to evaluate the composite rubric using the following sheet and considering the following criteria:

- How clearly is each criterion under each achievement level described?
- Identify overlap in descriptions or levels to ensure differentiation among all criteria according to a level of achievement.
- How clearly is each criterion differentiated along the continuum of achievement levels?
- Is any language unclear or ambiguous?

	Achievement Level or Levels	**Particular Observation Worth Sharing with the Larger Group**	
Criterion 1 Descriptor			
Criterion 2 Descriptor			
Criterion 3 Descriptor			
Criterion 4 Descriptor			
Criterion 5 Descriptor			Reviewer Name:

4. *Interrater Reliability:* Once a core working group has reached consensus about a scoring rubric, raters go through a calibration period to ascertain how well they consistently apply that rubric to samples of student work that are also representative of the institutional population. To pilot an internally developed rubric, ask raters to apply a final scoring rubric to sample student work. Go through the following process to ensure interrater reliability before the team of scorers undertakes the formal scoring process.

   a. Ask raters to independently score a set of student samples that reflects the range of texts students produce in response to a direct method.
   b. Bring raters together to review their responses to identify patterns of consistent and inconsistent responses.
   c. Discuss and then reconcile inconsistent responses, such as confusion about vocabulary in a performance descriptor that might require developing a key or glossary for scorers using the final rubric.
   d. Repeat the process of independent scoring on a new set of student samples.
   e. Again, bring all scorers together to review their responses to identify patterns of consistent and inconsistent responses.
   f. Discuss and then reconcile inconsistent responses until there is agreement among the scorers about how to apply each performance descriptor to student work.

5. *Interrater Reliability:* Use the following chart to identify discrepancies in scorers' responses and to discuss areas of disagreement before another scoring session is scheduled. After each round of scoring, use this sheet to continue to identify and then resolve discrepancies among scorers before they formally assess student work. In a formal process, establishing a resolution panel to address discrepancies will be important to ensure consistency in the application of criteria and scales of achievement.

	Rater Score	Rater Score	Area of Disagreement	Agreement Reached? (Yes/No) Final Resolution of Difference
Criterion 1 Descriptor				
Criterion 2 Descriptor				
Criterion 3 Descriptor				
Criterion 4 Descriptor				
Criterion 5 Descriptor				

6. If you find the following scoring rubric useful, develop a version of it to provide feedback to students at the end of their first year of study in a discipline. You may wish to create additional versions of this format to reflect increasingly more complex expectations as you conduct formative and summative assessment of students.

FRESHMAN YEAR PORTFOLIO REVIEW

This review is designed for evaluation and to provide feedback to students during their freshman year. The review is marked on a scale from 1 to 5. A mark of 1–2 indicates below-average progress, a mark of 3 is average, and a mark of 4 to 5 indicates above-average progress.

The student's work in general: 1 2 3 4 5

1. Is the body of work well-rounded and grounded in the fundamentals of art? — 1 2 3 4 5
2. Does the body of work form both a technical and an expressive base for the student's success in future studies? — 1 2 3 4 5
3. What level of problem-solving skills does the student demonstrate? — 1 2 3 4 5
4. Has the student developed his/her powers of observation? — 1 2 3 4 5
5. Does the student demonstrate the ability to make expressive/sensitive choices in his/her creative work? — 1 2 3 4 5
6. Does the student have the ability to critically and verbally analyze his/her own work? — 1 2 3 4 5
7. Does the student have the ability to make reference to philosophy/art history? — 1 2 3 4 5
8. Does the student have a professional attitude? — 1 2 3 4 5
9. Is the student well organized for the presentation? — 1 2 3 4 5

The student's specific skills: 1 2 3 4 5

1. Does the work show knowledge in the use of perspective? — 1 2 3 4 5
2. Does the work demonstrate abilities in 2-D design principles? — 1 2 3 4 5
3. Does the work demonstrate abilities in 3-D design principles? — 1 2 3 4 5
4. Does the work employ sensitive/expressive use of materials? — 1 2 3 4 5
5. Does the work show knowledge of color theory? — 1 2 3 4 5
6. Does the work demonstrate the abilities to draw:
   A) animate objects? — 1 2 3 4 5
   B) inanimate objects? — 1 2 3 4 5
7. Does the work demonstrate the abilities to draw the human figure? — 1 2 3 4 5

COMMENTS:

Student Name _____
Major _____
Faculty Reviewer _____
Date _____

Source: Julie Stewart-Pollack, Rocky Mountain College of Art and Design.

APPENDIX 6.1 INSTITUTIONAL EXAMPLE: *Hampden-Sydney College:* Department of Psychology Primary Trait Scoring Sheet for Senior Thesis

TITLE

5 Is appropriate in tone, structure, and length to psychology journals; fully explanatory of the study; identifies actual variables or theoretical issues of study; allows reader to anticipate design.

4 Is appropriate in tone, structure, and length; generally explanatory of the study; identifies some variables or theoretical issues of study; suggests design.

3 Suggests nature of the study; may identify only one variable of the study; does not allow reader to anticipate design; may contain superfluous information.

2 Identifies only one variable of the study; contains superfluous information; lacks design information or is misleading.

1 Patterned after another discipline or is missing.

ABSTRACT

5 Is appropriate in tone, structure, and length; fully descriptive of the study; identifies the problem, subjects, methods, findings, and conclusions or implications of the study.

4 Is appropriate in tone, structure, and length; generally descriptive of the study; identifies most but not all of the elements of the study; may contain some superfluous information.

3 May be lacking in tone, structure, or length; identifies only some elements of the study; does not summarize the article so that the reader understands what was done; contains superfluous information.

2 Inappropriate in tone, structure, and length; is not descriptive of the study; contains irrelevant, inappropriate, or incorrect information.

1 Inappropriate for the discipline or is missing.

INTRODUCTION: PROBLEM

5 Clear statement of problem under investigation; identifies the major construct or conceptual IV(s) and the behavior or conceptual DV(s) of interest; clearly states goal(s) of the study; problem identified in introductory paragraph.

4 Problem under investigation stated in general terms; identifies only some of the conceptual IV(s) and DV(s) of interest; goals of the study stated less clearly; problem identified in introductory paragraph.

3 Introductory paragraph may not identify problem under investigation; nature of problem being studied is not clear to the reader; conceptual IV(s) and DV(s) may not be identified; the reader has to find the goals of the study.

2 Problem not identified in introductory paragraph; reader may be unable to determine the problem being investigated; the purpose and/or goals of the study are not apparent to the reader.

1 Fails to identify purpose of the research.

INTRODUCTION: LITERATURE REVIEW

5 Articles reviewed are relevant to the problem being investigated; coverage of previous empirical and theoretical studies is thorough; issues are clearly explained; issues related to the problem are discussed in a logical progression; the number of articles cited is fully sufficient for the task.

4 Articles reviewed are relevant to the problem; coverage of previous empirical and theoretical studies may not be complete; some confusion over concepts or issues may be present; issues related to the problem may not be presented in a logical order; the number of articles is adequate for the task.

3 Some articles reviewed are irrelevant to the problem, or relevant articles from the literature are not reviewed; important information about articles being reviewed may be left out, and/or irrelevant information may be included; confusion about some concepts or issues being discussed; issues related to the problem are not organized in a way which effectively supports the argument, are arranged chronologically, or are arranged article-by-article; the number of articles is fewer than necessary for the task.

2 Articles reviewed are not directly related to the problem, though they may be in the same general conceptual area; important information from articles is ignored, and irrelevant information is included; lack of understanding of concepts or issues being discussed; presentation of previous research

and theory not organized in a logical manner; inadequate number of articles reviewed.

1   Research and theory related to current problem is not reviewed or discussed.

INTRODUCTION: HYPOTHESIS

5   Clear statement of expectation(s) for outcome of study, relating IV(s) and DV(s) as identified in statement of problem; is or can be stated in "if . . . then" form.

4   Expectation for outcome(s) of study is stated, but not entirely clearly; one or more IV(s) or DV(s) may be left out of statement of hypothesis; is or can be stated in "if . . . then" form.

3   Expectation for outcome(s) of study not clear; one or more IV(s) or DV(s) are left out; is not or cannot be stated in "if . . . then" format.

2   Confusion about expected outcome of study; IV(s) and DV(s) are not identified; cannot be stated in "if . . . then" form.

1   No statement of hypothesis or expected outcome of study.

METHODS: DESCRIPTION

5   Contains effective, quantifiable, concisely organized information that allows the experiment to be replicated; is written so that all information inherent to the document can be related back to this section; identifies sources of all data to be collected; identifies sequential information in an appropriate chronology; does not contain unnecessary, wordy descriptions of procedures.

4   As in 5, but contains unnecessary or superfluous information or wordy descriptions within the section.

3   Presents a study that is definitely replicable; all information in document may be related to this section, but fails to identify some sources of data or presents sequential information in a disorganized, difficult way; may contain unnecessary or superfluous information.

2   Presents a study that is marginally replicable; parts of the basic design must be inferred by the reader; procedures not quantitatively described; some information in Results or Discussion cannot be anticipated by reading the Methods section.

1   Describes the study so poorly or in such a nonscientific way that it cannot be replicated.

METHODS: EXPERIMENTAL DESIGN

5   Student selects experimental factors that are appropriate to the research purpose and audience; measures adequate aspects of these selected factors; establishes discrete subgroups for which data significance may vary; student demonstrates an ability to eliminate bias from the design and bias-ridden statements from the research; student selects appropriate sample size, equivalent groups, and statistics; student designs an elegant study.

4   As in 5, student designs an adequate study; choice of subgroups may exclude conditions that would make the study more complete, or may include conditions that are not necessary for answering the question.

3   Student selects experimental factors that are appropriate to the research purpose and audience; measures adequate aspects of these selected factors; establishes discrete subgroups for which data significance may vary; research is weakened by bias or by sample size of less than 10.

2   As above, but research is weakened by bias and inappropriate sample size.

1   Student designs a poor study.

METHODS: OPERATIONAL DEFINITIONS

5   Each of the independent (where appropriate) and dependent variables is stated in terms of clear and precise operational definitions.

4   Major independent (where appropriate) and dependent variables are stated in terms of clear and precise operational definitions; some variables may not be defined operationally, or operational definitions are not sufficiently precise and clear.

3   Only some of the variables are operationally defined, and the definitions given are not sufficiently precise and clear.

2   Major independent (where appropriate) and dependent variables are not operationally defined, and other variables are not defined in terms that are sufficiently clear and precise.

1   Variables are not operationally defined.

RESULTS: CHOICE OF STATISTICAL ANALYSIS

5   Student chooses methods of summarizing and analyzing data which are ideal for the dependent variable(s) (DVs), and for answering the research

question given the parameters of the study (e.g., experimental or correlational study; number of IVs; number of levels of IVs; between- or within-subjects IVs; independent or matched treatment conditions; level of measurement of DV); data analysis is complete and thorough; statistical analyses are performed properly.

4 Choice of methods of summarizing and analyzing data is appropriate for the DV(s), and for answering the fundamental research question; statistical analyses are performed properly; data analysis may be incomplete: basic analyses are done, but not all follow-up or post hoc analyses are performed; analyses, though correct, are lacking in thoroughness.

3 As for 4, but some analyses may not be appropriate for the research question or analyses may not have been properly performed; descriptive statistics may be adequate, but inferential statistics are inadequate.

2 Data are not analyzed beyond the descriptive level; inferential statistics are not performed or are performed incorrectly.

1 There is no attempt to summarize or evaluate the data and only raw data are reported.

RESULTS: REPORTING STATISTICAL ANALYSES

5 Student has reported results of all statistical analyses using proper format; all information that is necessary to validate statistical findings is reported.

3 Results of statistical analyses are not completely reported, or are reported in incorrect format.

1 Results of statistical analyses are not reported.

RESULTS: GRAPHS AND TABLES

5 Choice and format of tables and graphs are appropriate for the data; the correct type of graph, where used, is used for each type of DV; tables, where used, are clear and effectively represent the findings of the study; the graphs/tables are effectively captioned and labeled and have descriptive legends; graphs are visually "appealing" and do not have wasted space; one graph or table is presented per page.

4 As for 5, but with graphs or tables which do not present results as clearly; captions, labels, or leg-

ends are not completely descriptive of what is displayed in graph/table; graphs/tables may be more difficult to interpret; graphs may be lacking some visual "appeal."

3 Graphs/tables are not as clear as for 4; captions, labels, or legends may be inadequate or missing; an inappropriate type of graph may be used for the specific type of variable used; graphs may be too "busy," or have too much wasted space; size of graph as prepared is inappropriate (too small or large) for the circumstances; graph is lacking visual "appeal."

2 Graphs/tables do not clearly or effectively present the results; captions, labels, or legends are missing or inappropriate; too much or too little information is presented in the graphs or tables; graphs/tables are sloppy and appear to have been prepared in a haphazard manner.

1 Graphs/tables are missing or wholly inadequate for purposes of presenting the findings of the study; if present, graphs/tables have been prepared or drawn by hand.

DISCUSSION: INTERPRETATION

5 Student has summarized the purpose and findings of the research; has drawn inferences that are consistent with the data and scientific reasoning and relates these to the reader and intended audience; has identified whether findings are consistent or inconsistent with research hypothesis; has related results to previous research and theory; explains expected results and offers explanations for unexpected results; distinguishes between fact and implication.

4 As in 5, but may not adequately explain unexpected findings, or thoroughly relate findings to previous research or theory.

3 As in 4, but student overinterprets findings and draws conclusions from the data which may not be justified, or fails to draw conclusions which may reasonably be deduced from the findings.

2 Student summarizes the purpose and findings of the research; does not fully explain expected results, and ignores unexpected results.

1 Student does not relate findings to original hypothesis; results may or may not be summarized, but student fails to interpret their significance for the reader and the intended audience.

DISCUSSION: APPLICATIONS/ EXTENSIONS OF FINDINGS

5   Student discusses possible applications of findings to contexts outside that of the study (e.g, outside of the laboratory); methods of the study are critically evaluated; student identifies questions that are unanswered as a result of current study; suggestions for further research or follow-up studies are identified and described.

4   As in 5, but student does not discuss possible applications to contexts outside that of the study.

3   As in 4, but the methods of the study are not critically evaluated.

2   Applications and extensions of research findings do not follow logically from the original research question, or are not made in the context of a stated theoretical framework.

1   Student does not discuss applications or extensions of the research findings, or suggest further research or follow-up studies.

REFERENCES

5   List of reference citations is complete; all works cited in the body of the paper are listed, but only those works; references are listed in alphabetical order; proper APA reference citation format is followed.

4   As in 5, but references are listed which were not cited in the paper; minor errors in APA reference format may be present.

3   As in 4; student has not followed proper APA format for reference citations.

2   Student has failed to include all references cited in body of the paper; information in the references is incorrect or incomplete; references do not follow APA reference citation format.

1   Reference list is wholly inadequate, incomplete, or missing.

APA FORMAT

5   Student has followed all conventions for proper format of a research report as described in *APA Publication Manual* (current edition).

4   Student has made minor deviations in APA format: e.g., incorrect form of page headers, improper section headings, or incorrect citation format of references.

3   As if 4, but more serious and consistent errors in APA format: e.g., subsections (e.g., *Subjects* or *Apparatus*) are omitted, absence of page headers or numbers, non-APA-style citation format, improper tense or voice for the paper, figures/tables inserted in incorrect location of paper, incorrect information included on Title page or critical information omitted, incorrect references to figures and/or tables.

2   Major errors in APA format: e.g., major sections of paper omitted, absence of title page, information presented in incorrect sections, critical information omitted, figures or tables left out.

1   Paper does not follow APA format.

WRITING QUALITY

5   Student has written elegantly and cogently, using proper grammar, syntax, punctuation, spelling; the paper has a neat appearance and is free of typographical errors; wording is appropriate to the context; paragraphs are well constructed; paper exhibits a logical "flow" from section to section; student used proper voice for the paper.

4   As in 5, but with occasional uncorrected typographical errors, or a very few minor errors in spelling, grammar, syntax, or punctuation; however, errors do not detract from the overall ability to convey meaning; the paper is not as elegant as in 5.

3   The paper exhibits numerous typographical errors and repeated errors in basic elements of writing; the student has not expressed ideas with clarity and precision; transitions between paragraphs are awkward; wording of sentences tends to be simplistic in style and content.

2   The student has displayed serious and consistent problems in basic writing skill; the ability to express ideas is compromised by the poor writing quality.

1   The paper is seriously deficient in quality of writing.

SENIOR THESIS PRIMARY TRAIT ANALYSIS—SCORING SHEET

Student name _____

Rater name _____

Category	Weight	Rating	Score
Title	1	_____	_____
Abstract	1	_____	_____
Introduction: Problem	1	_____	_____
Introduction: Literature Review	2	_____	_____
Introduction: Hypothesis	1	_____	_____
Methods: Description	1	_____	_____
Methods: Experimental Design	2	_____	_____
Methods: Operational Definitions	1	_____	_____
Results: Choice of Statistical Analyses	1	_____	_____
Results: Reporting Statistical Analyses	1	_____	_____
Results: Graphs and Tables	1	_____	_____
Discussion: Interpretation	2	_____	_____
Discussion: Applications/Extensions of Findings	2	_____	_____
References	1	_____	_____
APA Format	1	_____	_____
Writing Quality	3	_____	_____
Total	**22**		_____

Letter grade conversion:

Letter Grade	Total Score	Average Rating		
			A	99–110
			A–	93–98
			B+	87–92
A	93–110	4.25–5	B	81–86
B	75–92	3.4–4.2	B–	75–80
C	57–74	2.6–3.35	C+	69–74
D	39–56	1.75–2.55	C	63–68
F	22–38	1.0–1.7	C–	57–62
			D+	51–56
			D	39–50
			F	22–38

Source: Robert T. Herdegen III, Hampden-Sydney College.

APPENDIX 6.2

Association of American Colleges and Universities

CREATIVE THINKING VALUE RUBRIC

for more information, please contact value@aacu.org

The VALUE rubrics were developed by teams of faculty experts representing colleges and universities across the United States through a process that examined many existing campus rubrics and related documents for each learning outcome and incorporated additional feedback from faculty. The rubrics articulate fundamental criteria for each learning outcome, with performance descriptors demonstrating progressively more sophisticated levels of attainment. The rubrics are intended for institutional-level use in evaluating and discussing student learning, not for grading. The core expectations articulated in all 15 of the VALUE rubrics can and should be translated into the language of individual campuses, disciplines, and even courses. The utility of the VALUE rubrics is to position learning at all undergraduate levels within a basic framework of expectations such that evidence of learning can by shared nationally through a common dialog and understanding of student success.

Definition

Creative thinking is both the capacity to combine or synthesize existing ideas, images, or expertise in original ways and the experience of thinking, reacting, and working in an imaginative way characterized by a high degree of innovation, divergent thinking, and risk taking.

Framing Language

Creative thinking, as it is fostered within higher education, must be distinguished from less focused types of creativity such as, for example, the creativity exhibited by a small child's drawing, which stems not from an understanding of connections, but from an ignorance of boundaries. Creative thinking in higher education can only be expressed productively within a particular domain. The student must have a strong foundation in the strategies and skills of the domain in order to make connections and synthesize. While demonstrating solid knowledge of the domain's parameters, the creative thinker, at the highest levels of performance, pushes beyond those boundaries in new, unique, or atypical recombinations, uncovering or critically perceiving new syntheses and using or recognizing creative risk-taking to achieve a solution.

The Creative Thinking VALUE Rubric is intended to help faculty assess creative thinking in a broad range of transdisciplinary or interdisciplinary work samples or collections of work. The rubric is made up of a set of attributes that are common to creative thinking across disciplines. Examples of work samples or collections of work that could be assessed for creative thinking may include research papers, lab reports, musical compositions, a mathematical equation that solves a problem, a prototype design, a reflective piece about the final product of an assignment, or other academic works. The work samples or collections of work may be completed by an individual student or a group of students.

Glossary

The definitions that follow were developed to clarify terms and concepts used in this rubric only.

- Exemplar: A model or pattern to be copied or imitated (quoted from www.dictionary.reference.com/browse/exemplar).
- Domain: Field of study or activity and a sphere of knowledge and influence.

CREATIVE THINKING VALUE RUBRIC

for more information, please contact value@aacu.org

Definition

Creative thinking is both the capacity to combine or synthesize existing ideas, images, or expertise in original ways and the experience of thinking, reacting, and working in an imaginative way characterized by a high degree of innovation, divergent thinking, and risk taking

Evaluators are encouraged to assign a zero to any work sample or collection of work that does not meet benchmark (cell one) level performance.

	Capstone 4	Milestones 3	2	Benchmark 1
Acquiring Competencies *This step refers to acquiring strategies and skills within a particular domain.*	Reflect: Evaluates creative process and product using domain-appropriate criteria.	Create: Creates an entirely new object, solution or idea that is appropriate to the domain.	Adapt: Successfully adapts an appropriate exemplar to his/her own specifications.	Model: Successfully reproduces an appropriate exemplar.
Taking Risks *May include personal risk (fear of embarrassment or rejection) or risk of failure in successfully completing assignment, i.e. going beyond original parameters of assignment, introducing new materials and forms, tackling controversial topics, advocating unpopular ideas or solutions.*	Actively seeks out and follows through on untested and potentially risky directions or approaches to the assignment in the final product.	Incorporates new directions or approaches to the assignment in the final product.	Considers new directions or approaches without going beyond the guidelines of the assignment.	Stays strictly within the guidelines of the assignment.
Solving Problems	Not only develops a logical, consistent plan to solve problem, but recognizes consequences of solution and can articulate reason for choosing solution.	Having selected from among alternatives, develops a logical, consistent plan to solve the problem.	Considers and rejects less acceptable approaches to solving problem.	Only a single approach is considered and is used to solve the problem.
Embracing Contradictions	Integrates alternate, divergent, or contradictory perspectives or ideas fully.	Incorporates alternate, divergent, or contradictory perspectives or ideas in an exploratory way.	Includes (recognizes the value of) alternate, divergent, or contradictory perspectives or ideas in a small way.	Acknowledges (mentions in passing) alternate, divergent, or contradictory perspectives or ideas.
Thinking Innovatively *Novelty or uniqueness (of idea, claim, question, form, etc.)*	Extends a novel or unique idea, question, format, or product to create new knowledge or knowledge that crosses boundaries.	Creates a novel or unique idea, question, format, or product.	Experiments with creating a novel or unique idea, question, format, or product.	Reformulates a collection of available ideas.
Connecting, Synthesizing, Transforming	Transforms ideas or solutions into entirely new forms.	Synthesizes ideas or solutions into a coherent whole.	Connects ideas or solutions in novel ways.	Recognizes existing connections among ideas or solutions.

Source: AAC&U. Used with permission.

APPENDIX 6.3

QUANTITATIVE LITERACY VALUE RUBRIC

for more information, please contact value@aacu.org

The VALUE rubrics were developed by teams of faculty experts representing colleges and universities across the United States through a process that examined many existing campus rubrics and related documents for each learning outcome and incorporated additional feedback from faculty. The rubrics articulate fundamental criteria for each learning outcome, with performance descriptors demonstrating progressively more sophisticated levels of attainment. The rubrics are intended for institutional-level use in evaluating and discussing student learning, not for grading. The core expectations articulated in all 15 of the VALUE rubrics can and should be translated into the language of individual campuses, disciplines, and even courses. The utility of the VALUE rubrics is to position learning at all undergraduate levels within a basic framework of expectations such that evidence of learning can by shared nationally through a common dialog and understanding of student success.

Definition

Quantitative Literacy (QL) – also known as Numeracy or Quantitative Reasoning (QR) – is a "habit of mind," competency, and comfort in working with numerical data. Individuals with strong QL skills possess the ability to reason and solve quantitative problems from a wide array of authentic contexts and everyday life situations. They understand and can create sophisticated arguments supported by quantitative evidence and they can clearly communicate those arguments in a variety of formats (using words, tables, graphs, mathematical equations, etc, as appropriate).

Quantitative Literacy Across the Disciplines

Current trends in general education reform demonstrate that faculty are recognizing the steadily growing importance of Quantitative Literacy (QL) in an increasingly quantitative and data-dense world. AAC&U's recent survey showed that concerns about QL skills are shared by employers, who recognize that many of today's students will need a wide range of high level quantitative skills to complete their work responsibilities. Virtually all of today's students, regardless of career choice, will need basic QL skills such as the ability to draw information from charts, graphs, and geometric figures, and the ability to accurately complete straightforward estimations and calculations.

Preliminary efforts to find student work products which demonstrate QL skills proved a challenge in this rubric creation process. It's possible to find pages of mathematical problems, but what those problem sets don't demonstrate is whether the student was able to think about and understand the meaning of her work. It's possible to find research papers that include quantitative information, but those papers often don't provide evidence that allows the evaluator to see how much of the thinking was done by the original source (often carefully cited in the paper) and how much was done by the student herself, or whether conclusions drawn from analysis of the source material are even accurate.

Given widespread agreement about the importance of QL, it becomes incumbent on faculty to develop new kinds of assignments which give students substantive, contextualized experience in using such skills as analyzing quantitative information, representing quantitative information in appropriate forms, completing calculations to answer meaningful questions, making judgments based on quantitative data and communicating the results of that work for various purposes and audiences. As students gain experience with those skills, faculty must develop assignments that require students to create work products which reveal their thought processes and demonstrate the range of their QL skills.

This rubric provides for faculty a definition for QL and a rubric describing four levels of QL achievement that might be observed in work products within work samples or collections of work. Members of AAC&U's rubric development team for QL hope that these materials will aid in the effort to more thoroughly embed QL across the curriculum of colleges and universities.

Framing Language

This rubric has been designed for the evaluation of work that addresses quantitative literacy (QL) in a substantive way. QL is not just computation, not just the citing of someone else's data. QL is a habit of mind, a way of thinking about the world that relies on data and on the mathematical analysis of data to make connections and draw conclusions. Teaching QL requires us to design assignments that address authentic, data-based problems. Such assignments may call for the traditional written paper, but we can imagine other alternatives: a video of a PowerPoint presentation, perhaps, or a well designed series of web pages. In any case, a successful demonstration of QL will place the mathematical work in the context of a full and robust discussion of the underlying issues addressed by the assignment.

Finally, QL skills can be applied to a wide array of problems of varying difficulty, confounding the use of this rubric. For example, the same student might demonstrate high levels of QL achievement when working on a simplistic problem and low levels of QL achievement when working on a very complex problem. Thus, to accurately assess a student's QL achievement it may be necessary to measure QL achievement within the context of problem complexity, much as is done in diving competitions where two scores are given, one for the difficulty of the dive, and the other for the skill in accomplishing the dive. In this context, that would mean giving one score for the complexity of the problem and another score for the QL achievement in solving the problem.

QUANTITATIVE LITERACY VALUE RUBRIC

for more information, please contact value@aacu.org

Definition

Quantitative Literacy (QL) – also known as Numeracy or Quantitative Reasoning (QR) – is a "habit of mind," competency, and comfort in working with numerical data. Individuals with strong QL skills possess the ability to reason and solve quantitative problems from a wide array of authentic contexts and everyday life situations. They understand and can create sophisticated arguments supported by quantitative evidence and they can clearly communicate those arguments in a variety of formats (using words, tables, graphs, mathematical equations, etc., as appropriate).

Evaluators are encouraged to assign a zero to any work sample or collection of work that does not meet benchmark (cell one) level performance.

	Capstone 4	Milestones 3	Milestones 2	1
Interpretation *Ability to explain information presented in mathematical forms (e.g., equations, graphs, diagrams, tables, words)*	Provides accurate explanations of information presented in mathematical forms. Makes appropriate inferences based on that information. *For example, accurately explains the trend data shown in a graph and makes reasonable predictions regarding what the data suggest about future events.*	Provides accurate explanations of information presented in mathematical forms. *For instance, accurately explains the trend data shown in a graph.*	Provides somewhat accurate explanations of information presented in mathematical forms, but occasionally makes minor errors related to computations or units. *For instance, accurately explains trend data shown in a graph, but may miscalculate the slope of the trend line.*	Attempts to explain information presented in mathematical forms, but draws incorrect conclusions about what the information means. *For example, attempts to explain the trend data shown in a graph, but will frequently misinterpret the nature of that trend, perhaps by confusing positive and negative trends.*
Representation *Ability to convert relevant information into various mathematical forms (e.g., equations, graphs, diagrams, tables, words)*	Skillfully converts relevant information into an insightful mathematical portrayal in a way that contributes to a further or deeper understanding.	Competently converts relevant information into an appropriate and desired mathematical portrayal.	Completes conversion of information but resulting mathematical portrayal is only partially appropriate or accurate.	Completes conversion of information but resulting mathematical portrayal is inappropriate or inaccurate.
Calculation	Calculations attempted are essentially all successful and sufficiently comprehensive to solve the problem. Calculations are also presented elegantly (clearly, concisely; etc.)	Calculations attempted are essentially all successful and sufficiently comprehensive to solve the problem.	Calculations attempted are either unsuccessful or represent only a portion of the calculations required to comprehensively solve the problem.	Calculations are attempted but are both unsuccessful and are not comprehensive.
Application / Analysis *Ability to make judgments and draw appropriate conclusions based on the quantitative analysis of data, while recognizing the limits of this analysis*	Uses the quantitative analysis of data as the basis for deep and thoughtful judgments, drawing insightful, carefully qualified conclusions from this work.	Uses the quantitative analysis of data as the basis for competent judgments, drawing reasonable and appropriately qualified conclusions from this work.	Uses the quantitative analysis of data as the basis for workmanlike (without inspiration or nuance, ordinary) judgments, drawing plausible conclusions from this work.	Uses the quantitative analysis of data as the basis for tentative, basic judgments, although is hesitant or uncertain about drawing conclusions from this work.
Assumptions *Ability to make and evaluate important assumptions in estimation, modeling, and data analysis*	Explicitly describes assumptions and provides compelling rationale for why each assumption is appropriate. Shows awareness that confidence in final conclusions is limited by the accuracy of the assumptions.	Explicitly describes assumptions and provides compelling rationale for why assumptions are appropriate.	Explicitly describes assumptions.	Attempts to describe assumptions.
Communication *Expressing quantitative evidence in support of the argument or purpose of the work (in terms of what evidence is used and how it is formatted, presented, and contextualized)*	Uses quantitative information in connection with the argument or purpose of the work, presents it in an effective format, and explicates it with consistently high quality.	Uses quantitative information in connection with the argument or purpose of the work, though data may be presented in a less than completely effective format or some parts of the explication may be uneven.	Uses quantitative information, but does not effectively connect it to the argument or purpose of the work.	Presents an argument for which quantitative evidence is pertinent, but does not provide adequate explicit numerical support. (May use quasi-quantitative words such as "many," "few," "increasing," "small," and the like in place of actual quantities.)

Source: AAC&U. Used with permission.

APPENDIX 6.4

Association of American Colleges and Universities

CIVIC ENGAGEMENT VALUE RUBRIC

for more information, please contact value@aacu.org

The VALUE rubrics were developed by teams of faculty experts representing colleges and universities across the United States through a process that examined many existing campus rubrics and related documents for each learning outcome and incorporated additional feedback from faculty. The rubrics articulate fundamental criteria for each learning outcome, with performance descriptors demonstrating progressively more sophisticated levels of attainment. The rubrics are intended for institutional-level use in evaluating and discussing student learning, not for grading. The core expectations articulated in all 15 of the VALUE rubrics can and should be translated into the language of individual campuses, disciplines, and even courses. The utility of the VALUE rubrics is to position learning at all undergraduate levels within a basic framework of expectations such that evidence of learning can by shared nationally through a common dialog and understanding of student success.

Definition

Civic engagement is "working to make a difference in the civic life of our communities and developing the combination of knowledge, skills, values and motivation to make that difference. It means promoting the quality of life in a community, through both political and non-political processes." (Excerpted from *Civic Responsibility and Higher Education*, edited by Thomas Ehrlich, published by Oryx Press, 2000, Preface, page vi.) In addition, civic engagement encompasses actions wherein individuals participate in activities of personal and public concern that are both individually life enriching and socially beneficial to the community.

Framing Language

Preparing graduates for their public lives as citizens, members of communities, and professionals in society has historically been a responsibility of higher education. Yet the outcome of a civic-minded graduate is a complex concept. Civic learning outcomes are framed by personal identity and commitments, disciplinary frameworks and traditions, pre-professional norms and practice, and the mission and values of colleges and universities. This rubric is designed to make the civic learning outcomes more explicit. Civic engagement can take many forms, from individual volunteerism to organizational involvement to electoral participation. For students this could include community-based learning through service-learning classes, community-based research, or service within the community. Multiple types of work samples or collections of work may be utilized to assess this, such as:

- The student creates and manages a service program that engages others (such as youth or members of a neighborhood) in learning about and taking action on an issue they care about. In the process, the student also teaches and models processes that engage others in deliberative democracy, in having a voice, participating in democratic processes, and taking specific actions to affect an issue.
- The student researches, organizes, and carries out a deliberative democracy forum on a particular issue, one that includes multiple perspectives on that issue and how best to make positive change through various courses of public action. As a result, other students, faculty, and community members are engaged to take action on an issue.
- The student works on and takes a leadership role in a complex campaign to bring about tangible changes in the public's awareness or education on a particular issue, or even a change in public policy. Through this process, the student demonstrates multiple types of civic action and skills.
- The student integrates their academic work with community engagement, producing a tangible product (piece of legislation or policy, a business, building or civic infrastructure, water quality or scientific assessment, needs survey, research paper, service program, or organization) that has engaged community constituents and responded to community needs and assets through the process.

In addition, the nature of this work lends itself to opening up the review process to include community constituents that may be a part of the work, such as teammates, colleagues, community/agency members, and those served or collaborating in the process.

Glossary

The definitions that follow were developed to clarify terms and concepts used in this rubric only.

- **Civic identity:** When one sees her or himself as an active participant in society with a strong commitment and responsibility to work with others towards public purposes.
- **Service-learning class:** A course-based educational experience in which students participate in an organized service activity and reflect on the experience in such a way as to gain further understanding of course content, a broader appreciation of the discipline, and an enhanced sense of personal values and civic responsibility.
- **Communication skills:** Listening, deliberation, negotiation, consensus building, and productive use of conflict.
- **Civic life:** The public life of the citizen concerned with the affairs of the community and nation as contrasted with private or personal life, which is devoted to the pursuit of private and personal interests.
- **Politics:** A process by which a group of people, whose opinions or interests might be divergent, reach collective decisions that are generally regarded as binding on the group and enforced as common policy. Political life enables people to accomplish goals they could not realize as individuals. Politics necessarily arises whenever groups of people live together, since they must always reach collective decisions of one kind or another.
- **Government:** "The formal institutions of a society with the authority to make and implement binding decisions about such matters as the distribution of resources, allocation of benefits and burdens, and the management of conflicts." (Retrieved from the Center for Civic Engagement Web site, May 5, 2009.)
- **Civic/community contexts:** Organizations, movements, campaigns, a place or locus where people and/or living creatures inhabit, which may be defined by a locality (school, national park, non-profit organization, town, state, nation) or defined by shared identity (i.e., African-Americans, North Carolinians, Americans, the Republican or Democratic Party, refugees, etc.). In addition, contexts for civic engagement may be defined by a variety of approaches intended to benefit a person, group, or community, including community service or volunteer work, academic work.

CIVIC ENGAGEMENT VALUE RUBRIC

for more information, please contact value@aacu.org

Definition

Civic engagement is "working to make a difference in the civic life of our communities and developing the combination of knowledge, skills, values, and motivation to make that difference. It means promoting the quality of life in a community, through both political and non-political processes." (Excerpted from *Civic Responsibility and Higher Education*, edited by Thomas Ehrlich, published by Oryx Press, 2000, Preface, page vi.) In addition, civic engagement encompasses actions wherein individuals participate in activities of personal and public concern that are both individually life enriching and socially beneficial to the community.

Evaluators are encouraged to assign a zero to any work sample or collection of work that does not meet benchmark (cell one) level performance.

	Capstone 4	Milestones 3	Milestones 2	Benchmark 1
Diversity of Communities and Cultures	Demonstrates evidence of adjustment in own attitudes and beliefs because of working within and learning from diversity of communities and cultures. Promotes others' engagement with diversity.	Reflects on how own attitudes and beliefs are different from those of other cultures and communities. Exhibits curiosity about what can be learned from diversity of communities and cultures.	Has awareness that own attitudes and beliefs are different from those of other cultures and communities. Exhibits little curiosity about what can be learned from diversity of communities and cultures.	Expresses attitudes and beliefs as an individual, from a one-sided view. Is indifferent or resistant to what can be learned from diversity of communities and cultures.
Analysis of Knowledge	Connects and extends knowledge (facts, theories, etc.) from one's own academic study/field/discipline to civic engagement and to one's own participation in civic life, politics, and government.	Analyzes knowledge (facts, theories, etc.) from one's own academic study/field/discipline making relevant connections to civic engagement and to one's own participation in civic life, politics, and government.	Begins to connect knowledge (facts, theories, etc.) from one's own academic study/field/discipline to civic engagement and to one's own participation in civic life, politics, and government.	Begins to identify knowledge (facts, theories, etc.) from one's own academic study/field/discipline that is relevant to civic engagement and to one's own participation in civic life, politics, and government.
Civic Identity and Commitment	Provides evidence of experience in civic-engagement activities and describes what she/he has learned about her or himself as it relates to a reinforced and clarified sense of civic identity and continued commitment to public action.	Provides evidence of experience in civic-engagement activities and describes what she/he has learned about her or himself as it relates to a growing sense of civic identity and commitment.	Evidence suggests involvement in civic-engagement activities is generated from expectations or course requirements rather than from a sense of civic identity.	Provides little evidence of her/his experience in civic-engagement activities and does not connect experiences to civic identity.
Civic Communication	Tailors communication strategies to effectively express, listen, and adapt to others to establish relationships to further civic action	Effectively communicates in civic context, showing ability to do all of the following: express, listen, and adapt ideas and messages based on others' perspectives.	Communicates in civic context, showing ability to do more than one of the following: express, listen, and adapt ideas and messages based on others' perspectives.	Communicates in civic context, showing ability to do one of the following: express, listen, and adapt ideas and messages based on others' perspectives.
Civic Action and Reflection	Demonstrates independent experience and *shows initiative in team leadership of* complex or multiple civic engagement activities, accompanied by reflective insights or analysis about the aims and accomplishments of one's actions.	Demonstrates independent experience and *team leadership of* civic action, with reflective insights or analysis about the aims and accomplishments of one's actions.	Has clearly *participated* in civically focused actions and begins to reflect or describe how these actions may benefit individual(s) or communities.	Has *experimented* with some civic activities but shows little internalized understanding of their aims or effects and little commitment to future action.
Civic Contexts/Structures	Demonstrates ability and commitment to *collaboratively work across and within community* contexts and structures *to achieve a civic aim.*	Demonstrates ability and commitment to work actively *within community* contexts and structures *to achieve a civic aim.*	Demonstrates experience identifying intentional ways to *participate in civic contexts* and structures.	Experiments with civic contexts and structures, *tries out a few to see what fits.*

Source: AAC&U. Used with permission.

APPENDIX 6.5

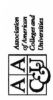

Association of American Colleges and Universities

INTEGRATIVE LEARNING VALUE RUBRIC

for more information, please contact value@aacu.org

The VALUE rubrics were developed by teams of faculty experts representing colleges and universities across the United States through a process that examined many existing campus rubrics and related documents for each learning outcome and incorporated additional feedback from faculty. The rubrics articulate fundamental criteria for each learning outcome, with performance descriptors demonstrating progressively more sophisticated levels of attainment. The rubrics are intended for institutional-level use in evaluating and discussing student learning, not for grading. The core expectations articulated in all 15 of the VALUE rubrics can and should be translated into the language of individual campuses, disciplines, and even courses. The utility of the VALUE rubrics is to position learning at all undergraduate levels within a basic framework of expectations such that evidence of learning can be shared nationally through a common dialog and understanding of student success.

Definition

Integrative learning is an understanding and a disposition that a student builds across the curriculum and co-curriculum, from making simple connections among ideas and experiences to synthesizing and transferring learning to new, complex situations within and beyond the campus.

Framing Language

Fostering students' abilities to integrate learning—across courses, over time, and between campus and community life—is one of the most important goals and challenges for higher education. Initially, students connect previous learning to new classroom learning. Later, significant knowledge within individual disciplines serves as the foundation, but integrative learning goes beyond academic boundaries. Indeed, integrative experiences often occur as learners address real-world problems, unscripted and sufficiently broad, to require multiple areas of knowledge and multiple modes of inquiry, offering multiple solutions and benefiting from multiple perspectives. Integrative learning also involves internal changes in the learner. These internal changes, which indicate growth as a confident, lifelong learner, include the ability to adapt one's intellectual skills, to contribute in a wide variety of situations, and to understand and develop individual purpose, values and ethics. Developing students' capacities for integrative learning is central to personal success, social responsibility, and civic engagement in today's rapidly changing and increasingly connected world where integrative learning becomes not just a benefit...but a necessity.

Because integrative learning is about making connections, this learning may not be as evident in traditional academic artifacts such as research papers and academic projects unless the student, for example, is prompted to draw implications for practice. These connections often surface, however, in reflective work, self-assessment, or creative endeavors of all kinds. Integrative assignments foster learning between courses or by connecting courses to experientially-based work. Work samples or collections of work that include such artifacts give evidence of integrative learning. Faculty are encouraged to look for evidence that the student connects the learning gained in classroom study to learning gained in real life situations that are related to other learning experiences, extra-curricular activities, or work. Through integrative learning, students pull together their entire experience inside and outside of the formal classroom; thus, artificial barriers between formal study and informal or tacit learning become permeable. Integrative learning, whatever the context or source, builds upon connecting both theory and practice toward a deepened understanding.

Assignments to foster such connections and understanding could include, for example, composition papers that focus on topics from biology, economics, or history; mathematics assignments that apply mathematical tools to important issues and require written analysis to explain the implications and limitations of the mathematical treatment, or art history presentations that demonstrate aesthetic connections between selected paintings and novels. In this regard, some majors (e.g., interdisciplinary majors or problem-based field studies) seem to inherently evoke characteristics of integrative learning and result in work samples or collections of work that significantly demonstrate this outcome. However, fields of study that require accumulation of extensive and high-consensus content knowledge (such as accounting, engineering, or chemistry) also involve the kinds of complex and integrative constructions (e.g., ethical dilemmas and social consciousness) that seem to be highlighted so extensively in self reflection in arts and humanities, but they may be embedded in individual performances and less evident. The key in the development of such work samples or collections of work will be in designing structures that include artifacts and reflective writing or feedback that support students' examination of their learning and give evidence that, as graduates, they will extend their integrative abilities into the challenges of personal, professional, and civic life.

Glossary

The definitions that follow were developed to clarify terms and concepts used in this rubric only.

- ⊚ **Academic knowledge:** Disciplinary learning: learning from academic study, texts, etc.
- ⊚ **Content:** The information conveyed in the work samples or collections of work.
- ⊚ **Contexts:** Actual or simulated situations in which a student demonstrates learning outcomes. New and challenging contexts encourage students to stretch beyond their current frames of reference.
- ⊚ **Co-curriculum:** A parallel component of the academic curriculum that is in addition to formal classroom (student government, community service, residence hall activities, student organizations, etc.).
- ⊚ **Experience:** Learning that takes place in a setting outside of the formal classroom, such as workplace, service learning site, internship site or another.
- ⊚ **Form:** The external frameworks in which information and evidence are presented, ranging from choices for particular work sample or collection of works (such as a research paper, PowerPoint, video recording, etc.) to choices in make-up of the eportfolio.
- ⊚ **Performance:** A dynamic and sustained act that brings together knowing and doing (creating a painting, solving an experimental design problem, developing a public relations strategy for a business, etc.); performance makes learning observable.
- ⊚ **Reflection:** A meta-cognitive act of examining a performance in order to explore its significance and consequences.
- ⊚ **Self-Assessment:** Describing, interpreting, and judging a performance based on stated or implied expectations followed by planning for further learning.

INTEGRATIVE LEARNING VALUE RUBRIC

for more information, please contact value@aacu.org

Definition

Integrative learning is an understanding and a disposition that a student builds across the curriculum and cocurriculum, from making simple connections among ideas and experiences to synthesizing and transferring learning to new, complex situations within and beyond the campus.

Evaluators are encouraged to assign a zero to any work sample or collection of work that does not meet benchmark (cell one) level performance.

	Capstone 4	Milestones 3	Milestones 2	Benchmark 1
Connections to Experience *Connects relevant experience and academic knowledge*	Meaningfully **synthesizes connections** among experiences outside of the formal classroom (including life experiences and academic experiences such as internships and travel abroad) to **deepen understanding** of fields of study and to broaden own points of view.	Effectively **selects and develops** examples of life experiences, drawn from a variety of contexts (e.g., family life, artistic participation, civic involvement, work experience), to **illuminate** concepts/theories/frameworks of fields of study.	**Compares** life experiences and academic knowledge to infer differences, as well as similarities, and **acknowledges perspectives** other than own.	**Identifies** connections between life experiences and those academic texts and ideas **perceived as similar and related** to own interests.
Connections to Discipline *Sees (makes) connections across disciplines, perspectives*	Independently creates wholes out of multiple parts (synthesizes) or draws conclusions by combining examples, facts, or theories from more than one field of study or perspective.	Independently connects examples, facts, or theories from more than one field of study or perspective.	When prompted, connects examples, facts, or theories from more than one field of study or perspective.	When prompted, presents examples, facts, or theories from more than one field of study or perspective.
Transfer *Adapts and applies skills, abilities, theories, or methodologies gained in one situation to new situations*	Adapts and applies, independently, skills, abilities, theories, or methodologies gained in one situation to new situations **to solve difficult problems or explore complex issues in original ways.**	Adapts and applies skills, abilities, theories, or methodologies gained in one situation **to new situations to solve problems or explore issues.**	Uses skills, abilities, theories, or methodologies gained in one situation in a new situation **to contribute to understanding of problems or issues.**	Uses, in a basic way, skills, abilities, theories, or methodologies gained in one **situation in a new situation.**
Integrated Communication	Fulfills the assignment(s) by choosing a format, language, or graph (or other visual representation) **in ways that enhance meaning,** making clear the interdependence of language and meaning, thought, and expression.	Fulfills the assignment(s) by choosing a format, language, or graph (or other visual representation) **to explicitly connect content and form,** demonstrating awareness of purpose and audience.	Fulfills the assignment(s) by choosing a format, language, or graph (or other visual representation) that **connects in a basic way** what is being communicated (content) with how it is said (form).	Fulfills the assignment(s) (i.e. to produce an essay, a poster, a video, a PowerPoint presentation, etc.) **in an appropriate form.**
Reflection and Self-Assessment *Demonstrates a developing sense of self as a learner, building on prior experiences to respond to new and challenging contexts (may be evident in self-assessment, reflective, or creative work)*	Envisions a future self (and possibly makes plans that build on past experiences that have occurred across multiple and diverse contexts).	Evaluates changes in own learning over time, recognizing complex contextual factors (e.g., works with ambiguity and risk, deals with frustration, considers ethical frameworks).	Articulates strengths and challenges (within specific performances or events) to increase effectiveness in different contexts (through increased self-awareness).	Describes own performances with general descriptors of success and failure.

Source: AAC&U. Used with permission.

APPENDIX 6.6 Division of Student Affairs Learning Outcome Assessment Rubric for Ethical Development

Student Name: _____   Date: _____

Department/Program: _____   Name of Assessor: _____

Assessment Criteria	Developing	Proficient	Accomplished
Students will be able to define and articulate a code of ethics and principles that guide their decision making and and actions in relation to the ethical standards of the campus community.	☐ Student has difficulty articulating personal values and ethics.	☐ Student identifies personal values and ethics but has difficulty relating them to personal or community behavior.	☐ Student solidly articulates and understands personal values and ethics, including how they guide personal life.
	☐ Student has difficulty identifying shared values and ethics of community.	☐ Student demonstrates some understanding of community values and ethics.	☐ Student demonstrates clear understanding of role of values and ethics in community.
	☐ Student has difficulty articulating how personal and community values relate to one another.	☐ Student can identify some ways in which personal and community values relate.	☐ Student demonstrates understanding of interrelatedness of personal and community values in shaping actions.
Students will be able to reflect upon and critique their behaviors and actions as they relate to their personal ethics and campus and societal communities.	☐ Student may acknowledge his or her behavior but continue to place blame elsewhere.	☐ Student accepts responsibility for personal behavior or its outcomes.	☐ Student accepts full responsibility for personal actions and can articulate its impact on self and community.
	☐ Student has difficulty expressing remorse outside of self.	☐ Student demonstrates some remorse regarding the outcome of his or her behaviors but shows little remorse as to the underlying behavior.	☐ Student demonstrates remorse for behavior and its consequences on self and others and articulates why behavior was inappropriate.
	☐ Student has difficulty articulating any changes to behavior, values or ethics as a result of the process.	☐ Student discusses some lessons and changes to personal behavior and, possibly, to values and ethics as a result of the process.	☐ Student articulates clear lessons from the experiences and has begun putting into action a revised personal code of conduct and ethics.
Students will develop and articulate a plan for incorporating ethics into their future academic, professional, and community life.	☐ Student has difficulty articulating any plan for incorporating ethics or values into future behaviors.	☐ Student identifies plans for incorporating ethics or values into certain future behaviors.	☐ Student articulates a comprehensive plan for incorporating ethics into personal, academic, professional, and community life.
	☐ Plan is unexpressed or simplistic and lacks reflective thought.	☐ Plan demonstrates some periodic reflective thought.	☐ Plan fully integrates self-reflection and self-monitoring into future behavior and actions.

Source: Contributed by Andrea Goodwin and the University of Maryland Student Affairs Learning Outcomes Group.

APPENDIX 6.7 Division of Student Affairs Learning Outcome Assessment Rubric for Time Management Skills

Student Name: _____ Date: _____

Department/Program: _____ Name of Assessor: _____

Assessment Criteria	Developing	Proficient	Accomplished
Student has developed To-Do List for the week that clearly identifies A, B and C priority items in both academic and extracurricular areas	☐ To-Do List incomplete; does not indicate understanding of prioritizing activities	☐ To-Do List demonstrates satisfactory understanding of prioritizing in some parts of student's life	☐ To-Do List demonstrates exceptional understanding of prioritizing in all areas of student's life
Student has created weekly schedule that demonstrates balance among academic, personal, social and extracurricular activities	☐ Schedule incomplete; beginning understanding of scheduling techniques; limited awareness of importance of balance	☐ Schedule demonstrates satisfactory understanding of scheduling techniques; balance in some parts of student's life is evident	☐ Schedule demonstrates exceptional understanding of scheduling techniques; balance among all areas of student's life is demonstrated
Student has demonstrated an understanding of the concept of flexible scheduling	☐ Schedule has every hour blocked out; no awareness of need for flexibility	☐ Schedule includes limited flexibility	☐ Schedule includes room for flexibility in all areas
Student has set aside two hours of study for each hour in class over the course of the week	☐ Schedule demonstrates study hours but below 2 hour minimum	☐ Schedule demonstrates adequate study hours (2 hours/class hour)	☐ Schedule demonstrates more than adequate study time
Student has created a semester schedule which shows all major exams, papers, tests and other academic obligations	☐ Semester schedule has some, but not all, academic obligations included	☐ Semester schedule adequately addresses academic obligations	☐ Semester schedule describes academic obligations in full detail
Student has reflected on and analyzed use of time for the week and identified areas for improvement	☐ Student has limited understanding of strengths and weaknesses in time use; has not demonstrated self-reflection; limited suggestions for improvement	☐ Adequate understanding and reflection of strengths and weaknesses in time use; has made some suggestions on ways to improve	☐ Clear, insightful reflection of strengths and weaknesses in time use; has made significant suggestions on ways to improve

Source: University of Maryland Student Affairs Learning Outcomes Group

APPENDIX 6.8

Name of Person completing form: _____   Date: _____

Name of Person being assessed: _____   Dept: _____

Person Completing Form is (circle one): Student Employee or Student's Supervisor

University of Rhode Island   Page 1 of 4

Assessment of Learning for URI Student Affairs Employees
University of Rhode Island 11/29/2006

Directions:

1. Please place a check in the space provided next to the learning items your department will assess this year.
2. Student and supervisor complete form independently.
3. For each learning item checked, circle the statement that best describes the level of learning for the person being assessed.
4. Compare answers and discuss with your student or supervisor.
5. Please write any necessary comments under the item (e.g., "Student has not been trained for this skill" or "Student has requested to be assessed on this item in addition to department requirements.")

EDUCATED PERSONS

Learning Outcome: *Student employee is able to show understanding of and be able to articulate his/her role and purpose in the organization.*

( ) 1. Student is able to explain the mission of the organization.

4	3	2	1
Student can articulate the mission in his/her own words and shows personal understanding.	Student can describe the mission, but shows less personal understanding.	Student vaguely cites the mission and has little personal understanding.	Student is not aware of the mission and shows no personal understanding.

Comments:

( ) 2. Student is able to articulate the daily operations of the organization and how those operations fulfill the mission.

4	3	2	1
Student has no difficulty articulating the daily functions and identifying the people responsible, and fully understands operations fulfill the mission.	Student has little difficulty articulating the daily functions and identifying the people responsible, and for the most part, understands how these fulfill the mission.	Student has a good deal of difficulty articulating the daily functions and identifying people responsible, and has some understanding of how these fulfill the mission.	Student is unable to articulate the daily functions and identifying people responsible, and does not understand how these fulfill the mission.

Comments:

( ) 3. Student is able to describe his/her role in the organization, and how that role fulfills the mission of the organization.

4	3	2	1
Student can almost always specifically describe her/his own duties and responsibilities, and is able to tie these to the mission.	Student can usually describe her/his own duties and responsibilities, and has a general awareness of how these tie to the mission.	Student can sometimes describe her/his own duties and responsibilities, and can vaguely tie these to the mission.	Student can rarely describe her/his own duties and responsibilities.

Comments:

Learning Outcome: *Student employee is able to gather, evaluate and apply information to solve work related problems.*

( ) 1. Student employee is able to gather, evaluate and apply information to solve work related problems.

4	3	2	1
Student can almost always identify work related problems and engages in a systematic, conscious process of gathering, evaluating and applying information to solve the problem.	Student can usually identify work related problems and for the most part engages in a systematic, conscious process of gathering, evaluating and applying information to solve the problem.	Student can sometimes identify work related problems and at times engages in parts of a conscious process of gathering, evaluating and applying information, but does so in an unsystematic way. For example, the student may leave out some of the process steps.	Student can rarely identify work related problems, and when does address them does so with little gathering, evaluating, and applying for information to solve the problem.

Comments:

( ) 2. Student employee seeks clarification about job-related tasks and issues when appropriate.

4	3	2	1
Student is able to seek clarification about job-related tasks and issues even when the situation may involve tension or conflict.	Student is usually able to seek clarification about job-related tasks and issues, but may avoid doing so if the situation involves tension or conflict.	Student is sometimes able to seek clarification about job-related tasks and issues, but usually avoids doing so if the situation involves tension or conflict.	Student is seldom or never able to seek clarification about job-related tasks and issues.

Comments:

University of Rhode Island

SKILLED WORKERS
Learning Outcome: *Student employee is able to demonstrate behaviors/skills appropriate for the work setting.*

( ) 1. Student employee performs duties independently without constant supervision.			
4	3	2	1
Student almost always performs expected daily tasks without reminders to do so from supervisor.	Student usually performs expected daily tasks without reminders to do so from supervisor.	Student sometimes performs expected daily tasks without reminders to do so from supervisor.	Student rarely performs expected daily tasks without reminders to do so from supervisor.

Comments:

( ) 2. Student employee uses time management skills.			
4	3	2	1
Student almost always uses time well throughout the day. Supervisor does not have to adjust deadlines or work responsibilities because of procrastination or inefficiency.	Student usually uses time well throughout the day. Supervisor does not have to adjust deadlines or work responsibilities because of procrastination or inefficiency.	Student sometimes uses time well throughout the day. Supervisor does not usually have to adjust deadlines or work responsibilities because of procrastination or inefficiency.	Student rarely uses time well throughout the day. Supervisor frequently needs to adjust deadlines or work responsibilities because of procrastination or inefficiency.

Comments:

( ) 3. Student employee presents image appropriate to the work setting.			
4	3	2	1
Student almost always attends work in appropriate attire.	Student usually attends work in appropriate attire.	Student sometimes attends work in appropriate attire.	Student rarely attends work in appropriate attire.

Comments:

( ) 4. Student employee produces high quality work to the specification given.			
4	3	2	1
Work produced is almost always of high quality.	Work produced is usually of high quality.	Work produced is sometimes of high quality.	Work produced is rarely of high quality.

Comments:

( ) 5. Student employee observes principles of confidentiality.			
4	3	2	1
Student always maintains confidentiality of sensitive information and can explain the importance of confidentiality.	Student, on a rare occasion, fails to maintain confidentiality of sensitive information, but can explain the importance of confidentiality.	Student sometimes fails to maintain confidentiality of sensitive information and cannot explain the importance of confidentiality.	Student often fails to maintain confidentiality of sensitive information and cannot explain the importance of confidentiality.

Comments:

( ) 6. Student employee seeks additional work, as time permits.			
4	3	2	1
Student often takes the opportunity to ask for additional work and/or also takes the initiative to carry out additional tasks.	Student sometimes takes the opportunity to ask for additional work and/or also takes the initiative to carry out additional tasks.	Student rarely takes the opportunity to ask for additional work and/or also takes the initiative to carry out additional tasks.	Student never takes the opportunity to ask for additional work and/or also takes the initiative to carry out additional tasks.

Comments:

LIFE SKILLS MANAGERS
Learning Outcome: *Student is able to communicate effectively with others.*

( ) 1. Student employee demonstrates an ability to work collaboratively with others.			
4	3	2	1
Student almost always listens to, shares with and supports the efforts of others. Tries to keep people working well together.	Student usually listens to, shares with and supports the efforts of others. Does not cause "waves" in the group.	Student sometimes listens to, shares with and supports the efforts of others, but is sometimes not a good team player.	Student rarely listens to, shares with and supports the efforts of others. Often is not a good team player.

Comments:

(continued)

APPENDIX 6.8   *(continued)*

University of Rhode Island

( )   2. Student employee demonstrates effective speaking skills.

4	3	2	1
Student almost always expresses self clearly and almost never uses language that is inappropriate for the work setting.	Student usually expresses self clearly and on occasion uses language that is inappropriate for the work setting.	Student sometimes struggles to express self clearly and sometimes uses language that is inappropriate for the work setting.	Student often struggles to express self clearly and frequently uses language that is inappropriate for the work setting.

Comments:

Learning Outcome: *Student is able to display effective self-management of his/her responsibilities and emotions.*

( )   1. Student employee is able to balance studies and other responsibilities with work availability.

4	3	2	1
Meeting academic demands and/or other responsibilities almost never interferes with work availability.	Meeting academic demands and/or other responsibilities sometimes interferes with work availability.	Meeting academic demands and/or other responsibilities usually interferes with work availability.	Meeting academic demands and/or other responsibilities almost always interferes with work availability.

Comments:

( )   2. Student employee uses criticism/feedback constructively.

4	3	2	1
Student sometimes seeks out feedback on his/her work, always responds positively to feedback & is able to modify work to those specifications.	Student, on occasion, seeks out feedback on his/her work, usually responds positively to feedback & is able to modify work to those specifications.	Student does not seek out feedback on his/her work, sometimes responds positively to feedback & is able to modify work to some specifications.	Student does not seek out feedback on his/her work, rarely responds positively to feedback & is not able to modify work to some specifications.

Comments:

( )   3. Student employee handles emotion in a manner appropriate to the work place.

4	3	2	1
Student almost always maintains positive & professional attitude despite personal or professional stress or turmoil. Work is not negatively affected.	Student usually maintains positive & professional attitude despite personal or professional stress or turmoil. Work is not negatively affected.	Student sometimes maintains positive & professional attitude despite personal or professional stress or turmoil. Work is sometimes negatively affected.	Student rarely maintains positive & professional attitude despite personal or professional stress or turmoil. Work is usually negatively affected.

Comments:

SELF-AWARE INDIVIDUALS

Learning Outcome: *Student employee is able to articulate awareness of and demonstrate personal characteristics that positively impact the work place.*

( )   1. Student employee demonstrates willingness to learn and train for job-related tasks.

4	3	2	1
Student almost always shows positive attitude toward learning & training for job-related tasks; rarely fails to show interest.	Student usually shows positive attitude toward learning & training for job-related tasks; sometimes fails to show interest.	Student sometimes shows positive attitude toward learning & training for job-related tasks; more usually fails to show interest.	Student rarely shows positive attitude toward learning & training for job-related tasks; consistently fails to show interest.

Comments:

( )   2. Student employee asks for assistance when appropriate.

4	3	2	1
Student almost always seeks help when appropriate; almost always seeks alternative sources and/or uses good judgment when help is not available.	Student usually seeks help when appropriate; usually seeks alternative sources and/or uses good judgment when help is not available.	Student sometimes seeks help when appropriate; sometimes seeks alternative sources and/or uses good judgment when help is not available.	Student rarely seeks help when appropriate; rarely seeks alternative sources and/or uses good judgment when help is not available

Comments:

( )   3. Student employee presents a self-confident image.

4	3	2	1
Student almost always acknowledges own abilities & performance appropriately; almost always expresses self-criticism appropriately & is never publicly critical of the work of others.	Student usually acknowledges own abilities & performance appropriately; usually expresses self-criticism appropriately & is rarely publicly critical of the work of others.	Student sometimes acknowledges own abilities & performance appropriately; sometimes expresses self-criticism appropriately & is sometimes publicly critical of the work of others.	Student almost never acknowledges own abilities & performance appropriately; almost never expresses self-criticism appropriately & is often publicly critical of the work of others.

Comments:

University of Rhode Island   Page 4 of 4

( )	4. Student employee takes responsibility for own choices and behaviors.		
4	3	2	1
Student almost always acknowledges own role in outcomes, positive or negative. Almost never makes excuses or blames others for negative outcomes.	Student usually acknowledges own role in outcomes, positive or negative. Sometimes makes excuses or blames others for negative outcomes.	Student sometimes acknowledges own role in outcomes, positive or negative. Usually makes excuses or blames others for negative outcomes.	Student rarely acknowledges own role in outcomes, positive or negative. Almost always makes excuses or blames others for negative outcomes.
Comments:			

INTERPERSONALLY AND CULTURALLY COMPETENT INDIVIDUALS
Learning Outcome: *Student employee is able to work and communicate effectively with others, including people from different cultures or backgrounds.*

( )	1. Student employee demonstrates knowledge of different cultural groups.		
4	3	2	1
Student shows deep reflection and respect for a wide variety of cultural and physical characteristics.	Student shows a high level of awareness and respect for cultural and physical characteristics.	Student shows some awareness and respect for cultural and physical characteristics.	Student shows little/no awareness and respect for cultural and physical characteristics.
Comments:			

( )	2. Student employee demonstrates inter-cultural respect and sensitivity.		
4	3	2	1
Student almost always speaks inclusively and sensitively; diverse characteristics are never an obstacle to communication.	Student usually speaks inclusively and sensitively; diverse characteristics are rarely an obstacle to communication.	Student sometimes speaks inclusively and sensitively; diverse characteristics are sometimes an obstacle to communication, but when insulting language is identified he/she shows willingness to improve communication and consider cultural differences.	Student rarely or never speaks inclusively and sensitively; diverse characteristics are often an obstacle to communication and when insulting language is identified he/she does not show willingness to improve communication and consider cultural differences.
Comments:			

( )	3. Student employee demonstrates ability to respond to cultural and interpersonal conflicts.		
4	3	2	1
Student is completely nonjudgmental, almost always considers multiple perspectives of the situation and shows excellent ability to negotiate solutions.	Student is usually nonjudgmental, usually considers multiple perspectives of the situation and shows good effort to negotiate solutions.	Student tries to remain nonjudgmental, sometimes considers multiple perspectives of the situation and shows willingness to negotiate solutions.	Student is unable to remain nonjudgmental, rarely considers multiple perspectives of the situation and does not show willingness to negotiate solutions.
Comments:			

DEMOCRATIC CITIZENS
Learning Outcome: *Student employee is able to understand the value of communicating own and others' perspectives and is willing to articulate those perspectives.*

( )	1. Student employee is able to understand the value of communicating own and others' perspectives and is willing to articulate those perspectives.		
4	3	2	1
Student has no difficulty articulating the value of sharing own and others' perspectives for the good of the community and is almost always wiling to communicate those perspectives.	Student has some difficulty articulating the value of sharing own and others' perspectives for the good of the community and is usually wiling to communicate those perspectives.	Student has a good deal of difficulty articulating the value of sharing own and others' perspectives for the good of the community and is sometimes wiling to communicate those perspectives.	Student is not able to articulate the value of sharing own and others' perspectives for the good of the community and is rarely wiling to communicate those perspectives.
Comments:			

Source: Student Affairs Assessment Committee, University of Rhode Island.

Chapter 7

DESIGNING A CYCLE OF INQUIRY

It is reasonable to expect a college student to be able to apply in a new context a law of physics, or a proof in geometry, or a concept in history of which she just demonstrated mastery in her class. If when the circumstances of testing are slightly altered, the sought-after competence can no longer be documented, then understanding—in any reasonable sense of the term—has simply not been achieved.

—John Gardner, 1991

OVERVIEW: Designed to assist institution- and program-level assessment committees or working groups orchestrate and then move through one cycle of assessment, this chapter describes strategies for collecting evidence of student learning; scoring student responses; analyzing, representing, and interpreting results to make decisions about educational practices; and then reentering the assessment cycle. Use this chapter to develop and implement a plan to assess one institution- or program-level outcome based on collectively agreed-upon assessment methods. Progressing through one cycle of inquiry helps an institution and its programs and services determine how to position assessment as a core institutional process—how to adapt existing processes, structures, and channels of communication or how to create new ones. The worksheets at the end of this chapter are designed to guide two processes: (1) an institution- or a program-level cycle of inquiry and (2) the development of periodic reports that chronicle the assessment process, results, and next steps for each cycle of inquiry. These reports build institution- and program-level knowledge about student learning; they also become a way for colleges and universities to document their achievements, as well as their continual learning.

A DESIGN FOR INSTITUTIONAL LEARNING

Executing a plan to derive and use evidence of student learning is more than a calendared sequence of tasks leading to a report of percentile results. Without reaching consensus about what we want to learn about our student population at the institution or program level, information gathering can become a sterile act leading to broad generalizations about student achievement.

These generalizations may not take into account representative student populations and their learning chronologies, such as what they knew or were able to demonstrate upon matriculation. Collective development of learning outcome statements, research or study questions that are coupled with outcome statements, assessment methods, and standards and criteria of judgment to assess student work clarify *what* members of an academic community want to learn about students' progression and eventual achievement. But to learn more specifically about students' learning in relation to educational practices, we need to ask, *whom* do we want to assess—all or samples of our students? And *how, where,* and *when* do we want to derive evidence—in what kinds of contexts? Answering these questions leads to a plan to collect, score, analyze, and interpret results of student achievement, processes that lead to institutional learning about the efficacy of educational practices.

Specifically, this chapter describes the primary tasks involved in collecting evidence of student learning and using the results to inform educational practices. These tasks include the following:

- Reaffirming agreement about what you want to learn shaped by your outcome statement and your research or study question
- Determining your sample size
- Identifying times and contexts for collecting evidence of student learning through direct and indirect assessment methods from which you can make inferences about students' performance levels and answer your research or study question
- Scoring student projects, products, work, or responses or administering instruments such as standardized tests or surveys
- Analyzing and representing results in ways that promote collective interpretation
- Collectively interpreting and making decisions based on results, such as adapting, modifying, or innovating new ways of teaching and learning or developing new approaches to services or support programs

- Reentering the assessment cycle to determine the efficacy of adaptations, modifications, and innovations

REAFFIRMING AGREEMENT ABOUT WHAT YOU WANT TO LEARN

Reestablishing agreement about what you specifically want to learn about student learning, that is, what you identified in your research or study question discussed in chapter 4, is essential as you determine how and when you will collect student work through the direct and indirect assessment methods you design or identify. Who our student populations are and what we want to learn about them affects how we gather evidence about their achievement. Identifying the shared goal of collective inquiry, your research or study question, is important to establish before launching into evidence gathering. Otherwise, the process of collecting evidence and data may not produce the kinds of results that members of the educational community will find useful. Assuring that members of a core inquiry group agree on a research or study question also shapes how assessment results will be reported to answer that question. For example, at the end of one cycle of assessment, the chemistry department at Clarke College specifically wanted to answer two questions about students' writing and analysis, along with answering questions about the adequacy of the scoring rubric they used (see Box 7.1).

The following kinds of questions also help guide consensus about what you want to learn:

- What do we want to know about achievement levels within your representative populations and their learning histories?

BOX 7.1   Chemistry Department Sample Questions

ASSESSMENT DATA COLLECTED AND ANALYZED (SPRING 2007–SPRING 2008)

1. Outcome(s) assessed: communication (writing) and analytical skills
2. What the department wanted to know about student performance:
   - Writing: Are students writing in appropriate technical style? Where do students need reinforcement?
   - Analytical skills: Can students interpret data based on what they know about precision and accuracy?
   - General: Do rubric categories and performance indicators match outcomes measured and do scores provide meaningful information?

Source: Chemistry Department, Clarke College.

- What's the story you want to tell at the end of your inquiry process?
- Are members of an academic community interested in making large-scale interpretations or targeted interpretations based on results? For example, is an institution or a program interested in pursuing the progress and attainment levels of students who place into college-level preparatory courses? How well do these students progress toward and eventually achieve institution- and program-level learning outcomes, especially as they transition out of those preparatory courses?
- Is your institution or are certain programs or departments interested in tracking students' achievement based on different dominant pedagogies or curricular design, such as programs that are offered online as well as face-to-face?
- Is your institution interested in tracking students according to their declared major, area of concentration, or area of specialization to learn how well students integrate general education or core curricular learning into their field of study?

If, for example, you are interested in learning about how effectively skills-based courses offered outside your discipline prepare students for disciplinary work, then you may plan to sample students as soon as they begin their first-level disciplinary courses. Then you can share those results with those who offer skills-based courses as well as collaboratively identify how both skills-based courses and introductory disciplinary courses might adapt new pedagogies that, together, improve students' abilities to transfer and use their skills-based course learning. Or, if you are interested in determining how well students transfer their general education learning into their major, such as critical-thinking abilities, then you could sample student work across introductory courses in disciplines or fields of study to ascertain the patterns of strength and weakness that are occurring.

If you have developed a Taxonomy of Student Weaknesses, Errors, or Fuzzy Thinking (described in chapter 4, pages 133–134), then you may decide to sample student work chronologically to determine how well students overcome those obstacles or continue to struggle with them based on new pedagogical approaches designed to help students overcome those obstacles. Results of this approach would bring together faculty in a department, for example, to discuss chronological samples of student work that track students' progress. Recall the physics example in chapter 4; typically entering physics students hold on to their naïve understanding of physics concepts. How to help students move beyond those naïve understandings so that they can develop chronologically more complex conceptual understanding became the focus of faculty work leading to the development of interactive online scenarios. If you have adapted a new face-to-face or online pedagogy, then your assessment can focus on determining how well that pedagogy is fostering enduring learning by selecting student work from the remaining coursework that students will take.

The institutional example in Box 7.2 illustrates how four open-ended guiding questions drove decisions about the multiple kinds of evidence an inquiry group needed to collect to learn how to improve the advising process at Indiana University–Purdue University in Indianapolis:

1. What have students learned from their advising experiences?
2. What aspects of the advising experience contribute to academic success and intended advising outcomes?
3. How does the University College Advising Center help students make successful transitions to degree-granting schools?
4. What role, if any, should the University College Advising Center play in advancing advising across the campus, particularly with faculty members in the degree-granting schools?

Some Key Institutional Contributors

Determining what you want to learn involves engaging the expertise of several key institutional contributors who also typically serve on core working groups that design or select assessment methods:

1. Institutional researchers
2. Registrars
3. Representatives from academic support services
4. Representatives from student affairs

These individuals are especially essential in guiding the actual collection, analysis, and interpretation of assessment results. Institutional researchers contribute expertise in the types and logistics of population sampling and in analyzing results that promote community interpretation. Registrars contribute in a variety of ways: They identify and track student cohorts, such as students enrolled in the same program but offered through different delivery methods—online versus face-to-face, for example; they provide course-taking patterns and information about student progression; and they identify students' placement starting points. At both the front and back ends of the process of assessing student learning, they provide valuable information about students' contexts for learning that assist collective interpretation. Individuals from student support services, including student tutors, contribute information about students' persistence in support services or the patterns of difficulty students experience. These kinds of information may correlate with levels of achievement and, thus, guide collective interpretation of results. Multiple experts work together, then, to prepare for the collection of students' evidence of learning and to provide information that will enrich collective interpretation of student results.

DETERMINING YOUR SAMPLE SIZE

The size of an institution's student body may prohibit assessing all students at both the institution and program levels. There are, however, opportunities in most institutions for assessing the student population as a whole. Examples include building in a common time at the end of a required course, for example; at the end of a program or service; or during a required assessment period integrated into a college or university's semester schedule. Sampling members of an institution- or program-level population may, however, be a more realistic and feasible option on which to make inferences about student learning. Three of the most commonly used sampling methods are the following:

1. *Simple random sampling.* This method draws a representative selection of students from the whole student population, with the aim that each student has an equal chance of being selected. Key to this sampling is developing a way to reduce bias of selection by using random number tables, for example.
2. *Stratified random sampling.* This method first categorizes students within the larger institutional population and then draws an independent random sampling within each

category. Possible categories within an institution may be based on the following:

- Educational background
- Professional and life experiences
- Student demographics (see also page 8 in chapter 1 for possible ways to categorize your student demographics)
- Levels of initial placement on matriculation
- Major program of study

3. *Cluster sampling.* In this method, heterogeneous groups or clusters are defined, representative of the institution- or program-level student population. Simple random sampling identifies students in each cluster; observers then sample students from each cluster (Levy & Lemeshow, 1999).

In the case of the large, public urban institution, IUPUI (Box 7.2), a core working group used several sample sizes to answer the multiple study questions the institution raised about the efficacy of its advising process, critical to its students' academic performance. Specifically, the group sampled all students who were enrolled in learning communities (a specific cohort that could be captured through a questionnaire); submitted a web-based questionnaire to reach as many students as possible; and selected individuals to interview to probe into their relevant experiences and perceptions.

Whether an institution and its programs assess all students or sample representative populations, reaching early consensus about the focus of inquiry within or across the student population helps target collective interpretation of results.

IDENTIFYING TIMES AND CONTEXTS FOR COLLECTING EVIDENCE

The kinds of collective discussions described in chapter 3 about the design of curriculum, instruction, the co-curriculum, and educational practices promote consensus about appropriate times to assess students' attainment. Building those times into a plan is a next step: When is it appropriate to assess for a particular outcome or sets of outcomes along the continuum of students' learning to answer a collaboratively agreed-upon research or study question: after each course, after a certain number of courses, or after a set of courses and related experiential opportunities? Selecting and designing assessment methods establishes the

BOX 7.2 Case Study: Using Assessment Data to Improve Academic Advising

Many students attending Indiana University-Purdue University in Indiana (IUPUI), a large, urban, commuter university, possess characteristics that place them at a greater risk for academic failure and attrition: not completing a rigorous high school college-preparatory curriculum, being first-generation college students, attending classes part-time, living off campus, and committing to significant off-campus work. These students are often juggling work and family responsibilities along with school and may need support to achieve their academic goals. Academic advising often provides students with the informational, personal, and academic support necessary for them to attain academic success. As such, providing effective academic advising to meet students' diverse needs is an essential priority at our institution.

Using assessment data to improve academic advising at IUPUI has many challenges given the complexity of organizational decision making and the diversity of perspectives among faculty, administration, staff, and students. Through a self-study and program review process conducted at IUPUI we successfully created campus-wide commitment and support for ongoing advising improvements. Assessment data were used to address several guiding questions and to examine fundamental assumptions.

The University College (UC) Academic Advising Unit provides support for students as they transition into college and to their degree-granting school. UC advisors provide individual advising, work with students during orientations, are integral members of instructional teams in learning communities, work with students on probation, and provide campus-wide workshops. In an effort to understand if the UC advising unit was successfully meeting the needs of students and the campus community, a comprehensive assessment plan was designed and implemented. The following major questions guided the development of the self-study assessment plan and data collection methods:

1. What have students learned from their advising experiences?
2. What aspects of the advising experience contribute to academic success and intended advising outcomes?
3. How does the University College Advising Center help students make successful transitions to degree-granting schools?
4. What role, if any, should the University College Advising Center play in advancing advising across the campus, particularly with faculty members in the degree-granting schools?

We employed a mixed-method design and collected data from diverse sources: web-based surveys were administered to a random sample of UC students and a random sample of students recently certified to schools, a pre-post questionnaire was administered to all students in learning community (LC) sections, and interviews and surveys were conducted with all UC advisors. Additionally, a review team consisting of internal faculty members and external experts conducted comprehensive interviews with various members of the campus community (e.g., advisors in UC and faculty advisors in the schools, faculty members, staff, administrators, and students). The quantitative and qualitative assessment data were analyzed and several reports were produced to help shed light on the guiding questions.

Results based on the pre-post questionnaire suggested that students made significant improvements in the following areas as a result of the advising interventions in LCs:

- Increased knowledge about campus resources and ways to become engaged in co-curricular activities
- Enhanced understanding of how to decide on a major or future career, the process of getting into a degree granting school
- Increased academic self-efficacy in terms of academic goal setting, planning, and dealing with school-related problems

(continued)

BOX 7.2 *(continued)*

The web-based survey results revealed that there were several significant and important differences between students who almost always met with the same advisor and students who almost always met with different advisors. Students who met with the same advisors were significantly more satisfied compared to students who met with different advisors with regard to advisor encounters in the following areas: advisors' interaction style, knowledge levels, ability to establish connections with students, professionalism, and effectiveness in helping students establish academic goals. Additionally, the more students experienced advisors who were *professional* (e.g., readily available, flexible in arranging meeting times, promptly returns phone calls, provides timely information), the higher their levels of academic performance were (first-year cumulative grade point averages). Students reported that UC advisors need to improve the accuracy of information, increase knowledge, and ensure information is up-to-date in order to help students make successful transitions to degree-granting schools. Another major finding was that there was no formal process for ensuring students make a successful transition to the schools and that no body or structure existed to coordinate advising services across the campus. Interviews conducted by the review teams revealed that students, advisors, and faculty were not aware of the intended learning goals for academic advising at IUPUI.

A number of data-driven changes were implemented based on the assessment results. One major assumption that was validated was that UC needed to continue helping students establish relationships with academic advisors by having advisors be an integral part of the instructional teams in learning communities. A pilot program was also implemented that ensured ongoing contact with the same academic advisor until the student was officially accepted into a degree-granting school. Advisors also hosted workshops and established more active relationships with the schools to ensure up-to-date knowledge requiring degree and major requirements. Another critical improvement in advisor functioning was that advisors intentionally designed learning experiences for students in individual advising sessions, group advising, and the learning communities to focus on stated learning outcomes. Additionally, advisor training and professional development opportunities were designed to be more aligned with articulated learning outcomes. A formal process was also established for transitioning students to schools with "dual" advisors who are instrumental in this process.

The UC Advising Center now plays an active role in advancing advising across the campus, particularly with faculty members in the degree-granting schools. The following initiatives were planned and implemented based on the assessment findings: A campus advising newsletter was created; campus-wide advising workshops were planned and conducted; a Campus Advising Council, with the UC Dean of Advising as the chair, was formed. Additionally, resources were expanded to provide support to involve advisors in the inquiry/scholarship of advising. Thus, by clearly and effectively communicating assessment findings, we were able to secure resources to implement proposed changes, ensure results were used to facilitate ongoing learning and change, and monitor progress toward achieving critical institutional and unit goals.

Source: Cathy A. Buyarski, Scott Hansen, and Scott Evenbeck, Indiana University-Purdue University Indianapolis

backbone of a chronology; commercially designed standardized tests, for example, are usually designed to be administered during a defined time period, such as at the end of a program of study, as is the case with Educational Testing Services' Major Field Tests. Locally designed formative assessment methods, developed to assess students' learning after each course or across courses, require a different timetable that builds in faculty and staff time to assess student work at these points along students' studies. Establishing a midpoint project designed to ascertain how well students integrate core curricular learning and other institutional learning outcomes into a major field of study requires setting up yet another timetable. Building in a long-term collaborative project designed to ascertain how well student groups develop and test a new product requires yet another timetable and set of responsibilities for faculty and staff.

Decisions about ways to collect evidence of student learning through direct and indirect assessment methods fall closely on the heels of establishing an assessment time line. Within what kinds of contexts will students demonstrate or represent their learning—in classes or programs, online, off campus, within the educational community, within the local external community, in web-based simulations? The following list represents some ways to collect evidence within that range of contexts:

1. Embed assessment methods into existing courses or services. This method requires that designated faculty, staff, and others who contribute to students' learning reserve time for students to respond to a prompt or task. In some cases an assignment can be woven into a course, service, or educational experience; students hand in their response to an assignment in duplicate. One response is returned to students with faculty or staff comments; the other is turned over to outside scorers for institution- or program-level assessment purposes. Integrating a case study into specific courses across a major program of study provides evidence of how well students are integrating, transferring, and applying new learning. This case study may also be in the form of a simulation that provides observers with an opportunity to assess how well students integrate knowledge, behaviors, and attitudes. If an institution asserts that its students reason quantitatively, regardless of their majors, then embedding a problem for them to solve in a non-quantitatively-based course that students take at the midpoint and end point of their studies would provide evidence of that sustained ability. Arranging for videotaping or observations of students' emerging abilities at various points along their studies, such as their ability to deliver oral presentations to a range of audiences with different knowledge backgrounds and needs, is another way to embed assessment within students' sequence of courses.

2. Extract samples of student work along the continuum of their studies based on agreed-upon assignments designed to prompt students to represent learning described in outcome statements so that there is a consistent kind of text to assess. One way to assess students' learning over time is to collect their work at designated points in their studies: on matriculation into the institution or their acceptance into a program or their entry into a particular service; at a midpoint in their studies or during participation in a service; and at the end of their studies or participation in a service. Results of applying scoring rubrics to these chronological samples provide evidence of students' patterns of progress.

Figure 7.1 illustrates where and when Clarke College collects evidence of students' general education learning over 4 years, using four outcome areas as examples. Baseline evidence and data about student learning are collected from embedded assignments during students' first year in cornerstone courses or introductory courses; midpoint evidence and data are collected in students' major program of study; and end point evidence and data are collected in students' final capstone projects. Larger institutions that follow this collection pattern may want to conduct a simple random sampling of students' work at points along the chronology of their studies or may want to sample work from across their student cohorts to identify those groups that may continue to exhibit patterns of weakness.

3. Establish a common institutional time—days or even a week—to assess student learning. Campuses are increasingly scheduling annual assessment weeks in their institutional calendars as opportunities to assess at the institution and program levels. This scheduled period may be the best time to administer standardized instruments if the week or days are built into students' calendars. More important, these times may also serve as celebrations of student achievement, during which students select work they believe represents their learning—performances, artwork, research projects, collaborative projects, local community projects—and share it with both internal and external audiences.

4. Sample student portfolios designed to include work that represents students' learning and responds to institution- and program-level learning outcome statements. Knowing that students are responsible for submitting certain kinds of work over the duration of their studies provides a rich set of evidence

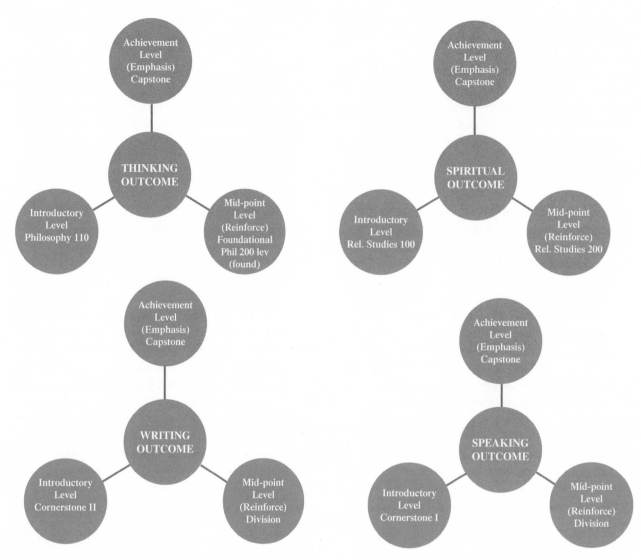

FIGURE 7.1   Clarke College Institutional Assessment of General Education Outcomes
Source: Kate Hendel, BVM, Ph.D., dean of adult and graduate studies, director of general education, Clarke College.

for an institution or program to assess. Furthermore, if students learn on matriculation that they are responsible for chronicling their learning, they are positioned early on to become assessors of their own work, represented through the texts they produce. E-portfolios facilitate sampling across representative student populations as well as provide evidence of students' learning progression (chapter 8 addresses the issue of students' consent to use or access their work for institution- or program-level assessment).

5. Develop inquiry groups consisting of faculty, staff, administrators, alumni, students, and members of advisory boards, for example, that track a cohort of students over time,

using multiple and often concurrent methods to learn more deeply about students' learning, such as assessing portfolios or embedded assignments and then conducting focus groups or interviews about the work.

6. Build in integrative projects, such as midpoint capstone projects, along the continuum of students' learning to assess how well students transfer and make meaning. These projects may become a component of existing courses or services, modules attached to courses, or credit-bearing or required courses themselves.

7. Conduct interviews or focus group discussions designed to complement direct methods. That is, use these indirect methods as ways to probe issues about what and how stu-

dents believe they learn. Refer also to pages 178–179 in chapter 5 about think alouds.

8. Allow students to identify work they believe represents their progress toward and achievement of learning outcomes, providing them with the opportunity to select their own texts. That is, they take ownership of their learning and chronicle that learning through key works. Peer and self-assessment, self-reflection, and students' analyses of how they developed a work may also accompany each piece.

9. Identify opportunities off campus, such as in internships, experiential learning opportunities, students' performances within the local community, and participation in community service projects, that also serve as evidence of their learning applied in more public contexts.

SCORING STUDENT WORK AND ADMINISTERING INSTRUMENTS

A plan for assessment also incorporates time to score students' work or administer and assemble responses from a survey or interview. Actual scoring of student texts or responses can occur in multiple contexts based on the sample strategies discussed in the previous pages. Testing services that develop commercially designed instruments build in scoring and analysis of results as part of the design of their instruments, using either automated scoring systems or scorers who have gone through calibration together to prepare to grade student responses, such as writing samples. Developments in technology have even led to automated scoring of writing samples and complex computer-based tasks that may also be used on campus (Shermis & Daniels, 2002, pp. 159–160; Williamson, Mislevy, & Bejar, 2006).

Typically, however, internal or external scorers or combinations of these scorers blind-score student texts using rubrics so that results can be analyzed according to students' performance under each criterion. Specific teams may be formed to observe student interactions, such as in a simulation, or to score written or visual texts. Using two raters to blind-score student work is another common method after those raters have gone through calibration sessions scoring sample student work. If there is a discrepancy between the two scorers, a third scorer may be brought in or a panel may be established to resolve discrepancies. The possible composition of scorers is variable; among those possibilities are the following:

- Internal scorers—faculty, staff, administrators, teaching assistants, graduate students, or other internal contributors to students' education
- External scorers—members of advisory boards, internship advisors, alumni, representatives from professional organizations, faculty from other institutions, or professionals from the local community.

The institutional example in Box 7.3 illustrates the practice of embedding a direct assessment method into courses along the continuum of students' learning. Interdisciplinary teams score students' writing to assess for three learning outcomes. One of these teams consists of students.

ANALYZING AND REPRESENTING RESULTS

The ability to make targeted interpretations about student learning stems from achieving consensus about the most useful ways to represent assessment results. Involving institutional researchers early on in decisions about what an institution and its programs wants to learn helps these professionals, in collaboration with assessment teams or core working groups, to identify ways to represent results that will promote targeted interpretations about pedagogy; the design of curriculum, co-curriculum, and instruction; and educational practices and services. What formats for presenting results will prompt those kinds of conversations? How will reporting formats help answer the major research or study question raised?

Just as multiple assessment methods provide more comprehensive evidence of student learning, multiple reporting formats assist understanding and appeal to different ways in which audiences make meaning. Analyzed results presented through digital diagrams, tables, charts, graphs, spreadsheets, or maps help many viewers visualize information (Harris, 1996; Tufte, 1990, 1997a, 1997b, 2001). Patterns of performance may be represented for different cohorts—nontraditional-aged and traditional-aged students, international students, commuter and residential students, majors in fields of study—promoting targeted discussions about how to improve specific cohorts' levels of achievement. Other kinds of patterns may include chronological performance patterns indicating high- and low-achievement areas based on a common scoring rubric; students' comparative performance patterns on a first-year assignment and a similar second-year assignment, such as a case study; or patterns that

---

BOX 7.3   INSTITUTIONAL EXAMPLE: *University of South Florida*

At the University of South Florida, the institution's General Education Assessment Advisory team, consisting of associate deans from the colleges of arts and sciences and undergraduate studies, faculty representatives, the vice president of student affairs, representatives from career services and advising, and students, establishes multidisciplinary teams to assess (1) students' writing, (2) intellectual development, and (3) key general education knowledge and understanding based on students' writing.

A Writing Assessment Committee, consisting of teaching assistants from English, philosophy, communications, and sociology, scores student essays to assess writing proficiency. Another team, the Intellectual Development Committee, consisting of five faculty, one associate dean, and two assessment directors, evaluates the intellectual development level exhibited in students' papers using the Measure of Intellectual Development (Moore, 1990). A third team composed of students analyzes the content of students' papers to determine characteristics valued in the classroom and to assess students' understanding of issues and attitudes emphasized in the general education curriculum. Writing skills and intellectual development, as defined by William Perry (1970), are assessed by two additional faculty teams at three points in the curriculum:

1. Upon entry into Composition I
2. After the completion of Composition II
3. During junior- and senior-level capstone courses

A student team analyzes the content of the first and third essays.

Because of the nature of the university's general education curriculum and its desire for students to take assessment seriously, students write all essays as part of their courses. Serving two purposes of assessment, these essays also enable the English department to use the initial essays in Composition I and final essays in Composition II to assess students' progress in the composition program. The final essay, written in capstone courses after students have achieved junior or senior status, also serves as a culminating example of students' progress in writing. A tripartite focus on intellectual development, writing, and content, in relationship to general education curricular goals, provides assessment results that are shared with students, programs, departments, and even colleges within the university. The content analysis, conducted by student teams, provides valuable information about what students have learned within the institution's educational context.

Source: Teresa L. Flateby, University of South Florida.

emerge from student think alouds. Results of observing group interaction or simulations, for example, or results of focus group exchanges may best be presented in a narrative format that represents results in terms of chronological observations or cause-and-effect relationships. Results presented narratively, accompanied with quantitative analyses of student performance based on scoring rubrics, provide two ways for groups to identify patterns of strong and weak performance. Often visual representations of assessment results are accompanied with an *assessment brief,* a summary of findings that describes the initial research or study question, the process of gathering evidence and data, and a concise description of results. Most important is that visual representations of assessment results do the following:

1. Highlight important features such as performance patterns or comparative performance patterns
2. Help viewers quickly perceive patterns
3. Contribute to answering the collaboratively developed research or study question that accompanies outcome statements

Figures 7.2 and 7.3 are two of many ways to represent patterns of performance. Faculty and graduate teaching assistants may ask, "How well do junior biology majors write lab reports based on our holistic scoring rubric?" Figure 7.2 charts those scoring results. Faculty and teaching assistants probably want to know more than this initial visual provides. For example, they may also want to see representation of patterns

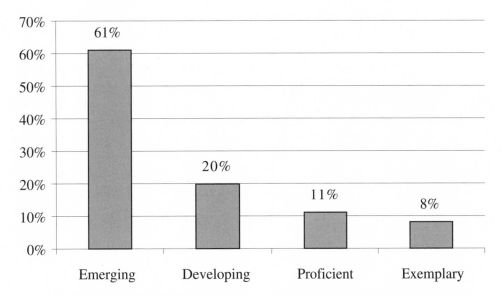

FIGURE 7.2   Bar Chart Representing Holistic Scoring Results of Junior-Level Lab Reports in Biology

of performance—both strong and weak—based on the criteria used in the holistic scoring rubric in order to identify the areas in which students are having difficulty. They may also want to see a comparison among cohorts of students majoring in biology, such as transfer students, first-generation students, developmental students, or honor students, to identify specific cohorts who are having difficulties.

Representing patterns for different cohorts of stu-

dents is Figure 7.3—a bar graph that initially answers the study question, "How well do students enrolled in our online and traditional health science program perform on our chronological examinations?" This comparative bar chart presents an overview of two cohorts' longitudinal performance on the same examinations: students enrolled in a traditional health sciences program and students enrolled in the online version of that same program. That visual helps viewers gain an

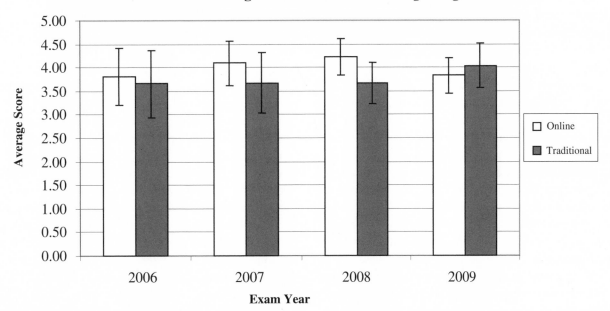

FIGURE 7.3   Chronological Comparison Bar Chart

overall sense of each cohort's achievement. Faculty would probably also want to see a visual representation of students' patterns of performance on questions or problems in the test. That kind of representation—patterns of students' responses to questions or problems—may lead to discussing the different ways of teaching and learning in each program. Alternatively, it may lead to identifying common obstacles that students face in both versions of the program, generating focused discussions about how both programs can improve practices to help students overcome patterns of weakness.

The assessment management systems described in chapter 8 include the capacity to report assessment results in various kinds of charts and graphs that aggregate and disaggregate data to promote collaborative discussion, reflection, and decision making. Additionally, numerous statistical software packages represent results in various kinds of formats after an individual has entered data or results into a program such as STATISTICA (www.statsoft.com). Online programs as well create graphs and charts such as the Bar Chart Generator (www.barchart.be).

Other kinds of institutional data that help answer a research or study question may also target interpretations and should be included in a representation and analysis of assessment results. For example, students' course-taking patterns could explain why certain groups of students perform well but others do not. Students' predisposition to navigate the curriculum to avoid taking certain kinds of courses, such as those that integrate writing or quantitative reasoning, may explain their weak performance in these areas. Looking at connections among students' participation in academic support services or programs and services offered through the co-curriculum may help explain results within cohorts. Because the results of the online survey Student Assessment of Their Learning Gains (SALG) represent students' responses to the components of a course, these results can contribute to educators' understanding of why patterns of performance exist in student work. SALG, for example, provides representations of student responses in multiple graphical formats. Coupling SALG results with scoring rubric results may expand discussion and reflection on how to improve students' levels of performance.

Comparing students' achievement against *baseline data* may also become another way to gauge students' achievement patterns. Information about student learning collected at the time of placement or matric-

ulation into an institution or its programs provides baseline data. Placement tests, portfolio reviews, samples from students' work, or results of assessment methods woven into early courses constitute baseline data. For example, results of the concept inventories (see page 125 in chapter 5) used to assess students' working knowledge of physics—before they take introductory physics courses—establish a baseline against which to assess how well students develop a more coherent understanding of physics concepts in relation to pedagogy and instructional design. In the absence of baseline information, we assume that our curriculum and educational practices advance all students' learning. Such an assumption would have the effect of obscuring or disguising such critical considerations as the following:

- How and what did they know, understand, and believe when they entered the institution or a program?
- What practices along the way revised or changed their conceptual understanding in a field of study?
- What practices challenged and even changed their long-held beliefs, attitudes, values, and interpretations? And what practices did not?

We can provide answers to those questions through baseline data that give us a beginning point to track what, how, and how well students learn within the context of educational practices.

COLLECTIVELY INTERPRETING RESULTS AND MAKING DECISIONS

Drawing on multiple analyzed results—results of assessment methods, course-taking patterns, or initial placement, for example—adds both depth and breadth to collective institution- and program-level interpretation. A community process involving both formal and informal occasions for dialogue, interpretation educates members of an educational community about the efficacy of its collective practices translated into student work. To deepen a shared commitment to assessment, an institution and its programs build occasions for dialogue into institutional rhythms. Chronologically, common institution- and program-level times to interpret and act on analyzed results unfold as follows:

- Initial time to hear and see analyzed results and ask questions about results

- Team-based time following an initial presentation to interpret those results. What interpretations emerge from teams of faculty, staff, students, and other members of the larger community? These teams may form around interdisciplinary perspectives of faculty, staff, and others who contribute to students' education or around focused perspectives, such as those of a team of students, a team of librarians, a team of student affairs staff, or a team of teaching assistants. These teams can contribute to collective institutional learning by establishing times to:

> Reach consensus about adaptations, modifications, or innovations to improve student performance
>
> Learn about the efficacy of changes once they have been implemented and student learning has been reassessed

Institution-level times also include opportunities for the larger community to hear about the results of program-level results and interpretations. What a program learns about its students' achievement informs institution-level discussions; what an institution learns about its students' achievement informs program-level discussions. Establishing reciprocal channels of communication increases awareness about patterns of student achievement and opens up the possibility for greater focus on improving areas of weak performance. That is, that reciprocal channel becomes the forum for revisions, changes, or innovations in pedagogy and the design of the curriculum, co-curriculum, and educational practices. Collective community dialogue based on results and interpretations of results is not designed to point fingers; rather it is designed to determine how members of an educational community can work together to improve student learning.

REENTERING THE ASSESSMENT CYCLE

Decisions about ways to innovate teaching and learning processes, adapt existing practices, or revise aspects of existing practices should emerge from the discussions and reflections that take place when results are shared in the larger communities discussed in the preceding pages. These decisions lead to developing a timetable to implement agreed-upon changes that may involve faculty and staff, such as partnering faculty in departments or partnering faculty with educators in academic or student services in designing a pilot project. Once changes have been developed or designed and then implemented, a timetable should be established to reassess the efficacy of new practices. The physics case study in chapter 4 builds in reassessment of students' conceptual understanding based on their learning through interactive online simulations. Change in itself is not enough. Ensuring that changes are improving learning is the final essential task in assessment.

A NARRATED CYCLE

How collaborative tasks and decisions come together to launch a cycle of inquiry is represented in Box 7.4, an example from Mesa Community College. This narrative chronicles how a core working group of faculty, in collaboration with representatives from the college's office of research and planning, designed, validated, and pilot-tested an assessment method it now uses to assess learning outcomes in the arts and humanities. The office of research and planning continues annually to compare results across years to ensure the integrity of the assessment method and the way in which it administers the method. The internally designed assessment method is embedded in non–arts and humanities courses to determine how well students transfer and apply valued ways of knowing, understanding, and interpreting in contexts outside such courses. The institutional process Mesa Community College designed to validate its assessment methods provides a close-up view of the interrelated decisions, tasks, and processes that define a cycle of inquiry into student learning.

DEVELOPMENT OF AN ONGOING COMMITMENT

Initial pilot projects focused on planning and carrying out an assessment cycle help educate a community about what is involved in the assessment process. A mature assessment system annually seeks evidence of student learning by cycling through one or more outcomes each year, including reassessing agreed-upon changes that educators have made based on results from a previous assessment cycle. Box 7.5 represents the annual cycle that the Graduate School of Library and Information Science at Simmons College follows to assess its doctoral program in managerial leadership in the information professions (MLIP). Using multiple methods and building in annual times to interpret

BOX 7.4   INSTITUTIONAL EXAMPLE: *Mesa Community College*

Arts and Humanities is one of seven collegewide general education areas at Mesa Community College. For five of the seven outcome areas, including Arts and Humanities, the faculty have developed their own assessment tools.

ARTS AND HUMANITIES STUDENT LEARNING OUTCOMES

Cross-disciplinary faculty clusters developed specific student learning outcome statements for each of the seven general education areas defined by the college community. Faculty members representing several arts and humanities disciplines defined the learning outcomes for Arts and Humanities to ensure balanced input across the disciplines. Staff from the Office of Research and Planning provided guidance by providing definitions and examples of good outcome statements and guiding the group to write outcomes that are measurable and independent of one another. The Arts and Humanities outcomes describe what students should be able to demonstrate:

1. Knowledge of human creations.
2. Awareness that different contexts and/or world views produce different human creations.
3. An understanding and awareness of the impact that a piece (artifact) has on the relationship and perspective of the audience.
4. An ability to evaluate human creations.

ARTS AND HUMANITIES ASSESSMENT TOOL

After the outcomes were written, the Arts and Humanities faculty cluster met to determine the most appropriate assessment tool. The research office provided support during this process by conducting searches for possible appropriate tools, reviewing items, and helping faculty align items to outcomes. Faculty decided to design their own instrument to assess the Arts and Humanities outcomes.

Faculty made all content decisions related to the development of the instrument; the research office provided structured feedback and technical support. The Arts and Humanities assessment is a four-part multimedia presentation that includes a photograph of an art exhibit, a videotape of a Shakespeare soliloquy, a musical composition, and a storytelling performance. Faculty selected the presentations and produced the CD-ROM. Students write responses to a series of questions about each presentation; the questions are aligned with the learning outcomes. Students are asked to write personal reactions to each piece, to interpret the piece in terms of its historical or social context, and to examine and evaluate artistic aspects of each.

A scoring rubric was developed by the cluster to measure a set of common constructs across all of the presentations. The rubric consists of a five-point scale describing elements that should be present in the responses. The scale rates the responses from lowest (1 = response is completely undeveloped) to highest (5 = response shows a high level of understanding in a broader view and illustrates coherent integrated thinking about the work).

VALIDITY AND RELIABILITY

Faculty conducted face and content validity measures to assure that the content was relevant and inclusive. The office of research and planning conducted other validity measures, as well as correlated students' GPA, course enrollment patterns, and overall student performance on the method. Reliability analysis and factor analysis were conducted to explore and improve the alignment of items to outcomes, such as measures of internal consistency among a group of items combined to form a single scale. Consistency in rater scoring was also built into this process to determine how well evaluators agreed in their responses.

SAMPLING AND SCORING

A cross-sectional research design was chosen for the assessment program. Beginning students who had completed zero to nine hours (pre-group) were compared to completing students who had completed a core of at least 30 hours of general education coursework distributed across the core curricular areas (post-group). The sampling was selected to represent the general population of the campus. Demographic characteristics of participating and nonparticipating students were also compared by cohort and overall. The proportion of students of color and male/female ratio were compared between groups to determine if there are significant differences in the samples.

Arts and Humanities response booklets were blind-scored by a group of faculty using the scoring rubric; each response was scored by two raters. At the beginning of the scoring session, a norming session was held during which raters scored several sample student responses and discussed the elements that comprise excellent, average, and poor responses. Statistical tests were used to compare the total scores and the scale scores for the learning outcomes to determine if there were significant differences between the two groups of students.

ADMINISTRATION OF THE ASSESSMENT

The Arts and Humanities assessment is currently administered to students during the College's annual assessment week; assessments are assigned across general education departments from a pool of more than 200 volunteered sections. In Spring 2003, 537 students took the Arts and Humanities assessment during a 75-minute scheduled class period. In order to ensure that the general education program, and not a particular department, is being assessed, measures that relate to particular disciplines are not administered in those disciplines (e.g., the Arts and Humanities assessment is not administered in art classes). Annually, faculty attend an orientation and follow standard administration procedures. At the end of the assessment cycle faculty provide feedback concerning the assessment process.

Assessment results are also compared over time. Although different student populations are assessed each year, results are compared between years to determine if the patterns and overall performance are similar.

Source: Mesa Community College.

results, the school has learned how to improve pedagogy, instructional design, and services that support its students.

Based on lessons learned from going through one cycle, an institution and its programs develop and periodically update assessment plans that build in cycles of inquiry. Each cycle includes assessing one to two student learning outcome statements, interpreting results, making changes to improve patterns of weakness, implementing those changes, and reassessing how well students improve based on implemented changes. Two of many possible annual report formats appear in Appendixes 7.1 and 7.2. Appendix 7.1 illustrates the format the Division of Student Affairs at the University of Maryland uses for its annual reports. Appendix 7.2 illustrates a detailed annual program-level report format (to report results and proposed changes for a limited number of outcomes each year) that can be streamlined once constituencies have become accustomed to the tasks that underlie effective assessment. Both examples seek documentation about what educators learned or discovered at the end of an assessment process and how they intend to use that knowledge to improve student learning.

A final view of how a core institutional process becomes embedded in the life of an institution, illustrated through several institutional examples, is the subject of chapter 8.

BOX 7.5   Ongoing Program Assessment in a Doctoral Program

In 2005, the Graduate School of Library and Information Science at Simmons College in Boston received its first multiyear grant from the Institute of Museum and Library Services (IMLS) to develop a Ph.D. program focused on managerial leadership in the information professions (MLIP). The program is intended for practitioners who work full time in managerial positions and are willing to make a substantial commitment to completing a doctorate. Courses meet at the beginning of a semester in 1-week intensive on-site sessions, followed by a suite of activities carried out remotely. This program is now educating its fourth year of students.

The MLIP program incorporates an extensive assessment framework designed to assist students in their development and to provide ongoing review of the program. This framework is centered on a leadership model adapted from one developed by the National Center for Healthcare Leadership (http://web.simmons.edu/~phdml/docs/phdmlip_models.pdf). Primary competencies for the Simmons MLIP program are listed above the dotted line under each heading in the model on this website; those below the line are secondary. Further, the text accompanying the model defines each competency. The model focuses on the following:

- Transformation: Visioning, energizing, and stimulating a change process that coalesces communities, patrons, and professionals around new models of managerial leadership
- Accomplishment: Translating vision and strategy into optimal organizational performance
- People: Creating an organizational climate that values employees from all backgrounds and provides an energizing environment for them. It also includes the leader's responsibility to understand his or her impact on others and to improve his or her capabilities, as well as the capabilities of others.

The annual review is a key component of student assessment. At the end of the first and second years, students meet with faculty to review their progress. The purpose of the review is to encourage students to reflect on their learning experiences, identify strengths that they can leverage and build upon, and pinpoint areas needing improvement as well as strategies for making those improvements. In addition, the review enables faculty to provide feedback and direction to students, and helps identify program strengths and weaknesses. Elements of the annual review include the following:

- Personal Leadership Competency Assessment (PLCA). At different points in the program, students evaluate their own competency levels with the skills and characteristics highlighted in the model.
- Course-level Leadership Competency Assessment (LCA). At the end of each term, the faculty who have engaged with the students evaluate students' competency levels with the assorted leadership skills and characteristics as well as their performance in courses.
- Managerial Leadership Development Plan (MLDP). Concurrent with their completion of the PLCAs, students prepare a narrative review of their progress and outline a plan for improvement moving forward.
- E-portfolio. Each student maintains an electronic portfolio containing artifacts demonstrating progress as outlined in the MLDP.

Coursework concludes with a capstone experience—a course that involves sustained interaction among the faculty, leaders in the professions, and students in examining issues critical to managerial leadership, drawing on the theories, abilities, and skills explored in previous coursework. The grade for this course represents an assessment of the student's cumulative knowledge and demonstrated practical growth. After the capstone, students take a written qualifying examination. The final stage of the program is the dissertation.

To gain experience as researchers and to prepare for the dissertation, students complete two research studies relating to managerial leadership or the evaluation of services offered by information professionals. They improve on their ability to understand and apply concepts such as those related to reflective inquiry (formulating a problem statement, developing a literature review with a theoretical component, and developing objectives, research questions, and hypotheses). As well, the faculty gather insights into their progress in writing a research report.

A multistakeholder assessment of the program provides critical insight and direction. Each summer the faculty gather to discuss the courses they teach and to consider ways to improve the learning experience. A 16-member board of advisers regularly reviews program documentation, raises questions and issues, and offers recommendations. A program assessment committee is composed of four external observers who are respected leaders in the information professions. Annually, a new set of committee members reviews program documentation, interviews students and faculty, and examines student papers to assess the program's effectiveness. The committee submits a written and oral report of its findings to program leadership.

This thorough and multifaceted approach to assessment has already led to improvements in the program such as the following:

- Review and adjustment of competencies listed in each syllabus once the course has been taught
- Enhancement of oral communication activities after discerning gaps in competency coverage
- Modification of course content and presentation to help students more effectively synthesize and demonstrate understanding of content
- Adaptation of course sequencing, allowing students from different cohorts to take an elective course together
- An increase in face-to-face meetings with instructors to strengthen continued guidance as students develop their first research proposal
- Improved assistance in developing written presentations for different types of audiences
- Increased flexibility regarding the types of technology used for course support

Ongoing assessment will undoubtedly suggest other additions and modifications. There are still challenges to overcome, such as finding ways to develop a realization among the students that a doctoral program is more than a set of courses and that successful doctoral students demonstrate highly self-motivated learning practices and persistent inquisitiveness that extend beyond course content.

In conclusion, developing an outcomes-based program requires fully integrated assessment at every level, which has been a challenge. Involvement of all stakeholders (students, faculty, advisers, and external reviewers) has been essential, and responding to their observations and concerns has required flexibility. The result, we believe, is a stronger, more dynamic program responsive to the evolving needs of the profession.

Source: Peter Hernon and Candy Schwartz, Simmons College.

WORKS CITED

Baxter Magolda, M. (1992). *Knowing and reasoning in college: Gender-related patterns in students' intellectual development.* San Francisco, CA: Jossey Bass.

Gardner, J. (1991). *The unschooled mind: How children think and how schools should teach.* New York: Basic Books.

Harris, R. L. (1996). *Information graphics: A comprehensive illustrated reference: Visual tools for analyzing, managing and communicating.* New York: Oxford University Press.

Levy, P. S., & Lemeshow, S. (1999). *Sampling of populations: Methods and applications* (3rd ed.). New York: Wiley.

Moore, W. S. (1990). *The measure of intellectual development: An instrument manual.* Olympia, WA: Center for the Study of Intellectual Development.

Perry, W. G. (1970). *Forms of intellectual and ethical development in the college years: A scheme.* New York: Holt, Rinehart, & Winston.

Shermis, M. D., & Daniels, K. E. (2002). Web applications in assessment. In Banta, T. W., & Associates, *Building a scholarship of assessment* (pp. 148–166). San Francisco: Jossey-Bass.

Tufte, E. (1990). *Envisioning information.* Cheshire, CT: Graphics Press.

Tufte, E. (1997a). *Visual explanations: Images and quantities, evidence and narrative.* Cheshire, CT: Graphics Press.

Tufte, E. (1997b). *Visual and statistical thinking: Displays of evidence for decision making.* Cheshire, CT: Graphics Press.

Tufte, E. (2001). *The visual display of quantitative information* (2nd ed.). Cheshire, CT: Graphics Press.

Williamson, D. M., Mislevy, R. J., & Bejar, I. I. (2006). *Automated scoring of complex tasks in computer-based testing.* Mahwah, NJ: Lawrence Erlbaum.

Yin, R. K.(2003). *Case study research: Design and methods.* (3rd ed.). Thousand Oaks, CA: Sage.

ADDITIONAL RESOURCES

Analyzing and Representing Results

Bounford, T., & Campbell, A. (2000). *Digital diagrams: How to design and present statistical information effectively.* New York: Watson-Guptill.

Cleveland, W. S. (1985). *The elements of graphing data.* Boston: Duxbury.

Cleveland, W. S. (1993). *Visualizing data.* Murray Hill, NJ: Hobart Press.

Dey, I. (1993). *Qualitative data analysis: A user-friendly guide for social scientists.* London: Routledge.

Fitz-Gibbon, C., & Morris, L. (1987). *How to analyze data.* Newbury Park, CA: Sage.

Frantz, R., Jr. (2003). *Graphs done right vs. graphs done wrong.* Cheshire, CT: Graphics Press.

Harris, J., & Samson, D. (2000). *Discerning is more than counting* (p. 3). Washington, DC: American Academy for Liberal Education.

Hartley, J. (1992). Presenting visual information orally. *Information Design Journal, 6,* 211–220.

Hartley, J. (1992, June–July). A postscript to Wine's "Understanding graphs and tables." *Educational Researcher, 21*(5), 25–26.

Henry, G. T. (1994). *Graphing data: Techniques for display and analysis.* Thousand Oaks, CA: Sage.

Howard, R. D., & Borland, K. W., Jr. (Eds.). (2001). *Balancing qualitative and quantitative information for effective decision support.* San Francisco: Jossey-Bass.

Kelle, U. (Ed.) (1995). *Computer-aided qualitative research.* Thousand Oaks, CA: Sage.

Lichtenberger, E. O., Mather, N., Kaufman, N. L., & Kaufman, A. S. (2004). *Essentials of assessment report writing.* Hoboken, NJ: Wiley.

Morris, L. L., Fitz-Gibbon, C. T., & Freeman, M. E. (1987). *How to communicate evaluation findings.* Newbury Park, CA: Sage.

Myatt, G. J. (2006). *Making sense of data: A practical guide to exploratory data analysis and data mining.* Hoboken, NJ: Wiley.

Myatt, G. J., & Johnson, W. P. (2009). *Making sense of data II: A practical guide to data visualization, advanced data mining methods, and applications.* Hoboken, NJ: Wiley.

Richardson, L. (1990). *Writing strategies: Reaching diverse audiences.* Newbury Park, CA: Sage.

Silverman, D. (1993). *Interpreting qualitative data: Methods for analyzing talk, text, and interaction.* Thousand Oaks, CA: Sage.

Stiles, W. (1992). *Describing talk.* Newbury, CA: Sage.

Tufte, E. R. (2003). *The cognitive style of PowerPoint.* Cheshire, CT: Graphics Press.

Wainer, H. (1992, January–February). Understanding graphs and tables. *Educational Researcher, 21*(1), 14–23.

Ware, C. (2000). *Information visualization.* San Francisco: Morgan Kaufmann.

Wolcott, H. F. (1990). *Writing up qualitative research.* Newbury Park, CA: Sage.

Wolcott, H. F. (1994). *Transforming qualitative data: Description, analysis, and interpretation.* Thousand Oaks, CA: Sage.

Automated Scoring

Brown, S., Race, P., & Bull, J. (1999). *Computer-assisted assessment in higher education.* London: Kogan Page.

Burstein, J., Marcu, D., & Knight, K. (2003, January–February). Finding the WRITE stuff: Automatic identification of discourse structure in student essays. *IEEE Intelligent Systems,* 32–39.

Cheville, J. (2004, March). Automated scoring technologies and the rising influence of error. *English Journal, 93*(4), 47–52. *http://www.people.iup.edu/qrkp/Cheville%202004.pdf*

Dikli, S. (2006, August). An overview of automated scoring of essays. *Journal of Technology, Learning and Assessment, 5*(1). *http://escholarship.bc.edu/cgi/viewcontent.cgi?article=1044&context=jtla*

Shermis, M. D., & Barrera, F. D. (2002). Automated essay scoring for electronic portfolios. *Assessment Update, 14*(4), 1–2, 10.

Shermis, M. D., & Barrera, F. D. (2002). Facing off on automated essay scoring. *Assessment Update*, 15(2), 4–5.

Shermis, M. D., & Burstein, J. (Eds.). (2003). *Automated essay scoring: A cross-disciplinary approach*. Mahwah, NJ: Erlbaum.

Interpreting Results

Strain, S. S. (2003, March–April). Keeping the faces of the students in the data. *Assessment Update*, 15(2), 1–2, 14–15.

Sampling

American Statistical Association. *www.amstat.org*

Chaudhuri, A., & Stenger, H. (2005). *Survey sampling: theory and methods* (2nd ed.). Boca Raton, FL: Chapman & Hall.

Federal Committee on Statistical Methodology. *Statistical Policy Working Papers*. *www.fcsm.gov*

Free Resources for Program Evaluation and Social Research Methods. *http://gsociology.icaap.org/methods/*

Healey, J. (2008). *Statistics: A tool for social research*. (8th ed.). Belmont, CA: Thomson Wadsworth.

Judd, C. M., & McClelland, G. H. (1990). *Data analysis: A model-comparison approach*. San Diego, CA: Harcourt Brace Jovanovich.

Sirkin, R. M. (1994). *Statistics for the social sciences*. Thousand Oaks, CA: Sage.

Sudman, S. (1976). *Applied sampling*. New York: Academic Press.

Yancey, B. D. (Ed.). (1988). *Applying statistics in institutional research. New Directions for Institutional Research*, 58. San Francisco: Jossey-Bass.

WORKSHEETS, GUIDES, AND EXERCISES

1. *Progressing Through a Cycle:* The following worksheet is designed to guide a cycle of inquiry that begins with collective articulation of a learning outcome statement and ends with collective interpretation of results. This sheet guides either an institution- or a program-level cycle.

Worksheet to Guide a Cycle of Inquiry

    a. List institution- or program-level learning outcome statement(s) that align with what and how students have learned.

          _____

          _____

          _____

    b. State the research or study question that you have coupled with your outcome statement(s).

          _____

          _____

          _____

    c. Identify the direct and indirect methods you will use that align with these outcome statement(s) and that together contribute to answering your research or study question.

          _____

          _____

          _____

    d. Identify the kinds of inferences you intend to make based on these methods and how a scoring rubric documents those inferences.

          _____

          _____

          _____

    e. Describe how you will test a method's properties of validity and reliability.

          _____

          _____

          _____

    f. Identify the times and contexts within which students will respond to these methods—for example, formative and summative assessment of entries into portfolios; formative and summative assessment of case studies; or formative and summative written responses to representative disciplinary problems included in a final examination.

          _____

          _____

          _____

g. Determine whom you will assess (sampling method) and how you will derive samples.

_____

_____

_____

h. Identify who will score the samples—for example, teams within the institution or external reviewers.

_____

_____

_____

i. Identify who will analyze the results and how results will be presented for collective interpretation.

_____

_____

_____

j. Schedule institution- and program-level times to interpret results, make decisions about changes, and develop a timetable to reassess students' learning after changes have been implemented.

_____

_____

_____

2. *Developing a Report:* As your institution and its programs complete cycles of inquiry, maintaining a history of this work is important in building knowledge about practices within a program as well as across the institution. For institutional purposes, campuswide committees may develop a format that requires documentation of cycles of inquiry into institution- and program-level learning outcome statements. This information, in turn, should move into the processes of institutional decision making, planning, and budgeting. External bodies, such as accreditors, seek evidence of institution- and program-level commitment to assessing students' learning as an indicator of institutional effectiveness. Maintaining a history of your assessment cycles, findings, interpretations, and implemented changes should become, then, one of the rhythms of this core process at both the institution and program levels. Use the program assessment form in Appendix 7.2 as a way to develop your own template for consistent annual reporting or identify an assessment management system (homegrown or commercially developed, as described in chapter 8) to store and maintain a chronological record of your institution-, program-, and department-level assessment plans and actions to improve student learning.

3. *Focusing on Actionable Findings:* The National Institute for Learning Outcome Assessment's leading 2009 recommendation to colleges and universities (see page 125 in chapter 4) is that institutions need to demonstrate how they use assessment results to take actions to improve student learning. Thus, assessment reports should include descriptions of patterns of weakness that educators identified in the assessment process. In addition, they should should include results of assessing student work once new educational practices have been implemented to address weaknesses documented in a Taxonomy of Student Weaknesses, Errors, or Fuzzy Thinking. It is essential to describe assessment results and plans to improve patterns of weakness through pedagogy, instruction, educational practices and curricular design as opposed to stating, "We will address these patterns." Recall the case studies in chapter 4. If you now have assessment results that answer your research or study question, use the following format—with two examples—to focus on your findings and identify ways to improve patterns of weakness.

Description of Findings

Comparison of online students' final projects with traditional students' projects revealed that online students conduct quick and often superficial online searches for their resources. They often turn to the Internet to find easily accessible websites or resources in lieu of identifying relevant traditional primary and secondary resources.

Assessment of sophomore biology students' laboratory assignments revealed that 99% of students' assignments illustrated students' inability to convert raw data into data summaries. In a focus group meeting with students across our five sections, we learned that students did not know what *conversion of raw data* means.

Proposed Actions for Improvement

Over this summer we will companion day faculty with those teaching in our online program to share research strategies already incorporated in the day program and then review online syllabi in the fall to determine how well faculty teaching online courses are incorporating effective research strategies into their online programs to improve students' repertoire of online research strategies.

This summer we will hold a retreat to identify strategies we can thread across our first- and second-year courses to help students understand what *conversion* means and to give them chronological opportunities to practice converting raw data into data summaries. Some strategies we may use include the following:

a. Online tutorials
b. Chronologically more difficult assignments requiring the creation and/or interpretation of graphs
c. Enhanced use of graphs in courses
d. Increased demonstrations of how raw data can be converted to data summaries from which conclusions can be drawn
e. Additional clicker questions in lectures regarding aspects of quantitative analysis

APPENDIX 7.1 Student Affairs Assessment Results for Cognitive and Diversity Skills in the Resident Life Common Ground Peer Dialogue Leader Training Program

For Time Period: March 2006–February 2007
Program Contact: Rhondie Voorhees, Jim Osteen
Submitted to Student Affairs Unit Head: February 27, 2007; March 14, 2007 (Revised)

Note: This assessment is part of an ongoing dissertation project. Data analysis for the study is currently in progress. Therefore, findings reported here are based on an initial review of the data only and are preliminary and speculative.

Program Description and Goals: The Common Ground Multicultural Dialogue Program is a cognitive-based, task-oriented approach to dialogue that provides structured opportunities for diverse groups of 12 to 15 undergraduate students to engage in peer-led dialogues about issues that have important implications in 21st-century American society such as affirmative action, abortion, the death penalty, and same-sex marriage. Overall goals of the dialogue program include teaching students dialogue skills that will enable them to engage in future conversations with people who have views that are different from their own and teaching students how to find common ground when multiple and competing points of view are expressed. The Common Ground program consists of two primary components: (1) a three-credit academic course titled BSOS 301–Leadership in a Multicultural Society, taught each fall and required of all sophomore students in the CIVICUS living and learning program, and (2) a Peer Dialogue Leader (PDL) Training Program, conducted each Spring for a select group of students who have performed well in the BSOS 301 class. The PDL Training Program also serves as one option for CIVICUS students to complete their required capstone experience for the living and learning program. At the culmination of their training, the newly trained PDLs co-lead a four-session dialogue group and then may continue to lead additional groups on a volunteer basis throughout the remainder of their undergraduate careers.

The primary goal of the PDL Training Program is to provide undergraduate students with the knowledge and skills necessary to effectively co-lead Common Ground dialogues with diverse groups of undergraduate students. These include an understanding of the nature of dialogue, an understanding of participant and leader behaviors in dialogue groups, self-awareness with regard to dialogue leader behaviors and personal communication styles, listening skills, and an ability to recognize and respond to hot buttons. Another fundamental goal and desired outcome of the PDL Training Program is that the experience of co-leading dialogue groups will enhance the undergraduate dialogue leaders' cognitive development and will help promote an increased ability to recognize and understand the multiple perspectives that exist on any given multicultural issue or societal dilemma.

The assessments of this program are being conducted as part of a dissertation study designed as a formal case study evaluation of student learning outcomes associated with participation in the Spring 2005 PDL Training Program. Specific outcomes of interest include students' cognitive development, students' experiences in the training phase of the program as compared to the leading phase (an evaluation of the impact of the experiential learning component of the training), and students' overall perceptions of their learning (an exploratory study to determine additional learning outcomes).

Relevance of goals to the mission and/or strategic plan of the University, College, or Program as applicable: The goals of enhancing students' cognitive development and their abilities to see multiple perspectives are consistent with the academic goals of the CIVICUS living and learning program, which centers on five tenets of civil society: citizenship, leadership, community building in a diverse society, scholarship, and community service-learning. They are also consistent with the Department of Resident Life's mission statement, which emphasizes student development and the promotion of academic excellence, and the "cognitive complexity" outcome category from *Learning Reconsidered.*

Methods: This study is a formal evaluation of student learning outcomes associated with participation in the spring 2005 Peer Dialogue Leader Training Program. The research questions are being studied through a mixed-methods evaluative case study in which the primary unit of analysis is the training program and the embedded units of analysis are eight sophomore students who participated in the spring 2005 training program and also agreed to participate in the study.

Data were collected from five sources: (1) a pre- and post-administration of the Measure of Intellectual Development (MID), a qualitative paper-and-pencil measure that uses open-ended essay prompts to assess cognitive development along the first five positions of William Perry's (1970) theory of cognitive development, (2) participant interviews, (3) observations of training sessions, (4) participant journals, and (5) a focus group with experienced PDLs from previous training years who were not participants in the study.

Student Learning Outcomes (list only those assessed during this time period)	Outcome Category* (I–VII)	Assessment Measure, Criteria, and Results	Impact of Results
Outcome 1: Peer Dialogue Leaders will demonstrate positive changes in their cognitive development as defined by William Perry's (1970) theory of cognitive development and Baxter Magolda's (1992) epistemological reflection model. Specifically, PDLs will show positive movement along Perry's continuum.	I. Cognitive complexity	**Measure:** Yin's (2003) view of the use of theory and research hypotheses in explanatory, evaluative case studies guides the data analysis for this research question. The research hypothesis will be tested using a pattern matching technique (Yin, 2003) in which patterns generated by the case study data will be compared to the pattern of cognitive development for college students that would be predicted by Perry's theory and the epistemological reflection model. Specifically, these theories would predict that undergraduate students would typically move from a position of dualistic thinking (absolute or either/or thinking) to one more consistent with multiplicity (an ability to see multiple perspectives). **Criteria:** At the end of the training semester, more than half of the students in the study will show positive change in cognitive development, most likely from dualistic to multiplistic thinking depending on each student's position at the start of the study. **Preliminary findings:** Preliminary findings indicate that the overall experience of participating in the training program and co-leading the dialogue group promotes cognitive development. For example: • Students report that being taught concepts of dualism and multiplicity in the training program promotes introspection and self-reflection on their own past and current ways of thinking which, in turn, promotes increased complexity in thinking • Pre- and post- interviews indicate that the students were thinking more complexly about the topic of the dialogue group they led (awareness of multiple perspectives) after leading the group than they were prior to leading the group. • Results from the MID indicated that six of the eight students showed positive change during the training semester along the Perry continuum and five of eight showed positive change of half a position or greater. Of the remaining two students who showed no change, one started at a very high position at the beginning of the study.	Still in progress

(continued)

Student Learning Outcomes (list only those assessed during this time period)	Outcome Category* (I–VII)	Assessment Measure, Criteria, and Results	Impact of Results
Outcome 2: Peer Dialogue Leaders will demonstrate an increased ability to see and understand multiple perspectives on multicultural societal dilemmas.	I. Cognitive complexity; III. Humanitarianism	**Measure:** Interpretative analysis will be used to analyze case study data from participant interviews and journals for examples of increased understanding of multiple perspectives. **Criteria:** At the end of the semester, a majority of students in the study will show positive change in their ability to see and understand multiple perspectives. **Preliminary findings:** Initial review of the data supports the supposition that the PDL training experience enhances exposure to and perception of multiple perspectives. For example: • PDLs report that exposure to the varying views expressed among participants in the groups broadens their own perspectives on the topics. • PDLs report that the experience of withholding their own opinions when co-leading the dialogue group (being a "neutral" facilitator) forces them to listen in a different way, which helps them gain increased insights into the multiple perspectives that dialogue group participants put forth on any given topic.	Still in progress
Outcome 3: Peer Dialogue Leaders will learn additional skills and/or perspectives as a result of their participation in the training program.	Yet to be determined because of the exploratory phase of assessment	**Measure:** Exploratory case study methods will examine additional learning outcomes due to participation in the PDL training program. **Criteria:** Relevant learning outcomes that emerge from the study will be highlighted as outcomes of the training program. **Preliminary findings:** Examples of self-reported learning outcomes that are emerging from an initial review of the data include the following: • Acquisition of dialogue facilitation skills (e.g., listening, effective questioning, paraphrasing, summarizing) • Increased understanding of dualistic and multiplistic thinking, including self-reflection and analysis • Increased awareness of personal communication style • Reduction of stereotypes • Increased self-confidence	Still in progress

*Outcome Categories for Student Affairs (adapted from *Learning Reconsidered*):

    I. Cognitive complexity
    II. Knowledge acquisition, integration, and application
   III. Humanitarianism
   IV. Civic engagement
    V. Interpersonal and intrapersonal competence
   VI. Practical competence
  VII. Persistence and academic achievement

Source: Rhonda Vorhees and the University of Maryland Student Affairs Learning Outcomes Group

APPENDIX 7.2   Annual Program Assessment Form

Program:

Degree:

Chair: Academic Year: 20__/20__ (Addressing Outcome # or Outcome # to #)

Student Learning Outcomes	Performance Criteria	Evidence of Intentional Commitment to Address and Assess Outcome(s) Across the Program	Program-Level Assessment Method(s) and Timing
Upon completion of program, students are expected to (know and be able to do): 1. 2. 3. 4. 5. 6. 7. (Or attach specialized or professional accreditors' standards)	List specific attributes—knowledge, skills, behaviors, etc. you expect students to exhibit that reveal achievement of specific outcome(s) assessed during this cycle. Attach a scoring rubric if you used one.	Identify the collaborative means you used to ascertain that students have multiple and varied opportunities to learn a program-level outcome or outcomes, such as through curricular mapping, an audit or review of syllabi, or an inventory of teaching, learning, and assessment practices.	Identify the direct and indirect methods you chose or will choose to gather evidence of students' attainment of the program-level outcomes and to answer your research or study question.

Expected Level of Achievement	Actual Level of Achievement	Analysis and Interpretation of Data	Actions Taken	Timetable for Reassessment
Identify the level of norm-based or criteria-based performance you expect graduating students to achieve.	Identify students' actual level of achievement against the expected performance level.	Identify the recommendations that emerged from your interpretation of student evidence and other data.	Describe the actions you have taken (or will take) with particular focus on improving teaching and learning.	Identify when you have reassessed or will reassess specific outcomes to ascertain the efficacy of actions you have taken or will take. If you have already reassessed, what did you find?

Chapter **8**

BUILDING A CORE INSTITUTIONAL PROCESS OF INQUIRY OVER TIME

Good-to-great transformations often look like dramatic, revolutionary events to those observing from the outside, but they feel like organic, cumulative processes to people on the inside. The confusion of end outcomes (dramatic results) with process (organic and cumulative) skews our perception of what really works over the long haul. No matter how dramatic the end result, the good-to-great transformations never happened in one fell swoop. There was no single beginning action, no grand program, no one killer innovation, no solitary lucky break, no miracle moment.

—Jim Collins, 2001

> **OVERVIEW:** The preceding chapters focused on the decisions and tasks that characterize progression through one cycle of inquiry. This final chapter explores how this initiative matures over time to become embedded into institutional life as a core institutional process. The maturational process occurs by establishing intentional links or connections with other campus structures, processes, decisions, and channels of communication, often resulting in complementary or new relationships or new institutional behaviors. Further, it advances through a commitment of human, financial, educational, and technological support. It also manifests itself through new campus practices that publicly and intentionally recognize the enduring value of this work in advancing both institutional and student learning. Representative campuses included in this chapter illustrate some of the ways that institutions are strengthening their commitment. The Worksheets, Guides, and Exercises at the end of this chapter are designed (1) to promote institutional self-reflection about a campus's current commitment to assessing for learning and (2) to stimulate collective discussion about ways in which that current commitment may deepen or expand into a core institutional process focused on advancing institutional and student learning.

A VIEW OF THE WHOLE

"We were doing fine until our provost left." "Our director of assessment left, so we haven't been able to sustain our commitment." "We are waiting to hire a new president." When assessment rests on the belief that one person sustains an institutional commitment, chances are that the commitment has not been deeply embedded into institutional life. It may be ingrained in some programs or services but not necessarily deeply rooted in campus life. Some members of the academic community may understand assessment's integral relationship to teaching and learning and its contribution to collective learning. Others may not share that understanding at all. An institutional commitment to assessing for learning builds over time as a campus or system learns how to develop, integrate, or adapt practices, structures, processes, and channels of communication that support and value a collective commitment to institutional learning. Further, as members of an academic community become more knowledgeable about the interdependent tasks that characterize a collective commitment, expertise grows as well.

Institutional size and resources may shape the practices, structures, processes, and channels of communication that support a collective commitment to assessment. Describing an absolute model that suits all institutions ignores issues of size and capacity and the ways in which a college or university achieves its mission and purposes. In some institutions, a collective commitment to assessment may be achieved by expanding the responsibilities of existing bodies, such as an office of institutional research and planning; or the curriculum committee may expand its work to include ownership of assessing institution-level outcomes. In other institutions a collective commitment may initiate new practices and structures, such as the creation of a campus assessment committee. How assessment translates into institutional life and rhythms, how it becomes visible, is the focus of this chapter. Seeding and growing a commitment to this process depends on numerous variables, such as identifying previous institutional strategies that contributed to and fostered successful change. Thus, rather than prescribing an absolute model, this chapter describes representative ways colleges and universities manifest and value a collective commitment to assessing for learning. Specifically, it describes the following:

1. Structures, processes, decisions, and channels and forms of communication

2. Resources and support: human, financial, educational, and technological

3. Campus practices that manifest an institutional commitment

SOME REPRESENTATIVE STRUCTURES, PROCESSES AND DECISIONS, AND CHANNELS AND FORMS OF COMMUNICATION

Representative Structures

Assessment Committees

Often beginning as an ad hoc committee or a task force, over time an *institutional assessment committee* evolves into a formal committee that develops a mission and purpose statement, describes its roles and responsibilities, and establishes rotational membership from across a campus to build a collective commitment to and advance understanding about the process of assessment. In collaboration with institutional constituencies such as division chairs from across the institution, it schedules and oversees cycles of inquiry and receives the results and interpretations of those cycles. Assessment committees channel these results and interpretations into annual budgeting cycles and into the larger institutional plans developed by the office of research and planning. Absent an institutional research and planning office on campus, an assessment committee may channel its annually collected results and interpretations into the institution's vice president's or provost's annual planning.

As the committee matures, it sustains inquiry into institution- and program-level inquiry by doing the following:

- Establishing, making public within the institution, and periodically revising a campus plan to improve student learning through assessment at the institution and program levels
- Coordinating assessment efforts across an institution to establish annual cycles of inquiry
- In conjunction with leadership, establishing formal institutional times for collective discussion of, reflection on, and interpretation of results leading to actions to improve student learning
- Distributing learning across the institution based on assessment results, interpretations, and actions to improve student learning, such as on a website
- Providing guidance to the larger educational community through in-house, web-based, and online resources about assessment practices and methods
- Providing peer or mentor assistance to support working groups as they progress through assessment cycles

- Periodically reviewing the efficacy of its role in improving student learning
- Recognizing exemplary accomplishments in assessment work across the institution

As you have read throughout this book, assessment committees, often named student learning committees, to capture the goal of assessment, may also create core working groups or arms to carry out specific assessment tasks. A core working group consisting of faculty, staff, administrators, students, local professionals, and alumni, for example, may develop an institution-level outcome statement that describes how students would demonstrate or represent civic responsibility. Another group may be formed to analyze results of direct and indirect methods and present them to the educational community, which, in turn, forms crossdisciplinary or specialized groups to interpret results and determine ways to improve student learning. Or, assessment committees may create inquiry circles, groups of faculty, staff, or even students who track students' learning over time through multiple methods of assessment. The specific arms at work at Portland State are described in Box. 8.1.

Building in times for its own self-assessment, an assessment committee periodically evaluates its practices for several purposes:

- To ensure that faculty, staff, and administrators use and act on interpretations of assessment results to improve student learning
- To ensure that interpretations of assessment results are channeled into short-term and long-term institutional planning and budgeting to focus institutional decision making and planning on student learning
- To ascertain how well institution- and program-level educational practices are evolving based on the learning emerging from cycles of inquiry—that is, how do members of an academic community learn, share, and build on that learning?

Over time, assessment committees link with other institutional bodies or infuse assessment into their work. Curriculum committees may begin to assume increased responsibility for reviewing course and program proposals or reviewing current courses and programs within agreed-upon institution- and program-level outcomes. Viewing courses and proposals within this larger context, they may seek, for example, to understand how components of a course or a program contribute to both institution- and program-level outcomes, that is, how they contribute to curricular coherence. Increasingly, teaching and learning centers, also called teaching, learning, and assessment centers, are integrating assessment practices and methods into their work and developing workshops to assist faculty and staff as they develop assessment methods and embed them along the continuum of student's learning. Faculty and staff development committees also recognize the significance of awarding funding to individuals or groups interested in designing an assessment project. Representatives from faculty governance committees often serve on assessment committees; some governance committees now embed assessment into their

---

BOX 8.1 INSTITUTIONAL EXAMPLE: *Portland State University*

Portland State University's deepened commitment to assessing student learning is reflected in the various arms of support that are available to the larger educational community. Among these arms are the following:

1. Implementation teams for each school or division, led by a dean, an associate dean, a lead faculty, faculty teams, and one graduate assistant
2. A cadre of graduate students who have taken the university's Academic Assessment Course designed for graduate students and assist in school or division assessment projects
3. A network of resources on assessment practices
4. Professional development opportunities that are organized based on the needs that faculty express

That is, the university has expanded its institutional commitment to support and sustain collective work.

Source: Terrel L. Rhodes, Portland State University.

routine discussions and decisions to position assessment as a core focus of their work, as illustrated in Figure 8.1.

Figure 8.1 represents the structure and process of assessment at the United States Naval Academy (USNA). As you will read in the institutional example in Box 8.2, the USNA's original assessment task force emerged as part of the institution's strategic planning and is now evolving into several central agencies that will assume responsibility for sustaining various inquiry cycles. These cycles focus on determining how well midshipmen achieve institution- and program-level learning outcomes. Significant in this model are channels of communication between the agencies and three working groups focused on specific aspects of assessment: developing criteria based on learning outcomes, developing methods or using instruments to

assess those outcomes, and developing ways to analyze results. In addition, the agencies of assessment receive analyses and interpretations of assessment data and direct analyses and community interpretations back into programs that then assume responsibility for improving and reassessing student learning.

Within an institution, individual schools, programs, and divisions, such as the Division of Student Services, also establish assessment committees, microcosms of an institution-level committee. These committees establish individual assessment plans that develop cycles of inquiry to assess several levels of outcomes: institution-level outcomes expected of all undergraduate and graduate students, those particular to the division itself, and those particular to the programs and services that are housed in student services. Similarly, academic divisions or schools within a uni-

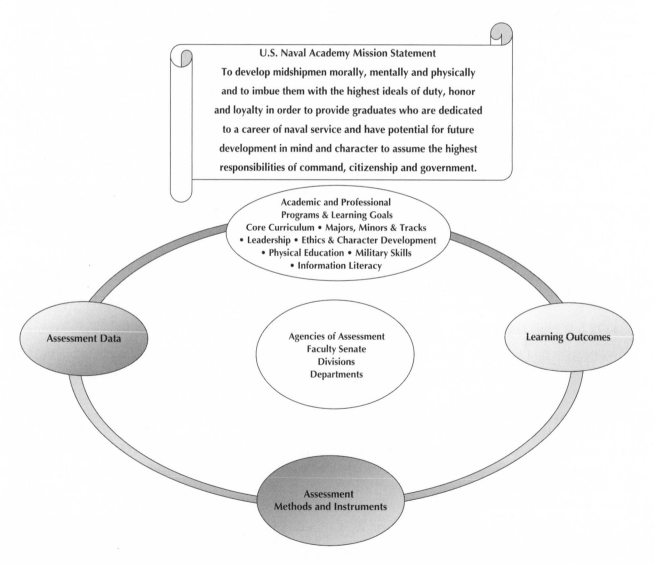

FIGURE 8.1   Structure and Process of Assessment at the USNA

BOX 8.2   INSTITUTIONAL EXAMPLE: *United States Naval Academy*

In the spring of 1999, the United States Naval Academy (USNA) completed a strategic plan that incorporates a list of 11 capabilities and attributes to be attained by graduates in support of the USNA mission to *develop midshipmen morally, mentally and physically and to imbue them with the highest ideals of duty, honor and loyalty in order to provide graduates who are dedicated to a career of naval service and have potential for future development in mind and character to assume the highest responsibilities of command, citizenship and government.*

The various mission-related expectations for graduates are that they should be highly effective communicators, exhibiting high moral and ethical behavior; be exemplars of academic, technical, and tactical competence; and able to understand and integrate geopolitical complexities in their decision making. In addition, one of the goals under the Strategic Plan Focus Area of Academic Excellence is to foster an educational environment that supports and encourages midshipmen in learning and critical thinking. The rationales for assessment at the naval academy are, first, to validate the academy's achievement of these capabilities and attributes in its graduates and, second, to guide continuous improvement.

Assessment at the USNA is designed to address the academy's full range of academic and professional programs, as shown at the top of the loop in Figure 8.1. These areas define the learning goals and educational experiences that constitute the USNA learning environment and form the starting point of assessment. The agencies responsible for assessment include the academy-wide Assessment Task Force that will be transformed into the newly established Faculty Senate Committee on Academic Assessment, the academic and professional development divisions, and other departments and centers with responsibility for student learning (listed in the center of the assessment loop in Figure 8.1).

Moving to the right from the Academic and Professional Programs and Learning Goals, the first step is to develop learning outcomes. The next step is to develop instruments and other methods for collecting and evaluating evidence of student learning. The third step is to analyze and interpret the results and feed them back into the program(s) responsible for the learning goals—that is, close the loop. Of course, it is possible to start at any point in the loop. For example, one could begin with data already collected to determine whether the desired learning has occurred or even whether the most reliable and valid methods were used. Or developing assessment criteria may help focus one's goals and develop or select appropriate assessment methods.

USNA implemented this model first by looking at institution-wide goals that are supported by the core curriculum and academic programs. The development of assessment plans by academic departments related to the goals associated with majors, minors, and tracks quickly followed. Recently, leadership assessment and the assessment of midshipmen ethics and character development have begun. Planning for the assessment of the core curriculum will begin in 2004.

This model provides a common language and process for communicating, coordinating, and integrating assessment at the United States Naval Academy and, ultimately, for validating graduates'

Source: Peter Gray, United States Naval Academy.

versity develop cycles of inquiry to assess similar levels of outcomes:

- Those expected of all undergraduate or graduate students
- Those particular to a school, for example, a school of design

- Those particular to a specific area of concentration, such as interior design

Similar to the various working groups that are established in institution-wide committees, these units may also form separate working groups or constitute themselves as a working group. Members may serve on an assessment committee for 2 to 3 years, after which a new member of a division or school would join the group. Just as an institution-wide assessment committee calendars cycles of inquiry, these program-level committees develop cycles that become a part of the campus's plan. That is, they present results and interpretations to the institution's assessment committee and share them during more formal institutional occasions.

Offices of Institutional Research and Planning

Offices of institutional research and planning or offices of institutional effectiveness often work with campus assessment committees as they establish an assessment plan or help support or coordinate their efforts. In addition, these offices assist core working teams as they select or design methods of assessment, develop rubrics, and collect, analyze, and interpret results. (See also pages 263 and 267–269 in chapter 6). Given their role of collecting data on numerous institutional fronts and for numerous purposes and given their expertise in assessment design, selection, and methods of collecting and analyzing results, offices of institutional research and planning support institutional assessment committees. Specifically, they do the following:

- Position groups to plan assessment backward—to identify the kinds of evidence or data they will need to gather to answer the research or study question coupled with an outcome or outcomes
- Offer expertise on both the selection and administration of assessment methods that contribute to answering research or study questions

- House additional institutional data that may deepen community-based interpretations
- Become a means to channel assessment results and interpretations into institutional decision making, planning, and budgeting

Box 8.3 describes the role of Rose-Hulman Institute of Technology's director of assessment.

Processes and Decisions

Institutional processes and decisions, such as those involved in annual professional reviews, may include criteria focused on an individual's contribution to program- or institution-level assessment. Promotion and tenure criteria may be revised to place value on a commitment to assessment as a form of scholarship (refer to pages 24 in chapter 1). Decisions about program- and institution-level budgeting may focus on ways to deepen an institutional commitment through allocation of human, financial, educational, and technological support. Further, developing an institutional annual and long-range planning calendar that synchronizes assessment results and interpretations with the timing of deliberations and decisions about planning and budgeting represents an institutional commitment. This scheduling recognizes that information about student learning and ways to improve it systematically guide decision making at the highest institutional level. Other institutional decisions and processes may eventually contribute to strengthening and deepening the commitment: decisions about hiring individuals who are experienced in or willing to learn more about various kinds of conventional or technology-enabled assessment methods; decisions about release time; or decisions about resource

---

BOX 8.3   INSTITUTIONAL EXAMPLE: *Rose-Hulman Institute of Technology*

At Rose-Hulman Institute of Technology, the college's Committee on the Assessment of Student Outcomes is co-chaired by a faculty member and the director of institutional research, planning, and assessment. The director's role is to relieve committee members of the administrative aspects of assessment and to serve as a resource. That is, the committee focuses on developing learning outcomes, methods of assessment, rubrics, scoring processes and scorer training, and review of results. The director focuses on ways to assist the decisions committee members make, thus enabling them to focus primarily on how to capture and score student learning and unburdening them from additional responsibility for the logistics of the process.

Source: Gloria Rogers, Rose-Hulman Institute of Technology.

allocation, for example, can reflect assessment as an institutional priority.

Channels and Forms of Communication

Expanding or developing channels and forms of communication also characterizes an institutional commitment to assessment as a core institutional process. These channels build on and distribute learning to do the following:

- Share information in order to promote discussions about teaching and learning at the institution and program levels
- Engage members of the community in interpretive dialogue that leads to change or innovation and builds on institutional learning
- Inform institutional decision making, planning, and budgeting focused on improving student learning

Figure 8.2 represents both channels of communication and decision making at Clarke College, illustrating how the assessment process has become a core institutional learning process, involving educators, institutional leaders, and board members as well. That is, the college has fully integrated assessment into a rhythm of its life.

At both the institution and program or department levels, building in formal times to focus on teaching and learning and the development of methods to assess learning becomes a hallmark of an institutional commitment to assessment. These times also provide professional opportunity for educators not only to share educational practices, but also to design sequences of practices that foster desired learning. Results of assessment provide evidence of the efficacy of those designs. These results contribute to institutional learning. Over time, educators do the following:

- Build on this learning
- Develop and share innovative practices or redesign the curriculum and co-curriculum
- More intentionally align the curriculum and co-curriculum
- Develop or adapt new educational practices to provide alternative ways of learning

Campuses can develop another channel of communication by bringing together members of a campus community to share and interpret institution- and program-level assessment results in formal campus-wide forums designed to (1) learn about institutional practices, (2) explore new practices, (3) learn about assessment results, and (4) build institutional learning based on those results. Based on assessment results, how do programs intentionally contribute to or build on institution-wide learning outcomes? Similarly, how does an institution's core curriculum contribute to learning outcomes within programs, such as students' abilities to bring multiple perspectives to solving problems? Program-level assessment results, such as patterns of students' inability to reflect and act on the ethical dimensions of disciplinary problems, need to come forward to the educational community at large, especially when those results reflect institutional intentions. Bringing program-level results to the larger community triggers collective interpretation and discussion about ways the institution and its programs and services can more intentionally foster desired learning. Breaking an educational community into groups that explore assessment results and then develop complementary approaches to improving student learning develops a collective commitment to learning. Public forums provide an opportunity for that kind of community dialogue.

Further, communication channels are necessary to funnel new initiatives into institutional decision making, planning, and budgeting. Assessment committees, institutional research and planning offices, and annual program- and institution-level budgets can serve as those channels. They can earmark support for financial or human resources or support that advances an institution's commitment to improving learning, such as opportunities for faculty and staff to learn about research on learning, developments in assessment practices, or developments in disciplinary pedagogy. For example, based on evidence of students' lower-than-expected quantitative reasoning abilities, an annual institutional budget may propose developing or providing workshops for faculty, staff, and administrators to help them develop additional ways to integrate quantitative reasoning across the curriculum so that students' continuum of learning includes multiple opportunities to develop this way of reasoning. Offices of institutional research and planning become a major communication channel that synthesizes interpretations and decisions to improve learning and transmits that information into annual and longer-range institutional planning and decision making.

Multiple forms of communication also reflect an institution's commitment to assessing for learning.

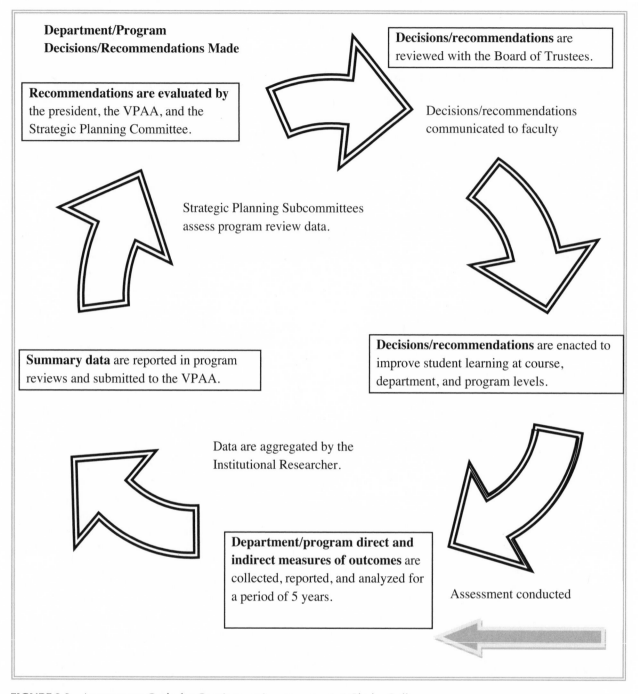

FIGURE 8.2   Assessment Cycle for Continuous Improvement at Clarke College
Source: M. Lynn Lester, BVM, Clarke College

Catalogs, recruitment materials, public documents, and an institution's website reflect this focus for external audiences. Internally, newsletters, resource websites, access to student data that informs interpretations, forms of recognition of assessment projects or leaders of these projects, and documents that help students map their learning exemplify some of the ways this focus translates into institutional life.

Institutional knowledge leads to change when it is distributed over multiple channels of communication. The institutional example described in Box 8.4 and illustrated in Figure 8.3 represents how institutional learning and change occur when a systematic and systemic process of assessment evolves. Institutional rhythms move information into institutional planning and decision making that support proposed changes.

BOX 8.4   INSTITUTIONAL EXAMPLE: *Indiana University–Purdue University Indianapolis*

Indiana University–Purdue University Indianapolis (IUPUI) is building a culture based on evidence (see Figure 8.3). Coordinated by the Office of Planning and Institutional Improvement (PAII), assessment begins with a planning phase in which the campus vision, mission, and goals are established and unit goals are aligned. In academic programs and individual courses, faculty set learning outcomes for students—some discipline-specific and all integrating IUPUI's six Principles of Undergraduate Learning (PULs). Developed over years of discussion involving faculty, students, and staff and approved by the Faculty Council in 1998 and reaffirmed in 2007, the PULs describe the intellectual competence and cultural awareness that every baccalaureate recipient should attain. They are Core Communication and Quantitative Skills; Critical Thinking; Integration and Application of Knowledge; Intellectual Depth, Breadth, and Adaptiveness; Understanding Society and Culture; and Values and Ethics.

Each year deans and vice chancellors use a web-based template organized according to campus goals (www.imir.iupui.edu/annualplan) to report progress on their goals and objectives. They draw on data the institution has assembled at the campus level (e.g., student enrollment and retention data, survey findings, financial ratios) as well as information gathered on their own. Members of the Program Review and Assessment Committee—faculty from each school, librarians, and student affairs staff—use a matrix format to report annual progress on learning outcomes as well as improvement actions taken on the basis of assessment findings (www.planning.iupui.edu/prac/prac.html). Using this top-down, bottom-up iterative approach over the past decade, PAII staff have created performance indicators that demonstrate campus progress on 10 mission-critical goals (iport.iupui.edu/pr/).

Currently IUPUI is developing an e-portfolio that will enable students to demonstrate their learning in connection with each of the PULs. Competence at introductory and intermediate levels is being defined by multidisciplinary campus groups, whereas competence at advanced levels is defined by faculty in each discipline. Planned assessment of the electronic portfolios by faculty will yield evidence for evaluating progress as a campus in advancing student learning of the PULs.

Although work on the student e-portfolio is still in a formative stage, comprehensive academic program reviews involving external disciplinary and community peers in campus visits have been underway since 1994. The university's first locally developed surveys for students were administered by PAII staff that same year. And since then the institution has developed companion surveys containing a core of similar items for IUPUI alumni, faculty, and staff. PAII maintains a rich array of management information to meet the needs of deans and vice chancellors and conduct detailed analyses for both academic and administrative units. Economic modeling services offered by PAII staff link budgets with unit planning and evaluation initiatives. Having become a leader in the development of web-based assessment tools such as placement tests, course evaluations, and surveys, in 2002 IUPUI became the first institution in the North Central region to use an electronic institutional portfolio to present its self-study for regional accreditation (www.iport.iupui.edu).

Institutional improvement is embedded in the PAII title and is always a paramount goal in collecting and using evidence. For example, enrollment data showing an increasingly younger student body on this urban commuter campus, coupled with disappointing retention statistics and student survey responses indicating the need for more campus programs and services, led to the creation in 1999 of University College. UC is the point of entry for all undergraduates and provides a variety of programs designed to enhance learning and increase retention, including freshman learning communities, peer mentoring, and supplemental instruction in reading and mathematics as well as other introductory courses. Assessment focused on each of UC's initiatives has led to refinements in the learning community model, a gateway initiative providing student support and engaging instructors of our largest introductory courses in faculty development experiences, and modification of supplemental instruction to institute a structured learning assistance model. Survey data have been used to suggest improvements and to monitor their impact in such areas as advising, registration, placement

(continued)

testing, and even campus parking! Program reviews, the university's most comprehensive assessment vehicles, have shaped faculty hiring, curricula and degree programs, departmental planning processes, and crossdisciplinary collaboration. Finally, IUPUI's ability to document claims of program progress and distinction using data and other forms of evidence has helped garner awards and recognition from the American Productivity and Quality Center, the Association of American Colleges and Universities, the American Association of State Colleges and Universities, the National Consortium for Continuous Improvement in Higher Education, and the Policy Center on the First Year of College. In addition, in 2002 IUPUI received a Theodore M. Hesburgh Certificate of Excellence for its gateway initiative, and in 2006 IUPUI was recognized by the Council for Higher Education Accreditation in its inaugural competition for Institutional Progress in Student Learning Outcomes.

Source: Trudy W. Banta, professor of higher education and Vice Chancellor for Planning and Institutional Improvement.

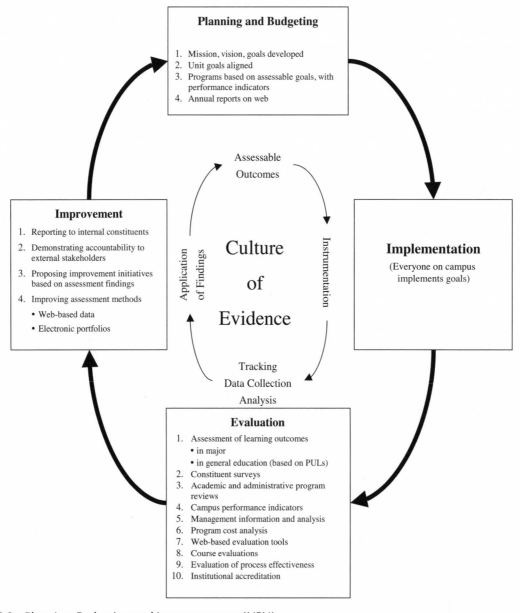

FIGURE 8.3 Planning, Evaluation and Improvement at IUPUI

Source: Trudy W. Banta, Indiana University—Purdue University Indianapolis.

RESOURCES AND SUPPORT: HUMAN, FINANCIAL, AND EDUCATIONAL

As is the case with other core institutional processes, commitment of human, financial, and educational support underlies the startup as well as sustainability of assessing for learning. Initially, a startup assessment committee may be the source of an institution's support, having received some institutional allocation of finances to do the following:

- Set up a website or an in-house resource that provides resources on assessment practices and methods
- Offer, often in conjunction with teaching and learning centers, workshops focused on assessment practices
- Establish a cadre of faculty and staff who mentor and help colleagues through various assessment-related tasks, such as developing outcome statements, designing or selecting assessment methods that align with what and how students learn, developing and pilot-testing scoring rubrics, or articulating research or study questions
- Support faculty and staff to attend assessment-related conferences or convenings, including disciplinary and professional meetings

Eventually, resources come from multiple institutional contributors, reflecting the depth and pervasiveness of a campus commitment, such as from institution- and program-level budgets, faculty and staff development budgets, teaching center budgets, and grants to support the following:

- Design or initiation of an institution- or program-level assessment project
- Personnel necessary to carry out a project
- Technological assistance such as in creating an institution- or program-level portfolio that documents efforts across the campus and builds institutional knowledge about practices, results, and innovations to improve learning
- Faculty and staff participation in conferences that contribute to their learning about assessment practices or to which they contribute
- Development of online or in-house resources
- Development of workshops that educate about new practices or bring together faculty and staff to share their practices

As the Portland State University example illustrates on page 285, a core institutional process requires not only physical resources to sustain the commitment, but also human support, such as through the assistance of graduate students. Human support may be needed for other purposes as well, such as in the following:

- Collecting students' responses or work
- Pilot-testing a rubric or proposed assessment methods
- Conducting indirect methods of assessment that require interaction with students, such as Small Group Instructional Diagnosis
- Videotaping teamwork or students' think alouds
- Scoring student work or responses
- Analyzing assessment results
- Preparing results for the educational community to interpret, leading to consensus about necessary institution- and program-level changes or innovations

As is increasingly becoming the case, centers for teaching and learning, now often called centers for teaching, learning, and assessment, have taken on the central role of integrating assessment into both the curriculum and co-curriculum. Annual workshops, presentations, symposia, and on-demand consultancies with faculty and other educators keep assessment at the forefront of curricular and co-curricular design. Placing a demand on center directors to continue to reach out to constituencies, some center directors have developed faculty fellow positions to assist the center with this ongoing commitment. The director of the Center for University Teaching, Learning, and Assessment (CUTLA) at the University of West Florida has created such a position: a CUTLA fellow helps the director meet requests for consultancies focused on instructional strategies, assessment, and other matters related to teaching and learning (http://uwf.edu/cutla/consult_services.cfm).

RESOURCES AND SUPPORT: TECHNOLOGICAL

Locally designed or commercially designed assessment management systems have become the means by which many institutions are now chronicling their annual assessment efforts. That is, one system provides relevant documentation of annual assessment cycles, findings, and interpretations; helps track and analyze assessment results from individual students and cohorts of students; and often also includes and supports e-portfolios.

Advancements in technology, namely locally designed or commercially designed assessment management systems, now make it possible to support and house the assessment process. Relying on shared formats and expectations for reporting, one repository can now store, track, and report the results of analyzing student work, including aggregating and disaggregating assessment results to inform collaborative decision making. In addition, constituencies can disaggregate populations to look more closely, for example, at sets of educational experiences students have had that may contribute to their levels of achievement. The advantage of these systems is their capacity to house and chronologically document the entire assessment process at the institution, department, and program levels so that one reliable source of evidence and data about student learning is accessible to members of an educational community in commonly agreed-upon formats and sets of reporting expectations.

Most of these systems can chronologically track not only individual student achievement but also cohorts' achievement of a specific outcome over time—from an outcome in a general education course to the same one in courses in a major program of study. In addition, most of these systems have now incorporated e-portfolios for faculty, students, and the institution itself and also store scoring rubrics that internal or external scorers apply to student work. These portfolios provide not only internal but multiple external audiences with diverse kinds of longitudinal evidence of student learning accessible through multiple paths of inquiry. What and how evidence of student learning will be stored and assessed will change as technology offers broader options and environments for representing students' processes and products of learning.

Locally Designed Assessment Management Systems

Box 8.4 describes the web-based system developed at Indiana University–Purdue University Indianapolis—a shared way for educators to post or store information that others can access as well, promoting a collective institutional commitment to assessment. Appendix 8.1 describes and illustrates the University of Nebraska–Lincoln's assessment model supported by an online assessment system (adapted from one at the University

of Colorado) that has centralized a faculty-led program-level assessment process. The PEARL Project (Program Excellence through Assessment, Research, and Learning), UNL's organizational assessment model, is anchored in a peer review process during which faculty outside a specific program or department comment on the program's or department's assessment plans, activities, and results. As illustrated in the pages extracted from the online system (pages 306–314), the peer review process (1) facilitates and supports conversations among faculty and other internal and external constituencies, such as dialogue about a program's lead research or study question, and (2) helps programs coordinate documentation for multiple reporting requirements through an established reporting template.

Some Representative Commercially Designed Assessment Management Systems

Given the time demands to develop a homegrown system, alternatively institutions have chosen to purchase commercially designed assessment management systems that chronologically, almost annually, develop capacities to mirror the assessment process, integrate developments in accreditation, and address institutions' requests for improvements based on their campus experiences using these systems. For example, as accreditation standards are revised or updated or when professional bodies develop criteria, such as is the case with Association of American Colleges & Universities' (AAC&U) Valid Assessment of Learning in Undergraduate Education (VALUE) rubrics, commercial vendors download these chronological developments into their systems so that educators can immediately align their outcomes, student work, and assessment results accordingly. These systems also mirror the assessment process by helping to develop outcomes, map outcomes, provide resources for or questions about aligned methods of assessment, incorporate (or even help design) scoring rubrics, aggregate and disaggregate results, and require documentation of assessment results, including reflection on and decisions about ways to improve students' patterns of weakness. Representative commercially designed assessment management systems are briefly described in Appendix 8.2 to provide an overview of their capacities.

Selecting a commercially designed assessment management system should become a collaborative decision involving constituencies across the institution so that everyone works within one system, understands how it functions, and learns how to enter and access relevant chronological data and evidence. These systems do not replace human judgment; rather, they provide the tools to facilitate and coordinate the underlying tasks that contribute to the assessment process and to the collaborative discussions focused on ways to improve student learning. The following considerations help in the selection process:

- Initial cost of the system
- Flexibility in incorporating specific institutional needs into initial cost
- Annual costs (such as per student or annual institutional allocation)
- Maintenance responsibilities and costs
- Ability to adapt, convert, or draw on current institutional data management systems
- Ease of use to attract educators to become accustomed to working with the system
- On-site and web-based training that is included in initial and ongoing cost of the system
- Cost of ongoing training as new developments occur in a system
- Support for troubleshooting
- Ease in accessing support
- System responsiveness to emerging needs or changes in assessment and accreditation requirements or demands
- Future design plans especially as they relate to your institution's projected needs, such as incorporating e-portfolios
- Compatibility with your institution's current or emerging model of assessment—such as a chronological problem-based approach to answering research or study questions coupled with your outcome statements (discussed in chapter 4).

CAMPUS PRACTICES THAT MANIFEST AN INSTITUTIONAL COMMITMENT

A commitment to assessing for learning translates itself into institutional practices that visibly represent an institution's level of commitment. These practices or norms of behavior include the ways in which institutions and programs orient students to their education and the ways in which institutions value—even celebrate—faculty and staff commitment. The following practices represent some of the major ways that manifest an institutional commitment to assessment:

1. Orientation of students to assessing for learning, beginning with their matriculation into the institution—that is, integration of this focus into students' first-year experiences or orientation seminars to prepare them to chronologically assess their achievements, as well as to inform them about institution- and program-level assessment practices designed to improve student learning (see Appendix 8.3 about the ethics of inquiry in relation to students)

2. Periods of formal and informal self-reflection built into institutional life as well as department- or program-level life focused on improving learning through collective interpretation of assessment results

3. Recognition of a commitment to assessment as professional and scholarly work through criteria established for promotion, tenure, or periodic review; these criteria recognize that this commitment contributes not only to institution- and program-level learning, but also to advancing practices in higher education through national, professional, and disciplinary projects and forums

4. Faculty and staff development opportunities dedicated to learning about research on learning and developments in educational practices that advance campus or disciplinary practices or build on current practices

5. Orientation of new faculty and staff to the institutional commitment with opportunity to shadow a current effort

6. Assessment days, weeks, or events that provide opportunities to calendar in assessment of student work through both direct and indirect methods. These times may also provide opportunities for students to present their work for public assessment from faculty, staff, administrators, peers, professional members of the community, members of advisory boards, and alumni, for example. That is, students represent their learning for multiple audiences who, in turn, assess their work. The example in Box 8.5 represents how an institution schedules an event that brings together members of an educational community.

7. Annual celebration of exemplary assessment plans and use of results to inform change

8. Annual symposia to share assessment practices and demonstrate interpretation of

assessment results that lead to changed educational practices

9. Incorporation of assessment results, agreed-upon changes in educational practices or pedagogy, and results of assessment of changed practices into periodic program review to focus on the centrality of student learning in our professional work. In contrast to traditional program review content that focused on inputs—number of faculty and their credentials, syllabi, number of majors, number of courses taught, and so on—more recent program reviews now also include a focus on assessment of student learning. Dunn, McCarthy, Baker, and Halonen (2011) identify assessment of student learning as one of the essential and most useful report elements of program review.

SIGNS OF MATURATION

A collective institutional commitment to assessing for learning emerges from intellectual curiosity about the efficacy of institutional practices in promoting student learning. Compelling questions, then, drive a process of discovery that brings a campus community together to gain knowledge about its students' learning and thereby build on, adapt, or innovate new practices designed to enhance learning. As assessment becomes incorporated into institutional life, relationships among learning outcome statements; the design of the curriculum, co-curriculum, instruction, pedagogy, and educational practices; and methods of assessment become a focus of collaborative work, creating new opportunities for institutional learning. Occasions for dialogue about teaching, learning, and assessment among all contributors to students' education, including students themselves, mark this collaboration.

As this collaboration deepens and becomes both systemic and systematic, the following developments will probably characterize this working relationship:

- Institutional forums designed to share research on learning or to discuss how to apply research on learning to pedagogy; the design of instruction, curriculum, and the co-curriculum; educational practices; or the use of educational tools
- Increased focus on how components of students' education build on each other to contribute to institution- and program-level learning outcomes
- Widened recognition of assessment as a field of scholarship that advances institution- and program-level knowledge that, in turn, advances educational practices within an institution and across the larger higher education community
- Increased responsiveness to research on how humans learn that prompts the development of varied educational practices and educational pathways

---

BOX 8.5   INSTITUTIONAL EXAMPLE: *University of Wisconsin–River Falls*

Patterned after a professional meeting poster session, the Assessment Fair is an opportunity for academic and co-curricular programs as well as individual faculty and staff members to showcase their assessment efforts to the entire university community. The poster session format allows participants to display their assessment efforts and share ideas, successes, and difficulties with others on campus.

Departments, committees or teams, and individuals are encouraged to present posters describing assessment activities they are involved in. Participants at all stages of developing and implementing assessment plans are sought. *A fully developed assessment plan is not necessary for participation.* Student organizations and others in the campus community involved in assessment are also encouraged to present their efforts.

The fair helps focus attention on assessment and is an excellent opportunity for all shareholders, whether faculty or students, to become more involved in continuing assessment efforts on campus. It is also an informal and nonthreatening means to gauge the progress the campus community is making toward a culture of effective assessment practices.

Source: Faculty Assessment Committee, University of Wisconsin–River Falls, Dr. Michael Middleton, Chair.

- Collaboration in the design of educational practices among members of an academic community, including instructional designers, and those outside the community who bring professional expertise to higher education, such as representatives from professional and disciplinary bodies who contribute national perspectives on and knowledge about developments in research and educational practices
- Collaboration with professional and national organizations, public audiences, alumni, professionals from the local community, or faculty from neighboring institutions to articulate criteria and quality standards of judgment
- Leadership from campus teaching and learning centers focused on integrating assessment into the processes of teaching and learning, developing conversations about philosophies or models of teaching and learning and the ways in which students progressively learn, and helping to design methods that align with what and how students learn in different contexts for learning
- Institution- and program-level representations of students' educational journey through curricula—co-curricular maps that help students visualize how courses and educational experiences contribute to their learning. These maps will also help students identify experiences that they believe will benefit them, encouraging them to take responsibility for their learning
- Integration of students into a culture of inquiry on matriculation so they become profilers of their own learning and self-reflective about how their learning builds over time
- Expansion of systematic ways to store and sample student work that can be aggregated and disaggregated for various internal and external audiences and purposes while humanizing, not standardizing, assessment based on the demographics of each of our institutions
- Given developments in technology, particularly the development of Web 2.0 e-portfolios, openness to identifying new forms of evidence of learning and new criteria to assess student work with particular focus on how

students draw on, blend, and integrate their learning, as opposed to compartmentalizing it
- Development of online learning communities focused on sharing (1) online or face-to-face pedagogies and educational practices that foster students' enduring learning in general education and in their major fields of study or professions, and (2) results of assessment methods that assess not only students' products but also their thinking-learning processes to prompt dialogue about ways to innovate or adapt educational practices to improve student learning

Actualizing a professional philosophy, repositioning oneself in relation to a concept, integrating disciplinary learning that shapes decision making, solving murky problems—these are among the complex issues that colleges and universities prepare students to address. Simplistic assessment methods by themselves cannot capture that complexity. Multiple assessment methods that align with what and how students learn can document the depth and breadth of students' achievement, representing the diverse ways in which students construct meaning.

WORKS CITED

American Council on Education. (2001). *On change 5: Riding the waves of change: Insights on transforming institutions.* Washington, D.C.: Author.

Collins, J. (2001). *From good to great.* New York: Harper-Collins.

Dunn, D. S., McCarthy, M. A., Baker, S., & Halonen, J. (2011, forthcoming). *Using quality benchmarks for assessing and developing undergraduate programs.* San Francisco, CA: Jossey Bass.

ADDITIONAL RESOURCES

Middaugh, M. F. (2010). *Planning and assessment in higher education.* San Francisco, CA: Jossey Bass.

Nichols, J. O., & Nichols, K. W. (2000). *The departmental guide and record book for student outcomes assessment and institutional effectiveness* (3rd ed.). New York: Agathon Press.

Nichols, J. O., et al. (1995). *A practitioner's handbook for institutional effectiveness and student learning outcomes assessment implementation* (3rd ed.). Edison, NJ: Agathon Press.

Palomba, C. A., & Banta, T. W. (1999). *Assessment essentials: Planning, implementing, improving.* San Francisco: Jossey-Bass.

Pet-Armacost, J., & Armacost, R. L. (2002, April). Creating an effective assessment organization and environment. NASPA *NetResults. www.naspa.org/pubs/mags/ nr/archive.cfm* (Restricted to NASPA members only.)

Primary Research Group. (2008). *Survey of assessment practices in higher education.* Rockville, MD: Market Research. A benchmark study of 80 institutions on how they structure, support, and conduct assessment.

Rogers, G. M., & Sando, Jean K. (1996). *Stepping ahead: An assessment plan development guide.* Terre Haute, IN: Rose-Hulman Institute of Technology.

Case Studies

Banta, T. W., Lund, L. P., Black, K. E., & Oblander, F. W. (1996). *Assessment in practice: Putting principles to work on college campuses.* San Francisco: Jossey-Bass.

Maki, P. (2010). *Coming to terms with assessment: Faculty and administrators' journeys to integrating assessment in their work and institutional culture.* Sterling, VA: Stylus. *http://stylus.styluspub.com/Books/BookDetail .aspx?productID=218787*

Nichols, J. O. (1995). *Assessment case studies: Common issues in implementation with various campus approaches to resolution.* Edison, NJ: Agathon Press.

Schwartz, P., & Webb, G. (Eds.). (2002). *Assessment: Case studies, experiences and practice from higher education.* Sterling, VA: Stylus.

Ethical Considerations in Assessment

American Educational Research Association. *www.aera.net/about/policy/ethics.htm*

American Psychological Association. *www.apa.org/ ethics/code/index.aspx*

American Sociological Association. *http://www.asanet.org/*

Hutchings, P. (Ed.). (2002). *The ethics of inquiry: Issues in the scholarship of teaching and learning.* Menlo Park, CA: The Carnegie Foundation for the Advancement of Teaching. Includes an annotated bibliography on issues of ethics related to the scholarship of teaching and learning, as well as to ethics within disciplines.

Hutchings, P. (2003, September–October). Competing goods: Ethical issues in the scholarship of teaching and learning. *Change,* 35(5), 27–33.

National Council on Measurement in Education. *www.ncme.org/about/*

National Research Council. (2002). *Scientific research in education* (pp. 154–157). Washington, DC: National Academy Press.

Outcomes Assessment Resources on the Web. Includes a listing of institutional websites that contain manuals, guides, and descriptions of college and university assessment process and procedures. *http://www.tamu.edu/mars/ assess/HTMLfiles/oabooks.html*

Program Review

Council of Graduate Schools. (2005). *Assessment and review of graduate programs: A policy statement.* Washington, DC: Author.

WORKSHEETS, GUIDES, AND EXERCISES

1. *An Overview of Your Current Institutional Commitment:* Periodically, developing collaborative perspectives on ways in which assessment is rooted in an institution's culture enables members of an academic community to appreciate the types and levels of commitment. Collaborative perspectives, then, lead the way to determining how to deepen or strengthen the commitment. Designed for campus leaders to work with constituencies across an institution, this worksheet asks those constituencies to identify ways in which assessment is already embedded into an institution's culture and to provide evidence that supports those perceptions. Asking constituencies who may not have been directly involved in launching or furthering the initiative to identify ways in which assessment is embedded into an institution's culture also provides a realistic read on the current institutional climate.

Structures, Processes, Decisions, and Channels and Forms of Communication	
Institutional Structures (committees, regularly scheduled retreats, centers, such as teaching and learning centers, regularly scheduled faculty and staff development opportunities, faculty and staff meetings, governance structures, new structures):	Evidence:
Institutional Processes (annual personnel reviews, faculty evaluations, approval of programs and courses):	Evidence:
Institutional Decisions (awards, forms of recognition, promotion and tenure, budgetary decisions, hiring decisions):	Evidence:

(continued)

Channels of Communication (with board, decision and planning bodies, wider public, current and future students, faculty and staff):	Evidence:
Forms of Communication (public documents, recruitment materials, catalog, website, newsletter, other):	Evidence:
Support (line item in budgets; use or development of technology to collect, store, or record assessment results and interpretations; grant support focused on assessment; human support to help carry out aspects of the process, such as graduate interns):	Evidence:
Human Support:	Evidence:
Financial Support:	Evidence:
Educational Support:	Evidence:
Technological Support:	Evidence:
Campus practices (new student orientation; new faculty orientation; assessment week; celebration of faculty-staff-student work; program- and institution-level times—common times—to focus dialogue on teaching, learning, and assessment and formal institutional times to receive and interpret results of assessment; collaboration across traditional boundaries to explore student learning from multiple lenses):	Evidence:

2. *Ways to Deepen or Strengthen the Commitment:* Using the preceding worksheet, ask members of the group to identify ways in which the institution can deepen or strengthen its commitment, including changing, revising, or modifying any of the criteria listed.

3. *New Practices:* After these two exercises, ask the group to think beyond the institutional norms that exist to invent new practices that promote campus commitment to teaching, learning, and assessment to improve both student and institutional learning. For example, might it be possible to develop a cadre of interdisciplinary teams (academic and student affairs, or academic and student support services, for example) that track cohorts of students over the continuum of their learning? Might it be possible for such teams to develop an entire program together, moving from agreed-upon outcomes to the collaborative design of a program, to collaborative development of assessment methods designed to track students' emerging learning, to collaborative interpretation of results along the way? That is, as an institution deepens its focus on learning through multiple avenues, can it change the ways in which it currently operates?

4. *Signs of Maturity:* Based on its research on 26 institutions that underwent institutional transformation, the American Council on Education (ACE) identifies four attributes that mark successful campus transformation: (1) that the institution changes its underlying assumptions, as well as overt institutional behaviors, processes, and structures; (2) that the transformation itself is deep and pervasive, affecting the whole institution; (3) that change is intentional; and (4) that it occurs over time (ACE, 2001, p. 5). Using these four attributes, with a core of individuals from across your campus, consider how your institution's current commitment may advance over time under these four attributes. Rather than inserting assessment as an "add-on," discuss how the rhythms of institutional life will intentionally incorporate this core institutional process of discovery or how new rhythms will be created to improve both student learning and institutional learning.

5. *New Evidence of Learning:* Given developments in technology and the ways in which students can demonstrate their learning in new contexts, such as in wikis, blogs, or multimedia presentations, what new kinds of assessment evidence might your institution or a program or department identify beyond conventional ones? How might these new kinds of evidence lead to new criteria to assess student achievement? (Recall Appendix 5 in chapter 4.)

6. *Development of a Scholarly Commitment:* Because there now is ample evidence that institutions are incorporating assessment into their work, using scoring rubrics, and sharing results internally as a basis on which to identify ways to adapt, change, or innovate new educational practices, with the appropriate body at your institution or by assembling representatives across the institution, consider how your campus might develop a scholarly commitment to assessment through intentionally doing the following:

   a. Drawing on research on learning to design one or more new programs that chronologically assess the efficacy of the educational practices that foster learning in those programs.

   b. Working with either institutions similar to yours or institutions in your area (such as transfer institutions) to share assessment results that prompt discussing ways to improve student learning

   c. Reaching out to other institutions to create a learning community focused on improving student performance through your shared commitment to one or more learning outcomes. Consider the possibility of establishing an online learning community to overcome geographical barriers. Also consider how sets of experts in this learning community might assess another campus's student work, discuss patterns of strength and weakness, and then engage members of the learning community in developing ways to improve patterns of weakness.

APPENDIX 8.1   University of Nebraska–Lincoln's Online Peer Review Assessment System

Two challenges in outcomes assessment are (a) building faculty support and engagement and (b) finding efficient and effective systems to manage the process. Collaboration among three colleges at University of Nebraska–Lincoln (UNL) addressed these challenges by implementing a faculty-led program-level process that is facilitated by an online assessment system. The Program Excellence through Assessment, Research, and Learning (PEARL) project at UNL initially involved the College of Education and Human Sciences, the College of Agricultural Sciences and Natural Resources, and the College of Journalism and Mass Communications (www.unl.edu/ous/pearl/pearl.shtml). The success of that initial pilot led to the use of the system by all colleges for the institutional reporting process. The senior vice chancellor for academic affairs and the Office of Undergraduate Studies provided significant support for piloting and sustaining the system and program for developing, validating, and assessing student outcomes.

The concept and features of the online system were developed by Kim Bender at Colorado State University (CSU), who entered into a partnership with UNL to pilot the system. UNL adopted many of the features and structures of CSU's software but developed a unique organizational model to better fit UNL's culture, where colleges are autonomous and decision making is often decentralized. This required a bottom-up approach driven by the faculty and supported at the college level. Three features of the online system are key in the organizational model:

1. Shared format for reporting assessment activities across academic programs
2. Mechanisms for faculty and academic programs to access and share plans, best practices, methods/instruments, and potential contributions to program improvement
3. Structure for capturing dialogue between programs and peer faculty reviewers about the program's assessment activities and results

The organizational model developed a process around these key features to achieve the following goals:

- Encourage conversations among faculty and other internal and external constituents about what learning is valued and how programs will know whether students are achieving that learning
- Prompt academic programs to "close the loop" on the assessment process by reflecting on the meaning and implications of results, instead of stopping once the exercise in data collection is complete
- Raise the visibility of assessment and its potential impacts by documenting the gradual but significant growth in how academic programs explore, assess, and improve using evidence of student learning
- Assist programs in coordinating documentation for multiple reporting requirements, including an institutional reporting process, accreditation, and/or academic program review. (An example of an institutional report using PEARL documentation can be found at www.unl.edu/ous/faculty_resources/assessment/page1.shtml)

THE ORGANIZATIONAL MODEL

The organizational model developed at UNL is structured to support more efficient and effective campuswide coordination and discussion of outcomes assessment (OA) among faculty. Although not all colleges use precisely the same model, Figure 1 generally describes the key constituents involved in the PEARL process and their roles:

The key group in this organizational model is a group of faculty members who play a leadership role in the system's process as peer reviewers. Peer reviewers are provided professional development activities that allow them to develop expertise in assessment, play a consultative role in the development of the PEARL system, and provide faculty leadership for the system in their college and home departments. The peer reviewers have also contributed to the development of a rubric of shared expectations for program's assessment plans that is then used when they review and provide feedback on programs' assessment plans. The steps in this process for each program are tracked in PEARL as described below and illustrated in Table 1.

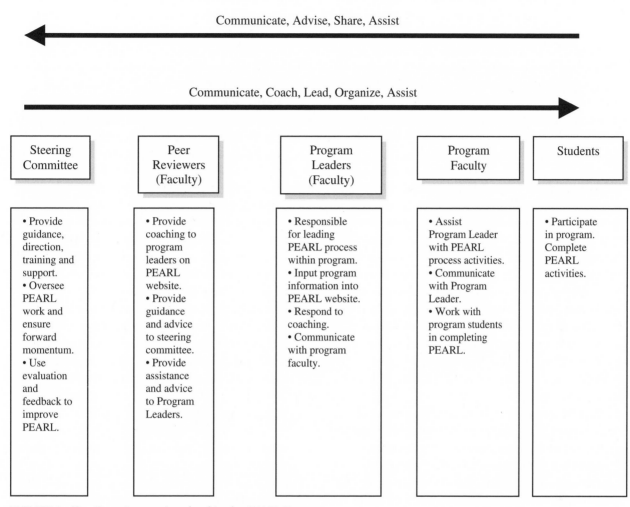

FIGURE 1 Key Constituents Involved in the PEARL Process

Table 1: Steps in the PEARL Process With One Department Example

College: Example College

Department: Example Department

	October 1, 2010	November 2010	December 2010	September 2011	October 2011	December 2011	January 2012
Example Department Academic Year 1	Programs input plan	Peer reviewers provide feedback on plan	Update on progress and respond to feedback	Programs report results	Peer reviewers provide feedback on results	Programs respond to feedback on results	AY1 Plan Complete

	October 1, 2011	November 2011	December 2011	September 2012	October 2012	December 2012	January 2013
Example Department Academic Year 2	Programs input plan	Peer reviewers provide feedback on plan	Update on progress and respond to feedback	Programs report results	Peer reviewers provide feedback on results	Programs respond to feedback on results	AY2 Plan Complete

1. In the fall of each academic year, every program is asked to specify an assessment plan for three learning outcomes using the PEARL online reporting site. For each learning outcome the program is to (1) state the outcome, (2) identify opportunities for achieving the outcome, (3) pose a question that the assessment will answer about the outcome, and (4) describe methods to be used for assessing the outcome.

2. In late fall the peer reviewers are divided into teams of three who review the plans individually and as a group. Their review is structured with a rubric that describes effective characteristics for each of the four components and results in a rating (Well-Developed or Developing) and descriptive feedback. Their review is not considered an approval process that is evaluative, but instead is developmental and collegial by affirming good assessment practices and encouraging better assessment practices. (The PEARL rubric can be found at http://www.unl.edu/ous/pearl/PEARL_Rubric _Current.pdf.)

3. In early winter every academic program then reviews the feedback, responds if needed, and determines how to proceed. This feedback is provided within 3–4 weeks of the program's submission, and the dialogue between peer reviewers and the program is documented in the PEARL system.

4. Programs then implement their assessment activities and compile and discuss the results with faculty in their program. The results, conclusions, and intended uses are then entered into the PEARL program early the following fall.

5. In that same time period the peer faculty reviewers again use the rubric to rate and provide feedback on the documented results, conclusions, and intended uses.

6. By late fall programs respond to faculty reviews of documented results, conclusions, and intended uses. This concludes the assessment cycle from the previous year.

7. To foster a process of continuous improvement, programs are prompted to start the next assessment cycle in the Fall once they have reported their results from the previous year (see Year 2 in Table 1). This promotes using lessons learned from one cycle to inform the next cycle by fine-tuning previously identified outcomes and plans, as well as adding new outcomes to broaden the learning assessed by the program.

PROGRAMMATIC EXAMPLES

The following are actual examples of programmatic assessment reported in the PEARL system. The examples have been abbreviated to provide an illustration of what programs have found and how they intend to improve based on that evidence.

Example 1

Outcome 1 **Student Learning/Development**	**Last modified on: 08/29/06** **Classify Outcome**	NEXT ▶
Description & Methodology		

Outcome

By their senior year, majors will be able to write effectively and to communicate research results and opinions in a manner appropriate to an audience.

This outcome addresses a skill that many potential employers care about and will need in the future. On both a national and local level, potential employers have identified the poor preparation in writing of the entry-level pool of graduates. Our graduates also go on to graduate school, in which effective written communication is critical to their long-term success. This outcome is consistent with the institution's core value related to developing a learning environment that prepares students for success and leadership in their lives and their careers.

Opportunities to Learn

The department's core curriculum provides a common foundation of knowledge essential for majors and emphasizes an interdisciplinary approach. Our course of study is expected to provide our students with the opportunity to gain technical expertise and communication skills. In most departments, oral and written reports are requirements. Communication skills are also stressed under the institution's general education program.

Question of Interest

Can graduates write a well-researched, referenced, logical, and well-composed research paper?

Assessment Method(s)

To assess this outcome we will evaluate at least 33% of the papers from our senior capstone courses each semester in which they are offered. These courses enroll approximately 10 to 40 seniors. We will collect a minimum number of 10 students, if available, or 50% of a student population of 20 or more. To assist in the archiving and organizing the review of papers, the department's associate director will work with capstone instructors to develop a protocol for electronic submission of papers.

The instructors for the capstone courses will require that students hand in two copies of their paper—one for grading and one for assessment. The associate director will randomly select from this set of papers for the assessment. An external faculty review panel will be convened by the associate director. This panel will evaluate the randomly selected sample of papers with a rubric that will examine the writer's ability to define the purpose of the paper; logically present content; organize ideas; sustain the reader's interest; use a professional tone, sentence structure, and appropriate terminology; use appropriate grammar, spelling, and writing mechanics; use references; and provide quality references. For each rubric category, the criteria of exemplary, good, acceptable, and unacceptable will be used. For each criterion, a description of what the students should demonstrate will be described. Each paper will be reviewed by two review panel members. Review panel members will represent one or more of the following groups: faculty, alumni, and employers. If the two panel members differ on their evaluation in more than 50% of the criteria, they will get together to discuss their reviews and reach a consensus.

The ratings of the review panel will be summarized and presented to the Undergraduate Curriculum Committee and the capstone course instructors for discussion and recommendations. A summary of the results and recommendations will then be presented to the department as a whole for their consideration and potential action.

Committee Comments and Program Responses

Comment 38	Outcome: **Well Developed.** The outcome is clear and uses active verbs to describe what students are to have learned.
10/5/20XX 10:11 AM J. Doe 123-456-7890 jdoe@email.edu	Are the papers intended to be written for any audience, or a specific audience? If it is specific, please clarify the intended audience. Question of interest: **Developing.** The question you ask cannot be answered by this assessment method. The assessment method will answer the question, "Can our students write?" not whether the requirements are appropriate. Assessment method: **Developing.** Please clarify the writing assignment and attach the rubric as a supplemental when it is available. Because you are concerned with employers, is there a way to include

employers in this process? How many capstone courses are included in this process? If there are only 10 students, 33% is only three papers, and that seems to be too small a sample. Does the sample come equally from all of the different capstone courses? Are you really asking: "Are our writing requirements effective in light of the results we are seeing in the papers coming out of these capstone courses?"

Suggestions:

The task of collecting and sorting all of the paper copies can be burdensome. Has use of an electronic system to add efficiency to this process been considered? This could also become an ongoing archive of papers for students to use when they are working on this assignment as a resource.

PEARL Peer Reviewers: J. Doe, A. Johnson, & C. Anderson

Response	Thank you for your comments. We have modified the question of interest to "Can our students write . . . ?" We have also modified the sample number criteria to a minimum of 10, if available, or 50% of a student population over 20. The idea of an electronic paper archive has been incorporated and will be developed through the interaction of the associate director and the capstone course instructors. We will attach the rubric when it is developed. Our review panel now includes the possibility of faculty, alumni, and employer members.
11/7/20XX 2:47 PM J. Smith 123-456-7890 jsmith@email.edu	

Results and Planning

Summary of Assessment Evidence/Results

Assessment Methods

In our initial design of the assessment approach for this learning outcome, our intent was to evaluate papers from capstone courses. Unfortunately, these courses did not yield enough papers to evaluate, so we modified our assessment methods. We took a more holistic approach and collected 28 papers from 300 and 400/800 level classes. Twelve faculty members volunteered to serve on an external review panel. A rubric was used to examine the writer's ability to define the purpose of the paper; logically present content; organize ideas; sustain the reader's interest; use a professional tone; employ appropriate sentence structure and terminology; use appropriate grammar, spelling, and writing mechanics; use references; and provide quality references. For each rubric category, the criteria of exemplary (3 points), good (2 points), marginal (1 point), and unacceptable (0 points) were used. For each criterion, a description of what the students should demonstrate was described. The rubric can be found in the supplemental files on the PEARL site. Each paper was assigned a number and reviewed by two panel members. The names of the author(s) and the course number were removed from the title page of each paper.

Summary of Assessment Evidence/Results

Outcome 1, Table 1 (Supplemental Information), is the summary of the review of student papers for each course. The maximum score on any given survey item was 3 and the maximum total survey score was 30. The individual average category scores that are highlighted indicate average scores below a good rating (<2 points). Data for individual categories indicate that regardless of the course, the writers struggled with paper organization in the context of expressing ideas in a logical fashion; sentence structure, which influences the flow of the paper; and word choice, which reflects the range of words used and the extent to which they are used appropriately.

Conclusion

These data clearly indicate that students taking upper-division courses struggle with writing a well organized, logically presented paper.

Use of Assessment Evidence/Results

The data collection for this assessment activity was completed in late July and early August, which coincided with the department's move into a new building. As a result, one of the first items on the agenda for the Undergraduate Curriculum Committee at their meeting in early September will be to develop recommendations for creating additional opportunities for students to develop their writing skills. Potential recommendations include, but are not limited to the creation of a technical writing class; development of a writing across the curriculum project; professional development for faculty related to best practices for integrating writing into the curriculum; reduction in the use of group writing projects; and development of a plan for the evaluation of writing skills from enrollment to graduation.

Lessons Learned

Although the paper review process generally worked, there were at times fundamentally different expectations of the reviewers for the various papers. One of the reasons for these different expectations was that an assumption was apparently made that all these papers were written to achieve the same objective. This unfortunately was not the case in that the objectives of the papers from the various classes were different. Before they use this review process in the future, the members of the faculty review panel will convene to discuss the process, the rubric, and the expectations of the review. This will reduce the disparity between the reviews of the same paper by different reviewers.

Committee Comments and Program Responses

Comment 360

8/24/20XX
9:27 AM
J. Doe
123-456-7890
jdoe@email.edu
Peer PEARL
Reviewer

Summary of Assessment Evidence/Results

Well Developed

Results presented evidence that can be understood by persons outside the content area and discussed what was learned about the effectiveness of the assessment process. The rubric was well developed and provided specific information related to strengths and weaknesses of students' writing skills. Twelve faculty members volunteered to serve on an external review panel, which represents strong faculty support for the assessment process. Despite the fact that the program had to modify the initial assessment design and select papers from a variety of courses, the program was able to identify some meaningful results.

Use of Assessment Evidence/Results

Developing

Because of the move, it is understandable that the program has had limited opportunity to identify how it will use the results related to future program changes. The program has indicated some potential recommendations for addressing writing weaknesses identified by the assessment process and strategies to reduce disparity between the reviews of the same paper by different reviewers. Once the assessment process has been solidified, it may be helpful to share program assessment results with employers, program graduates, and other stakeholders to obtain their thoughts about strategies for program improvement.

Peer PEARL Reviewers: J. Doe, A. Johnson, & C. Anderson

Supplemental Materials

Outcome 1, Table 1: *Data Summary*
Undergraduate Paper Rubric: *Student Paper Rubric*

Example 2

| Outcome 1 | Last modified on: 08/11/06 | |
| Student Learning/Development | Classify Outcome | |

Description & Methodology

Outcome

During their senior year, majors will be able to demonstrate the ability to communicate to patients, clients, and the public accurate information based on science (evidence-based practice).

The outcome addresses a skill that is important to majors and the profession. The public is continuously bombarded with claims and recommendations, which leaves them confused about what is accurate and true. Professionals are expected to provide the public with accurate information based on science. To maintain individual credibility and the credibility of the profession, a professional must do the following:

- Rely on scientific data when available as the basis for practice decisions and information provided to the public (evidence-based practice)
- Provide both sides of an issue when there is not clear consensus

Opportunities to Learn

Majors have the opportunity to develop these skills through the following courses:

COURSE 344 (taken fall of junior year): Students must research the validity of a "myth."

COURSE 356 (taken spring of junior year): Students must prepare and present an education session to an audience in the community that must be based on current research evidence and adapted to meet the needs of the selected audience.

COURSE 344: Students begin to explore and interpret the validity and accuracy of information available to the public and the opportunity to create an accurate "bottom line" statement related to the scientific accuracy of the myth.

COURSE 356: Students must interpret and evaluate information as it relates to a particular audience and develop an effective education message.

The assessment of the question of interest will occur in COURSE 453, which builds on the experiences in COURSES 344 and 356. The assignment requires students to interpret and evaluate research and other sources of information and then translate that information to a specific case scenario.

Question of Interest

Given counseling scenarios based on product claims, websites, newspapers, popular magazines, and so on, can students demonstrate the ability to use appropriate resources and determine the strength of evidence to support a specific claim or recommendation and communicate accurate information to patients/clients or the public?

Assessment Method(s)

All students in COURSE 453 will be given a counseling scenario that incorporates an example of a claim or recommendation. The student will complete a Determining Strength of Evidence adapted from the protocol used for the Evidence Analysis Library of the Professional Association for a minimum of two peer-reviewed research articles and two websites. This assignment will be graded and incorporated into the determination of the final grade for the course.

A rubric will be used to score the student's response, and 80% of the students will score at a level documenting that they possess this skill at a level appropriate for entry-level practice. Results of the assessment will be used to modify the course and the assignment to enhance students' development of this desired learning outcome.

Committee Comments and Program Responses

Comment 65

1/10/20XX
4:55 PM
J. Doe
123-456-7890
jdoe@email.edu

Outcome: **Well Developed.** The outcome is clearly stated, describes why it is important, and clearly identifies learning that can reasonably be measured. Some wording change is suggested to reflect the use of active verbs: "During their senior year, majors will demonstrate the ability . . ."

Question of Interest: **Well Developed.** The program clearly states a question that is related to the outcome and can be answered by the assessment process. Counseling Scenario attachment provides an excellent example of the scenario to which students will be asked to respond. Adding parenthesis may clarify the question: "Given counseling scenarios (based on product claims, websites, newspapers, popular magazines, and so on), can students demonstrate . . . ?"

Assessment Method: **Well Developed.** All students in COURSE 453 will be given a counseling scenario to which they will respond. It is assumed that this is a required course for all students in the program (essential for a true determination of the ability of students in the program to use appropriate resources). The attachment, "Determining Strength of Evidence," provides guidelines for evaluating the responses consistently over time and instructors. By making the scenarios a part of the course grade, this guarantees that students will be motivated to perform well. Wording changes are suggested to clarify the method, where [] indicates changes: ". . . to facilitate behavior change in patients/clients leading to a more healthful. . . ."; "The student will complete a "Determining Strength of Evidence" [report (]adapted from the protocol used for the Evidence Analysis Library of the Professional Association[)] for a. . . ." Clarify the rubric results. Is it meant that success is evaluated when 80% of the students score at a level appropriate for entry-level practice? Please clarify.

PEARL Peer Reviewers: J. Doe, A. Johnson, & C. Anderson

Response 5/18/20XX 10:34 AM T. Smith 123-456-7890 tsmith@email.edu	Thank you for the valuable feedback. A sample of the final project and a grading rubric has been developed and will be posted.

Results and Planning

Summary of Assessment Evidence/Results

Assessment Process

Each student in the class completed one randomly assigned counseling scenario.

In order for students to learn information from each of the counseling scenarios and to share the evidence to support their recommendations with students who completed the identical counseling scenario, students presented their consensus findings to the entire class. Students were organized by their assigned counseling scenario and instructed to do the following:

Discuss the counseling scenario:
- Share the research and website references identified for the assignment
- Share responses to each of the three questions

As a group:
- Identify two reference sources from peer-reviewed research journals to share with the class
- Identify two website sources to share with the class
- Come to consensus in answers to the three questions

The skill that was being evaluated was the students' success in demonstrating the ability to use appropriate resources and determine the strength of evidence to support a specific claim or recommendation and communicate accurate information to patients/clients or the public.

Each student received an individual score using the grading rubric. The target measure was identified as "80% of the students will score at a level documenting that they possess the skill at a level appropriate for entry-level practice," which would equal a score of 15–18 points (Competent) on the rubric. This was an error and should have read "greater than 80% of the students will score at a level documenting that they possess the skill at a level appropriate for entry into a internship program" which would equal a score of 12–14 points (Beginner) on the rubric. In the Education Model for Lifelong Learning, Competent occurs at the end of the internship program and Beginner occurs at the end of the undergraduate education component of professional growth. Consequently, scoring at the Beginner level would be a more appropriate goal for student performance.

The grading rubric was effective in evaluating the overall quality of the assignment. However, it was not effective in providing specific feedback to individual students related to how their answers could be enhanced. Feedback provided in class during the group presentations addressed the shortcomings of some answers in general, but specific feedback for each answer for each student would enhance student learning and understanding of what the assignment was designed to accomplish.

There was a variance among the counseling scenarios related to their complexity. Three of the counseling scenarios required less critical-thinking ability.

Results

Fifty-three students were enrolled in the class; 83% scored at the Beginner level and 17% scored at the Competent level. The assessment results did meet the outcome target of "greater than 80% of the students will score at a level documenting that they possess the skill at a level appropriate for entry into an internship program," which would equate to the score of 12–14 points (Beginner) on the rubric.

Overall, students received the maximum number of points for the following Outcome Assessed categories of the rubric—Scientific Data; Web Sites; and Recency of Information. Points were most often lost in the following Outcome Assessed categories: Interpretation of Information, Answers to Questions, and Completeness of Answers to Questions. Completeness of Answers to Questions tended to be the weakest component of the assignment response.

Sharing and Discussion of Results

Results were shared at the spring faculty retreat. Results were shared as part of the discussion related to PEARL and during discussions related to learning outcomes for all students in the department. Results have also been discussed on an individual basis related to coordination of course content between COURSE 401 and COURSE 453. There was consensus that interpretation and application of research continues to be an area that needs to be a continual focus in course development and course activities/assignments.

Use of Assessment Evidence/Results

Using Results and Interpretations and Future Plans

As a result of the assessment process, several changes will be made to the assignment for the spring semester of 2007 (the next time the course will be taught).

1. The grading scale will be changed on the rubric to indicate levels of professional performance as Novice, Beginner, and Advanced Beginner. It is inaccurate and inappropriate to indicate that someone is Competent based on one class assignment.
2. The assignment will be due earlier in the semester to allow for more individualized and specific feedback to students to enhance student learning.
3. Three of the counseling scenarios will be revised or replaced to result in a more comparable degree of difficulty in finding evidence-based information and in requiring higher-level critical-thinking skills.
4. The rubric will be revised to provide more guidance to assist students in the completeness of their answers (the component of the assignment where students most often lose points).

This question of interest will continue to be part of the PEARL assessment program for next academic year. The changes proposed for the assignment will help students develop their critical-thinking skills. The target measure is that 50% of students will score at the Beginner level and 50% will score at the Advanced Beginner level.

Committee Comments and Program Responses

Comment 331	Sharing and Interpretation of Results: **Well Developed.** The results thoroughly address the question of interest. Results present evidence so that it can be understood by persons outside the content area fairly well. One suggestion to improve this is to define or list the "three questions" that the student group needs to answer as part of the counseling scenario. The method collected sufficient evidence to formulate recommendations; although they did not answer all that was wished, the results have
9/25/20XX 1:58 PM J. Doe 123-456-7890 jdoe@email.edu	

led to several recommendations. The interpretation reflects what was learned about the effectiveness of the assessment process. The results state that "... specific feedback for each answer for students would enhance student learning and understanding of what the assignment was designed to accomplish." The results were shared at the department spring faculty retreat; areas of improvement were suggested with a recommendation that this question of interest be a continued focus for the program.

Using Results and Interpretations and Future Plans: **Well Developed.** The program indicates that some modifications will be made based on what was learned addressing the question of interest. Changes include a changed grading scale, an earlier assignment date for more feedback opportunities, revision of some of the counseling scenarios to equalize difficulty among all scenarios, and revision of the rubric. The program indicates how the use will be implemented next time the class is offered. The study will continue with the revised program to determine whether it led to the intended effect.

PEARL Peer Reviewers: J. Doe, A. Johnson, & C. Anderson

| **Response**
10/30/20XX
3:34 PM
T. Smith
123-456-7890
tsmith@email.edu | Thank you for your feedback and review of the assessment results.

T. Smith |

Supplemental Materials

Answers to Counseling Scenario: *Select Instrument Type Below*
Assignment Guidelines: *Select Instrument Type Below*
Counseling Scenario: *Select Instrument Type Below*
Determining Strength of Evidence: *Learning Project Description*
Grading Rubric: *Learning Rubric*

Source: Dr. Jessica Jonson, director of institutional assessment at the University of Nebraska–Lincoln, and Dr. Jeremy Penn, formerly program assessment coordinator at the University of Nebraska–Lincoln and currently director of assessment and testing at Oklahoma State University.

APPENDIX 8.2 Representative Commercially Designed Assessment Management Systems

BLACKBOARD LEARN FOR OUTCOMES ASSESSMENT

Blackboard Learn for Outcomes Assessment (www .blackboard.com/outcomes) extends the existing Blackboard teaching and learning environment with a complete assessment management solution that makes it easy to measure and improve student learning. It enables an institution to document, analyze, and report on educational outcomes so it can meet external accountability requirements and make informed budgetary and policy decisions based on real evidence.

Assessment Toolbox

The Blackboard Learn platform includes both direct and indirect measurement tools so individuals can collect all the data they need in a single platform. Surveys and course evaluations help measure student attitudes while portfolios, artifacts, and observations provide direct evidence of student learning.

Institutional Planning and Alignment

Colleges, schools, and departments often pursue separate assessment strategies without unified goals and methods. The Blackboard Learn platform enables every unit of an institution to map its goals and objectives to broader institutional goals and standards and report on activity and alignment for true institution-wide visibility.

Assessment Reporting and Tracking

Assessment data are critical to making informed budgetary and policy decisions. It is difficult to get true visibility into student learning and program effectiveness without extraordinary effort and cost. Blackboard Learn can help an institution realize the true value of visibility by generating, capturing, and analyzing institutional assessment data in a single system.

Comprehensive Assessment Management

In a single platform, Blackboard Learn provides assessment instruments, workflow management, collaboration, and enterprise reporting to support all of an institution's evidence-based improvement initiatives. (See Figure 1.)

CHALK & WIRE

Chalk & Wire (www.chalkandwire.com) is a full-featured, web-based, assessment data gathering and analysis tool. Created in 1996, it provides a simple way to organize, share, and assess work samples and other data related to performance for whole organizations or groups within them. The system is branded to the institution and adapts and evolves with the institution as it grows its assessment culture. External institutional standards and goals are all custom loaded for the institution. All aspects of the system can be changed at will to respond to trends reported by the data analysis tools provided. The system can be hosted by Chalk & Wire or by the institution.

The solution features an individual and cooperative WYSIWYG, point-and-click e-portfolio editor that supports the upload of all file types and solves the challenge of large videos by converting uploads into much smaller, streaming Flash video. There is support for embedded forms and surveys as data gatherers as well as imports of data from spreadsheets and enterprise databases and information systems. A programmable, open API is also provided to automate imports of assessment and demographic data. There is support for Single Sign On and integration with Blackboard, Moodle, and Turnitin.

Chalk & Wire completes its tool set with a full range of robust statistical tests and data visualization options to provide organizations with strategic information about learning patterns and trends. Urgent reports are automatically moved to users' Dashboards to indicate the need for action; all other reporting is available on a permissions basis. Reports can be organized and shared securely within the system and outside it. This solution is widely used for accreditation, program audit, and action and pure research in the United States, Canada, and Australia.

FIGURE 1: Blackboard Learn for Outcomes Assessment

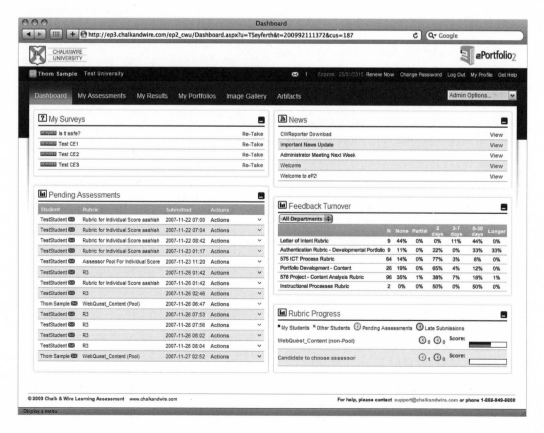

FIGURE 2: Chalk & Wire

EDUMETRY

EduMetry (www.edumetry.com) is a provider of assessment-of-learning services to universities and colleges, offering an end-to-end service ("map, measure, monitor, morph") to help university administrators manage student learning outcomes (SLOs) at the program, college, campus, or university level. Its services include assisting with the development of learning outcomes and assisting in the design of rubrics, as well as collecting, scoring, analyzing, and triangulating data.

The EduMetry Five-Step Process

STEP 1	STEP 2	STEP 3	STEP 4	STEP 5
DEVELOP SLOs	DESIGN RUBRICS	GENERATE SLO DATA	ANALYZE SLO DATA	RECOMMEND ACTION

In addition, Virtual-TA™ is an outsourced grading service that helps faculty provide students with rich feedback on their weekly assignments. The two services are synergistic in that the Virtual-TA forms the foundation for the generation of SLO data, which can then be harvested and aggregated to carry out analytics. EduMetry currently offers a simple Learning Dashboard based on Excel and custom-produced on demand for the client; plans are afoot for a more sophisticated, portalized version.

ELUMEN

eLumen (www.elumen.info) offers a qualitatively different system, an institution-wide "outcomes plat-

form" that everyone can directly access through a Web browser. Assessment leaders can craft a virtual model of the institution as an integrated structure for comprehensive and precise visibility of actual student achievement and nonachievement. Departments have options within an integrated set of academic processes that encompasses the entire assessment process and supports four different ways to electronically capture assessment data relative to student learning outcomes and rubrics. A course instructor has choices in setting up assessment in his or her own course section, selecting recommended assessments from faculty committees, bringing forward assessments he or she has used in a previous course, or creating his or her own new connection between a specific student activity and the searchable contents of the institution's virtual library of student learning outcomes and rubrics.

Numerous on-demand reports directly serve the expectations of accreditation, but more is possible. This can be more than assessment in courses; instructional support, student support services, student life, and student work-study can all become part of the context within which the strengths and weaknesses of any student (and any set of students) come into and remain in focus. If it chooses, a college can achieve "educational GPS"—the capacity for authorized individuals to know (and respond accordingly) in real time where any student or any set of students stands relative to any defined set of expected student learning outcomes. (See Figure 3.)

EPSILEN ENVIRONMENT

Epsilen Environment (www.epsilen.com) provides assessment through its Epsilen Learning Matrix (ELM).

User-customized report: An institution can know where any set of students stands in real time relative to any defined set of expected student learning outcomes.

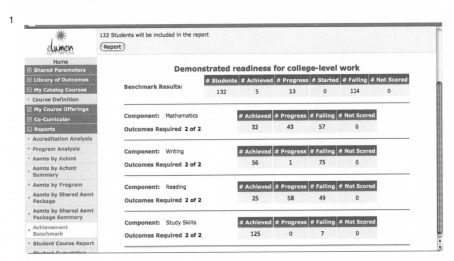

FIGURE 3: eLumen

The ELM is a comprehensive management tool for both formative and summative learning outcome assessment. Students within an Epsilen-licensed institution may use the ELM to collect, select, reflect, and present their learning accomplishments in an easy-to-use, Web-based "*x, y*" grid format. The *x* (horizontal) dimension is composed of Categories (criteria or levels of accomplishment or competency), and the *y* (vertical) dimension is composed of Principles (learning objectives, outcomes, or guidelines). A typical Matrix Template contains between 2 and 4 Categories; however, as many or as few categories as needed may be defined. A typical Matrix Template contains between 3 and 10 Principles; however, again, as many or as few Principles as needed may be gener-

ated. The Epsilen Learning Matrix offers capabilities for both K–12 and higher education institutions to create any number of customized outcome-based matrices for different colleges or academic programs within an institution. For instance, School of Business students would use a matrix optimized according to the School of Business learning outcome principles, whereas the College of Nursing may use an entirely different matrix. A faculty member can use the simple five-step ELM Wizard (see screenshot) to quickly produce and develop a unique Learning Matrix template based on campus, school, or department learning-outcome needs. That template would be available for evaluation and demonstration purposes only unless the faculty member's campus acquires

FIGURE 4: Epsilen Environment

an Epsilen license that includes the ELM option, whereby the template automatically becomes available to some or all campus students, faculty, or academic assessors or for accreditation assessment. An institution can easily generate a universal Epsilen Learning Matrix template. Academic advisers may use the ELM to securely review and assess student learning outcomes, both formative and summative. Potential employers may access the ELM to view student learning credentials. (See Figure 4.)

ESTAR

eSTAR (www.estar.com) is a web-based, comprehensive student advising and assessment system that allows department staff and faculty to administer, manage, and monitor students' progress and performance throughout their entire university experience—from prospect to alumnus. eSTAR allows administrators to set up goals and standards for a specific course, program, or unit and specific transition points, as well as tracking assessments, field experience, portfolios, transition points and other custom reviews. The eSTAR system is designed to support benchmarks so that institutions can measure students' performance against established program goals and objectives and compare performance with peers on key factors. The system associates standards and goals set for a specific course and/or transition points automatically when a student enrolls in that course or reaches a transition point. The tool provides support for conducting 360-degree assessment while preserving the assessor's confidentiality. eSTAR promotes assessment using uniform methods (rubrics/standards) to evaluate students. This system maintains a repository of standards of reports and the alignment of these standards with those of the department or program through its standards director; allows users to create rubrics using standard spreadsheet editing features through its rubrics director; offers advisers point-and-click options to track meetings with students; and has a "rules-based engine" to adapt to specific rules of an institution and to help track at-risk students.

FOLIOTEK ASSESSMENT

Foliotek (www.foliotek.com) delivers standards-based assessment, data collection, and reporting through the paradigm of electronic portfolios. Foliotek's creative blending of comprehensive data collection, reporting, assessment, and portfolio capabilities provides educators with a flexible tool for student and program

accreditation. Rubrics are configured to facilitate the assessment paradigm of any program. Programs can score student work against any set of competencies with their choice of performance levels and evidences. A second level of assessment can be added to any unit to track performance on subcompetencies or any other expectation. Programs may also choose to score any group of artifacts or a single artifact as a unit. Thus, Foliotek gives each program the ability to configure its assessment process, which may include any number of evaluation checkpoints. Foliotek may also be configured to collect program-specific profile information. Each profile field answer may be used as a filter for any assessment report. Programs may also compile pass-rate reports on every profile field answer for a selected question. The online reporting tools facilitate the gathering of assessment data at any time. Foliotek offers automated reports on interrater reliability, student activity, customizable forms, surveys, any assessment, or any group of assessments that uses the same set of rubrics. Furthermore, evaluation records on every student are archived, which aids in the process of monitoring student progress across evaluation checkpoints. A copy of the student's work is saved along with the scores and comments left by the assessor. Foliotek's newest additions to its product line include the Institutional Portfolio and eDossier products. All combined, Foliotek's products offer educators 360 degrees of coverage for their program accreditation and professional development needs. (See Figure 5.)

LIVETEXT

LiveText (www.livetext.com) is a leading innovator and provider of learning assessment, accreditation management, and e-portfolio services. Dedicated to keeping LiveText members at the forefront of technology and practice, LiveText makes powerful web-based tools, shared resources, and practice innovations available to participants in the LiveText Community. Institutions, programs, and students construct or adapt best practices frameworks for assessment at each level.

LiveText brings experience and tools to plan, implement, and sustain direct and indirect assessment; align outcomes and standards; gather real-time data; glean insights; tie data to inquiry and decisions; track effects of change; delve into evidence; tailor assignments and templates; validate assessment instruments; and more. These capabilities enable accreditation committees, institutional effectiveness offices, assessment teams, program leaders, faculty, and students along with field, global, and nonacademic stakeholders.

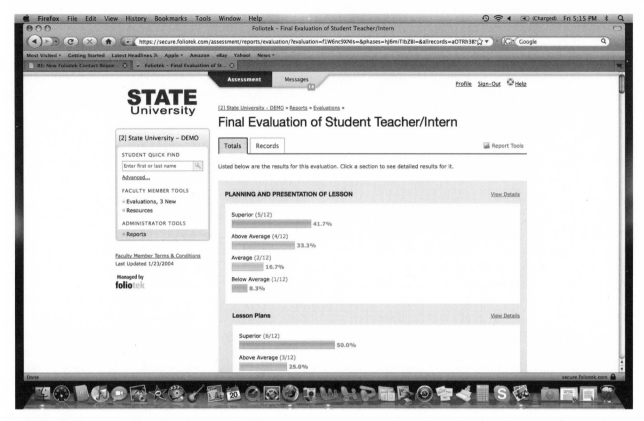

FIGURE 5: Foliotek

The primary focus of these efforts remains attainment of ever higher levels of learning efficacy for LiveText's members, often the students seeking a higher education.

When adopted for student use, LiveText services include authoring and publishing tools and secure storage. Students make or house capstone and team projects, selected assignments, or various e-portfolios (e.g., writing, growth, program, resume) as instructed and at their own initiative.

In the LiveText Community, assessment is purposefully systemic, fostering longitudinal awareness of learning and cumulative progress vis-à-vis standards and outcomes for the individual, program, and institution. Experiences involve a blend of instruments and voices through direct and indirect assessment for formative or summative purposes, coaching, mentoring, reflection, and feedback to continuously improve learning at all levels. (See Figure 6.)

NUVENTIVE ENTERPRISE OUTCOMES ASSESSMENT SOLUTION

The central obstacle to achieving continuous improvement in education is often the lack of a common framework for managing change toward the agreed-upon goals. Nuventive (www.nuventive.com) offers an Enterprise Planning and Outcomes Assessment Solution that provides institutions an electronic system for defining, assessing, and measuring the progress the institution is making in meeting the education quality goals defined in its mission. Nuventive's solution helps drive institutional effectiveness from data through to goal-aligned action.

TracDat, the core component of Nuventive's solution, provides a shared framework for broad-based planning and quality improvement that is used in both academic and administrative areas of an institution or across multiple institutions. TracDat manages the planning and assessment process by effectively supporting strategic planning, outcomes assessment from the course through the institutional level, and accreditation at multiple levels from a single solution. Goals can be defined and linked at multiple levels within an organization or across many organizations and tied to a common process for implementing and monitoring progress. The framework allows individuals and groups to maintain discrete levels of autonomy and yet, when appropriate, have shared goals, data, and plans.

FIGURE 6: LiveText

The iWebfolio electronic portfolio platform, an optional part of the Enterprise Planning and Outcomes Assessment Solution, allows the institution to gather assessment data at the individual and course/program levels. Evidence of student learning can be collected from portfolios along with aggregate data captured in reports. Institutions may also demonstrate meeting accountability requirements via a presentation portfolio at the program, department, division, and institutional levels. (See Figure 7.)

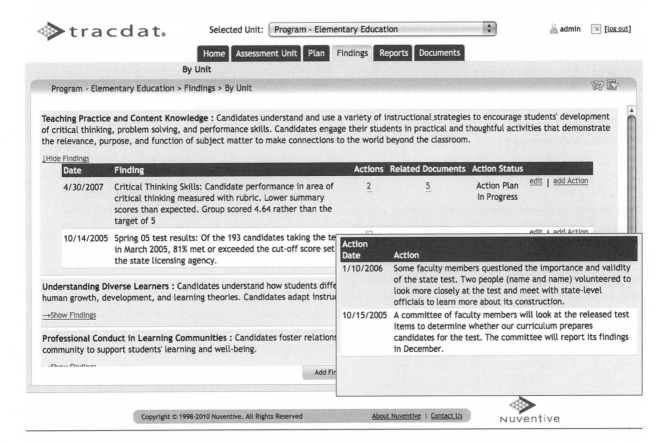

FIGURE 7: Nuventive Enterprise Outcomes Assessment Solution

STUDENTVOICE

StudentVoice (www.studentvoice.com) offers a comprehensive solution that includes cutting-edge technology, higher education–specific resources, and expert consultation to support assessment initiatives. By providing a centralized platform for managing assessment and participation data throughout the student life cycle, participating institutions gain a clear understanding of the student experience at every stage: recruitment, retention, alumni relations, and development.

Although assessment professionals have historically had to adapt their processes to off-the-shelf software packages that weren't designed with the unique needs of higher education in mind, StudentVoice was built, from the ground up, for administrators in assessment, advising, and institutional research and effectiveness roles. The StudentVoice platform integrates data from across the institution and provides user-friendly tools for data collection and reporting, peer benchmarking, and project management to meet academic, strategic, and process requirements, such as the measurement of student engagement and learning. Ultimately, StudentVoice helps institutions save time and resources to accomplish annual planning, budgeting, and accreditation requirements.

The StudentVoice program has been accepted equally by all types of campuses, with more than 400 campuses using elements of the platform to guide educational and decision-making processes. The platform is entirely web-based and delivered through a software-by-subscription model to colleges and universities that aspire to build a culture of assessment around student and program development.

TASKSTREAM

TaskStream (www.taskstream.com) provides solutions to help efficiently plan and manage assessment processes, demonstrate learning achievement, and foster continuous improvement in the interest of promoting genuine inquiry into student learning and institutional effectiveness. The Accountability Management System (AMS) provides a central, collaborative environment for managing assessment processes. The Learning Achievement Tools (LAT) facilitate gathering and analyzing outcomes assessment data from performance measures, such as portfolios, capstone projects, fieldwork, surveys, and key assignments.

With AMS, institutions can examine effectiveness at achieving their mission and strategic goals by doing the following:

- Customizing process requirements for collecting information from academic and nonacademic areas (e.g., learning outcomes, operational objectives, assessment plans, improvement actions)
- Engaging faculty and staff through collaborative "workspaces," discussion areas, and shared resources
- Documenting and aligning outcomes across the institution with higher-order goals, including pre-populated accreditation standards
- Analyzing where outcomes and objectives are addressed and measured via alignment reports and curriculum maps
- Managing quality assurance and content approval with defined review processes and reports

Employing a portfolio-based model, LAT enables the assessment of learning over time and beyond course boundaries:

- Institutions can assess student achievement of outcomes and standards, based on direct evidence of learning, using custom rubrics or forms.
- Institutions can implement multiple assessments of student artifacts and generate inter-rater reliability reports for comparative analysis.
- Faculty and assessment coordinators can aggregate and analyze performance data for program effectiveness purposes, as well as for reporting to external stakeholders.
- Students can build personal portfolios for showcasing achievements. (See Figure 8.)

WEAVEONLINE

WEAVEonline (www.weaveonline.com) is a hosted subscription service that integrates assessment and planning solutions so that universities, colleges, and community colleges can better address these critical processes. WEAVEonline features integrated software, plus supporting webinars, experienced assessment and planning professionals, and a consultative peer learning community.

Developed by faculty and administrators to address

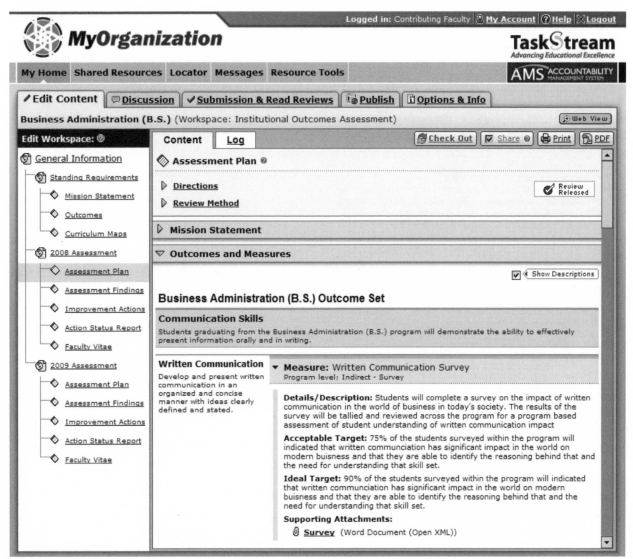

FIGURE 8: TaskStream

assessment within the context of accreditation, WEAVEonline focuses on institution- and program-level processes for quality assurance and quality enhancement. It allows institutions to associate student learning and other important outcomes and objectives in academic and administrative units with general education, multilevel strategic planning, and other institutional priorities. It also allows the institution to align the work with external requirements for regional and programmatic accreditation and other types of professional standards. To facilitate this, WEAVEonline includes a flexible mapping module to demonstrate the alignment of courses and experiences with higher-level outcomes and objectives.

Setup of the software is determined by member institutions to reflect their needs for assessment and/or planning—organizational chart entities, grants, action projects, faculty and staff, accreditation or strategic planning sections, or other areas of interest. Each of these can establish purpose, goals, outcomes/objectives, measures, and targets and then enter findings and action plans. The institution can pose questions to facilitate reflection or gather information for other processes, such as program reviews. There is an option to include annual or special reporting sections as well. Throughout the system, users can display point-of-reference documentation, using almost any type of electronic file. (See Figure 9.)

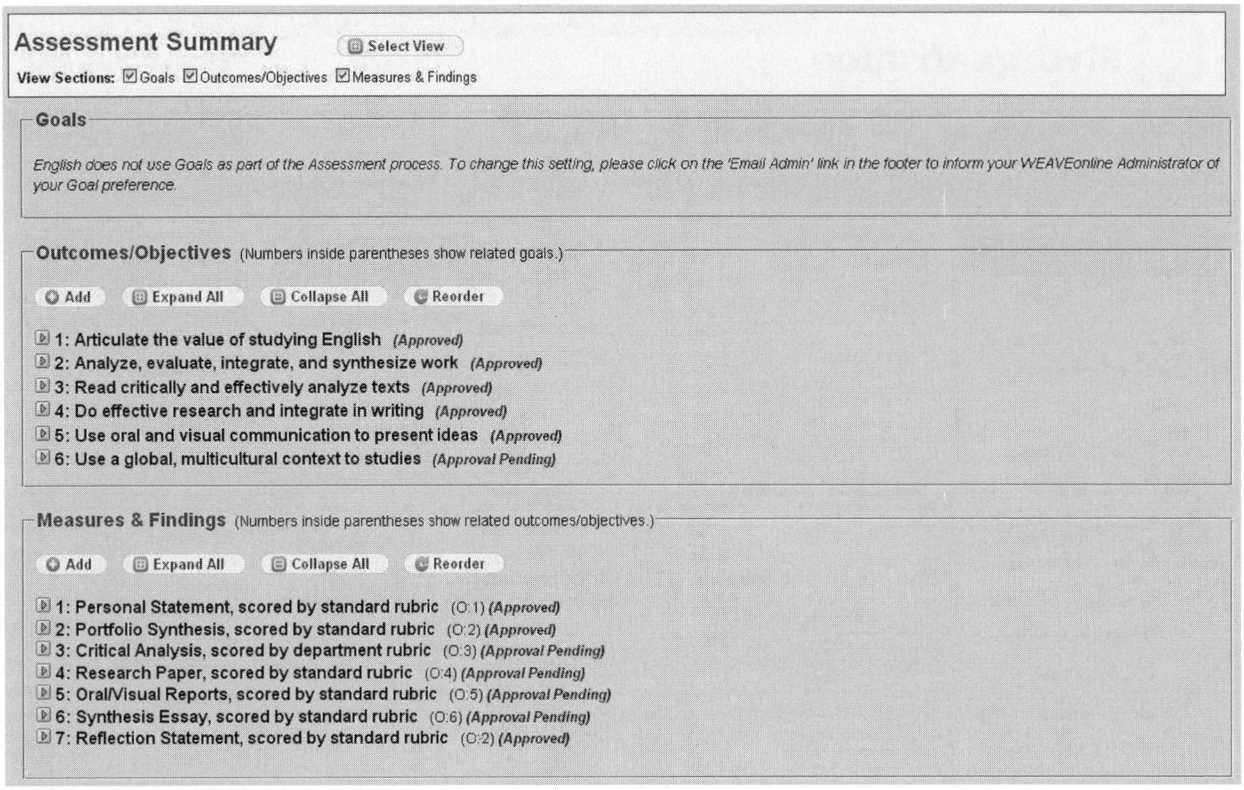

Assessment Summary   [▣ Select View]

View Sections: ☑ Goals   ☑ Outcomes/Objectives   ☑ Measures & Findings

Goals

English does not use Goals as part of the Assessment process. To change this setting, please click on the 'Email Admin' link in the footer to inform your WEAVEonline Administrator of your Goal preference.

Outcomes/Objectives   (Numbers inside parentheses show related goals.)

[⊕ Add]   [▣ Expand All]   [▣ Collapse All]   [⟳ Reorder]

▶ 1: **Articulate the value of studying English** *(Approved)*
▶ 2: **Analyze, evaluate, integrate, and synthesize work** *(Approved)*
▶ 3: **Read critically and effectively analyze texts** *(Approved)*
▶ 4: **Do effective research and integrate in writing** *(Approved)*
▶ 5: **Use oral and visual communication to present ideas** *(Approved)*
▶ 6: **Use a global, multicultural context to studies** *(Approval Pending)*

Measures & Findings   (Numbers inside parentheses show related outcomes/objectives.)

[⊕ Add]   [▣ Expand All]   [▣ Collapse All]   [⟳ Reorder]

▶ 1: **Personal Statement, scored by standard rubric**   (O:1) *(Approved)*
▶ 2: **Portfolio Synthesis, scored by standard rubric**   (O:2) *(Approved)*
▶ 3: **Critical Analysis, scored by department rubric**   (O:3) *(Approval Pending)*
▶ 4: **Research Paper, scored by standard rubric**   (O:4) *(Approval Pending)*
▶ 5: **Oral/Visual Reports, scored by standard rubric**   (O:5) *(Approval Pending)*
▶ 6: **Synthesis Essay, scored by standard rubric**   (O:6) *(Approval Pending)*
▶ 7: **Reflection Statement, scored by standard rubric**   (O:2) *(Approved)*

FIGURE 9: WEAVEonline

APPENDIX 8.3   Consent Form

Involving students in institution- and program-level assessment efforts carries with it ethical considerations about the use of their work. Beyond informing students that the institution and its programs will assess their work over time, an institution is ethically responsible for providing students with the opportunity to accept or decline the use of their work for institutional learning and improvement. Federal guidelines exempt the following kinds of research from U.S. Regulations Governing Research Ethics Requirements, so long as human subjects cannot be identified or linked to the research:

1. Research conducted in "established or commonly accepted education settings involving normal education practices"
2. Research "involving the use of educational tests (cognitive, diagnostic, aptitude, achievement), survey procedures, or observation of public behavior"
3. Research involving the "collection or study of existing data, documents, records, pathological specimens, or diagnostic specimens" (Code of Federal Regulations, Title 45, Part 46:Protection of Human Subjects, 2009) http://www.hhs.gov/ohrp/humansubjects/ guidance/45cfr46.htm

However, institutional review boards may require approval of any institution- or program-level assessment methods under their human subjects policies, even if students' names are not identified in the results. For that reason, institutions should make clear to members of their community the necessary policies and procedures that guide conducting assessment across the campus and within programs.

Viewing assessment as a process of inquiry that advances both student and institutional learning creates a learning partnership between students and the larger educational community. Providing students with opportunities to learn about the institutional commitment during their orientation to the institution, as well as providing them with an opportunity to accept or decline to participate in large-scale institutional efforts, values their role in the assessment process. For that reason, many institutions develop student consent forms that explain the process of assessment or the methods of assessment that the institution will use at points in students' studies. Washington State University presents students with the following consent form before students participate in one of the university's institution-level assessment projects. This form provides students with a full understanding of the purposes of the assessment project and their role in this project:

- Explains the purpose of the project within the institution's context
- Acknowledges the value of the project to students
- Describes the process students will be involved in
- Ensures confidentiality
- Makes public students' right to participate or decline
- Demonstrates compliance with the institution's review board

CONSENT FORM FOR CRITICAL THINKING STUDY

Student Participation at Washington State University

Your instructor is participating in a study which is further implementing and developing an assessment instrument, a "Critical Thinking Rubric," originally designed at WSU, which would afford a rough measure of student progress in achieving the higher intellectual skills over the course of their college careers. This study is a component of the grant received by General Education, the Center for Teaching, Learning and Technology and the Campus Writing Programs from the Fund for the Improvement of Post-Secondary Education.

The researchers for this project will collect student papers from this class and evaluate them using a group of trained faculty readers to determine the effectiveness of the Critical Thinking rubric. Your instructor will collect assignments from at least two points in the semester.

Data collected will be strictly confidential and your name will not be recorded. Only the research team will have access to the data. Your performance in your class will have no relation to your participation in this study.

By participating in this project, you will help WSU faculty refine instructional and evaluative methods which will encourage higher intellectual skills over the course of students' college careers. Washington State University and the Center for Teaching, Learning and Technology, Campus Writing Programs and General Education Program support the practice of protection of the rights of research participants. Accordingly, this project was reviewed and approved by the WSU Institutional Review Board. The information in this consent form is provided so that you can decide whether you wish to participate in our study. It is important that you understand that your participation is considered voluntary. This means that even if you agree to participate you are free to withdraw from the experiment at any time, without penalty.

Critical Thinking Study Principal Investigator
Diane Kelly-Riley, Campus Writing Programs

CONSENT STATEMENT:

I have read the above comments and agree to participate in this project. I understand that if I have any questions or concerns regarding this project I can contact the investigator at the above location or the WSU Institutional Review Board.

_____   _____
Participant's Signature   Date

_____   _____
Print Name   WSU ID Number

Course Name and Number _____

Source: Diane Kelly-Riley, WSU, and the Washington State University Critical Thinking Project.

INDEX